A Time To Remember

V. G. Gallagher

A Time to Remember
By V. G. Gallagher

Photos are from the author's collection unless otherwise noted. Photos from istock.com are noted accordingly. Roses on cover are also from istock.com

Some names mentioned in the narrative are fictitious. However, the names of the soldiers and the military units are true names with the exception of those soldier names the author no longer remembered or purposefully made fictitious. The entire narrative is based on the author's memories of actual experiences from his early childhood and his days of service as both a non-commissioned and also a commissioned officer, together with his photographs and the records he maintained over the years.

Published by Blue Spruce Publishing Company
2175 Golf Isle Drive, Suite 1024
Melbourne, FL 32935
610-647-8863
info@BlueSprucePublishing.com

Visit author's website which includes
interesting full color pictures, stories and books.
VinceGallagherBooks.com

ISBN 978-1-943581-09-2

DEDICATION

This book is dedicated to my best friend Max Ries, and all those who marched out of the 12th Regiment Armory to serve in four of our nation's wars:

The Spanish American War - 1898
World War I - May 1918
World War II - May 1941
Korean War - May 1951

Courtesy of Fordham University School of Law

The War Memorial, at Fordham University School of Law,120 West 62nd Street, New York City - the former address of the old armory. The Memorial was created by the 12th Infantry New York National Guard.

iii

Table of Contents

Prologue

The desire to write a narrative about my early life growing up in Woodside, Queens in New York City, was never on my bucket list of "Things to Do." Being an avid reader of fact over fiction I happened to pick up a book about World War II and some of the smaller and lessor known battles in Asia. In 1944, my 19 year old first Cousin PVT Vincent Cavallo was killed in action in Burma leaving his parents and younger brother devastated, the sorrow was shared by everyone in the entire Cavallo Family. Vincent was drafted, quickly trained, sent overseas to an unknown destination in Asia and within weeks, the tragic telegram arrived. The only knowledge his parents had was his address and that he was killed in a strange sounding place called "Myitkyina, Burma."

As a 12 year old I wrote my cousin one letter that was never answered. His address was unusual and remained in my memory. I came across this odd address while reading that history book. The 5307th Composite Unit Provisional, otherwise known in code as "Galahad" or unofficially "Merrill's Marauders." This was never known by anyone in the family.

Years later when I checked in with the VA to have my hearing tested, I asked to check my cousin's records which were quickly shown on the computer screen with, date of death, Purple Heart Medal, Asiatic Pacific Service Medal and WW II Victory Medal and Camp Swift, Texas.

With my curiosity now aroused and taking advantage of "The Freedom of Information Act," I wrote and requested copies of my cousin's records. I dug deeper and paid a fee to the U.S. Army Military History Institute for additional research and found my cousins awards and decorations were never added to his record. It allowed me to record a chronology of his service from the time he was drafted, to the day a US Army Form 52B was attached to his body hastily stating, *"PVT Vincent Cavallo, Company F 2nd GAL (2nd Galahad)...killed in line of duty."* At the moment of his death, he became another KIA statistic.

That is until, as his first cousin and sharing the same given name in honor, of our Grandfather Vincenzo Cavallo, I decided to to tell his story for him.

After completing my research, I requested the Department or Defense to update Vincent's records detailing his service together with the medals and awards that he earned at the cost of his young life. When complete I wrote a narrative, had copies printed and sent this history to the extended Cavallo family including some of whom, I never knew; my cousin Jackie Cavalla was the Cavallo historian and she provided me with the addresses. All the records I received from the Department of the Army were sent to Vincent's namesake and nephew in New York. He never knew his Uncle and only recalled some talk from his Dad Raymond, Vincent's younger brother which, helped me to complete the narrative.

The Department of Defense sent me acknowledgments of my cousin decorations and awards and assured me his army record would be updated with this information. My Aunt and Uncle would never know about their son's heroism having only, a trivial knowledge of his service. It was a sad day for this 14-year-old boy back in 1946 when I attended funeral services in the Bronx. The images of my Cousin Vincent's flag draped coffin and his grieving mother, father and brother still remain very clear in my memory. No one in our family knew anything at all about Vincent's service and wartime story. I was sorry it took me so many years to open that window again to look back and honor my cousin.

This made me think about my own time in the military so, I wrote a brief narrative about my service for my family. When I researched my cousin's records I only needed his name and serial number. Anyone researching my military life would have to access not one, but four different sources. Army records using my name and enlisted serial number then, my officer's serial number and then, the same two sources from the Army National Guard records. And, this would only happen if they knew exactly where to search.

As I wrote the words I relived the past which became a book. I did not experience close combat but, I did serve in harm's way as a young soldier and wanted my true story told.

This is a memoir written by a curious person who served willingly and proudly with great men. The memories of those men I served with are cherished for their integrity, a quality rarely found in others I was to meet later in life's adventure. The many records, orders, photos and paraphernalia from those days were stored in a box in my garage for over 50 years. Once opened, they re-awakened my vivid memory which I inherited from my Dad, John Aloysius Gallagher. This memoir is also my love story with Lee from the first moment I met her in her parent's living room to this day more than 64 years ago. I am thankful to the Good Lord for her love and for His blessing on us for our long life together.

Now, much older and maybe a little wiser and along with millions of American Veterans, I still feel pride in my service and the uniform I wore in those days. I wish God's Blessing for those brave American men and women, active, guard, and reserve, whom today volunteer to walk in harm's way for our protection.

V. G. Gallagher

The reader will enjoy viewing the illustrated website:
VinceGallagherBooks.com

Chapter 1

Woodside in the 1930s and 1940s

In 1941 on my ninth birthday I was introduced to the military but first, some background. I was then a decent but not an exceptional student at P.S. 152 elementary school located on 62nd street and Northern Boulevard. The school was a recently constructed four story all brick building. My folks John and Nellie owned our two story two family home on 59th Street a few avenues south of Northern Boulevard. I had a healthy walk to and from school every day, in fair and inclement weather. In those days, only the handicapped and unhealthy children in the Open Air class at P.S. 152 were bused to school.

Most homes in Woodside were single or two family dwellings interspersed with an apartment building 4 to 5 stories high. All the streets were paved and had side-walks, curbs, water mains, sewers, fire hydrants and telephone poles carrying power and telephone lines. We did not have a phone until later and still had an ice-box. Cloths were washed by hand with a scrubbing board. In the 1940's my folks added a phone and an electric refrigerator.

Woodside was a mixed neighborhood with many different nationalities, races and religions. Whites, Hispanics, some Blacks, some Asians and some from the Middle East including, Christians, Jews and some Muslim families in the mix. I do not recall hateful acts between any races or religions as I grew up. Woodside's popularity was its convenient access to public transportation, just a short walk to the elevated or subway train lines and then, only minutes to Manhattan.

Located just across the East River from Manhattan, Woodside had many empty lots resulting from the end of the building boom of the 1920's and the onset of the Great Depression of the 1930's. Many lots were overgrown and now semi-wooded, giving kids plenty of open areas to play Football, Base Ball and act out their fantasies. 59th Street served as a playground for Stickball, kick the can, kick the stick, hide and seek and Ring O'Leary O, Ring O'Leary O and Caught, Caught, Caught, a rowdy form of tag. When the winter rolled around with snow on the ground and, no snow plows to remove it, the snow packed solid to form ice. Our street sloped downhill and starting on 39th Avenue we ran down hill and jumped on our sleds belly first, called "Belly Whopping." Our sleds swiftly sped on the ice all the way down to 37th Avenue. Remember, this is before the advent of computer games and kids spent their leisure time outdoors during all seasons, winter, spring, summer and fall.

Home entertainment was the popular radio programs and serials. Table games with Checkers, Chinese Checkers and Pick-Up Sticks most popular. This was during some of Hollywood's golden years and most adults went to the movies once a week. The kids in Woodside went every Saturday to the matinee at the Deluxe movie house on Roosevelt Avenue. Admission was only 10 cents which included a free comic book for the first 100 kids. We lined up at 9 AM and remained until we saw the double feature movies and cartoons twice. Parents welcomed this private time, with the kids out of the house for a few hours every Saturday morning if you catch my drift!!!

After the matinee was over, the theater management turned on all the lights and the ushers escorted all the kids out to make room for the afternoon showings for adults.

The public library was a magnet attracting many kids who loved to read. I made frequent visits to the public library and read quite a bit as a youngster. Adventure books interested me the most, from Stevenson, Dickens and Melville to the true-life adventures of Roy Chapman Andrews and Osa and Martin Johnson. Andrews was an adventurer and director of the New York Museum of Natural History famous for his travels to the Gobi Desert in Mongolia in his quest of dinosaur bones. The Johnsons were an American adventure couple who wrote books and made documentary film about their travels to Africa, the Pacific Islands and Borneo. Robert Louis Stevenson and Percival Christopher Wren were among my favorite adventure novel authors and *Treasure Island* and *Beau Geste* my two favorite novels.

A nasty chore in those days was cleaning the chicken coop, yes, we had chickens for most of my early childhood in Woodside. We enjoyed fresh eggs, both brown shell and white from a dozen Rhode Island Red and Leghorn chickens. Big brother John, six years my senior, assigned this duty to me with a promise to give me his much admired two wheeler bike when, he felt I was ready to ride it. He was true to his word and after stretching my legs to reach the pedals I was soon mobile.

We were all proud of John when he saved Aunt Mamie from the treacherous undertow at Rockaway Beach. The scratches across his chest and loss of his holy medal when Aunt Mamie panicked, scratched him and broke his miraculous medal chain, attested to his bravery.

I knew nothing about the concern my folks had when my Dad was out of work and how they struggled to make mortgage payments during the Great Depression. Deep in my memory are glimpses accompanying my Mom as she drove our gray Model A Ford across the 59th Street Bridge which spanned the East River connecting Queens County to Manhattan. We drove the few blocks south to a Sutton Place address overlooking the East River and the name Paris or Parish remain in my memory.

I recall my Dad mentioning years later that the bank did not foreclose because they told him they did not want to own all the homes in Woodside. Remember, this was in the pit of the Depression and I can only assume the banks sold the mortgages to private investors and Paris or Parish owned ours. I was in my teens before I heard about how my folks almost lost our home.

Back then, a few coins always jingled in my pocket. A couple nickels and dimes plus a few pennies could take you by subway all over the five boroughs of New York City, with enough left over for a hot dog and a soda.

At about the age of ten, and as promised, my big brother John gave me his bike and now I had "wings" to travel all over Queens on my bike. I started working part time jobs, one was delivering chickens for a kosher chicken market down the street on 37th Avenue. The market was only opened on Saturday and the live chickens were stored in big wooden cages. I remember whom I

3

assume was a rabbi, a big and burly man with red hair and a full red beard. He would grab a bird selected by the customer, carry it back to the "Operating Room," and do the "Coup" with his knife. Then, he dipped the chicken in a large pot of boiling water and cleaned the feathers off on a rotating wheel with many rubber fingers.

I do recall the rabbi eating a whole boiled chicken for his lunch with a loaf of yellow Jewish challah bread, and drinking tea in a glass. Now, with a large metal basket attached to my bike and all loaded up with bagged chickens, I was off to deliver the orders. I always reminded the boss when he attached that big wire basket to be careful not to scratch the paint on my fender which I was always touching up. Funny how these images remain after so many years.

One stop was fun at a Chinese laundry on Skillman Avenue. The family including the mother, the father, and a store full of kids all smiles and all noisy and busy. I never really knew what they were saying but their smiles were contagious and I smiled right along with them. Their order was for several chickens and the dad always gave me a quarter which was a huge tip in those days ... my memory as I write this brings back to my mind, the picture of their bright smiles and their shiny straight black hair.

I also delivered the newspaper to a group of apartment houses and collected the 18 cents a week charge. The more generous paid with a quarter, leaving seven cents for the delivery boy, but most only gave a few pennies tip. Mom Nellie arranged for me to work covertly from time to time at Benny's grocery store on Roosevelt Avenue, candling eggs and packing and weighing candy in the basement.

I remember my two favorite teachers, Mrs. Hirsh was small and pretty and Mrs. Pfeiffer a tall lady I would walk with a few blocks on my way home, as she continued on to the 61st train station. My only sad memories are the asthma attacks I suffered in the summer months from about the age of four or five to about nine or ten. The empty lots I played in were all overgrown with ragweed and it was later found that I was terribly allergic to the ragweed.

I remember coming home after playing all day in the dense growths of ragweed with welts all over my arms and legs, unable to breathe at night, and my dad sitting with me by an open window as I panted for breath, he not knowing what was wrong with me. This was before home air conditioning so I was just breathing in more ragweed pollen.

My folks took me to Dr. Fletcher in Flushing to confirm my allergy after a scratch test. I went to the public clinic at Queens General Hospital where I received weekly de-sensitizing injections at a cost of only twenty-five or fifty cents a week. By the time I was nine or ten I found complete relief and was no longer bothered with the ragweed allergy until my late senior years. Mom took me to the hospital in the early years and once I knew the way at about from eight years old, I started to go alone. I took the elevated train from Roosevelt Avenue and 61st Street train station to the end of the line in Flushing, and then took the Q-65 bus to Queens General Hospital. I enjoyed the trip all by myself and it gave me a sense of independence. This encouraged me to start traveling all over the five boroughs including the boat ride on the Staten Island Ferry from Manhattan's Lower East Side across the harbor to Staten Island. These adventures were without my Mom's knowledge. I had that desire to explore from an early age and enjoyed my excursions to new places.

Mom Nellie became an activist to pressure Queens County officials to rid the area of the ragweed which she accomplished very successfully. Within a year or two the county removed all the offensive weed. For years, people talked about how Nellie Gallagher helped rid Woodside of ragweed. Later on, when I took the long walk to Bryant High School in Astoria, I would take short cuts through those same lots and don't remember seeing any ragweed. Nellie did a good job.

The desensitizing injections enabled me to play in the lots to my heart's content. One of the lots was on 58th Street directly behind our home. Together with my street chums we dug a trench to protect us from the imaginary enemy. The trench was about four feet deep and ten or so feet long. It took quite some time to dig this trench but a half dozen boys all pitched in with shovels, sometimes working until dark, then starting a fire and roasting "Mickey's" - this was very popular with Woodside kids in those days. We would toss our potatoes into the fire and cook them until the potato was black, peel away the skin and eat the "Roast Mickey." Someone always had a salt shaker to share.

We decided the trench needed an escape tunnel and started digging a horizontal escape tunnel through the wall of the trench. Work was done at different times by me and my pals and sometimes all alone. One afternoon with my army entrenching tool that I bought at an Army & Navy store in Flushing on those weekly hospital visits, I crawled quite deep into the tunnel head first on my stomach and started scooping out dirt. I was making good progress as I squeezed in deeper and deeper. I remember it was chilly and I was wearing a coat that day and must have twisted to make room to scoop out the dirt when I accidentally wedged myself in the escape tunnel, unable now to back out. No one was around and my shouts probably could not even be heard anyway. I was stuck head first deep inside the tunnel.

Did I panic?? You bet I did. After a cold chill ran up my spine and the hair on the back of my head stood up, I took a deep breath and tried to relax my body. I was finally able to wiggle out. That trench remained with an unfinished escape tunnel for a long, long time. It sat unfinished until after World War II when a garage was built on that lot for the use of Hellman's Mayonnaise delivery trucks.

My dad was a steam-fitter and plumber and in the 1920's earned a very good income before the Great Depression struck in 1930 and lasted until 1942. Skilled building tradesmen, especially electricians and plumbers were highly paid and respected in those days. Mom told stories about when newlywed she was embarrassed when she deposited large weekly sums in their savings account and the bank tellers appeared to have questioning looks on their faces. But the Depression ended the building boom and with it, steady employment. My folks bought the house in Woodside in 1930 and Dad became "idle" in 1932, the year I was born. I remember the expression "being idle," for it was quite common for a decade until the onset of World War II.

Although Dad suffered the lack of steady employment the same as many others, as a child I never realized this. He also had a plumbing business with a partner Billie Hahn and Gallagher and Hahn were not as active as previous years. We always had plenty to eat and a warm, clean and cozy home. I remember great Christmas holidays and one in particular when I received a basic Gilbert Chemistry set.

The only disappointment I recall is my mom's reluctance to ever buy me a pair of knee high lace-up leather boots, just like the boots Roy Chapman Andrews wore in the Gobi Desert. She issued me instead big brother's hand-me-down oversized rubber galoshes.

In Dad's Model A Ford we traveled on some summer vacations to Scranton, Pennsylvania, my dad's hometown to visit family. At home on summer weekends, Dad would take us to Rockaway Beach or to Jones Beach to enjoy the waves on the ocean side as well as the calm waters of the bay. On the way there, me and my brother Johnny, sitting in the back seat, would strain our young eyes trying to spot the prominent Jones Beach Tower. The first to spot the tower would be rewarded with a whole nickel.

In the summer, a special treat was when big brother John would take me to Astoria Pool where he taught me how to swim and I've loved the water all my life. Mom would give big brother enough for admission which was only a few cents each. The bus fare was five cents each way to Steinway Street where we transferred free to the Ditmars Boulevard bus and then a short ride to the beautiful new and spacious Queensboro Astoria Pool complex. We also had enough for a hot dog and an orange drink at Nedick's on the corner of Broadway and Steinway Street. We waited there for the bus to take us to the pool each holding under our arms, our swim trunks neatly wrapped up in a clean fresh towel.

At the pool, we were given a metal basket for our clothes and an elasticized tag with a numbered metal medallion and entered into a large open changing room. We attached the medallion on our arm or leg then slipped into our bathing suits and turned in our clothing stacked basket covered by our towels.

We then walked through the required shower and the chemically treated foot bath and finally, through an opening to the huge three pool complex. The sounds of hundreds of kids yelling and screaming and laughing while having a great time still ring in my ears. No gangs, no bullies, no drugs, no race hatred, no fights or violence of any kind.

My folks read the New York Daily News, the Herald Tribune, Journal American and others I have forgotten plus a local Long Island paper that I delivered but now cannot recall that name. My dad was an avid newspaper reader in those days and I remember stacks of newspapers my brother had stored in the basement to later   bring to a re-cycler who paid him a few cents a pound. A dim memory remains of Mayor LaGuardia reading the Sunday comics to kids on the radio when one of the papers was on strike.

The large general pool in the middle of the Astoria Pool complex was probably four or maybe five feet deep at the deepest part which is where I spent all my time. There was a kiddie pool with sprinklers on one end and a deep diving pool for the more experienced swimmers on the other end. This is where Brother John would venture to see how high he could dive. The diving platforms were at several levels and John was an excellent swimmer. There was also a refreshment pavilion but Mom told us to buy our refreshment at Nedick's because prices were too expensive at the pool. I don't remember ever eating or drinking anything there. (For interesting images go online to "Images Astoria Pool Queens County, NYC").

On Sunday, we all went to Saint Sebastian's Church on 58th Street, a few avenues from our home, to attend mass. As a public school student I also attended religious instruction at the St. Sebastian Catholic School every Wednesday afternoon. This was to prepare for First Holy Communion and Confirmation. I was always uncomfortable there and never got used to the very stern nuns whom I felt treated public school kids with some disdain compared to the Saint Sebastian's Catholic School children.

Some Sundays after church, we would drive in the Model A to the Lower East Side of Manhattan, to a Jewish tenement neighborhood to shop for clothing. The stores were open all day on Sunday and the area was alive with activity. Barrels of kosher dill pickles and pickled herring were on the sidewalks and in colder seasons, yams and chestnuts roasted on open grills right on the streets. It was there my dad introduced me to pickled herring which I still enjoy to this day.

The streets were lined up with push carts and the stores were located on the first level of the tenement buildings. Some of the buildings were adorned with wrought iron grating along with signs announcing the wares inside. Many of the signs were printed both in English and Hebrew script.

When first married in 1925, Mom and Dad lived in a Jewish neighborhood in the South Bronx where they made many life-long friends. As a child I thought Aunt Tillie and Uncle Joe Levy and daughter Anita were actually relatives. Tillie was a big vivacious red-haired woman with a happy demeanor and Joe was tall and lanky with a gruff voice and a warm smile. Anita was older and quite beautiful and about John's age. John knew the Levy's were not actual relatives and always had a crush on Anita. My childhood memories of the Levy family are all happy ones of a family who lived in a luxurious apartment on the Grand Concourse in the Bronx. Mom learned many Yiddish words from her friends. "Make Shana" (nice) and "Shana Madel" (nice girl) still remain in my memory.

Mom bought all of our clothing in the same stores she shopped in with her mother earlier in the century. This was when the large Cavallo family lived in an apartment on West 28th Street in Manhattan. She knew several generations of shopkeepers personally and it was like visiting family. I remember one store where we bought dry goods such as sheets and towels. The man was in tears and Mom Nellie was comforting the mother or grandmother. She was told one of their babies was just born with a club foot and everyone was crying. I remembered this but I was more interested in the pastrami sandwich at Katz's Deli which Dad promised at the end of the day.

The prices in the stores on the Lower East Side were never marked, they were negotiated or better yet, they were "haggled."

Mom knew many Yiddish expressions and spoke the language to the older vendors and she was a pretty good "haggler" herself. In good times Dad took us all to Katz's Delicatessen on East Houston and Ludlow Streets for an overflowing hand carved hot pastrami sandwich on Jewish rye bread, with mustard and a new dill pickle accompanied by a cream soda. I savored pastrami in famous Deli's both in Hollywood and at Manhattan's Stage Deli on 7th Avenue, but Katz's was better. I lick my lips just writing about it. Christmas of 2012, son John surprised us with a gift package from Katz's Delicatessen and I was to again enjoy the famous pastrami with Lee.

At that time Dad and his partner Billie Hahn had their Gallagher and Hahn Plumbing business located near Delancey Street and my Mom's sister Aunt Lucy worked there as a secretary. The old antique Remington Typewriter she used was a prop in one of son John's early movies.

My ninth birthday was a milestone because I could now join the Junior Blue Jackets of America, (JBA). This was also an important time for our family because our new baby brother James Martin also joined us in 1941. Jimmy was a beautiful baby and everyone fussed over him. He had blonde curly hair and blue eyes.

There was quite a span of years between Jimmy and his two older brothers, nine years for me and fifteen years for John, so Jim missed out on much of the closeness brothers had with each other. Jim grew up to become a loving and caring son to our Mom and Dad and, together with his beautiful wife Katherine, took good care of our folks and embraced Mom after our Dad passed away. When in their pre and early teens our sons John and Vincent enjoyed Aunt Kay and Uncle Jim's love and attention when the boys spent many summers with my folks in Woodside. This was at a time when Lee and I were building our new business in Philadelphia.

The JBA was a popular Queens County naval oriented organization. I was introduced to the JBA by my brother John who was a member for a while. Speaking of Brother John and before it slips my mind, I must mention his inclination to scare the hell out of me as often as he could. Before I ever saw the movie *Dracula*, the name incurred a shudder of fear in me ... it just sounded evil.

John told me Count Dracula lived in our garage in the backyard right outside our bedroom window and at night he would purposely open the window .... "Shhhh, be very quiet or 'D' will hear you sooooo just go to sleeeeep." "Mom, Mom ... Johnny is scaring me again!" Which, he would vehemently deny with a hurt expression on his face.

When I joined the JBA, I had to sign up and pay, I think, twenty five cents weekly dues. All the senior officers had U. S. Navy or Merchant Marine experience. The training program consisted of military subjects such as close order drill, manual of arms, military courtesy and discipline, first aid, semaphore and Morse code, knot tying, map reading and any subjects that would work within the confines of the school gymnasium at P. S. 152. Members attended drill in a modified blue navy uniform and were inspected to make sure their uniform and appearance was "ship shape". The white hat, belt and leggings must be freshly washed since last drill and the blues pressed and cleaned. Pride in one's appearance was important and the boys strived for that approval.

The drill was always followed by basketball games. After taking orders for a couple hours, this was a welcomed break to allow the boys to let off some steam before they went home. After the drill and followed by the basketball game, the young sailors were in less than the neat well-appointed form they started out with and this gave them the responsibility to make sure their "blues" were clean and pressed and their "whites" would be sparkling clean for next Friday night's drill.

Looking back, it was good training for young boys and gave them a sense of right and wrong, some discipline and respect for authority, added was some knowledge about personal cleanliness and hygiene which helped impart some pride in appearance and self-esteem.

These were simple and carefree days for a nine-year-old boy. That is until, one Sunday after church on the way to go shopping in the Lower East Side, a dramatic event occurred that changed our lives and the lives of all Americans.

We were stopped at a red light on Delancey Street on the Manhattan side of the Williamsburg Bridge when we noticed a great deal of excitement that seemed to electrify the crowds of people moving about. Dad opened the window of our Model A Ford and asked a policeman what was happening.

The policeman replied with shocking news: "The Japs bombed Pearl Harbor." This was about 2:00 PM Sunday, December 7th, 1941. When we got home, out came the world globe map and encyclopedia to see where Pearl Harbor was located and the radio turned on for more news.

My uncle and cousins on both the Gallagher and the Cavallo families served in World War II. Brother Johnny served in the Navy and his picture in uniform was displayed in our dining room next to the picture of our cousin Private Vincent Cavallo, killed in Burma in 1944. Among the Cavallo's serving were Mom's brother, Louie Cavallo, cousins and brothers Joe, Frank, Jimmie and Angelo Chiara and cousin Jerry Longo...Aunt Lucy Cavalla's husband Jack Toland served in the Merchant Marine. On the Gallagher side of the family our cousins Michael George (M.G.) McGraw, an Annapolis graduate, served as a naval officer and his brother Bill McGraw served in the army. Cousins Frank (Bud) Dougher served in the army and his brother Bill in the navy.

During the years of World War II, my Aunt Lucy's husband Jack Toland would take me to the U. S. Merchant Marine office and lounge in lower Manhattan. This is where merchant sailors would await job openings for seamen, specialty ratings and officers for duty on ships leaving the Port of New York. Jack was a Chief Steward and wore an officers uniform so he had access to areas most were not allowed.

This was early in the war when German submarines threatened the shipping lanes on the eastern seaboard. Many merchant ships and crews were lost to torpedo attack within sight of the New York City skyline. This was before blackouts were mandated and the bright lights of Manhattan silhouetted the ships outlines. This made the merchant ships easy targets for German submarines. German espionage and sabotage was also a threat, so only select persons could enter restricted areas. For this reason,

Uncle Jack thought it a good idea for me to wear my JBA uniform when I accompanied him to the Merchant Marine offices.

We were never refused entry but I took a lot of kidding from the real seamen. I was proud to accompany Uncle Jack even if it meant taking a lot of joking from the old seasoned and sometimes slightly, or more than slightly, inebriated merchant sailors. They would be surprised to see a ten or eleven-year-old kid in uniform with petty officer stripes and hash marks on his sleeve.

Wisecracks were common. "They're takin' them younger every day." "How old are you, boy, with all those hash marks?" Regular U. S. Navy sailors wore one red stripe hash mark for each four years served while JBA sailors wore one for every year served. My reply, "Eleven years old, sir," always resulted in an unbelieving shake of their heads. Some of the old salts had been going to sea since they were youngsters themselves.

Later in 1944 brother John was drafted into the Navy. I can remember that sad day when we waved farewell to Johnny as he boarded the train at Grand Central Station and headed for boot camp at Sampson Naval Training Center. Around that same time in 1944 my Grandma Maria Cavallo, at home alone, received the dreaded telegram from the War Department with the wrenching news that read, "We regret to inform you that your son, PFC Louis Cavallo, is missing in action." She could not read or write and the telegram terrorized her with fright not knowing what bad news the telegram was announcing. My memory rewinds to that day when I saw my Grandma Maria half walking and half running down our street.

Her face was streaked with tears and her hair was blowing in the wind and all the while she was holding a crumpled telegram in her hand and shouting for my mother, "Nellie, Nellie, what it says about Louie." Uncle Louie was an infantryman fighting in France and separated from his unit. Soon afterwards, we received a letter from Louie assuring us he was all right. I kept up a correspondence with my Uncle Louie all during the war and recall his joyous "Welcome Home Louie" party at Grandma Cavallo's house at the end of the war.

It is interesting to note Louie and my Mom devised a code just before Louie was sent overseas. In a letter, Louie disclosed the word FRANCE hidden from the censors so my Mom knew where he was. They created a code about the first letter of the second word in a complicated number of sentences that she kept on record. Overseas in those days could mean any number of places in the world.

Mom Nellie was born in Colliano, Italy and arrived in the U.S. when she was only one-year old in 1903, nevertheless, she could speak, read and write Italian and of course English without any accent and did not even speak with the marked New York accent we all have. Italian was spoken at home. For years she served as translator for family, friends and neighbors receiving letters from loved ones in Italy and, in some cases, served as the scribe also.

Mom's name was always a mystery and as our little family grew up we never learned how she acquired the name Nellie. The manifest dated 1903 from the German ship Palatia shows Nellie listed as Donatello Cavallo a one year old boy... her given name was Donatella. Both her parents were illiterate and when asked questions probably said "Si" to everyone to avoid any problems in transit to the new world. Once becoming of age to attend school in New York City and wishing to become more Americanized, many Eastern and Southern Europeans selected more American sounding names. I would not doubt for a minute that Nellie hand-picked her own name but cannot imagine why "Nellie"...she probably thought it sounded very American!

My Mom was a sweetheart and loved by all but, she was also a strong-minded woman. Her sister Aunt Lucy Cavalla went a step further to show her independence by replacing the male gender vowel O with the feminine vowel A in her surname. Both girls grew up with seven brothers and their Dad made for eight males all living in one apartment but, Grandma Maria was still the Matriarch of the Cavallo clan. I remember hearing stories about Grandma standing at the front door every Friday, as all the men dropped their week's wages in her opened apron and she decided how much weekly spending money each one deserved. Keeping with old country tradition, she also bought the bedroom set for each son when they married. Lee reminds me when Uncle John and Aunt Tina Cavallo showed us their home in Forest Hills years later, she commented about Grandma Cavallo's extravagant taste in bedroom furniture. Lee reminded me that her parents owned the very same bedroom set.

All the Cavallo siblings Americanized their names; Giuseppe the oldest became Joseph, Donato, Fred, Dominick Daniel, Carmine Charles, Giovanni John and Luigi Louis…Uncle Angelo remained Angelo. All the Cavallo's had sky blue eyes and fair complexions and spoke with not a hint of an accent. Although Italian was spoken at home, I recall all the siblings urging their parents to speak more English at home. All the siblings were educated in New York City public schools to the eighth grade and all had beautiful handwriting…the youngest may have gone to high school.

Within days of Grandma Cavallo's receipt of the telegram about Uncle Louie the Cavallo family was again struck by tragedy. My Aunt Mary and Uncle Freddy Cavallo received the devastating telegram telling them their 19-yearold son Vincent was killed in action in Myitkyina, Burma. Louie arrived in France on D-Day, June 6th, 1944 and Vincent was killed in Burma on June 28th, 1944.

My brother John received a medical discharge from the Navy some months after because he could no longer hide from the Navy the fact that he experienced occasional seizures. During his time in the service he secreted his Dilantin capsules to control the seizures in a tin tooth powder can (Tooth Powder quite popular in the 1940's). After boot camp he trained at the Naval Air Station in Opa-Loka, Florida. While there, he had a seizure and received an unwanted medical discharge. We were more than happy to see him home again.

It was common to see the white banner with the red border and blue star displayed in the front windows showing that an individual from that household served in the military. Too many windows in Woodside displayed a gold star on the banner indicating a loved one who served from that family had been killed in action. With great relief, Mom removed the Blue Star banner from our front window, thankful that John was home again and under our roof safe and sound. It was indeed rare to see a front window in Woodside without a Blue or Gold Star banner.

One summer, many years before the war, we were in Scranton visiting with my dad's sister Aunt Marguerite Gallagher McGraw whom we called "Aunt Reety." Brother John was running around the house with Cousin Bill McGraw when John went crashing into a glass window or door. He cut and split his temple and carried the star shaped scar on his temple all his life. The doctors thought this may have caused the epileptic seizures from which no one else in either the Gallagher or the Cavallo family suffered. He was about 10 or 11 when it happened and the first seizure occurred back in Woodside some- time later.

When at home and in between ships, Uncle Jack Toland took me to visit vessels he sailed on that were docked in Brooklyn and Manhattan. The ship yards during the war were heavily guarded and shipyards operated under strict war time security. I remember guards looking at me and shaking their heads in disbelief at how young they were taking seaman.

For me at the time, it was an education and a thrill to be aboard these huge seagoing vessels that smelled from diesel oil topside and the aroma of food cooking in the galley below deck. It seemed to me they ate well in the Merchant Marine. Even though the ships were tied up and not under way it was always a thrill for me. My Uncle Jack treated me like an adult and it was good to be with him. I think he was a little proud of me for taking the joking and remarks from the old salts while keeping a smile on my face. Addressing the old timers with a "yes sir" and "no sir" always threw them off guard and I always said it with a big grin.

The JBA had a sailing vessel of its own named *James A. Webster*. The *Webster* was a far cry from those huge gray steel ships I visited. She was an old wooden schooner carrying double masts with fore and aft sails and about 150 feet long.

The *Webster* was built in Maine in the 19th century and started life hauling granite and lumber from Rockland, Maine to ports along the east coast. The *Webster* became a training ship for the JBA and was berthed at Port Washington on the north shore of Long Island on the Long Island Sound.

During the spring, summer and fall, weekend training cruises were offered for a few dollars to those kids who had their parents' written permission.

The young sailors would arrive on a Friday evening and board ship. Following U. S. Naval tradition upon boarding ship, the youngsters were instructed to first turn aft to salute the American flag flown on the flagstaff and then turn to face and salute the Officer of the Deck. Upon boarding they would be assigned to either the starboard or the port watch.

After climbing down to the lower deck, they would find their assigned bunks which were lined up on both sides of the ship. The starboard watch bunked on the right side and the port watch on the left side. The older JBA petty officers would give them instruction about shipboard living and what their individual responsibilities would be while aboard, which was simply to obey all orders.

Life jackets were issued to all hands and then they were shown the proper way to wear them. The boys were drilled in the procedure to abandon ship if this became necessary. The Long Island sound is a large body of water and could be a dangerous place to be when a sudden storm struck. Back in the 1940's we did not get minute to minute weather reports. This added a hint of risk to help keep the boys alert. The JBA was very strict especially when the younger boys were aboard. When cruises were restricted to the older boys somewhat more freedom was allowed but no nonsense was tolerated while aboard the *James A. Webster*.

When stepping down to the lower deck the old ship had a smell to her which was not offensive, but smelled of wood, tar and I guess the sea, which all the young sailors noticed.

Because the *Webster* was originally a cargo vessel there were no port holes. When below deck within the cramped quarters and low overhead some felt a little confining at first. But this was soon overcome, after a full day of working both the ship and the body. That bunk was a welcome relief and made one feel kind of warm and secure to be wrapped up in the protection of that old ship. It felt good to me and I'm certain the other boys felt the same way. The soft rolling of the ship helped me to fall asleep, waking up the next morning and loving the *Webster*.

I took many cruises aboard the *Webster* and enjoyed every one of them. With not much to comment about the food, I do remember pancakes one morning served with jam. The pancakes were all loose and runny inside but I ate them anyway without making a complaint.

The *Webster* had the original top rigging removed to prevent the boys from attempting to climb aloft...all Rat Lines (climbing lines) were removed from the shrouds which were off limits to the younger boys. The wind was the only source of power provided by the huge fore and aft sails and jibs. The main deck was open and gave plenty of room to haul and lower the sails. Only older boys were permitted to climb out on the bowsprit to set and haul in the *jib s'ls*...jib sails for you landlubbers.

The anchor was hoisted with the aid of a small gas-powered winch. We could not operate the hand powered capstan. The capstan was used before power assists on all sailing vessels to haul in the anchor and perform other more strenuous functions. The sailing master showed us how the old capstan was used but we could not even budge it. Recalling the old adage, "Wooden ships manned by Iron Men." No "Iron Men" among the kids from Queens County, New York City.

The little power winch was the only engine aboard and when under way the *Webster* relied totally on wind power. Moving her from dockside into the wind was accomplished with the aid of a motor powered launch. The sailing master would direct the launch to come along side of the *Webster*. The order to remove the bow and stern lines was given and with padded prow the launch would slowly push the ship from the dock into the channel and then out and into the wind. While the ship was sailing, the launch was covered with a tarpaulin and towed behind the ship. The *Webster* also had a smaller skiff that when under sail was hoisted on davits aft on the quarter deck. The launch together with the skiff could accommodate all hands in case of emergency.

Some form of lighting was provided by a battery system for the few light bulbs below decks. It was very dim light and we were in a total blackout when lights out was ordered. All hands were instructed to bring flashlights for use at night if they were on watch or had to use the head (toilet).

While at sea, a watch crew was stationed at the helm 24 hours a day and, everyone had his turn at night watch. I forgot the salty terms we used and the number of bells that rang when the watch was changed, but that was all part of the experience aboard ship.

The duties were equally divided from swabbing the decks to preparing chow, cleaning the galley and setting and hauling in the sail. The days were filled with classes and shipboard duties. Each young sailor was given a "Trick at the Wheel." We learned about navigating with the stars on clear evenings and were also entertained by hearing ship lore yarns at night.

Having 30 or so young boys on board was a big responsibility for the officers and Ship's Master, and military courtesy and discipline were strictly enforced. No practical joking was tolerated; that was to come later when I joined the National Guard and then entered active service. When told to do something, you did it. If you had a question about it, you could discuss it later.

Sounds a little undemocratic but one must remember the JBA was working an old sailing vessel with young boys and the seniors were there to help make it a safe and interesting voyage. Most of us young boys would later serve in the active military and would not be surprised to hear the old adage about when ordered to do something, just do it now and then, "Bitch about it later."

Depending on weather and the ages of the sailors the destinations were to places like a short trip to City Island for the younger kids where they would debark for an ice cream sundae. The older boys sailed across the Long Island Sound to Greenwich, Connecticut.

The weekend cruises were something to look forward to and I still use the knowledge I learned aboard the Webster. By the time I was 15 in 1947, the JBA had lost its appeal. Dressing up in a sailor suit, and having to wash my white hat, belt and leggings every week to pass inspection for Friday night's drill, was becoming humdrum.

My petty officer rank was Boatswain Mate First Class and my Mom altered my uniform for the last time. When I joined the JBA in 1941, a neighbor of ours had access to naval stores at the Brooklyn Navy Yard and for a few dollars my mom purchased a regulation woolen U. S. Navy uniform. The uniform was purchased large enough so it could be altered as I grew. Mom's mother taught her to take in the seams and then letting them out again as I grew. She took in and shortened everything when I first joined and let out a little each year until it could not be taken out any more. My next promotion would be to Chief Petty Officer which required a new officer's type uniform and this was totally out of the question.

Several of my JBA friends were all feeling the same desire to move on. Chief Petty Officer Page told us about his dad's friend who was a Sergeant in the 12th Infantry Regiment, New York State Guard. They were issued summer, winter and field uniforms at no cost, and trained and fired real weapons, some right in the armory. Best of all you were paid for the two week summer camp tour.

That opened a new and interesting window. One Friday night, Page mentioned he was going to the 12th Regiment Armory the next Monday night and invited some of us to come along. The old 12th Regiment Armory was located on West 62nd Street and Columbus Avenue in Manhattan.

That Monday several of us went to the armory where we met Page's father's friend. We were introduced to the G Company commander, Captain Klopfer, and the First Sergeant, Master Sergeant Hirsch. All went well and some of the guys said they would think it over but I signed on the spot along with Neuman and Miller. Page never did join.

I was aware that 17 was the minimum age and I was only 15 so I told Sergeant Hirsch I was 17 and he handed me a parental consent form for those under the age of 18. I wondered if this was going to be an obstacle. I thought I could convince my dad to sign the form. When I went home and asked him to sign for me, his reply was a big and loud, "absolutely NO."

My Dad was born in 1896, and raised in an Irish Catholic Anthracite coal mining community in Scranton, Pennsylvania. When his father Michael first came to America from County Mayo, Ireland, he worked in the coal mines. I recall many stories about how hard the miners worked and the dangers they faced both to their health and the all too common mine accidents. Later in life, my grandfather was able to advance himself so he no longer had to work in the coal mines.

Although my father never actually worked in the mines as a young boy, he worked after school and in the summer tending the mules that were used to haul the coal cars in the mines. He also "picked slate," an expression to describe the job youngsters were hired for at a few pennies a day to separate the pieces of coal falling off the coal shipments from the slate or stone on the ground. It must have been back breaking work, imagine any kids doing that today.

He recalled the stories about the violence between the miners and the militia. The mine owners, the police and the militia were all allied against the miners who were trying to organize. The fledgling unions were fighting for better pay, shorter working hours, and safer working conditions and many miners were beaten and some killed during those turbulent times.

Dad grew up with this history fresh in his mind. To the working families with their men toiling in the mines the militia members were a much hated group. My Dad said no son of his would be a strike breaker so that pretty much ended my enlistment desires. I nagged and pleaded and finally my Dad agreed to sign the form. My Dad in his younger day was a tough Irishman to deal with but I always had a way to persuade him. I was now in G Company, reconnaissance squad, 12th Infantry Regiment New York State Guard. This was sometime in early 1947.

Thanks to our prior training we three received immediate promotions, Neuman was promoted to Staff Sergeant, Miller to Buck Sergeant and I was now a Corporal ... my navy blues were cleaned, folded, moth balled and stored in a trunk ... Nellie never threw anything away and found a use for everything.

I seem to remember that old navy blue blouse later converted to an attractive and warm woolen vest.

Dangerous Youthful Antic

The Gilbert Chemistry set opened a whole new world to me. My curiosity urged me to take things a step further, which could have resulted in tragedy. I soon wearied of adding chemicals that changed red water to a colorless liquid and other dull experiments and while snooping around the library I came across an old chemistry book. As I thumbed through the book I came upon a chapter titled "Black Gun Powder." I was probably 10 or maybe 11. I checked out the book and took it home and for the next few days I absorbed the content.

This was of course prior to the internet access and I do not remember how I discovered the source for the material I would need for my experiments. But, I did find John H. Winn Chemical Company on West 23rd Street in Manhattan. John H. Winn's management would be arrested and sued out of business if they attempted to sell those same chemicals to children today. Apparently, I was not the only curious kid to buy my dangerous chemicals from John H. Winn. I found a forum online about like-minded children and now adults posting tidbits about the dangerous chemicals they bought from John H Winn.

I walked up to the 61st and Roosevelt Avenue train station and journeyed into Manhattan with the contents of my piggy bank and a check list of needed ingredients stuffed in my pocket. With absolutely no questions asked about my age the clerk acknowledged my order. He left and quickly returned and placed on the counter three blue one pound containers similar to Morton Salt containers with small John H. Winn's labels attached. Each container was packed with one of the three necessary ingredients for making black gun powder. I will not repeat the exact ingredients here for obvious reasons. Trying to remember how old I was on my first trip to Winn's is difficult but, I do recall looking up at that counter top to retrieve my chemicals.

I am sure today's youths could go on line and find this detail and much more to satisfy any curiosity so, I will only explain the process. A ceramic mortar and pestle is needed to avoid any metal to metal spark. The ingredients must be

23

thoroughly mixed wet to prevent an explosion. Black powder can explode by a spark from static electricity or any other means. The drying process is also critical so it should be left undisturbed until dry and then very carefully handled. I added a lock to the roll top desk and Mom asked, "Why the lock." I simply commented, "I didn't want anyone touching my chemical set.

In those days, I was not yet close to the Lord but my folks were devout. It was their prayers for me that protected me from myself even though they did not know what I was doing with my Gilbert Chemistry set.

I made little round golf ball sizes of wet paste wrapped in Kleenex tissues, previously soaked in a solution of XXXX and H2O and then set to dry. Not being contained they would only burn violently when ignited.

After school I took them out to the empty lots and lit them with a fuse made by soaking and then drying the string which I borrowed from my Mom's ball of cotton thread she used to wrap her fowl and meat roasts and "Braciole" (Italian wrapped and stuffed beef).

Further research revealed to me that by adding other chemicals to the mixture, I could change the flame color. Strontium nitrate added red, Barium blue and Zinc Oxide added green to the blaze.

It was not long before my older pal Marty O'Grady from across the street became my accomplice. The flares now increased to baseball size. My Mom often asked Dad, "John, have you used any tissues from my Kleenex box, I think I just put a full box on the cabinet." Naturally, I made like I hadn't heard a thing Mom said. Mom Nellie never missed the cotton string but this did prompt me to buy my own supply of Kleenex tissues before my experiments were exposed!!!

My part time jobs always sustained my piggy bank jingling and, it allowed me to operate in the black having, a very low overhead.

With my buddy Marty, I experimented with different types of fuse material before settling on a particular brand which we bought and added to our supply of material. Trips to John H. Winn became more frequent.

Marty had a stop watch so we further experimented with timing our fuse. Marty entered high school a year or so before I did and then we both lost further interest in our array of colored flares. We finally burned everything in an empty lot. I believe my folks' prayers were answered even though they never knew about these antics.

Woodside Wanderings in the Model A Ford

The Model A Ford
istock.com

Pictured is a 1931 Model A Ford Tudor Gray 2 door sedan just like the one my Dad owned. I do not remember the model year it was. Ford made almost 5 million Model A's in several styles in gray, green or black using the same basic design between 1927 and 1931.

On the floor in the rear of the car, was a storage compartment and that is where we stored live crabs after catching them in Freeport. In the 1930's Freeport in Nassau County Long Island, was a beach town on the south shore. It was developed with streets and all improvements but the depression halted the planned new construction.

Mom would pack a lunch and prepare our big gallon Thermos jug filled with homemade lemonade or Kool-Aid, a very popular depression era beverage. For just a few pennies, a family could make a gallon of colored sweet tasting sugar water.

In those days, the Freeport streets were separated by canals. It was designed so that the new homeowners could moor their boats alongside the proposed new homes, which never happened. Dad would park our Ford next to one of these canals and we would set up the beach chairs and improvised table, and start "Crabbing." Mom would meanwhile prepare our lunch.

The drill was to just tie a chicken back onto a long piece of string, drop it into the canal and let it sink to the bottom. Then we would slowly retrieve it all the while watching if any crabs attached their claws to the chicken back. When the crab took hold you continued to pull the string very slowly being sure the crab did not let go. When the crab was within scooping range, Dad would reach out with a long handled net, scoop up the crab and chicken back with one clean stroke. We would shout, "Hooray for Dad." Dad used a work glove or rag to snatch up the crab and put it in the "Crab Locker" in the floor of the car.

Some crabs got away and we all scrambled to catch them before the crab could make it back to the canal wall and slip back into the water. All the way back to our home in Woodside we could hear the crabs rattling around in the "Crab Locker."

I also remember the clear blue sky and the fresh smell of the seashore in Freeport in the 1930's, still untouched by the future building boom in the late 1940's and 1950's. These were happy times before World War II when strict gas rationing restricted these fun day excursions.

Vinny and the Pop Gun

Between the age of about 4 to about 6 or so, one of my favorite toys was a pop gun that Dad bought for me. With a pullback on the bolt to compress a spring, a cork tied on a string was loaded in the muzzle. A squeeze of the trigger would send the cork flying out. The cork moved along at a pretty good clip. I soon realized I could extend the range of the cork by simply cutting off the string. I found similar sized old corks which gave me a supply of projectiles. In the 1930's, corks were plentiful and used on almost every glass container. Today, everything is made of plastic with closures that are almost impossible to remove without tools.

I aimed my pop gun at many objects and practiced until I became quite proficient. One afternoon while seated as usual in the rear seat of the Model A directly in back of my dad, I noticed his big Irish ears (which by the way, I inherited from him). My curiosity and impishness got the better of me and I wondered if I popped my Dad's ear, would he think this was funny?? So, I aimed and squeezed off a perfect shot!!! John Aloysius Gallagher, a man with a sense of humor did not think *this* was funny. John A. pulled over to the side of the road and gave me a couple of good smacks on the rear end. He threatened to break and throw away that "damned pop gun" if I ever did it AGAIN. I never, ever, did it AGAIN.

When big brother John and I got into a scuffle in the back seat, which was all of the time, Dad would pull over to the side of the road and give us a couple of slaps on the butt. We would cry out in agony but slyly giggle at each other over the light-handed smacks. Following our butt smacks, if we passed a Howard Johnsons, Dad would buy us an ice cream cone and he would have one of his own favorites, Strawberry or Pistachio!!! Our dad had a harsh word but a soft heart…I always loved him and I still do.

Vinny with his popgun in front of a neighbors home.

Woodside Tenants

We had a varied assortment of tenants in our upstairs apartment over the years. When Dad converted the six-room apartment to two very nice one-bedroom, one-bath apartments with living rooms and eat-in kitchens, this limited tenant occupancy to maybe one or two people for each apartment. Before the conversion, our tenants were usually large families which increased the activity and maintenance of our home.

Early in my memory is a large Irish family by the name of McGroarty. I could not pronounce the name as a child and still

28

have trouble spelling and pronouncing it today. Mr. and Mrs. McGroarty spoke with strong Irish brogues. She was a housewife and he was a Fifth Avenue bus driver whom I always thought was a policeman because of his uniform. They pronounced my name with a strong accent, "VEN-cint." I remember them talking about my skinny physique and advising my Mom, "Now Nellie darlin', give VEN-cint a bit of beer because you know dear, its nurrishin', yes, yes beer is nurrishin'."

Whenever friends or relatives came over from the old sod they would stay with the McGroarty's until the relative became…"Sit-she-ayted." I remember the laughter and partying upstairs of a large Irish family.

The McGroarty's would bring their newly arrived clansman downstairs to meet the "Galla'hers," and I remember one in particular who may have been Billie O'Malley. After introductions and handshakes, the Irishman noticed a small dish of mom's homemade hot red cherry peppers left over from dinner. The Irishmen asked mom, "Mrs. Galla'her, now, what are them little red things on the table?" She replied, "Oh, I don't think you would like them Billie, they are very hot." In a wink, he popped one in his mouth, bit down and did an Irish jig right in our dining room. The colder the water he drank the hotter the pepper burned as he howled, "Be-jaysus I never taysted such fire." "Eat some bread," Nellie advised. I do recall Billie O'Malley encouraging one of his newly arrived greenhorn clansmen to try the "Galla'hers' sweet red peppers", followed by more Irish jigs.

I got to know Billie O'Malley as he became well known in Woodside. He was always in one of the bars along 39th Avenue and there were many. He would see me and buy me a beer. This is when I was in my early- to mid-teens and the bartenders would not hesitate to give me a short beer; they were all Irishmen and would take a sip of beer along with us. Billie's "profession," if that's what we shall call it, was "helper" for any carpenter, painter, plumber or tradesman who would give him a day's work whenever he was sober. He worked for my Dad from time to time. Billie smoked his cigarettes all the way down to almost his lip before he tossed it out…long before filter tips. Dad always warned me to stay away from Billie O'Malley because he drank too much.

My memory of Billie O'Malley was of a good-natured Irishman who always had a laugh and a smile for everyone. Yes, he did drink too much but I never saw him falling down drunk, or without a smile on his face.

By the time I was 12 or 13, the McGroaty's had long since moved out and Mr. McG was retired from the 5th Avenue Bus Company. He was now working with a relative in East Durham in the Catskill Mountains who owned an Irish-American boarding house and cottages. These resorts were very popular in the Catskills Mountains where, they served ethnic food and offered popular entertainment for many different cultures and nationalities for city folk wishing to spend some leisure time in the mountains. We vacationed there twice, the food was great and the parties every night were very loud with Irish music and Irish laughter.

I was not happy there until I discovered a trout stream in a meadow behind the resort but at the time, did not have the skill or proper fishing tackle necessary to catch one. I could clearly see the fish darting about in the stream. I later learned they were rainbow trout. I could see their pinkish paint brush-like splash along the side of their bodies as they sped by and I really wanted to catch one.

Many years were to pass before I became proficient with a spinning rod, and was always the neophyte with a fly rod. I caught many wild trout, rainbows, browns and brook trout in the streams of upstate New York and the rolling Pennsylvania countryside and, many years later, on the Big Horn River in Montana and the Brazos River in New Mexico. A trout stream runs right through Chesterbrook full of wild brown trout brought here from Germany back in the 19th century and today, flourish in Valley Creek. Unfortunately, the stream is polluted from the old Main Line railroad facilities in Paoli. The toxins do not affect the fish themselves but do affect those who would consume the fish so, the stream is posted "Catch and Release Only."

Tenants came and went and some stand out clearly in my memory mainly because the memories included food. Mom was a wonderful cook and Thursday night was always Spaghetti and Meatball night sometimes with homemade Italian sausage or cubes of beef or on special occasions Braciole …a tasty stuffed and rolled beef braised then cooked in the tomato sauce. The stuffing was made with fresh chopped parsley, grated parmigiana cheese, garlic and bread crumbs. Hmmm I think I will suggest this to Lee but, I will have to make it because she will skimp on the garlic. The dinner table back in Woodside always had a salad, Mom listened to Victor H. Lindlahr a 1930's nutritionist who coined the phrase "You are what you eat", the name of his popular book.

Mom cooked many dishes taught her by her Irish Mother-in-law and from the flow of tenants which assured a varied diet. I remember Mrs. Robbins, who taught Mom how to make a Jewish apple cake. Mrs. Robbins' son and daughter-in-law were tenants. I also remember Mrs. Bauer's pickled whitefish, which was a big hit with all of us. The only fish I remember eating as a kid was pickled herring, smoked whitefish and Mom Nellie's pickled whitefish. Mrs. Bauer was an older Austrian woman who showed me pictures and told me stories about her relative in the Austrian Army in World War One, then part of the Austro-Hungarian Empire at war with Imperial Russia. She told me about her relative's experience when confronted by a huge, burly and bedraggled Russian soldier who only wanted food and not war.

Mom exchanged recipes with all our tenants and neighbors. I remember a relish, for I can think of no better word for it, made by Mrs. Nardi our next door neighbor. I have tried for years to duplicate it but always missed. It was made with chopped walnuts, flavored with butter, olive oil and garlic, and crisped in a pan. I tried making it several ways and it was tasty but, never the way our neighbor made it. It was always a treat for the family when Mrs. Nardi would bring a big bowl full on a Thursday, our Spaghetti night.

I have a warm remembrance of a very nice couple and this was when I was still quite young. They owned a small boat, a cabin cruiser, moored in Flushing Bay across from what later became La Guardia Airport and once was the Marine Air Terminal where Pan American Clipper planes arrived and departed.

The couple offered to take me for a ride on their boat and then dine with the wife's family in Flushing. Mom did not like boats and said no until Dad interceded and said, "Oh Nellie ... let him go." I remember going on the boat for a ride with them and then having dinner at her family's home. The folks were German and spoke with strong accents. I recall the man asking the daughter in half German and half English what amounted to "Vell Shotsy, Vat does he look like, more Irish or more Ee-talian?" as I ate to my surprise a dinner of spaghetti and meatballs. Shotsy was the name her husband used to address her with also.

Shotsy was a tiny German lady with a big personality. For some reason, I remember an image of her rowing a little skiff they had tied up to the pier to take them back and forth to the moored boat. I also recall the sweet tasting tomato sauce that was much sweeter than I ever remember Nellie's tomato sauce tasting. Over the years some tenants left vivid memories and others only tidbits of images in my young brain.

After meeting Lee and discovering her family summer home in the Catskill Mountains, I often went deer hunting and trout fishing there with my pal Jim Merget another lover of the fields and streams. Usually, the family house was quite busy during deer season and we preferred hunting alone. At times, we would stay at Butler's Old Empire Guest House located on Route 23 in the town of Lexington. The Butlers were an Austrian couple with a tuneful sound to their accents who catered to Austrian and German-American families from Manhattan in the summer time and to hunters in the fall. The food was great at the Butlers' and one evening we had spaghetti and meatballs with the same sweet tasting tomato sauce. The Butlers said all German people put sugar in the sauce to cut down on the acid of the tomatoes. Now that I have strayed so far from my story, I might just as well continue on to another anecdote about of all people, Arnold Schwarzenegger.

The villages of Lexington and Hunter in the Catskills attracted German, Austrian and Ukrainian people from New York City probably reminding them, of the forest and mountains of their homelands. Sometime in the 1990s, after many years of absence from Lexington, I returned to go trout fishing. On the way, I noticed on NY State Highway 42, approaching the bridge that crossed the Schoharie Creek into Lexington, some road signs proclaiming "Arnold Schwarzenegger slept here."

The arrow pointed into the road leading to the tiny hamlet of West Kill. I passed the signs several times at a restaurant called Marie's Dream House. Interested only in trout fishing I just ignored the signs and went on my way. I did find out later that Marie was Arnold's aunt by marriage to his Uncle Otto Schwarzenegger, Arnold's dad's brother.

By this time both Mr. and Mrs. Butler had passed away and their large Old Empire Guest House was still standing but now vacant. That wooden-framed many-gabled structure with the old fashioned wrap around porch was always so inviting after a day spent in the beautiful outdoors of Greene County in the Catskill Mountains. I was saddened now as I passed by to see it empty on Route 23. So, I double backed to Schwarzenegger's and met the gracious family. The Schwarzenegger's had great accommodations and even greater food including tomato sauce made with a little sugar added.

Otto Schwarzenegger was a big man like his nephew Arnold and also had a band. He traveled with his band all over the Catskill Mountains entertaining at resorts. Arnold's pictures and mementos were placed all over his uncle's resort and Arnold had actually slept there.

Mom got recipes from everyone from Orange Marmalade to German Sauerkraut to hot cherry peppers, tasty bread and butter pickles and other goodies. Brother John and I would treat ourselves from time to time...John knew where the key was for the cool pantry in the basement.

My job every Saturday was to scrub the tile entry way to our home and vacuum the carpet on the stairs leading to the apartments then, wax the exposed hard wood. Especially remembered is when I would climb the ladder outside to clean the windows on the first floor of our home with the popular Bon-Ami cleaner. Nellie remained on the inside vigorously pointing out the spots I missed and the look of disappointment when I continued to miss the same spots. Yes, at times she could be a tough top Sergeant.

As a kid growing up in Woodside I have nothing but wonderful memories of my Mom and Dad, big brother John and baby brother Jimmy. We all may not have shown it at the time but, there was a lot of love in that family and there still is in my heart.

Whitney & Kemmerer

As soon as I was 14 years old I got the required legal working papers and looked for a summer job. No more working under the radar at Benny Eisen's grocery store and delivering dead chickens every Saturday on my bike. It was now time to put on a white shirt and a nice tie to step up a notch and find a good full time summer job in an office.

Our tenant Gerald Robbins was an accountant who dressed in very good taste with expensive clothing. He had a wonderful wardrobe, pieces of which he often passed down to Mom when he tired of something. His suits, slacks and sport coats were all high ticket items with labels like Brooks Brothers and Hart, Schaffner and Marx. Mom was expert in tailoring Gerald's hand- me-downs and I was better dressed than most of my school teachers as long as you didn't look too close. Sometimes the two back pockets on the trousers were right next to each other when Mom took in the waist. I guess the Ironized Yeast Tabs and all those double and triple dinners that I ate added some height and weight to my teen-aged frame. I was a well turned-out young man all during high school years and filled out Gerald's clothing pretty well.

I think Dad was a little disappointed that I did not follow him into the plumbing trade. When Billy Hahn retired, Dad moved the Gallagher & Hahn business to First Avenue and 60th Streets in Manhattan now, Gallagher & Son. The new location was a short hop over the bridge to our home in Woodside.

Someone must have mentioned the Equitable Life Building at 120 Broadway in lower Manhattan which was my target to seek a job as office boy. On the first Monday morning of my summer vacation, I dressed, passed Mom's inspection, took the train to

34

lower Manhattan and found 120 Broadway. I took the elevator to the top floor of the 38-story office building and worked my way down. "Any openings for office boy?" "Nope." "OK. Thank you," and ran to the next office to repeat the question. I was not disheartened one bit by any of the frowns and answer of no. I was encouraged by the many smiles which kept my energy level up to continue knocking on doors.

Halfway down and still with a full head of steam, I repeated the question as I opened the door to Whitney & Kemmerer. I had a feeling this was going to be IT! There were maybe a dozen employees, both male and female, seated at desks when I entered. My first encounter was when a matronly and attractive well-dressed woman answered my announcement with "Yes, young man, we do need an office boy. Come in and sit down and talk to Mr. I Don't Remember His Name."

The pay $18-a-week salary, the hours were 9 to 5 five days a week with a three-quarter-hour lunch break and a quarter-hour AM and PM coffee break. I was shown around the office and introduced to all. The names are all lost to my aged old brain but they are all remembered as being very nice to me. I would start the next day for a few days trial. If it worked out, I had my job for the summer. Well, one could imagine how happy this 14-year-old felt … it was a great feeling and I could not wait to tell my Mom.

As I was leaving the building I could smell the aroma of fresh brewed coffee emanating from the luncheonette in the lobby. Having some silver in my pocket, I stopped in and spotted a mini-apple crumb pie. I ordered one with a glass of milk. That tasty pie was to be my afternoon break snack for the entire two months working there. The smell of coffee always tempted me in the AM snack time. Mom was a wonderful cook with many recipes and also an excellent baker. But, she did not drink regular coffee, Sanka or Postum were served at home so a hot cup of genuine coffee was a real treat.

Mom was happy and made sure I had a fresh laundered and ironed shirt and pressed trousers every morning. " Even tenant Gerald Robbins would say, "That suit looks better on you than it ever did on me." Gerald tired of his wardrobe while the clothing was still in very good condition.

There was no requirement to turn in any part of my pay at home and I was able to treat myself well. I started out having lunch in the lobby luncheonette but later found other places to eat, though I was still loyal to that apple crumb pie in the afternoon.

All the Whitney & Kemmerer staff treated me very kindly. I simply did everything I was asked to do, all with a smile and a sense of urgency. I had to file papers and sometimes deliver small packages to other offices or banks so about half my time was spent out of the office. I visited Trinity Church, peeked into Fraunces Tavern, visited Battery Park and took long looks at the Statue of Liberty. Wall Street meant nothing to me at age 14 except that in the 1600's Peter Stuyvesant built a log wall to protect New Amsterdam from attack by the Native Indians, Pirates and the British.

My further travels and inquiries led me to a discount sporting goods store somewhere in the area where I purchased a good quality fresh water casting rod and reel which was used for years fishing the ponds, lakes and streams of Long Island.

I also discovered Wally Frank Tobacconists. I could not resist the enticing smell of all the pipe tobacco flowing from the open door so I stepped right in. I was partial to a pipe and enjoyed the smell of great-uncle Martin Molloy's pipe which he always had with him. I treated myself to a mushroom-shaped good quality French briar pipe and a few ounces of a Wally Frank tobacco mixture and puffed away, it was not to last.

Now I did not smoke this pipe often but did keep it with me. Later that fall the pipe would cause me some woe and led to the confiscation of my Wally Frank Imported Mushroom Style Fancy French Briar Pipe.

Upon reporting to Bryant High School in September 1946 I re-connected with a sweet Southern blonde, blue eyed girl named Stacy. Some years earlier, my then single Aunt Lucy Cavalla befriended a southern gentlemen whom the entire family liked. He was a dapper dresser and debonair gentleman who worked in an exclusive gentlemen's clothing shop on Fifth Avenue. He looked the part with gray curly hair and mustache to match, impeccably dressed with tons of Southern charm and a pretty daughter named Stacy. I remember he smoked Old Gold cigarettes, maybe because I may have sneaked one.

Stacy came on the scene and lived with her Dad in an apartment in Jackson Heights an up-scale community bordering Woodside. We would see each other at Grandma Cavallo's gatherings from time to time.

I remember Mom taking me and Stacy to the DeLuxe Theater in Woodside when I was quite young, Stacy being a year or so older. I sat next to Stacy and held her hand and remember she smelled so nice, like pineapple I thought. Funny what us old guys remember. Somewhere along the way, Stacy left to live some place down south. I later learned her parents were divorced and she went to live down south with her mother.

When I started high school I was surprised to see Stacy there. She was already at Bryant, a year ahead of me. I forgot if we ran into each other when I joined the camera club or before but, we were both members and renewed our friendship. I hadn't seen her for some time and at 15 years old she had developed into a well-proportioned and a very beautiful young girl. She still had the same sweet disposition and cute Southern drawl. I noticed a marked renewal of our mutual interest in each other.

It was fun being with Stacy again and she taught me how to develop film and print photos in the darkroom. Every once in a while, when we were alone, we would pause for an innocent squeeze and a kiss but never progressed to anything beyond that.

Later that fall while wearing my new cold weather Red Buffalo plaid wool jacket Mom just bought for me, I was walking along 37th Avenue to 74th Street to see Stacy, all the while smoking my Wally Frank Imported Mushroom Style Fancy French Briar Pipe. There was an autumn chill in the air and I did not notice ashes blowing out of my pipe and into my Red Buffalo plaid jacket breast pocket until the sting of fire seared my chest. Looking down, I saw my jacket aflame and being fed more oxygen from the brisk headwind. What would I do now and, even worse, how do I tell my Mom? I thought that maybe Stacy could help as I snuffed out the fire and double-timed it to her apartment.

"Vinny, what ever happened to youuu?" Stacy called out with her Dixie drawl as she wrinkled her pretty little nose. "Golly you stink but come on in." We cleaned me up as best we could and Stacy applied some burn ointment on my chest and believe me that is about as carnal I ever got with her. Luckily the burn was only a minor one. I think she loaned me one of her dad's coats or heavy sweaters so we could at least go to the movies as planned. My memory now blanks out. I know we went to the movie but forget what movie we saw. I didn't even want to squeeze and kiss pretty little Stacy goodnight! All of my thoughts were on facing my Mom with my ruined new Red Buffalo plaid jacket.

Mom Nellie was never a demonstrative woman, she just looked at me, aired out the coat and proceeded to mend it. Mom made a very presentable new pocket with some matching Red Buffalo plaid material she had in her scraps basket. Nellie never threw anything away and I was soon as good as new.

Nellie now looked at me and with authority in her voice, ordered, "Now give me the pipe." I later learned she didn't even throw the pipe away. The next time I saw my Wally Frank Imported Mushroom Style Fancy French Briar Pipe, great-uncle Martin Molloy was smoking it.

Although I thoroughly enjoyed my summer and new surroundings I did not believe that I would like to make a career of working in an office in New York City. I thought a sales job would be more to my liking but not in New York City. For some reason, I had the fields and streams and the lakes and mountains in my heart and mind and, that's where they still remain.

THE MAGIC OF CHEMISTRY FOR CHILDREN

Picture of bench was purchased from Shutterstock

In an effort to find information online about John H. Winn
Chemical Company I came upon a Blog Site TIKIBLOG-
False Chemical Memory. To avoid any copyright
infringement I did not copy the webpage and merely refer
to it. If your curiosity is aroused just logon and read for
your own amusement. The site of course is all about young
kids buying explosive chemicals without their parent's
approval or, barriers of any kind.

To recall my age when I first traveled by subway from
Queens to West 23rd Street in Manhattan, I am counting
backwards. Maybe this was a latent effect of playing with
dangerous chemicals at an early age. I entered High School
when I just turned 14 and that is when my neighbor Marty
O' Grady who was 15 helped me burn all evidence in an
empty lot. We made sure the fire was out before we left.
So, that would take me back to 13? Realizing I had been on
the job for about 2 years I was probably only 11 years old
when I first climbed the stairs at Winn's Chemicals to make
my first purchase. I recall looking up at a very high sales
counter and stretching to make the payment. I am very
thankful to still be here to write about it.

Dad and Brother Michael John in the Bronx, 1926. A prosperous time for New York City. Just look at that baby carriage and Dad's stylish overcoat.

Mom Nellie and Michael John in 1928.
I think they were at Katonah Park.

Mom and
Dad with
Brother
Michael John
at Rye Beach,
Westchester
County, NY.

Mom Nellie, Michael
John and Anita Levy.
Older brother had a
crush on her for years.
I thought she was my
cousin. But what the
hell did I know, all I
cared about was my
Mickey Mouse,
Popgun and Duck-A-
Duck pull toy. Bronx,
1927.

Dad and Michael John at Katonah Park, Bronx, 1927.

Jones Beach 1930 where Dad taught brother how to
swim on the calm bay side.

Woodside 1934? Mom & Dad's bedroom windows. Dad out of work. Rare to see Big Brother smiling in my presence.

Jones Beach 1935. Aunt Freda's parents, the Stefan's, he was a German U-Boat Signals Officer in World War One, Mom and Dad. You could see I could not stand against big brother. He told me he could feed me to Dracula and I believed him.

Garage Outside bedroom window where brother told me Dracula lived. My expression and brother's posturing show that I believed him. His shoes look big, maybe they were Uncle Louis' hand me downs.

There's my Mickey Mouse. Odd to see big brother's hand on my shoulder, how sweet. Probably planning some mayhem for that night.

Jones Beach
1936.
Vinny with
Cousin Charlie
Cavallo, before
Ironized Yeast
tablets.
Open Air
Class???

Rockaway
Beach 1940.
Vinny after
Ironized Yeast
Tablets.
No Open Air
Class now.

Brother Michael John's Confirmation 1935. Romer's
wooden frame house seen over his right shoulder.
Dempsey brick house similar to ours over left shoulder.
Behind all the homes were the expansive empty semi-
wooded lots before the WW II building boom. Brother
was not that much older when he rescued Aunt Mamie
from the dangerous undertow at Rockaway Beach. Also
around the time he accidentally hit Aunt Lucy on the
head with an apple when the extended family visited an
apple orchard. He tossed apples found on the ground like
baseballs practicing his pitch for the baseball team.

Dad enclosed part of the empty lot in back of our house and built a chicken coop on legs to keep the critters off the ground. We had about 12 assorted White Leghorn and Rhode Island Reds and collected both white and brown eggs every AM. Sometime during or after WWII, we got rid of the chickens.

James A. Webster built in Rockland, Maine in the 19th Century

Gallagher, Bartolomea, Hoffman and Donnelly aft under full sail probably by the looks of their ages, sailing to or from Greenwhich, Connecticut or return Port Washington, Long Island.

All hands worked the shipboard duties including swabbing the deck. Rank had no special privileges on the Webster. If you wanted a drink, you helped yourself at the white scuttlebutts you see in the picture

Sailors had to be sixteen years old before allowed to work the sails on the bowsprit. Neuman qualified for this job.

One cold early morning after abandon ship drill. These sailors are hungry waiting for breakfast. L to R, Gallagher, Hoffman, Unknown, Bartolomea, and Neuman.

Bartolomea, Hoffman and Sailing Master name now a salty mist...he was always on deck and present for all night watches

Boatswain Mate 2nd Class Gallagher lowers colors, Chief Petty Officer Donnelly sounds retreat. CPO Page in lower right on Starboard side. Port Watch is out of camera range

City Island Shore Liberty. In exotic Pelham Island Group, Bronx, NYC. Ice cream sodas for these sailors. Palm trees and dancing girls await the future. Curfew was 20:00 hours; that is 8 PM for you landlubbers.

Chapter 2

12TH Regiment, New York State Guard

Every Monday night I traveled by subway from Woodside to Columbus Circle in Manhattan. The armory was a few blocks west of Central Park.

The old 12th Regiment was a melting pot of ethnicity, characters, personalities, religions and races. Puerto Ricans, Blacks, Whites, Christians, Jews and all nationalities trained together. New York City characters from all walks of life from the trendy Upper East Side to the West Side, from Hell's Kitchen to the Lower East Side and the Bowery were all welcomed by the 12th. The location of the armory on Manhattan's West Side attracted some real tough characters from Hell's Kitchen, just a few blocks south of the armory. Oddballs and some felons filled the ranks. No screening was necessary; the 12th opened their doors to all. The 12th wanted to fill the ranks so anyone at any reasonable age and physical or mental condition was welcomed.

Shortly after I joined G Company, the Commanding Officer Captain Klopfer asked me to serve with several others on an honor guard detail for a recently deceased officer of the Jewish faith. Being a school kid with no full-time job, I was available and the Commanding Officer appointed me NCO (Non-Commissioned Officer) in charge. None of us ever served on an honor guard before so we were all given special instructions and taught how to load and fire the blank ammunition in the 1917 rifle and how to conduct ourselves at the graveside during the service.

Loading blank cartridges can be tricky - the cartridge case mouth is blunt because it does not contain the streamlined shape of a pointed bullet. At the armory, we practiced loading and firing blank ammo and the proper procedure to follow at the cemetery. One of the volunteers was a chap named Rubin. He was a real character with a stocky build, close cropped hair and a round face which gave him a slight physical resemblance to Curly of Three Stooges fame.

Rubin was a happy camper – a good natured person always with a ready smile. During our practice, he had some difficulty when loading the blank ammo in the bolt action rifle. He just fumbled and his jovial demeanor changed to one of anxiety.

On the day of the funeral we reported to the armory to dress into the heavy wool winter uniforms, helmet liners, leggings, web cartridge belts with first aid packets and 1917 bayonets attached. The day started out gray and cold with a dreary overcast so, the warmth of the heavy wool uniform was indeed welcomed.

The full-time armory caretakers checked out the 1917 rifles and I was issued a quantity of blank ammunition. I remember there were five of us but do not remember how many rounds we had to fire and think it was probably three rounds each. The instruction we received at the armory helped us to perform the ceremony. We were soon picked up by a limo and began the long drive to the cemetery located somewhere in the Bronx or Westchester County.

Rubin was quiet and pensive during the long drive and was worried about loading and firing his weapon smoothly. We tried to make him feel better with words of encouragement but we were all concerned about him. Actually, we were all a little nervous because this was the very first time we served on an honor guard and did not want to make any mistakes.

When we arrived at the cemetery, we were surprised to see such a large crowd of mourners and spectators including, some high ranking uniformed police and military among the multitudes of people. When we climbed out of the limo and saw the crowd, we heard Rubin mumble, "Oh shit." I gave each man several blank cartridges to load in the magazines of their rifles and made sure the bolts were closed on an empty chamber and the rifle safety levers were on "safe" with special attention given to Rubin.

We quietly marched at right shoulder arms to the gravesite. I gave the order to "Halt" and then "Order Arms," in hushed commands. I waited for the rabbi to say his words and to give me the sign to proceed. I do not remember eye contact with anyone because my attention was focused on the rabbi. I gave the commands to present and fire the volleys and to my surprise, all our shots resounded in perfect unison. I ordered the honor guard again in subdued tones, "Right Shoulder Arms," "Right Face," and "Forward March" as, we marched off in quiet cadence directly to the waiting limo. The driver was beside himself with a big smile on his face patting us all on the back and saying, "Great job, great job," with special congratulations to Rubin. The driver even grabbed Rubin and hugged him. Rubin's glow returned and he stood there with a huge smile across his round face.

I remember driving to a restaurant and telling the driver to lock the rifles in the trunk of the limo while we all entered the restaurant to have our meal with the family and their friends. I vaguely recall some people approaching our table as we ate and offering their thanks.

On the long drive back to the armory we had to listen to Rubin expound about his rifle handling, "Did you see me? What a soldier! Did you see me? I did it like a real pro, right?" "Did you see me, did you see me?" "How'd I do? Like a pro, right?" We all commented, "Rubin, you were great now…shut up already!"

Two characters from G Company are well remembered, Private Pedro Ortiz and Private Velázquez. Ortiz was nicknamed "Cuban Pete." Although Pete was Puerto Rican, he accepted the appellation because of a popular Desi Arnaz song at the time about "Cuban Pete, the guy with the rumba beat." Aside from his Zoot Suit, switch blade knife and phony zip-gun, he was really a good guy with a ready smile. Ortiz always bragged about all the girlfriends he had and took a lot of kidding from the troops. Later on in the National Guard and then on active service, Ortiz proved himself to be an excellent soldier serving in the machine gun section. Private Velázquez was another story. He was a loner and a real bad apple with a police record, a menacing sneer and a pimpled face. He had no friends that I can recall. Unfortunately, I had a run-in with Velázquez while at camp that summer.

During the summer of 1947, the 12th Regiment went to Camp Smith in Peekskill, New York for the two week camp tour and quartered in the eight-man squad tents in wide use then. The middle weekend we had a general inspection of quarters, equipment and in ranks. We were all outside in the company street waiting for the order to fall in for inspection in ranks. All of our field equipment was spread out in military fashion on our bunks with personal items stored in a duffel bag next to our bunk. With a few minutes to spare, I dashed into my tent for a last minute check to make any adjustment to my squad's accoutrements displayed on their cots. Instead, I discovered Velázquez rummaging through someone's personal duffel bag.

He glared at me when I surprised him and he snarled out something in Spanish which was not "*como esta usted*;" he pulled out his 17-inch WWI bayonet we all wore attached to our cartridge belts. He waved the blade menacingly in my face and threatened something if I reported him. My attention was focused on the bayonet. No, I did not pull out my bayonet to challenge him, I forgot exactly what I did say to him but he returned his bayonet to its scabbard and also returned the item he took. I hoped that would be the end of it. I did not want to have to sleep with one eye open with one more week of camp ahead of me. After that, I was on cordial but not too friendly terms with Velázquez and I was always wary of him.

Fortunately, a couple months later when the outfit was federalized to National Guard status Velasquez disappeared.

My memory returns to the day we left for summer camp and I remember anxiously waiting that day from the time I first joined the 12th. While walking the few blocks from the subway station at Columbus Circle to the armory, I was surprised to hear martial music blasting and it got louder as I approached the armory.

Much to my surprise and just outside the armory the 12th Regiment Band was playing an array of marching music. I did not know the 12th had such a band. Outside the big fortress-type double doors on 61st Street a large crowd was assembling creating, a circus-like atmosphere. When stepping inside the armory, I noticed many new faces bustling about. There were more people in uniform than I ever saw before on the usual Monday night drills. It was then I realized the 12th had two battalions; the first battalion drilled on Thursday night and my second battalion drilled on Monday night.

The G Company room was busy with a frenzy of activity as we all hastily dressed into our khaki uniforms with steel helmet, canvas leggings, and high quarter shoes, cartridge belts with canteen, canteen cup, first aid packet and bayonet attached. Everyone was checking to make sure everything was hooked on correctly. Most of us needed help to properly pack the old World War I roll pack with blankets, pup tent shelter half, tent pole sections, wooden tent pegs, rain poncho and mess kit. Some were "helped" by others, as bricks were also placed in their packs as a practical joke, not discovered until peeling off all this gear at camp. I learned to keep an alert eye out for some of those practical jokers from the West Side. You could imagine the shouts and laughs once this unfolded at camp.

There was a smell of alcohol in the well-packed G company room. There were Guardsmen in attendance I had never seen before, proving that many neglected the unpaid drill night but showed up for paid summer camp. Some of the old-time characters had their canteens laced with whiskey. My canteen was filled to the brim with fresh cold water flowing through the aqueducts of the New York City water system from reservoirs located in the then pristine Catskill Mountains.

The First Sergeant gave the order to fall in with rifles at sling arms on our right shoulder, gas masks over left shoulder with packs all adjusted, we marched down to the drill floor.

What was thought to be a simple train ride some 30 miles north of New York City to Camp Smith in Peekskill was now becoming a major operation. This surprised me. The regiment assembled on the huge armory drill floor and lined up by company and battalion. The Regiment was then called to attention and given the order to march out through the fortress sized double doors onto West 61st Street.

The band led the way, followed by the four man color guard one carrying the U. S. flag, a second carrying the 12th blue infantry regimental flag dipped slightly lower and, an armed guard on each side of the flags carrying their rifles at right shoulder arms. This was also the first time I saw the 12th's color guard. Following the color guard was the regimental staff, the First

Battalion staff and troops and finally the Second Battalion staff and troops along with G Company.

The regiment marched twenty blocks south on Amsterdam Avenue to the train yards in Manhattan's West Side, only blocks away from 42nd Street and Times Square. I felt a little self-conscious to be seen marching along the West Side in front of so many people. I thought we would appear to the public to be a shoddy group of out-of-step imitation soldiers each, marching to his own pace. As we moved along the men were all trying to keep in step with the music.

Some kids laughed at us, some saluted as we passed, and New York City policemen halted traffic and directed the traffic out of our way. The police saluted the colors as the color guard passed by in front of them. Some New Yorkers stopped what they were doing and just looked, wondering the reason for the parade. The sound of the marching music motivated everyone to keep in step with the tempo of the band. I never heard music like this before and it made one want to look his best.

Marching along were the characters and oddballs in G Company. I thought about the guys who took their Monday night drills as a joke that is, the guys who even bothered to show up to attend. Some missed Monday night drills but went to camp for the pay and the experience. Now, these same men had a serious expression which replaced the usual "I don't give a damn" smirk on their faces. Now they looked straight ahead and directly at the back of the helmet of the man in front of them. Their shoulders squared, chests puffed out, heads erect and swinging off to the cadence of the band. All the wisecracks and sneers now gone. G Company marched along finally with everyone including Rubin strutting off proudly like real soldiers all, in step with the band.

Our path to the train yard in the West 40's took us in front of the spectators no longer laughing but now, clapping and yelling as we swung by, marching right through Hell's Kitchen. Tenement windows opened and people leaned out to see what the racket was all about.

We were warned people may throw trash at us as they had done in previous years and it was for this reason the regiment wore the heavy steel helmets instead of the lightweight plastic helmet liners. Instead, they waved at us from the windows along with the people standing by the curbside. Some called out names of native sons who were among the troops, both the kids and adults clapping as we marched by.

Out of the corner of my eye I noticed a couple of grubby looking drunks standing in the doorway of a bar as they snapped to attention, almost tripping over each other and saluting as we marched by. I chuckled to myself thinking maybe they were 12th members who stopped at the local bar for a quick drink on the way to the armory and, after a second and third drink, they were now AWOL from camp tour.

Bars opened early in Hell's Kitchen to cater to those longshoremen on the way to the West Side docks to "shape up" to load and unload cargo from the many ships passing in and out of the Port of New York.

The longshoremen reported to the docks every morning where they eagerly waited to be selected for a day's work. There was no guarantee work would be available to them and many days they just returned home hoping to find work tomorrow. This was called "shaping up." It was hard work for hard men at an insecure job.

The sound of the band resonating throughout the streets and tenements on Manhattan's West Side, attracted everyone's attention. It made me feel good about G Company and the 12th. I only joined to be able to handle and shoot real guns and to get paid for going to camp. This experience was turning out to be much more than this 15-year old kid from Woodside bargained for.

As we approached the troop train, we saw trucks unloading our duffel bags for storage on the train. The band now lined up next to the rail head. This time the music was different. They were now playing show tunes and old New York tunes like "Give My Regards to Broadway," "The Sidewalks of New York" and the song every WW II and Korean War era veteran heard when boarding a troop ship for duty overseas, "So Long, It's Been Good To Know Ya."

The 12th Regiment Band played until every last man and boy was aboard the troop train; one could also smell the alcohol as you marched past the band. Later on, I heard that the 12th was one of the best military bands in the east. Many musicians in the 12th band played professionally at Carnegie Hall and in the many Broadway shows in Manhattan's show district.

Every morning at camp, the 12th band marched along the Camp Smith main street, each member neatly dressed in clean khakis and blasting martial music.

The Drum Major was a real character. He would be seen leading the band, a tall skinny guy strutting like a peacock and fancifully twirling his baton, all decked out wearing only red Long John underwear and combat boots, his head topped off with a shiny helmet liner marked "The 12th." That's a sight that kind of stays with you.

We de-trained at Peekskill and marched up the hill to Camp Smith to be soldiers for two weeks. We trained using fixed bayonets and discovered what tear gas smells like. Camp Smith had a mock village and we trained to attack and then switched sides to become defenders of the village. We fired plenty of blank ammo; pyrotechnics and smoke grenades were set off to add to the realism.

After preliminary practice dry firing, we were taught how to slowly squeeze the trigger and not to jerk it, and how to take a deep breath before each shot then slowly exhale as you slowly squeezed the trigger as well as how to sight the target properly. This gave us confidence when it was our time to fire.

The weapon was the .30 caliber Model of 1917 commonly called the Enfield. In World War One England awarded contracts to American gun makers Winchester, Remington and Eddystone to manufacture the new British Pattern 14 Enfield bolt action rifle in .303 British Caliber.

Later in 1917 when the United States entered the war, we needed rifles in a hurry and the contract with England was cancelled. With a simple change to the US 30-06 cartridge, the US Rifle Caliber .30 Model of 1917 was created. This was the weapon most doughboys took to France in 1917.

After qualifying with the rifle, we were then trained to mark the targets. We were taught how to raise and lower the big 100-yard target frames and mark the hits and misses. Hits were marked by placing a round disc in either black or white with a wooden plug that was placed in the bullet hole and then raise the target frame so the coach could mark the shooters score card.

A miss was marked by waving a red flag in front of the target for each miss. That red flag was called "Maggie's Drawers." I don't know when it started but every American serviceman or women knew about "Maggie's Drawers."

We were all apprehensive about going through the Gas Chamber. After a presentation and demonstration on the proper use of the gas mask, we entered a darkened building while wearing the gas mask. The instructors proceeded to pull the pins on tear gas and smoke canisters and the building was immersed in a white, blue and gray smoke. Not knowing what was next, we were ordered to remove the gas mask which we all did reluctantly. We got a good smell and the effect of tear gas as we double-timed out of the gas chamber. In case we ever had to be in a tear gas environment, we knew what it smelled like, and we were confident that we knew how to clear a gas mask before putting it on.

The last day at camp we lined up for "Pay Call." In those days, the military paid with cash. The procedure sure to be remembered by any old vet was to report for pay with a proper hand salute, "Sir, Corporal Vincent G. Gallagher reporting for pay." The company commander was seated at a table with a G.I. blanket spread out on top of the table and a cash box full of cash. The First Sergeant armed with a loaded .45 caliber pistol, was posted to guard the cash box. The exact amount was counted out and given to the soldier. The soldier was then ordered to sign the pay receipt form within the space provided with no lines going outside that space. This was one order each soldier obeyed with precision. I put my two weeks' pay in my left hand, saluted the CO with my right hand and walked off with a smile on my face. I thought these two weeks were a grand experience. In those days, the army had a bugle call for everything from "Reveille" in the morning to "Taps" in the evening and every event in between; the two most remembered were "Mess Call" and "Pay Call."

When the two weeks drew to a close we "policed the area" (cleaned up), assuring everything was ready for the next outfit. The tent floors were cleaned as well as the latrines and mess halls and we raked the dirt smooth and clean in the company street in front of our tents.

We marched to the Peekskill railroad station and boarded with everyone in good humor. Once back in New York City, without marching music or fanfare and with flags and guidons cased, we marched back to the armory and returned through the big double doors. My pockets jingled but some were not so fortunate. I was not fooled into gambling that last night at camp, something just didn't look right to me as I strolled around from tent to tent watching the poker and blackjack games. I found out later it was unwise to play cards with some of the Hell's Kitchen card sharks.

There was nothing new about Monday drill for the balance of that summer until one Monday in September we were surprised to hear an important announcement. The 212th Artillery Regiment New York Army National Guard was again federally activated.

The 212th was to be comprised of two battalions: the 773rd AAA Gun Battalion (90mm) and the 142nd AAA Automatic Weapons Battalion (40mm). The 773rd drilled Mondays and 142nd drilled Thursdays. Many 12th Regiment members did not join the National Guard for medical or personal reasons but all the WWII veterans welcomed the transition. Being offered a choice of drill nights I chose Monday night and was now a corporal in C Battery 773rd AAA Gun BN (90mm) NY Army National Guard. None of my JBA buddies joined me.

12th Regiment Armory 120 West 62nd Street, NYC. Built 1887 demolished in 1960 to make way for Fordham University Law School now sharing the same address. Ninth Avenue elevated train line later torn down. I remember the Cobblestones when walking to the Armory.

Massive drill floor afforded training areas for thousands of Guardsmen over the years. Also hosted elaborate fair well ceremonies for those marching out to answer the call in four of the nation's wars.
Both photographs Courtesy of the New York State Military Museum, Saratoga Springs, NY

Camp Smith summer 1947. Sergeant Corson or Clausen, G Company before entering battle in Mock Village between Red and Blue Army. He has a Red or Blue band on his helmet to ID him as friend or foe.

Same year, same Sergeant readying troops for inspection of field equipment with accoutrements and pup-tents

Camp Smith Company Street with eight
man squad tents then in use.

Demonstration of Riot Control with
sheathed bayonets and tear gas at Mock
Village. Everyone had his gas mask handy.

Company Street showing the concrete
block mess hall.

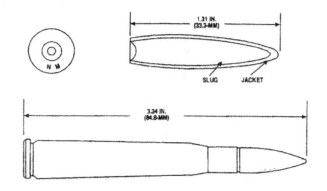

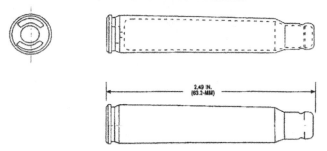

Comparing Ball with Blank Ammunition.
U.S Army Training Manual TM 43-0001-27

212th Regimental Crest with lineage going back to the 1920's when, the Antiaircraft Artillery units were classified as Coast Artillery branch through the end of World War Two. Later in the 1950's the classification was changed to Artillery Branch.

Chapter 3

C Battery 773rd AAA Gun Battalion

As a 15 year old high school student I was happy to receive a drill check from Uncle Sam every three months. The fact that the National Guard could be called to active duty by order of the president for any national emergency did not enter my mind. But, it was for this very reason many state guard members chose not to join the National Guard. Some could not pass the physical or meet the mental aptitude requisite, as simple as they were. Many just disappeared.

The 773rd was comprised of four firing battery's A, B, C & D, the Headquarters Staff and Headquarters Battery. Battery C (Charlie Battery) was to be my home for more years than I realized.

During my time in the guard and active duty through the 1960s, the U.S. had two armies. The Regular Army (RA) is the "United States Army" made up of soldiers joining the army as volunteers and advancing to officer rank and those officers graduating from the U.S. Military Academy at West Point. The serial numbers for RA enlisted men began with 1 and the RA officers begin with 01. The National Guard soldier's serial numbers began with 2 and in 1947 I received enlisted man's serial number 21 9XX XXX. Guard officers serial number began with 02.

All National Guard, Army Reserve (ER), ROTC (Reserve Officers Training Corps) and draftees were in "The Army of the United States." It was an odd arrangement that caused much good natured and in some cases ill-natured competition between the RA's and NG's which probably still exists today.

We heard an officer read to us The Articles of War, Code of Conduct and other doctrine aloud to the troops. After which we raised our right hand and swore to some oath I have long ago forgotten. This explained to all what legal rights the individual soldier had and what authority the military had.

I remember a few smirks in ranks when the officer

addressed "Capture by an enemy." "Only give your Name, Rank and Serial Number." We were not at war, World War II ended two years prior and the world as we knew it was at peace. No one knew in only three short years thousands of U.S. service personnel would be taken prisoner and mistreated by a brutal enemy and some even murdered in cold blood by North Korean soldiers. The enemy did not discriminate nor cared if the soldier was an RA, NG, ER or a Draftee; they were all mistreated equally. The next step taken in the process of becoming a National Guard soldier was to receive our army ID "Dog Tags" and then march by battery up to the Medics room to receive the first in a series of immunization injections. I still chuckle when I review this scene in my memory.

You can bet the vets laid it on pretty thick to us neophytes about the horror of being stabbed by the six inch needles. As a young kid, I had plenty of experience getting weekly allergy injections at Queens General Hospital. Even so, I was still somewhat apprehensive. The vets were very convincing and I thought that maybe they did use special needles for those exotic immunization shots. I was able to put on a brave face and with eyes wide open, spotted the tiny needles the medics were wielding. I took my shots without a cringe. But when asked by those still in line, I said it was awful! Cuban Pete smiled, closed his eyes then clenched his teeth as he stepped up to the plate. Most of the others did the same.

Other "Tough Guys," were forced as their turn came and panicked when the medic just wiped the cold alcohol swab on their arm. Some had never received an injection that they could remember. Some swooned just from the smell of the medics room so it was open season for the prankster, "Listen buddy, be sure to fall backward when they stick you so, I can catch you," was heard throughout the long line of nervous Guardsmen.

One Monday night we were issued our individual weapons. Mine was an M1 Rifle and it came thick with Cosmoline, a widely used military preservative used on all weaponry. I was very attentive to the instruction about disassembly and reassembly of the M1. It was no easy chore at first but later mastered.

We received hands-on training and viewed army training films. Prior to the semi-automatic M1 Garand rifle, the army used bolt action rifles. After firing a round, the bolt was simply opened to eject the spent cartridge case. Closing the bolt picked up a fresh round from the 5 shot magazine and the gun was ready for another squeeze of the trigger. The semi-automatic gas operated M1 required more knowledge and manipulation to fully understand its function.

The M1 was loaded with an eight round clip of ammo and every squeeze of the trigger fired a round, the bolt automatically opened and ejected the fired case and slammed shut while loading a fresh round. Another squeeze of the trigger repeated the process. When the last of the eight rounds were fired the last spent case and the clip are both ejected and the action locked open ready for another fresh clip of eight rounds.

Just to the rear of the barrel muzzle on the M1 rifle, a small hole was drilled to bleed off some of the gas caused by the firing of the cartridge. This gas pushed on a piston forcing the operating rod connected to the bolt to open, eject a case and load a fresh round. Every squeeze of the trigger fired a round.

The army termed the nomenclature, "US Rifle Caliber .30 Gas Operated Semi-Automatic M1." It was developed at the U.S. Springfield Arsenal in Springfield, Massachusetts by employee John C. Garand of French Canadian origin. The rifle was sometimes referred to as the "M1 Garand." Limited production and issue began in 1936. A total of some 6 million M1 rifles were manufactured by Springfield and other arms manufacturers during WWII and the Korean War.

When it was known the 212th had re-organized, the flood of enlistments really began. Many veterans who marched out of the armory in 1941 returned to their old outfit. Followed by men and boys from all walks of life with a desire to join the National Guard. The drill pay was an incentive…the check came every three months like clockwork and it came in handy.

The trained veterans were welcomed because artillery is a highly technical branch and the unit needed experienced veterans to teach us about all this new equipment. We received four 90mm

AA guns that is about 3.5 inches in diameter, four Quad mount 50 caliber machine guns, SCR-584 Radar van, M-9 gun director with optical trackers, radio and telephone and multitudes of vehicles making up an artillery battery. So, every specialty was needed including most importantly experienced cooks and mess personnel.

Many who left in 1941 with the 212th were now returning as non-commissioned officers and some returned as Lieutenants and Captains. Corporal Ivan Oppenlander, from the lower east side who marched out with the regiment in 1941 and went to war in Europe, returned as an artillery officer after serving in Patton's Third Army in Europe. He was enjoying a successful business career but something brought him back to the 212th in 1947 and, with a new name, "Ivan O. Turner." His name tempted the Hell's Kitchen crowd to call him "Ivanhoe" behind his back, of course.

Almost every Monday night new faces were appearing, both officers and NCOs. Except for a few of the officers, nearly the entire battalion staff left with the outfit in 1941 except the Battalion Medical Officer Lieutenant Josephson. Lucky for me he was actually a Dentist but, more on that later.

That year the battalion numbered about the same as an active duty firing battery 150 or so men. Instead of the normal Table of Organization and Equipment (TO&E) where each battery had its own four 90mm AA guns and four quad mount .50 Caliber Machine Guns, its own radar and fire control director. We all trained together with the battalion having the equipment for a single firing battery. Each battery had their own motor, communications and mess sections. The only section not receiving good training in the confines of the armory was the radar section. But, static tests simulating target tracking and emplacement, and maintenance procedures, could be performed under the armory roof.

Many veterans of the 773rd could draw upon recent experience firing the 90's and Quad Mounts against aerial and ground enemy targets.

Extensive training was conducted in the armory to prepare the battalion for the forthcoming two week training at Camp Edwards, Massachusetts. There we would be actually firing the guns at towed aerial targets and towed water borne targets simulating ground direct anti-tank fire. The gun crews were by now familiar with the placement and the march order of the guns as well as those of us in fire control training on the SCR-584 Radar and the M-9 Fire Control Director. The gun crews received training with practice dummy rounds and we in fire control were able to use static tests to simulate tracking a target and sending firing data to the guns. There was a lot of fumbling the ball but each Monday night we were improving and anticipating Camp tour the summer of 1948.

Because most of the work on a 90 was indeed manual work, the brawniest and not the brainiest were assigned to the gun platoon earning the nick name "Brawn Platoon."

The fire control platoon had two sections, the radar and the director sections. This equipment was much more technical than the gun platoon. The brighter soldier was assigned to Fire Control, nicknamed the "Brain Platoon." My job was assistant director section leader in charge of the three man optical Tracking Head (TH) which took four guys to lift out of the trailer and place it on its very heavy pedestal. We were not at all Brawny! The TH had two high power telescopes, an Azimuth scope for Lateral tracking and an Elevation scope. The Tracking Head provided the M-9 Director with the present azimuth and elevation of the target whether the target was aerial or ground.

The radar provided the director with an aerial target's present slant range, which was the distance in a straight line from the radar antenna directly to the target measured in yards. The moving target constantly changes position and it is this rate of change which the M-9 Director must calculate to predict a FUTURE position for the projectiles to meet and explode in the immediate vicinity of the moving target.

Unlike depicted in the movies, the AA guns did not necessarily directly hit a target with a round but instead caused a dense field of high explosive projectiles to destroy aircraft with hot pieces of shrapnel ripping into their thin aluminum air frames. The smaller automatic weapons like the quad mount 50's were used for direct fire on low flying aircraft. These were deadly against vehicles and personnel, and the defense of an artillery battery against enemy ground attack.

The fire control platoon included the radar and director sections. The M-9 Director was nothing more than an early computer. It was contained in a square metal cabinet about four feet high and about three feet square. The director section leader was a Sergeant First Class (SFC).

The radar section leader was also an SFC and was the Chief Radar Operator or CRO. The SCR-584 had a maximum search range of 70,000 yards and an engaging range of within 35,000 yards. This meant that the radar could lock on and track a target once it came within 32,000 yards. The 90 was effective up to 34,000 feet altitude and approximately 20,000 yards horizontal range.

The most important phase of training was to learn and understand orienting and synchronizing all the equipment. This could be taught right on the huge armory drill floor. It assured all pointed in the same direction and the dials on all the equipment had the same azimuth and elevation readings to start with.

I will cover the very first camp tour in 1948, the subsequent camp tours in 1949 and 1950 being somewhat redundant. 1950 did bring in a new group of recruits to the National Guard because of the recent offering of relief from the draft for anyone joining an active reserve or guard unit for a three-year enlistment. That is when I talked two of my Astoria buddies Bob Dema and Max Ries into joining the guard. Many college students took advantage of this draft relief and our ranks began to swell. Bob Dema served on a gun crew and Max Ries was the battery gun mechanic.

Built into the equipment was the ability to run static tests which was no more than recreating tracking a target, sending data to the M-9 Director and then converting that input to firing data sent to the guns without using an actual target…all training aids.

This technical aspect of soldiering opened a whole new world for me as I absorbed this knowledge. Before I realized it, I was not only learning but also training others on the tracking head and M-9 Director. I took the training seriously because it interested me while others just went through the motions to serve their time and do their jobs. I asked plenty of questions until I found the answers.

An important lesson was learned at that time that served me well in later years. When asked a question and unable to answer it, I simple said, "I don't know but will find out for you." I found this to be a leader's best answer and then followed up by actually finding the answer or finding someone who did know and then read the Field or Technical Manual to verify it. I asked plenty of questions as a youngster and still do. In the corporate world, I knew many who tried to get away with double talk and "fancy footwork," afraid to say or lacked the confidence to admit, "I don't know." In the army, you could not fool the troops and get away with it. In the army and especially in the artillery, guessing did not work.

The radar, director, tracking head and guns were all connected by cables that delivered power and data to all components. This electric power was provided by a gasoline powered generator. When in the armory, the generator was parked near the open double doors to dissipate the exhaust fumes. Each station had a field telephone powered by flashlight batteries and a hand cranked magneto. So, the entire firing battery was all connected and communicating by wire.

The dials on the guns' azimuth and elevation displays (Clocks) each had a three-position switch that read, MAN-AID-AUTO. MAN was for manually elevating and traversing the gun; AID was for manually following an inner dial which was moving as it was receiving data from the director, all the setter had to do was crank his wheel to match the dial. When set in AUTO, the M-9 Director took control of the guns and all the setters needed to do was sit back and watch. If everything was perfect, you could see the four guns slowly rotating and all pointing in the same direction ready to fire. But add some human error and things could and did go wrong

In artillery lingo a 360-degree circle consists of 6400 mils. During back sighting, if the adding or subtracting of 3200 mils is not done correctly, the radar and tracking head would point in one direction and the guns in another. The following is an explanation

73

of back-sighting…pointing two components at each other. Each station is connected by field phone for precise alignment of all the components.

Each piece is leveled and on the firing range or active deployment the guns fire "Settling Rounds" and then re-leveled. The AC (Aiming Circle) is mounted on a tripod and oriented with the needle pointing at Magnetic North which will read 0 mils one of the three norths (True, Grid & Magnetic) which will vary depending on the fire mission. The AC is then pointed at the (TH) Tracking Head Azimuth scope maybe 40 or so yards away and cross hairs on both are perfectly aligned with each other…thus back sighting. The AC operator, usually the fire control officer or Sergeant, tells the TH operator the azimuth reading on the AC in "mils." The TH operator then adds or subtracts 3200 mils, one half of the 6400 mil circle, and enters that number in the azimuth dial of the TH. The TH now aims the azimuth scope on the radar antenna elbow telescope located on the radar antenna until perfectly aligned and the TH operator tells the radar the azimuth reading and the radar adds or subtracts 3200 mils from that number and sets the azimuth on the radar antenna. The fire control equipment is now oriented and synchronized (O&S'd)

While that was happening, the four gun commanders opened the breech of the 90's, placed cross wires on the muzzle, and the guns are then pointed at the Tracking Head. The Gun Commander looks through the barrel of the 90 and aligns the cross wire on the muzzle with the Tracking Head azimuth scope. The TH operator tells the gunner the azimuth in mils on the TH. The gunner adds or subtracts the 3200 mils from the Tracking Head azimuth reading and enters that azimuth in the guns azimuth clock. This process is repeated on all four guns. If each component traverses to zero mils azimuth all will be pointing in the same direction of zero mils Magnetic north reading on all the azimuth dials. The battery is now O&S'd. It may sound confusing but achieved in minutes by a trained battery.

Enter Major Kraus the battalion executive officer. Formerly a Regular Army officer with vast experience having served in a 90 outfit in WWII. He strived for exactness and demanded it. The battalion commander Lieutenant Colonel Slavin was a much more patient man and between these two personalities they were a good team in such a technical unit.

The executive officer is the guy on the firing line responsible for the entire operation made more serious when using live ammunition in AA guns pointing at a friendly aircraft towing an aerial target...serious business. Everything had to be done by the book to make certain those live rounds exploded where they were supposed to explode. Zero tolerance was for real here and we were all green at the time except for the vets. We had a long way to go in our training for camp tour next summer. That left only about 40 Monday night drills to get ready to fire those 90's. I'm sure Kraus thought long and hard about that.

That first camp tour in 1948 and subsequent summer camp tours were all at Camp Edwards, Massachusetts located on Cape Cod and were indeed interesting experiences. We took a troop train out of the same rail yards located in the west 40's. The guns, radar and heavy equipment were all transported by rail on flat cars. This was accomplished by the full-time armorer's who were also soldiers in the battalion. Each battery had a full-time administrator who was also a guardsman working in the armory. His job was to keep the paperwork flowing and to maintain all the battery documents, records and equipment in proper order. This is before the age of computers when typewriters and triplicate carbon copies was the drill.

The first week was spent in Camp and we lived in wooden framed two story barracks built during WWII and typical for that time period. We slept in cots with mattresses under clean sheets and had hot showers every night. We ate three hot meals every day in a mess hall and the food was not at all bad but we complained about it anyway.

That first week we had some basic infantry training and some more training on the equipment. With Otis Air Force Base being close to Camp Edwards, there were always aircraft flying day and night giving ample opportunity to track real targets. We tracked targets manually and then the radar locked on targets transmitting present position to the director. Seeing things in broad daylight that we may have overlooked in the armory at night under indoor lighting made us more proficient. It also gave us more confidence as we looked forward to the second week when we would actually fire the 90's. But first, we had some excitement during that middle weekend.

A special unit of RA Paratroopers were stationed at Camp Edwards for demonstration purposes. I remember seeing some of them at the PX a time or two. They were a sharp group of soldiers wearing highly polished Corcoran jump boots and tailored, starched uniforms - they were indeed an impressive looking group of show troops.

Now compare them with the guys in the 773rd, dressed in ill-fitting uniforms with dusty combat boots the old issue with the rough side outside. These boots were originally made for the 1942 invasion of North Africa and were impossible to shine. One could easily see a marked distinction between the soldierly smart look of the RA paratroopers and the grimy G.I. Joe appearance of the NG's. I may have even noticed a sneer or two directed at this young National Guard Corporal while at the PX myself but, who cared.

That Saturday, Mistretta and I both got passes to go to town. We showered, shaved and put on clean Khaki uniforms and hitched a ride to either Hyannis or Buzzards Bay. We had a meal, drank some beers and cokes, and browsed around town. We walked to a beach intending to look at the girls and, with any luck, maybe even meet some, which we did!

We returned to camp and hit the sack only to be awakened by a frenzy of excitement in the wee hours of the morning. This is what happened.

A group of "Hell's Kitchen" boys led by Corporal John Zurla from the motor section, decided to "borrow" a 3/4 ton weapons carrier from the motor pool, a vehicle about the size of one of today's pickup trucks.

Accompanying Zurla were some of his pals from the west side. All were a couple of years older than I was at the time. I was 16 and didn't even have a driver's license. When Zurla's party arrived in town he parked the truck out of sight and they went looking to get some adult refreshment which they did. Somewhere along the way, they ran into a larger group of paratroopers, mostly southern boys.

In 1948, most RA's we knew were from the south. Well, when mixing sharp RA's from the south and sloppy NG's from "NU YAWK CITY" and all under the influence, this could set the stage for trouble. Some remarks were passed back and forth about Yankees not being able to find their "Assholes with a Roadmap" and NG's not even being able to read a "Road Map." Other comments included "Girl Scouts make better soldiers than NG's", and other smart-ass witty sayings that the southern boys are famous for... Who threw the first punch is now lost to history but I can only guess it was one of our guys. A gas house brawl soon followed that took place right in the middle of the town of Hyannis.

The young, starched and confident show troop paratroopers did not realize who these poorly dressed, sloppily clad and misfit NG's from New York City really were. They had never walked the mean streets along 8th, 9th, and 10th Avenues in the 30's and 40's on Manhattan's west side. Most of the southern boys' Daddies were farmers and not rugged New York City longshoremen working on the docks on the Hudson River. They never heard of Hell's Kitchen and, if they had, they probably thought it was a mess hall run by a particularly grouchy mess Sergeant. I do not remember the exact casualty list suffered by the overconfident paratroopers but we later heard "PVT No Name," a quiet soft spoken and very likeable guy, built like a refrigerator, put some RA's in the base hospital. Pity to those who tangled with the "West Siders."

After sweeping up the street with the paratroopers and damaging a public park where the scuffle occurred, Zurla and company hastily returned to camp, parked the truck in the motor pool and dashed into the barracks. That's when the M.P.'s caught up with them. It was not about the fight, which at the time was unknown but about Zurla's speeding in camp. The speed limit in those days on an army base was 25 MPH and the M.P.'s, especially during summer National Guard camp time, were out in force.

Most of us were now up and awake. The First Sergeant ordered all to go back to bed while he talked to the M.P.'s and that ended the incident. I do recall some talk about the First Sergeant checking with the base hospital the next day to make sure no one was dead. We all got the gory details for the balance of the camp tour. I do recall dashing into the PX for the last time while still in my dirty field uniform worn for a week at Wellfleet. With only a few minutes to spare I purchased a full box of Hershey bars and yes, cigarettes for only a dollar a carton. I passed by some sparkling paratroopers with their shiny brass and stiffly starched uniforms eyeing this 16 year old NG Corporal wearing a grimy field uniform and scruffy combat boots but there were no sneers this time...if looks could kill I would not be writing this.

Me and Mistretta were both glad to have missed the brawl and, anyway, I had a much better time having met a cute girl from Brewster, New York, vacationing on Cape Cod.

The artillery firing range was not located in Camp Edwards but 50 miles away at Wellfleet only 12 miles from the tip of the Cape. This will be the very first time the 773rd will travel as a unit in convoy and challenges would be faced all the way to Wellfleet.

To go to Wellfleet, we had to travel through small and picturesque towns and hamlets. There were no highways at that time and the roads meandered through some of the most beautiful areas on the famous Cape. The roads twisted and turned and winded through very narrow streets and small lanes, making it difficult for the inexperienced drivers and in particular the CAT (Caterpillar) drivers towing the 90's. Most vehicles also towed cargo trailers which compounded the challenges for the new drivers.

That Monday morning at 06:00 hours, there was a slight chill in the air as the convoy assembled after an early breakfast. The battalion commander was seated in the lead Jeep next to the driver. A radio operator sat in the back seat to maintain communications with the convoy with the aid of an Army Signal Corp radio, the ANC-9, AKA in G.I. parlance as the "Angry 9." The assistant driver sat in the rear with his copy of the Strip Map issued to every assistant driver in case of separation from the convoy. This was SOP (Standard Operating Procedure) whenever a unit traveled in convoy.

The tailgates were lowered as we climbed into the rear of a 2 ½ ton truck. The men folded down the wooden seats for those lucky enough to get a seat...others just sat on the metal floor of the truck bed. We were to be bounced around for that fifty mile drive to Wellfleet. Each man carried his weapon some had the heavy M1 rifle while others the lighter M1 carbine, packs contained all personal and field equipment including blankets, poncho, shelter half, steel helmet, change of socks and underwear, K rations seen for the first time, and a canteen full of water. "Where the hell is the food in this "K ration?" "Hey what are you supposed to eat in this Cracker Jack box? Do they come with a prize?" The soldiers were heard complaining all the way to Wellfleet about the ride, about the K rations and everything else soldiers could find to gripe about.

An electric buzz permeated the air as the Colonels Jeep moved out, followed by the unit rolling along to begin the first of the many convoy moves the future held for the 773rd Gun Battalion. We rolled due east as the sun rose to glare directly into the eyes of the drivers and the column would proceed north at the Cape's elbow and then continue on to our final destination at Wellfleet. My eyes and ears were wide open as I took in everything and... was still having fun. My guess, many years later, was the convoy consisted of about 20 or so vehicles.

An advance party also equipped with an "Angry 9" was sent ahead to check the terrain and the road conditions and to direct the vehicles as they arrived at Wellfleet. Upon arrival, the advance party officers and NCO's staked out exactly where to position the guns and fire control equipment on the firing range. This party was made up of the more senior experienced men who were accustomed to leading the way but, with trained drivers.

Proper convoy discipline called for the slowest vehicle to follow right after the lead Jeep to avoid being lost if the column was spread out too far. So, off rolled the clumsy radar van towed by a tractor truck driven by Corporal John Zurla, followed by the four CATS towing the 90's. They were followed by the four quad mount 50's in trailers each towed by a 2 1/2 ton truck called a "Deuce and a half." Following the guns came the M-9 Director and more trucks loaded with troops and also towing trailers. The ambulance with the Medical Officer and the medical section were close behind.

Last in line was the battalion motor section led by Chief Warrant Officer Manny Mazzarella AKA by the denizens from "Hell's Kitchen," as "Mr. Motorola." The motor section included all the battalion mechanics so necessary in a mobile artillery unit including the battalion wrecker that was designed to tow any vehicle in the column. The 773rd was rolling.

Wellfleet Artillery Firing Range

When practical in training, an advanced mess detail is sent ahead to set up a field kitchen and Lister Bags full of chemically treated drinking water. Enter Sergeant First Class Lew Davis, a character whom, could fill an entire book chapter. Davis was the Battery C mess Sergeant and a colorful fellow indeed. I served with him from 1947 to 1953, when I rotated back to the States from Korea and he continued his regular army career.

As a teen, Davis emigrated from Italy to escape Mussolini's Fascist Italy together with his older sister. They were of the Jewish faith and thankful to arrive in New York City. Sometime after their arrival in the 1930's Davis joined the National Guard at the armory on West 62nd Street. He marched out of that armory in 1941 to serve in World War II, rejoined in 1947 and then marched out to war again in 1951 when the 773rd was activated to serve in the Korean War.

Davis was a big six-foot-plus, overweight, cigar chomping Mess Sergeant with a colorful Italian accent and a guy you just do not ever forget. After years as a National Guardsman, Davis went on to become a Regular Army soldier together with other top two grade NCO's, taking the Army's offer to re-enlist RA and retain their current rank which then would be made permanent. I almost joined him but more on that later. When Davis went RA he would always proudly boast in his husky voice, "No more Nashana Guard, I'ma now Regala Army." You could imagine the jeers he received from his brother NG's.

Davis served as a mess Sergeant in an artillery battery in three wars: in the Aleutians and Europe in WWII, in Korea with the 773rd, and later in the 1960's in Vietnam. During the Vietnam War, my good buddy John Zurla, at the time a pilot with Air America and living in Saigon, ran into SFC Lew Davis, and marine vet M/SGT Bill Barker. Together, they re-enlisted in the Regular Army and now serving with Chief Warrant Officer Warren Burns, all soldiers formerly with Charlie Battery and all served in the same three wars. Burns was a young Southern teen while in an artillery unit in Hawaii on December 7th, 1941 and, spent three years in the Pacific area in WWII. As an RA replacement, SFC Burns joined C Battery in Fort Hamilton, New York when we were preparing for deployment to Korea. He served in my Fire Control Platoon as the Radar Section Leader. The three men were all serving in the same Army Hawk missile unit in Vietnam.

Davis with his Italian accent called me, "Gahlic" or in front of the troops, "Sargena Gahlic." Sergeant's John and Brother Joe Zurla were called "Zurl" or "Sargena Zurl." I will not repeat the names Davis had for others in the battery, but cannot resist one in particular Davis named and it stuck: "F- - K Upa McCarry," another New York character from Hell's Kitchen, although not totally crazy was nonetheless missing a few parts! I will definitely not pass on to the readers with tender ears the cadence count lyrics that Gun Platoon Sergeant Barker bellowed out about Davis while Barker drilled the troops and sharpened up Charlie Battery's marching ability. If you are envisioning a John Wayne, Hollywood-type Drill Sergeant, forget it. Barker was a couple inches shorter than my five foot nine height and slightly built with a round cherubic face and the loudest voice you could imagine. Charlie Battery heard a lot from Barker; his voice drowned out all competition. He did however have one weakness...a fear? Well no, let's just say a dislike or better yet a misunderstanding of electricity...I will tell you more about that later.

The privates hated to be on K.P. (Kitchen Police) when

Davis was on duty. It was a little less stressful for them when the first or second cooks were in charge. When in Camp Stewart, first cook Corporal Demopolis once got so mad at Davis that he chased Davis out of the kitchen with a meat cleaver in his hand. You guessed right, Demopolis was also a Hell's Kitchen son and also missing a few parts - no one messed with him!

Davis and the other battery mess Sergeants on the advance detail arrived to set up their kitchens at Wellfleet. The portable gasoline fired field combination stoves/ovens could be set up in minutes anywhere. Here at Wellfleet, they were set up right in the beds of the two-and-a-half ton trucks which, was a common practice when units were in the field.

Lunch that day was the infamous K ration eaten in transit as the battalion traveled. The hot meal that night consisted of warmed ten-ounce cans of C rations washed down with hot G.I. coffee and a piece of cake for dessert baked in the field oven and an extra provided by Davis's crew with the small fund the battery had. Large G.I. garbage cans were filled with water and gasoline fired immersion heaters placed inside the garbage cans to heat the water. The gas fired burners and chimneys were attached to the top rim of the can. The cooks dropped the cans in the hot water to heat them and issued one to each man. I thought the C ration was not half bad and over the years consumed many and tasted all the different offerings. Franks and beans, chicken and rice, ham and lima beans, and meat and spaghetti to name a few, that guys would barter and trade. A G.I. from the North could always trade a chicken and rice to a Southern trooper for a meat and spaghetti anytime, maybe even kicking in a couple cigarettes from the four-pack found in the K's and C's. The K's were the least appetizing with the word appetizing used very loosely here. (Any reader curious about army rations can go on line and just write in the address bar "K or C Rations Images" to view images of all the variations.)

By the time we went on active duty, the battery could understand four languages: English, New Yorkese, some Spanish and some "Sagina Davis." The southern boys who later came to the outfit had a hell of a time understanding anything Davis said and it was comical to hear Davis trying to mimic the southern drawl. You would be correct if you assume I am smiling while writing this.

It was a long drive to Wellfleet so the battalion CO tried to be as discreet as possible when halting the column alongside of the road with some cover to allow the troops to relieve themselves. Using the then-current army vernacular, the rest stop was simply called, "Piss Call." I imagine with today's political correctness and the fact that now many women serve with their brothers-in-arms, the army must now call it something else, maybe "Tinkle Time."

The fun really started when the battalion had to maneuver the vehicles through the quaint little towns with their small narrow lanes that appeared on the maps as roads. This was in 1948 and many Cape Cod villages looked the same as they did in colonial times. Guys were hanging off the trucks ogling and wolf whistling at all the females young and old, pretty or plain in these quiet and sedate Cape Cod towns.

The journey to Wellfleet meandered through the maze of hamlets and villages making tight turns around narrow lanes all the while knocking down fences, signs and mail boxes. The corners of some buildings were damaged.

It was a miracle that all of Cape Cod did not lose power considering the damage to the telephone poles carrying the power lines. The populace, businesses and the public utilities did not hang out signs spelling out, "Cape Cod Welcomes the 773rd."

Arriving at the firing range at Wellfleet was a shocker. There were no facilities at all, just scrub pine, sand and the 100 or more foot drop from the sand dunes to the beach below and as far as the eye could see, the vast expanse of the Atlantic Ocean.

We were ordered to set up our pup tents right in the scrub pine and to camouflage the tent and area with the pine branches then set up a perimeter defense to simulate combat conditions. The battery machetes were distributed to all sections. I wondered if I would still have a good time here.

Soon after, the First Sergeant started picking "volunteers" to dig latrines and at the same time, key personnel were ordered to report to their equipment positions on the range. That required me to set up the tracking head...that was more like it.

The mess Sergeants would travel to Camp Edwards on a daily schedule and return with rations and potable water towed in tank trailers. We learned how to fill the steel helmet with water and do the best we could to wash with it. Sometimes Davis would even heat up some water for the troops to use to shave. As much as Davis was disliked, I did see in him an experience that benefitted the troops in C Battery. In Korea, many RA's from other units served in C Battery and when they saw Davis ordering the cooks to warm up some water for shaving whenever he could, they were quite happily surprised. No showers at Wellfleet, that luxury would have to wait until we returned to Camp Edwards. It was a good thing we had those clean refreshing Atlantic Ocean breezes flowing in over the sand dunes and embracing the 773rd.

We all went to work placing the guns, radar and fire control equipment. The battalion was quite green but we had a cadre of vets who knew how to get the job at hand done. First, the 90's fired several settling rounds then were re-leveled. This was the very first time most of us ever heard the blast of the 90's as the gunners pulled the operating handle. After that first resounding blast, an awed silence followed for those of us who were paying attention. We just looked at each other with surprise and wonder. Those pre-occupied with other duties were startled by the guns sudden discharge and just jumped up while yelling "What the hell was that!" or some more vulgar expletive.

Because the radar was the center of fire control, we had to measure the distance in yards from the center of the four guns to the radar antenna. Out came the aiming circle and tape measure as we taped the distance N, S, E, and W and entered this distance in yards on a dial in the Director. This theoretically picked up the four guns and placed them directly on top of the radar, the Parallax Correction now complete. Several other technical adjustments were entered in the director to prepare the 90's to accurately explode their twenty pound warheads in the path of an oncoming target. Artillerymen called this path the "Future Predicted Position."

Colonel Slavin was a quiet gentleman who never had to raise his voice. He instilled a degree of confidence to all and displayed a slight smile as Major Kraus reported "Sir, the battalion is ready to fire." With a broader smile and field phone in hand, the Colonel reported to the range control officer positioned in a rustic wooden range tower, "The 773rd is ready to fire and requests a direct fire target."

An announcement was heard on a loud speaker that the range was hot and for all personnel to stand to the rear of the safety stakes to protect against muzzle blast. Upon looking out at the ocean, we saw the towed water target with the silhouette outline of a tank. Elbow scopes were installed on the 90's now and guided by aiming stakes in the sand to help keep the gun crews from traversing too far out of their safety zone. One at a time, the guns fired at the moving target. Next to shoot were the quad mounted .50 caliber machine guns. Many in fire control were not too involved with the direct fire but just kept the SCR-584 radar and the M-9 director humming.

My position tracking the target with the azimuth scope was to spot the hits and misses while an officer viewed through the elevation scope to verify. The 90's were tracking and leading the towed water target as we observed to see how many hits were made. It took a while before the gun crews scored but this was the very first time.

We were now ready for an aerial target and the sun was shining over the Atlantic Ocean and the sky was blue when, a summer thunderstorm burst sending the 773rd scrambling for their rain ponchos...it quickly subsided and the sun broke through the clouds again and now the sky turned a beautiful cobalt blue as it does right after a storm. That was talked about and from that time on, the 773rd was stuck with the nickname, "The Rain Makers."

An Air Force B-25 twin engine medium bomber towed a red target sleeve about 30 feet long attached to a steel cable a few hundred yards behind the bomber. The target frame was made of a reflective material to reflect back a signal so the radar could track and then lock on the target. Target sleeves were used in 1948 but when we returned to Edwards in 1949 and again in 1950, Radio Controlled Aerial Targets (RCAT's) replaced the towed target sleeve.

The battalion was now ready to fire and the Colonel requested a target. The B-25 from Otis Air base was soon located by the Tracking Head; the Radar locked on and tracked the target sleeve. Kraus looked through the scope on the radar antenna to visually verify the radar was locked on the target sleeve and not the B-25, which was a possibility. Imagine how the crew of that B-25 felt, knowing the unit down there on the ground was a green National Guard outfit with little to no experience now pointing four lethal 90mm guns loaded with high explosive ammunition in their direction.

The radar was now tracking the target sleeve smoothly all the while under Kraus's observation on the roof of the radar van. The gun control "Clocks" on the 90's were in the AID position and the setters were manually tracking by matching the dials, and you could see the guns moving with jerking motions. When the data finally settled, the order to switch to AUTO was given and the guns tracked smoothly. When all was ready the command was given to "FIRE."

The cannoneers rapidly passed the ammo to the Fuse Setter Loader who placed the round in the Fuse setter. The Fuse Setter cranked the handle setting the fuse then the loader passed the round to the opened breech. The gunner, in one fluid motion with his left fist closed, rammed the round into the breech. The upward movement of the breech block slamming shut pushed the gunner's closed-fisted hand up and out of the way as he yanked the firing handle with his right hand. Simultaneously, the gunner pivoted to his left rear out of the path of the recoiling gun. When the gun fired, the recoil action re-opened the breech block ejecting the spent shell case, the gunner kicked the spent shell case out of the way while loading another round, the gun crew all keeping time like a choreographed dance.

This is how it plays in my mind but never thought of in that way at the time. I was looking through the TH scope watching the shell bursts. The many hundreds of 90 rounds I witnessed firing never created an image of dancers and those multitudes of ex-gunners would laugh at my description but that is how it is remembered now. I served with 90's from 1948 to 1959 when we transitioned from 90mm guns to Nike-Ajax Missiles and never actually pulled that firing handle on a hot 90 round.

It was important for the gunner to keep his left hand in a tight fist when pushing the round to avoid losing fingers in a slamming breech block, a not uncommon hazard for many an artilleryman. I knew many who were missing some digits including my pal Max Ries. He lost a fingertip in Camp Stewart while working on a 90.

It took several tries before we actually bracketed the target sleeve with black shell bursts and tore up the red sleeve with hot shrapnel indicating hits. Much to our surprise, the pilot buzzed the range and to our amazement released the target as we all watched the shredded target float down. Many of us thought that was SOP (Standard Operational Procedure) but the vets said they never saw that happen before.

Maybe the pilot was overwhelmed with relief and just wanted an excuse to make a mad dash back to the Otis air base officers club for a quick drink of an adult beverage! Or, maybe the 773rd's accurate fire shredded the sleeve making it unusable!! We all yelled at the top of our lungs as the damaged red sleeve floated to earth and guys cut off samples. That day we were all happy campers in Wellfleet in 1948.

Thanks again to many of that cadre of experienced vets, Sergeants Red Haroldsen, Cacciotti, Bill Mauro, Faust, Monahan, Murray and Sergeant Major Jake Bond to name only a few. Jake Bond lied about his age twice, once when he joined in the 1930's to make himself older and again in later years when reenlisting, making himself younger. Later, as an officer and Battery Commander of Headquarters Battery, Jake Bond was my First Sergeant before he was promoted to the well-deserved rank of Battalion Sergeant Major. I don't know why, but as I write their names and remember their faces, I get a little choked up. Maybe my age and Irish sentimentality is showing.

One day, while the machine gunners were firing the Quad Mount .50 Calibers, the firing range was closed until some whales or porpoises swam out of harm's way. Again, the Tracking Head was the best seat in the house! It's too bad it was long before today's digital camera technology…it would have been fun to have taken digital pictures through those powerful lenses.

With firing complete, it was now time to return to Camp Edwards. We all looked forward to a much needed hot shower and to prepare for the trip home. While at Wellfleet, the drivers received additional training and were somewhat more experienced. Everyone was ordered to keep a low profile and be on their best behavior while traveling through the villages. The 773rd made its way back to Camp Edwards with no further incidents.

We did notice, however, all those curious locals who crowded the byways on our way out were now making themselves invisible and some were even seen curiously peeking from behind their curtains! Hmm…maybe during that week, some of the more adventurous troopers sneaked out while still wearing their grimy field uniforms, to meet and get to know some of the more daring Cape Cod Lassies?

Those years of 1948, 1949, and 1950 were memorable ones, before Camp Wellfleet was later developed into a permanent base for artillery firing. Barracks and all modern facilities were later constructed but, when the 773rd was there, it was still a barren part of the dunes on Cape Cod. Now it is part of the Cape Cod National Seashore. No one in the 773rd ever mentioned or even knew we were on almost the exact spot where Guglielmo Marconi had wireless towers built in the early 1900's. This was when Marconi was pioneering and perfecting the transmission of wireless communication between the continents of North America and Europe.

We returned to Camp Edwards, got paid, and ate our last hot meal in Davis's mess hall until the fall small arms shoot. That last night most of us were attracted to the many floating poker, black jack and crap games. I indulged but very, very cautiously. I do not remember if I even won or lost but either way, it was not much. I do remember, however, some less cautious guys being taken advantage of. As a corporal, I just minded my own business and warned my comrades in the Fire Control Platoon to stay away from Dennison and Corman, both card sharks from Hell's Kitchen.

Dennison was a card shark who would cheat on his mother

but, was nonetheless a likeable character. I remember later that fall at annual weapons qualification at Camp Smith when we were riding in the back of a truck with Dennison sitting across from me. "Hey Dennison, that's the sharpest I ever saw you dress, your brass all polished and your jacket pressed. You usually look like a sad sack." It was then I noticed Corporal stripes on his sleeve. The SOB was wearing my "Ike" jacket but, for some reason, you just could not get mad at Dennison.

Corman on the other hand by nature, was mean and vindictive and had few friends. I had as little as possible to do with him even though we crossed paths when he ran wire and phones to the FC equipment and later promoted to Commo Chief.

Corman was among those not chosen to go to Korea with the outfit. He was replaced by RA Communications Sergeant Haldane Irwin, a professional and highly competent NCO who brought so much more to Charlie Battery then Corman ever did.

The Camp tours of 1949 and 1950 are somewhat redundant. We had more men in the unit, a somewhat higher military bearing and a much better trained 773rd. The battalion's previous bad reputation was all but forgotten as we seemed to glide in and out of the same lanes and hamlets on Cape Cod. The drivers now much better trained and the troops more disciplined.

I went to Camp Edwards in 1950 as a Sergeant and M-9 Director Section leader. The rumors circulated throughout the Wellfleet range that we would not be going home at the end of the two-week camp tour and that training would be extended to include mobilization to active duty status. How this or any other rumors begin in the army is anyone's guess but it sounded convincing at the time.

June of 1950, a few weeks before camp tour and almost to the day I graduated from Bryant High School, the North Korean People's Army stormed across the 38th parallel to attack The Republic of Korea. The Cold War was now a Hot War and a massive National Guard mobilization took place. At the same time the draft was stepped up, National Guard units from all over the country were being alerted for activation as they had for all the nation's previous wars.

The rumors about activation put many troopers on edge so, when volunteers were called upon for an advanced detail to return to the armory a day ahead of time, many raised their hands. I warned the guys in my section to hold off, I saw these advanced details before and knew how they played out.

The day before we were scheduled to return to New York, the advanced detail of about 25 green troop volunteers from the battalion climbed into a two-and-a-half ton truck with all their gear and weapons and smiled as they waved good bye. The truck pulled out and drove all the way to the rail head at the other end of Camp Edwards where, the men in the advanced detail were deposited and they were told to wait for the train as, the truck pulled away. The advanced detail soon realized this was a hoax and they would have to march all the way back to the barracks and, the raucous cheers of their comrades who had just finished chow. This was the summer of 1950 and the last camp tour at Camp Edwards, Massachusetts for the 773rd gun battalion.

The Monday night drill became more intense. All Section Leaders were required to attend Thursday night headquarters non-paid drill to prepare for next Monday night's training sessions.

My two Astoria pals Bill Tierney and Bob Partos who did not join the guard both served in the army. Bill was drafted, trained and sent to the 7th Division in Korea as a rifleman and returned as a SFC and recoilless rifle section leader. Bob enlisted to pick his spot and after training served in an Artic clothing and equipment research unit in Keene, New Hampshire. I took a lot of good natured kidding from them about my later guard time.

September 1950 was school time for me and I attended New York State University on Pearl Street in Brooklyn. The industrial sales course was interesting enough and included an industrial lab with all types of machinery that we studied to become familiar with lathes, drill presses, milling machines and the like. Some of the students later went off to successful sales positions selling industrial equipment but, I was preoccupied with the guard, hearing almost weekly about guard units activated and just waiting for our turn.

Sometime in the fall of 1950 Chief Warrant Officer

Nicholetti, the battery's full time administrator asked me to meet with him before drill when, he presented an offer to me. Nicholetti knew the 773rd was to be activated but did not know exactly when. He told me the battery needed a trained Fire Control NCO and that it could lead to promotions. He reminded me that SFC Haroldsen who had trained us was in A Battery and we needed our own trained Fire Control NCO. He felt I was the best candidate for the five month Fire Control Gun course in Fort Bliss, Texas.

All the experienced artillerymen, both officers and enlisted men were familiar with Fort Bliss because it was and still is the army's foremost anti-aircraft artillery and guided missile school and training center. Missile and artillery ranges are located in the desert not too far from White Sands, New Mexico. Bliss is also where the Patriot anti-missile system was developed and who knows what advanced anti-missile technology is being perfected there today, at least I hope that is true.

To sweeten the pie Nicholetti fortified the many stories I heard from others about Fort Bliss being just minutes across the Rio Grande River from the *Turista* fun town of Juarez in Old Mexico. He told me about the .75 cent full course sirloin steak dinners and fifteen cent mixed drinks, fifteen cent Carta Blanca and Cruz Blanca Mexican Cerveza, the bull fights, the marimba and mariachi bands …and of course, the pretty dark eyed *senoritas* thrown in to close the deal.

In 1950, Juarez was not the crime ridden violent drug battle zone it is today. Juarez was a wonderfully colorful town for tourists and for a few cent bus ride from Fort Bliss to the International Bridge, it was a great place for a G.I. on a pass. I thanked Nicholetti and told him I wanted to at least complete my first semester at college and he said that would be fine. I could plan to go sometime after the first of January.

Sergeant Parisi's Cigar

SFC Joseph Parisi was an older, sober and serious NCO in C Battery and an experienced veteran, well respected by the troops. He enjoyed his cigars and on the train ride back from summer camp he dozed off while his cigar was still lit. The cigar apparently slipped and made its way down to the train seat and the seat of his pants. Parisi suddenly jumped up yelling and screaming. He frightened the hell out of everyone sitting nearby. I was seated a couple of rows in back of him and thought the old soldier just cracked up.

No one knew his problem until he turned around exposing a smoking mass of black smoldering Khaki pants, burnt shorts and singed buttocks. "Hey," someone yelled, "Is Sergeant Davis cooking something?"

"Who the hell is burning a fur coat?" yelled Monte. "Better not let that fire spread, Sarge," until it was realized Parisi was badly burned. The medics were a couple of cars away and soon appeared with medics bags in hand. Parisi was then further humiliated when the medics went to work on him cleaning and dressing his wound.

"Hey Sarge, why the hell did you do that while I'm still eating?" another quipped. More joking was called out by another of Parisi's West Side neighbors. "Ugh Sarge, that's the most disgusting thing I ever saw after seeing Davis taking a shower!" A laugh fest followed and even Parisi was laughing in between his cries of pain.

The Sarge proved his mettle when the officers suggested a cab ride back to the armory for him. Instead, he asked to borrow a Russet bag to sling over his shoulder to cover his butt and hide the burned seat of his pants. Parisi marched the twenty city blocks from the railhead on 42nd Street back to the armory together with his troops. His many friends and neighbors waved as the 773rd marched right through Parisi's West Side neighborhood and back to the armory on West 62nd Street.

A Soldiers Heartache

A tragic and heart-breaking event happened to one of our battery's top sergeants and although I used his family name in my initial narrative I can't with an easy heart use his real name that may open old wounds to his family. This Top Sergeant lived on Manhattan's, Upper East Side. This was not the fashionable 70's, 80's and 90's but, on East 115th Street in a crowded tenement neighborhood. This was in the 1950's when East Harlem was the largest Italian-American community in the country. When I was a little boy, the Cavallo family led by my Grandma Maria, ventured to 115th Street to go to the church there and celebrate the Italian Feast every summer in honor of the Lady of Mount Carmel. I can still recall the sound of Italian music, the crowds and the aroma and sound of Italian sausage and peppers sizzling on an open grill. As a child I remembered, "La Fiesta" without the religious significance only for the souvenir stands where I pestered my Mom to buy me a swell looking toy sword. "No, No," she kept on saying… "Here have some candy." But, I do recall admiring that sword on the way home and I think Grandma Cavallo bought it for me.

The Sergeant joined the unit sometime in 1948. He was a World War II veteran, having served in Europe as a 90mm Gun Commander with the U. S. Seventh Army. He served in combat in Italy, France and Germany. He was the army's best example of what an NCO should be and everyone officers, NCO's and enlisted men alike respected him.

Right after camp and returning to the armory we were marching up the wide stairway to the battery rooms when we all noticed a few civilian men on the staircase landing. The men had very somber expressions on their faces and you could tell something was wrong. We also noticed their resemblance to our Sergeant. Several of his brothers and cousins were sent to meet him at the armory. This was to prepare him for the terrible news that his beautiful two year old baby boy met with a tragic accident that day and now was at rest in a funeral parlor.

The battery paid their respects to the family and attended

the viewing. It was the saddest experience to witness and the images are still there. The Sergeant's face appeared as a marble mask and you could see he was holding back his feeling of immense grief. His wife was lost in indescribable sorrow. Elderly Italian women all dressed in black were seen kneeling in prayer and crying. Family, neighbors and the local Parish priests all crowded the funeral parlor sharing this terrible loss with the family.

The family all stood tall that evening, showing the strong family ties of a brave and dignified Italian American family. We all walked past the little boy's funeral bier and viewed his tiny body all dressed in a white suit. The family thanked us all for coming to pay our respects and to show our sympathy for their loss.

We stepped out on the crowded street in front of the funeral home and saw a steady line of mourners waiting their turn to comfort the family when someone suggested having a beer at the Olympus Bar on 8th Avenue.

We all took the train back to the armory to change into our civilian clothing and then had a quiet beer at the Olympus. The owner insisted on picking up the tab that night. I took the long train ride from Manhattan's West Side back to my home in Woodside. All the while, I was thinking about that little baby boy dressed in his white suit and laid out in a tiny white coffin.

Garcia Pharmacy

Summer 1950 was both work and play with plans to go to college in September. All during high school, I had two part-time jobs. One was at a local corner drug store, Garcia's Pharmacy on 61st Street and 39th Avenue. I worked there every Wednesday evening and every other Sunday as a "Soda Jerk" and, if the pharmacist was busy filling prescriptions, I helped out behind the counter waiting on customers. Sometimes a young school girl chum would walk in and see me behind the counter and stop, sit at the soda fountain and order a nickel Coke. I knew she came in to buy something else until she saw me behind the counter and we had trouble making eye contact and small talk. That never happened when men came in to buy condoms and it made no difference if I knew them or not. They just slammed down their fifty cents and ordered 3 Sheiks or Trojans and hurried out. Most married men ordered them in the dozen package....no small talk with me, there was something else on their minds. I also worked at the A&P every Saturday tossing cases of canned food and stacking shelves. My Uncle Danny Cavallo who was the meat manager at the local A&P got me the job.

Mr. Manuel Garcia was born in Puerto Rico and came to New York when in his teens. He worked days for the New York City Transit system and went to Pharmacy school at night. He owned the neighborhood drug store and was highly respected and admired. He was of medium height with full lips, an olive complexion and a bald head with white bushy hair around his ears. He looked a little like the actor who played "Uncle Remus" in the Disney flick "Song of the South." Mr. Garcia had a delightful Spanish accent and called me "Benny." To some Hispanics, "V" and "B" are interchangeable.

Mrs. Genevieve Garcia was a tall full-figured Scandinavian woman who wore her lengthy blond hair up in braids just like a Diva right out of a Wagner Opera. When they were together, they were a striking couple. She was a good deal taller than her Manny and you could tell they adored each other. Every Sunday at about 6 P.M., Mrs. Garcia carried in their Sunday meal which always looked so appetizing to me. They lived just two streets away on 63rd Street. They sat in the back of the store dining and listening to the Sunday Symphony and I can still hear her singing or humming along with the music. I have warm memories about my time with the Garcia's and I am sure many felt the same way about them. You could always tell about a person by the friends they have and the Garcia's s had many wonderful friends who visited the store and loved them.

Thirty-five cents an hour was the pay rate at the time...kind of unbelievable but true. Lee just verified it, she also earned 35 cents an hour working at a bakery in Brooklyn during her high school days.

We had some excitement one Sunday evening at Garcia's Drug Store when we were held up at gunpoint. Just before I was to attach the steel screen over the front door and start to clean up the soda fountain to close for the evening, a tall slim man with brown unruly hair wearing a grey tweed overcoat briskly walked in. One hand was in his pocket, the other holding a handkerchief on his eye as though he had something in his eye. This was quite normal for, in those days, many people walked in asking Mr. Garcia to remove a speck from their eye. Mr. Garcia always obliged for it was good for business. I know that could court disaster today for a potential law suit but it was highly acceptable in the 1940's.

I leaned around from in front of the cash register to address Mr. Garcia sitting in his rocking chair in the back room. I announced as I have done many times before, "Mr. Garcia, this man has something in his...his...his... he has a gun!" The man was already behind the counter standing in back of me and as I turned, I looked down at the gaping barrel of an army 45 caliber automatic pistol. I knew what they looked like, having seen several at the National Guard armory. This one was nickel or chrome plated making it look even more menacing.

"Both of you get on the floor...now!" the crook snarled. "But I have a bad leg," said Garcia. "On the floor, both of you!!!" I didn't have to be asked twice. I was already breathing dust as I lay face down on the hard wood floor of the back room of the pharmacy.

"Give me your wallets....no false moves," ordered the gunman. In a micro second my wallet with two one dollar bills was passed up to the counter.

"I do not have a wallet," claimed Garcia "All thee money is in thee register. "I knew this was a lie; before closing, Garcia emptied the register except for a few dollars and hid the day's receipts in the back room in an old brown paper bag...that was the nightly drill. The thief hit a register key and the register opened almost at the same time a young kid came in... "Hey anybody there? I want to buy some ice cream." Garcia answered, "Just a meenute, Benny will be there in a meenute." "Shut up," yelled the robber as we heard his heavy footsteps running out of the store.

Before I realized what was happening Garcia jumped up and grabbed a bottle from his array of chemicals on a back shelf and ran out after the crook who was running past the soda fountain with some bills in his hand and stuffing them in his pocket. Without even giving it a second thought, I stupidly followed after grabbing two bottles from a case of quart-sized Canada Dry Ginger Ale. With a bottle in each hand, I followed my leader chasing the thief out of the store. I had no plan what I would do with the bottles if challenged but it gave me a feeling of at least being armed with something I could throw at him. Garcia was splashing the contents of the bottle and it splattered all over the fleeing crooks neck and hair as he ran out and disappeared in the darkness of 39th Avenue. Garcia jumped into the phone booth at the front of the store and called the police.

"Hey, what's that smell? I want to buy some ice cream?" The kid yelled.

"Get the hell out of here, don't you know we were just held up at gun point?" I answered him.

An after-action report revealed how dumb Mr. Garcia's move was and that it could have resulted in a tragedy for three Woodside families that eventful evening. First off, the register only contained a few dollars because most of the day's take was already concealed in the paper bags, already hidden away. He apologized to me and the kid saying he was very sorry for putting our lives at risk.

The bottle he grabbed contained 28% ammonia water, a very potent strength. I do not know for what purpose he even had that strength in the store. The fumes were overpowering and Mr. Garcia turned on a standing floor fan as we waited outside until the police arrived. The cops didn't even want to enter the store until the ammonia fumes dissipated. Apparently, this was not the first time the store was held up. So my guess is that instead of a handgun for self- defense, he chose ammonia water 28%. When to submit and when to react is a question we all ask ourselves…you know, it does not always happen to the other guy or gal.

We gave the police a description of the thief and our names, addresses and phone numbers. I told them I had not seen the man's full face and described what I actually did see. I don't remember when I told my Dad about the hold-up. But I soon heard from the detective, apparently they had a suspect in custody and wanted me and Mr. Garcia to make a positive identification. My Dad said to me, "Be 100% sure before you identify anyone." Mr. Garcia drove me in his 1930's era Lincoln auto, to the 110th Precinct Police Station in Elmhurst.

The detectives were very nice to us and asked if he would like a cup of coffee or hot chocolate...we both declined. The drill was to be as follows. We were seated on a bench in the hallway with rooms on each side of the hall. They told us they would open a door slightly where they were holding the suspect. They would crack open the door so we could see the suspect without the suspect seeing us. They would make him turn around so we could view all sides of his face and he would not even know we were there. It seemed OK but, that's not how it actually played out.

As we were seated, the police had another idea. Within seconds, the door directly in front of us was opened and the police paraded this guy in plain view right in front of us as several detectives observed the suspect and both me and Garcia. The suspect was about the same height and weight and fit the description but I could not be sure without a doubt that this was the same guy. I never actually saw his full face...my focus was on that chrome-plated 45 automatic pointing at me which he purposely stuck in my face to distract me. I remembered the gun, the unruly hair, the tweed overcoat and, a white handkerchief partially covering his face. He was now just wearing a white shirt and trousers with both hands restrained behind his back in handcuffs. We were surprised when the suspect was paraded directly in front of us and we all made eyeball to eyeball contact with him as he walked by and into an adjoining room. He had no discernible marks, scars, tattoos or outstanding features to make identification obvious to us. To see him a little slumped over and tired looking he was actually quite plain looking. Or, possibly a good actor! We were then invited into an adjacent room and asked by the detectives to sit down.

"Well, that's our man, right?" a detective said with a smile on his face. Garcia and I looked at each other and I told the policemen I could not be 100% sure. "I only saw the back of his head and part of his face." Garcia told them he only saw the back of the suspects head. The policemen seemed annoyed and thanked us as we left.

On the way home, Mr. Garcia asked if I noticed the back of the suspect's neck and hair, and I said that I did not. I just remembered his stare at me, as he passed by. As I was trying to associate the face with that evening, all I could come up with was an image of a big shiny .45 automatic...the distraction had worked. Garcia told me the hair on the back of the suspects head had a vague red tint and the back of his neck was still a little red which may have been the effect of being doused with the strong ammonia water 28%. But he said that if he saw his full face and could have positively identified the suspect, he would have gladly told the police.

All the local drug stores were on alert in that part of Queens. The thief favored late night hold-ups of drug stores in the areas darkened streets. Sometime shortly after, the thief with the fancy .45 automatic was finally caught during a holdup and the story appeared in the Long Island newspaper.

My dad was annoyed with Garcia and told my Mom not to go to the store anymore. I still worked there on and off during my high school years with no more hold-ups. Sunday evenings close to closing time seemed the likely time for a robbery so, most Sundays the Garcia's friends would come in to visit and join them to listen to the symphony or an opera; they lingered until closing time. One of his friends smoked a pipe and I savored the aroma. I also enjoyed the setting, the company, and the music on those Sunday evenings in Garcia's.

Mr. Garcia's favorite treat which he would make for himself was a pineapple chocolate ice cream soda. A heaping spoonful of his homemade chunky pineapple syrup and a big scoop of chocolate ice cream. He showed me how to make the ice cream sodas in the large heavy glasses that were then placed in a shiny chrome plated metal holder and served. First, a generous portion of syrup then add about a 1/4 cup of milk and a big scoop of ice cream, and then slowly pour in the fresh carbonated water from the big spotless chrome fountain dispenser. His sodas and malted milks were like having a meal. Mrs. Garcia liked a big scoop of vanilla ice cream in her black coffee that always smelled so good as it was percolating on the stove.

Garcia made all the syrups for the fountain on that same stove in the back room where he also filled all the prescriptions. The aroma of the Pineapple syrup made with fresh chunky pieces of fresh Pineapple and the Strawberry Syrup with chopped fresh Strawberries were heavenly. My favorite was his special Chocolate Syrup made with big chunks of Chocolate. It seemed any one of these syrups were always simmering on the stove. Whenever a customer entered to fill an RX they would sit to wait at the fountain and before long were enjoying their fountain favorite. He told me he made smaller quantities to maintain freshness it also increased fountain business. He sold nickel candies but also had a large display of boxed chocolates and would order increased quantities when he made the special chocolate syrup. Customers would always comment "Oh Mr. Garcia, that chocolate syrup smells delicious." They would leave the store with their prescription and a nicely wrapped expensive box of chocolate candy

Whenever I entered for my work tour and syrup was brewing I knew I would have a busy night at the fountain and would partake in more than my normal goodies…so did Garcia. If Pineapple syrup was brewing that's when he indulged with his favorite chocolate and Pineapple ice cream soda.

The perks allowed me to also take home a pint of ice cream for my Mom and while working, to enjoy whatever I wished from the fountain. My treat needed to be consumed in the back room where I could listen to the music and still keep an eye on the store. Garcia was very strict about showing me how to wash the glassware and spoons in hot soapy water and to keep the fountain area spotless.

As I write down these memories, I keep on thinking about my sweetheart Lee working after school in Genovese Bakery many miles away from Woodside for the same 35 cents an hour. She had no thought that, someday, this boy from Woodside would arrive in Bensonhurst and, carry her off into the sunset.

New York State University & Fort Bliss

In September 1950, I started classes at New York State University, later known as Brooklyn Community College. My course of study was Industrial Sales. Classes were held in the main building at Pearl Street in Brooklyn and at the annex on Flushing Avenue, also in Brooklyn. Two high school chums, Bill Young and Wally Gratz, were in the same course and we three traveled to school every day on the subway. The studies were quite interesting and I felt good about a sales career in a technical field. In September 1950, my first three year enlistment in the National Guard was up and I re-enlisted for another three years. The Korean War started that previous June and the draft was already in effect; I thought it was better to be an Artillery Sergeant rather than a draftee Private in the infantry. Nothing against the infantry for I have the greatest respect for those who served our country as infantrymen. I felt I was just marking time at school until something more important and inevitable would happen

Massive National Guard mobilization was under way. Units were activated almost immediately following the attack on The Republic of South Korea. (See Korean War Project on line.) Every US armed forces unit serving in Korea has a message board I even wrote a paragraph there some years ago when I discovered the website.

In the meantime, life went on and school became more interesting. We had a small clique of like-minded youths joining me and my two pals. Bill, Wally, John M, Manny, Irv, Ed and Bernie swapped stories and experiences and we developed a nice social life while becoming active in the "Indales," a fraternity-like group with instructor Mr. McClusky as head of the Industrial Sales Department.

At school I met Ariana, an appealing dark-eyed young woman a little older than I was. She was attractive, bright and personable. She lived with her family in a lovely apartment a few blocks from the Grand Concourse in the Bronx. Two of her older sisters were already married with small children and lived in the neighborhood offering cozy baby-sitting evenings for us.

The relationship which started out as a mutual attraction for us was now beginning to take on a serious turn. We were spending more time together, babysitting her nieces and nephews in their cozy apartments and cuddling while the babies slept in the next room. I did like her very much but the cloud of "Guard Activation" and the prospect of going to Fort Bliss and not finishing college distracted me from this romance. She was a sophisticated young woman and perhaps more mature than this kid from Woodside.

I remember a party she invited me to that was held at her girlfriend's parent's splendid apartment on the Grand Concourse with a sunken living room and beautifully furnished. I was familiar with the luxurious Bronx Grand Concourse apartments because my parents' friends Joe and Tillie Levy lived there also and we visited them frequently. Ariana asked me to bring along a friend so I invited my school pal Bill Young who knew Ariana and he was happy to go.

My dad would let me take the 1937 Ford from time to time for local jaunts but I doubted he would agree to a sojourn all the way up to the Grand Concourse to the Bronx. So I just told him me and a pal were taking a couple of local girls out to the movies. One white lie is still a lie which will lead to another and the truth will eventually come out. I learned this lesson the hard way.

In those days, most teens I knew drank alcohol, and yes, even hard liquor was served to friends at home. Imagine that being done today. But, no one in my family or group of friends were ever drunk and disorderly. Drugs in any form were unheard of.

Bill Young was a fun loving guy but not, as I can remember, fool hardy. Bill had relatives down south living in one of the Carolinas and he mentioned "White lightning" from time to time. Dad gave me the keys to the Ford with the usual rule, drive carefully, no drinking and return the car with a full tank of gasoline. I agreed to all of the above.

That Saturday night behind the wheel of the 1937 Ford, I pulled up in front of Bill's house as he was waiting for me. He was carrying a large brown bulging paper bag in his hand. "What's in the bag, Bill?" "White lightning," Bill answered, followed by, "We need to pick up some grapefruit juice." I don't recall the following dialog but we did buy a quart size can of grapefruit juice and went off to the party…two real sophisticates.

We arrived at the party and met a friendly and attractive group of Ariana's friends and proceeded to enjoy ourselves. Most of the people appeared to be a little older and everyone was very friendly; the atmosphere was quite congenial. Some of the Bronx boys and maybe some of the girls also ventured a taste of the white lightning and grapefruit juice but, for the most part, they just made a face and went back to sipping a beer or a soda. I don't remember seeing any hard liquor at the party nor do I ever remember my girlfriend ever drinking any alcohol.

At the party I tasted a bit of "southern history" and thought it tasted like you would imagine rubbing alcohol and grapefruit juice would taste and didn't go back for more. Bill thought it was great. I nursed a beer and indulged in the beautiful spread of food. There were several types of bread, bagels and bialys, a soft bagel that was very popular with New Yorkers but mostly unknown in other parts of the country as I was to learn later on.

The buffet table was adorned with a spread of food including turkey, roast beef, assorted cold cuts, cream cheese, lox, potato salad and cole slaw, followed by cakes, cookies, and coffee.

There was a lot of dancing which left me flat-footed for that is a grace I never really mastered. Ariana and her girlfriends had some fun trying to teach me how easy it was but found I just didn't have the rhythm. When a slow love song played on the record player, I was OK. I knew how to closely caress my partner and dance cheek to cheek which was the only way I liked to dance anyway. And, it was the only dance step I ever knew. A girl in Bryant High School taught me a simple two-step I remember and if forced to dance today, that would have to be it. Big Brother John was a great dancer and knew all the popular steps and the girls liked to dance with him. But, I was left out in the cold when it came to dancing.

Lee and her entire family are all good dancers, and her Dad, Andy Reres, in his younger years was an award-winning ballroom dancer specializing in the Tango. All the women wanted to dance with him at the family weddings. Lee's brother Tony Reres has very competently filled his Dad's shoes over the years being a real "Twinkle Toes" in his own right. Lee and her sisters Rosemarie and Vincenza were all good dancers and Rose was also a singer in the 1950's. She sang professionally with a group of four other pretty teenage girls known as The Rosebuds. They cut a record titled "Dearest Darling," which enjoyed quite a bit of play in the 1950's.

The Rosebuds were an attractive and talented group of girls whom, if properly managed and financed could have gone on to greater heights. As a little boy, our son John called them the "Roe-Buds. John found a "Dearest Darling" record that was played at our wonderful 50th Anniversary party in 2003 to honor his aunt and godmother Rosemarie Reres DeSantis. Rosie was our Maid of Honor on our wedding day.

At the party in the Bronx, everyone had a few laughs about drinking White Lightning and grapefruit juice. A couple of the more adventurous Bronx guys may have had a slight bit more with Bill before the party ended. No one I can recall was the least bit intoxicated and I knew what a drunk looked like and sounded like from my youthful experience at the Merchant Marine hall and the old 12th Regiment. That's probably the reason why I chose not wanting to become one.

Now that it was time to leave, I was sorry Bill was here because I would not be able to linger with my girl in Dad's '37 Ford. But we would make up for that the next time we fulfilled our babysitting duties. Don't misread what I am saying: this never went beyond a certain point so don't get any ideas. Even if it did, I would not write about it...but it never did.

We said our good nights to Ariana's Grand Concourse hostess and thanked her for the swell time we had. Bill collected his still quite full bottle of moonshine, wrapped it up in the brown paper bag and we proceeded to drive my girl home. After dropping off Ariana and kissing her goodnight, I continued south on the Grand Concourse and over the Triborough Bridge to Queens.

The Triborough Bridge linked Queens, Manhattan and the Bronx boroughs and was completed in 1936. Since 2008 it's been called the Robert F. Kennedy Bridge. I remember as a child waiting with my parents on the Queens Borough side of the Bridge to see President Franklin Delano Roosevelt drive by on the bridge dedication day. Sure enough, there he was, led by a group of motorcycle police and FDR following in a shiny gray open-topped touring car. The President was waving his arms and flashing that famous smile as the crowd cheered him on and we all waved back. I vividly remember that scene from when I was only four years old.

When we arrived back at Bill's house, he reached in the back of the car for the half gallon bottle of White Lighting and discovered the lid was not on tight. The remainder of the liquor spilled all over the floor of my Dad's 1937 Ford. Bill was feeling a little sick, I was glad to have only tasted a little and Ariana smartly refused to have any at all.

Seeing Dad the next day and owning up to the night's events was not fun. I only had a little taste of the White Lightning and felt fine. When I told him about the moonshine, he was livid. Now I would have to pass inspection from my Dad to make sure I was not showing signs of alcohol poisoning. He read me the riot act but, not on drinking in general because I was not drunk nor had I ever gotten drunk. Dad raised hell about my being so stupid to drink that unknown rot gut. I swore never to drink anything I did not see opened from a sealed bottle and I never did.

Also, Dad cautioned me about drinking and putting my drink down unattended. He warned that if I must leave it even for just seconds, not to drink another drop of that drink and just walk away from it. You never know who the jokers are in the crowd and to what extent they will go to by slipping something in your drink for laughs or worse. This applied to any venue from family barbecues to hospitality suites at business events from simply emptying your Classic Coke can and filling it with water to slipping you a Mickey to destroy a career. I remembered that advice and passed it on to my sons and grandchildren.

Dad told me about the tragedies of moonshine booze and bathtub gin blinding and killing people during Prohibition. He also told me about the pranks he saw as a young man in his cousin's bar in Scranton before his Mom moved his family from their home in Scranton to Manhattan's West 28th Street. I always remembered his words to never leave a can of beer or soda unattended at an outdoor barbecue. If yellow jackets or other critters are flying about, the sweet will invite them right into the can or bottle in a flash. OUCH.

Sometime around this same time period I had the opportunity to purchase a real neat black 1939 Lincoln Zephyr two door coupe with my buddy Max Ries. It was a long sleek classic car that would be worth thousands of dollars today. We bought the car from pal Jim Merget and paid him only $50 each. The only negative was it burned a little oil and left a smoke trail. We drove it around and really enjoyed it until I left for Fort Bliss and we sold the car for what we paid for it.

Between Christmas and New Year's 1950-51 I made the decision to volunteer for Fire Control School in Fort Bliss. The five-month school would begin in March so I would not be returning to college in January. Forgotten is how this was discussed with my folks, my brothers and my girl.

The course at Fort Bliss was to start in March so I took a job at James Mont Modern Mode Furniture at East 51st Street between Second and Third Avenues in Manhattan.

Two Astoria buddies worked there and one of the fathers managed the finishing department where I would be working. This high-end custom furniture designer and manufacturer sold to the rich and famous. I was a sander working in an atmosphere of zany proportions, even too wild to write about it in this narrative. I also worked there the previous summer of 1950.

The time was fast approaching as I prepared to leave home for Fort Bliss. I do not remember how I addressed this decision with my family and friends. I do not remember packing or even traveling to Grand Central Station and getting on the train but do recall the activities in preparation to go.

I was issued a one-way first class rail ticket to El Paso, Texas, advising me that return transportation would be arranged at Ft. Bliss. I was given a file with my travel orders and records to be presented to the Artillery School once I arrived at Bliss or to show to any M.P.'s who may stop me on the way. Before I left, I was paid per diem travel funds so I was flush when I departed Woodside.

I do not remember actually leaving home. My memory seems to just fast forward to when the train arrived at St. Louis, Missouri. This is where I had to change trains to the Texas Pacific Line and the last leg of my journey to El Paso. There was a wait at the station and it is there I experienced the stark surprise and awakening to the reality of conditions in America in 1951. "Colored Only," "Whites Only" ... what the hell did that mean? I was quickly told when a porter stopped me from going into the men's room marked "Colored Only." I was shocked to see segregated lunch counters, waiting areas, drinking fountains and rest rooms. Cute little black kids did not look me in the eye but stared down when I looked at them with a smile on my face. I could not understand any of this.

All during World War II my dad car pooled to the ship yard in Port Kearney, New Jersey with our black neighbor Mr. Abrams. The Abrams boys had no Mom that I recall and went to school with me and Brother John. Mrs. Brown, a Caribbean Island black woman who lived in Corona, was Mom's friend who introduced her to apple butter and canned date nut bread that Nellie always had on hand. Brother John's adult job was with a black partner who had lunch at our house many times. I had a lot to learn about our country beyond the borders of New York City; I thought I had better pay attention.

At this period in our lives Dad had just passed the NYC Civil Service examination and would be starting his new job as an Inspector for the city's water department. He no longer worked in the plumbing trade while brother John was still employed in the trade and was at the time working on new high rise apartment's under construction in Manhattan. As the building went up with only the open steel skeleton the plumbers installed all the interior piping which exposed the workers to the danger of falling to their deaths. Many who did not watch their every move were killed and hurt in that dangerous occupation. Dad was concerned about Brother John's history of seizures and worried enough to talk John into taking every NYC Civil Service test available to him to get John away from the dangerous high paying construction field. So, John took and passed the Department of Sanitation test and started work as a sanitation worker which he hated; I recall him talking about this with his black partner when having lunch at our house many times. John finally left the job for a position with Boche Electronics which launched his career doing plant layout work which he enjoyed until his retirement.

The heat in the terminal in St. Louis was oppressive, maybe because I just didn't feel comfortable there. I strolled outside and found it to be even worse for I was still wearing the winter woolen O.D. uniform. A vague recall of being stopped by a couple of patrolling M.P.'s and asked to produce my travel orders.

The loudspeaker finally announced that the Texas Pacific Eagle to El Paso was ready for boarding and I entered the most luxurious train I could ever imagine. Upon presenting my ticket to a porter, he directed me to a private compartment complete with a sofa that became a fold down bed and a private shower and toilet. I think I spent two nights on the train for it made a number of stops; one in particular was at Texarkana. This is where movie actor Dennis O'Keefe boarded the train with a group of attractive and very well dressed people. I don't know how Mr. Nicholetti convinced the army to approve First Class Rail for this young National Guard Sergeant but that is how I traveled to El Paso.

While reading the paper after lunch I was sitting in the comfortable lounge/dining car when I met a charming young lady. She told me she was traveling to El Paso to join her husband stationed at either Fort Bliss or Biggs Air Force base. She was traveling coach and sat in the lounge car where she told me it was much more comfortable than her hard coach seat. During our conversation I casually remarked about my luxurious private compartment. As we talked, the O'Keefe party entered and sat at a table across from us and O'Keefe smiled and waved a hello sign to me and my travel companion whom he thought was my wife. I recall his blue eyes and big smile; his very lovely female friends looked on as O'Keefe happily signed his autograph on a menu for me. I attached a copy of this menu and you will be surprised at the prices...realize this was 1951 when gasoline was twenty five cents a gallon.

It wasn't long before I sat with my new travel companion for dinner and chatted some more and it was inevitable that her very uncomfortable coach seat would remain empty. Upon our arrival in El Paso I did catch a glimpse of her as she walked off to meet a uniformed young man and, that was the last I ever saw of her.

El Paso impressed me with the clear blue sky, white cotton candy clouds and the air seemed to be lighter. I was becoming acclimated to the dry desert air and thought it was invigorating. It was this weather pattern that convinced the army to make Fort Bliss the Antiaircraft and Guided Missile Training Center. It was very warm but army O. D.'s were still in season. My orders required me to report on a Monday morning and the train arrived in El Paso on a Saturday so I checked into the Knox Hotel a few blocks from the train station and the Greyhound bus terminal. I walked around town for a while and had something to eat.

The beautiful view of a mountain range greatly impressed me. As an Easterner, I enjoyed the Catskill Mountains back home but they were not as majestic as these desert mountains were right here before my eyes. I found later they were the Franklin Mountains that contained a natural pass for ancients to travel from the arid dry land of the south to the cooler country to the north. Thus, christened by the Spanish who were the first pioneers, "*El Paso Del Norte,*" The Pass to the North!

Also noticed during my stroll through El Paso was a huge, fancy, and obviously very expensive hotel named Hotel Paso Del Norte, and remember wondering whether I would ever be able to stay in such a magnificent palace like hotel.

That evening, I returned to my shabby hotel room with no bath only a tiny sink, slipped off my clothes and neatly hung them up. I stared up at the ceiling and noticed paint peeling off the walls and thought about the new adventure I was to face, then I closed my eyes and soon drifted off to a peaceful sleep.

The next morning came early and I washed and shaved as best I could in the tiny sink. I dressed and checked out, grabbed a quick cup of coffee, hailed a cab and was on my way to Fort Bliss. The cabbie drove through the main entrance and stopped at the Provost Marshall's office where I had to report to the M.P. Major on duty. It seemed all casuals like myself had to see the Provost to be briefed on safe driving conditions while at Fort Bliss. He scanned my orders and gave a speech about the 25 mile an hour speed limit, stopping at the approach to all full stop signs and not passing the sign, and then stopping and in general about driving safety. I was at Bliss twice and never had a car or drove a car while I was on base but that was the drill. Funny, it riles me today when I see people zip right through full stops or just slow down a bit half way out in the intersection. Again, the images remain.

Upon arrival at the Enlisted Students Detachment, I paid the cabbie, shouldered my barracks bag and reported to the First Sergeant. He checked me in and assigned me to a barrack and mess hall. His clerk issued me a fresh clean mattress cover, clean sheets and a pillow case and two wool O. D. blankets and topped off the issue with a wooden foot locker.

The first Sergeant saw I was a little confused about what to do with all this gear and, knowing I was a green NG, he just smiled and pointed to a two-wheel push cart just outside for all my new belongings. As I was leaving I noticed the RA Top Sergeant's tailored and sharply pressed O.D. uniform and his set of six stripes, three above and three below with a diamond in the middle denoting a Master Sergeant and the higher rank of First Sergeant. I never thought for a moment I would be wearing Master Sergeant Stripe's before the end of the year. My new address would be:

SGT Vincent G. Gallagher NG21XXXXXX
4054 Enlisted Students Detachment
Fort Bliss, Texas

COFFEE BREAK NO DONUTS

One picture is worth a thousand words, taken in Korea 1952 and, that is how I remember Mess SGT Lew Davis. He was always chewing on one of those cigars. The only one smiling is the Korean on the right and he could not understand any English or Davis's growling. K.P. Machine Gunner PFC Wells was not too happy to be taking orders from Davis

Immersion Heaters used during World War II and the Korean War and maybe before and used to clean mess kits by troops. Troops scraped food into one G.I. garbage cans then rinsed and scrubbed kits in another hot soapy water and advanced to hot clear water rinse finishing with a second hot clear water rinse. The mess kit and canteen cup were designed to hold in one hand with knife, fork and spoon attached.

Photo taken at Replacement Depot Pusan Korea March 1953. G.I.'s assembled waiting for enough troops to fill a troop ship to begin processing home...not any sad faces here.

Immunization Register carried by every G.I and known as a Shot Record. No computers in those days, each man was responsible to keep his own record to avoid taking the shots all over again if he was transferred to another unit.

ENLISTED RECORD		
1. NAME (Last, first, middle initial)	2. SERIAL NO.	3. GRADE	4. ARM OR SERVICE

ENLISTED RECORD

1. NAME (Last, first, middle initial) GALLAGHER Vincent G	2. SERIAL NO. 21▮▮▮▮	3. GRADE Sgt Gr E-5	4. ARM OR SERVICE ARTY
5. ORGANIZATION Btry C 773d AAA Gun Bn	6. SEPARATION DATE 10 Sep 1950	7. PLACE OF SEPARATION 120 West 62d Street	
8. PERMANENT MAILING ADDRESS ▮▮▮▮▮▮▮▮▮▮	9. DATE OF BIRTH ▮▮▮ 1930	10. PLACE OF BIRTH New York City	
11. CIVILIAN OCCUPATION Student			12. NUMBER OF DEPENDENTS None
13. COLOR EYES Blue	14. COLOR HAIR Brown	15. HEIGHT 5 FT 9 IN	16. WEIGHT 150 LB	17. CITIZEN Yes	18. RACE ☒ WHITE ☐ NEGRO OTHER	19. MARITAL STATUS ☐ SINGLE ☐ MARRIED

MILITARY HISTORY

20. ENLISTMENT DATE 11 Sep 1947	21. MILITARY OCCUPATION Section Leader, Range (527)

22. MILITARY QUALIFICATIONS AND DATES (Expert infantryman, marksmanship, etc.)

Rifel M-1 Marksman 21 Aug 1948
Rifle M-1 Marksman 25 Sep 1949

23. LATEST IMMUNIZATION DATES				24. HIGHEST GRADE HELD IN SERVICE	25. CHARACTER
SMALLPOX 5Nov47	TYPHOID 6Feb50	TETANUS 6Feb50	OTHER (Specify) None	Sgt Gr E-5	Excellent

26. EDUCATION (Circle highest grade completed) GRAMMAR SCHOOL 1 2 3 4 5 6 7 8 HIGH SCHOOL 1 2 3 4 COLLEGE ①234	27. SERVICE SCHOOLS ATTENDED None

28. PRIOR SERVICE

None

29. REASON AND AUTHORITY FOR SEPARATION Expiration Term of Service	30. LONGEVITY (For pay purposes) 3 YR 0 MO 0 DA

31. REMARKS

Retirement points accrued 207

32. SIGNATURE OF SOLDIER Vincent G. Gallagher	36. RIGHT THUMB PRINT
33. SIGNATURE OF OFFICER George J. Byrnes	
34. TYPED NAME AND GRADE OF OFFICER 1st Lt. GEORGE J. BYRNES	35. ORGANIZATION Btry C 773d AAA Gun Battalion

U. S. GOVERNMENT PRINTING OFFICE 20—58383-1

114

Camp Edwards 1948. Officers, Warrant Officers and Senior
NCO's absent from this photo may be at a meeting. The
overhang covering the first floor windows play a part in an
incident at Fort Bliss in 1951.

Sand Dunes at Wellfleet Artillery Range with hundred
foot drop to the beach. Forbidden for any attempt to
climb down to the beach. Wellfleet later developed with
permanent quarters and modern facilities which became
the National Seashore in the 1970's. *Photo from iStock.com*

Corporal Frank Mistretta a close friend for years since first tour in 1948. We were both responsible for close order drill that first week and rewarded with a toss in the shower, clothing and all by the West Siders the last night in camp. We both laughed right along with Charlie Battery cussing...At least you NOW know your @#$% ing Left foot from your Right foot.

Before posting guard for the evening Corporals Mistretta and Gallagher posed with West Sider PFC Dell Orto.

Camp Edwards 1949
hitching a ride to
Hyannis or Buzzards Bay.

Wellfleet firing range
1949, Mistretta now a
Sergeant, our pup tent
under camouflage. Any
wonder why I was in the
Brain Platoon and not the
Brawn Platoon.

1950 Wellfleet SFC
Red Haroldsen from A
Battery. He helped all
the Fire Control men
in the battalion to be
better prepared for
active duty less than a
short year away.

March Order at
Wellfleet 1950. This
was the most intense
camp tour at Camp
Edwards and we all
went home tired. Only
one month following the
outbreak of the Korean
war and the rumors
were rampant.

Vintage picture of original Marconi station in Wellfleet exactly where the 773ʳᵈ fired at camp tour. I do not recall anyone ever mentioning that historic advancement in communication technology to any of us. I may have even munched my C Rations while sitting on those old concrete and wood relics of one of the 210 foot towers.

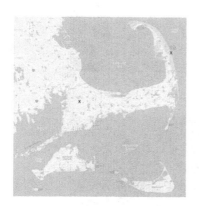

X marks the spot from Camp Edwards to the Wellfleet firing range. It would have been a delightful drive in my 1939 Lincoln Zephyr with a pretty girl sitting next to me. Clocked out at 50 miles one way, it was a long ride with your butt bouncing on the hard wooden seats in an army 2 ½ ton truck.

Both pictures courtesy US National Park Service,
National Seashore, Wellfleet, MA

119

Camp Smith, Fall 1948:
First Small Arms Qualification Weekend.

CPL Gallagher, PFC Monte, PVT McGann, CPL Calvano
pipe-lined to Korea from Camp Stewart 1951 as SGT Calvano,
Commo Section Leader.

CPL Sclafani pipelined to Korea from Camp Stewart
1951 as SFC Sclafani Gun Commander, PVT McGann,
CPL Gallagher, and PFC Monte

CPL Calvano, PFC Monte, PVT McGann, CPL Gallagher.
Don't recall if it was beer or soda in the cans.

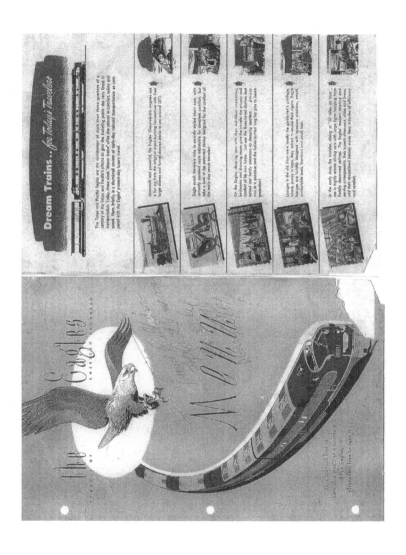

the *Eagles*

TABLE D'HOTE DINNER

Price of Entree Includes Complete Meal

Please Indicate on Meal Check Items Desired

Relish

Choice of —

Chilled Tomato Juice — Grapefruit Juice

Special Onion Soup — Fresh Vegetable Soup

Jellied or Hot Consomme — Fruit Cup, Grenadine

Omelette with Minced Ham 2.00

Fried or Broiled Fresh Fish, Tartar Sauce 2.25

Roast Young Turkey, Fresh Cranberries 2.50

Fried Young Chicken, Half, Disjointed, Country Style 2.75

Braised Veal Cutlets with Cream Sauce 1.85

Potatoes — Fresh Vegetable

Salad

Assorted Breads

Ice Cream with Wafers — Fresh Baked Pie

Half Grapefruit — Fruited Jello

Individual Cheese with Crackers

Coffee, Tea, Cocoa, Instant Postum, Grade "A" Milk

*

The Texas and Pacific Railway Reserves the Right to Designate Section of Passengers in Cafe Lounge

J. R. PURLEY, Superintendent Dining Car Service, Fort Worth, Texas

Passengers will please write their order on meal check.

Waiters can not serve verbal orders.

5-041

A La Carte (Selections)

"Truly Good Food"

Chilled Tomato Juice 20 — Chilled Grapefruit Juice 20

Special Onion Soup, Cup 24 — Hours of Celery 35 — Fresh Vegetable Soup, Cup 25

Jellied or Hot Consomme, Cup 25 — Fruit Cup, Grenadine 40

ENTREES

Omelette with Minced Ham 1.25

Fried or Broiled Fresh Fish, Tartar Sauce 1.35

Fried or Broiled Young Chicken, (Disjointed) 1.50

Special Corned Beef Hash, Poached Egg 1.00

Roast Young Turkey, Fresh Cranberries 1.50

Bread and Butter served with the above Entrees

SANDWICHES

Club Steves 1.25 — Special Chicken 1.30 — Ham or American Cheese .75

SALADS

Potato Salad (Individual Portion) 35 — Chicken Salad (Mayonnaise) 1.25

Head Lettuce (Individual Portion) (French Dressing) 75

Individual 1 and 2 Salad Bowl with Rq-Zfrg 65

Imported Sardines with Crackers .75

VEGETABLES

Fresh Vegetable 30 — Potatoes, Hash Brown, French Fried 30

BREAD, TOAST, ETC.

Assorted Bread—Hot 20, Cold 15 — Milk Toast 50 — Cream Toast 75

Texas Figs in Syrup with Cream 50 — Fresh Baked Pie 30 — Ice Cream with Wafers 30

Fruited Jello 30 — Individual Cheese with Crackers 25

COFFEE, TEA, ETC.

Coffee, Pot 20 — Hot or Iced Tea, Pot 30 — Instant Postum, Pot 25

Sanka Coffee 20 — Nescafe 25 — Cocoa, Pot 20

Iced Coffee, Pot 30 — Grade "A" Milk, Individual Bottle 20 — Malted Milk 30

Meals served in Pullman space, 50 cents extra per person except to ladies with small children, elderly or sick persons. Service includes poly when entire meal is served from Dining Car.

Parcels may show their portion with entrees without extra charge.

THE TEXAS AND PACIFIC RAILWAY

1939 Black Lincoln Zephyr 12 Cylinder 2-Door Coupe

In 1950, with Astoria buddy Max Ries, I purchased a 1939 Lincoln Zephyr for $100 from our auto mechanic pal Jim Merget in Corona. The car would be worth thousands of dollars today on the collectors' market. The condition was just like the museum piece on display in the Shanghai Auto Museum. The only downside and reason for such a great price was because the car needed a ring job and burned some oil.

Jim, in his usual display of exuberance, said it would be easy to jack up the car and rest it on sturdy milk crates - the strong steel and wood milk crates dairies used in the 1950's. Then, we would drop the pan, disconnect the connecting rods, remove the cylinders, install the new rings and, just put it all back together. Jim promised that after the work, the engine would run like new. It all sounded so easy but never happened. That would be simple for a mechanic with proper tools and facilities. But for us, it was a downer.

My lingering memory is seeing the Lincoln resting on the milk cartons pointing skyward like a Black Guided Missile awaiting count-down to launch. Soon after, I was launched on my own trip to Fort Bliss, Texas.

Lincoln Zephyr 1939 created common attribution-Share Alike 2.0 via Wikipedia Commons.

Chapter 4

Fort Bliss Artillery School March 1951

Fort Bliss, Texas, was an immense army base with the entire military reservation spread over West Texas and Southern New Mexico. The military installation includes a main post area where the old original 1st Cavalry Barracks were located and all the administration buildings. The service buildings, warehouses, post engineering and rail terminal were located further across from the main base. The other end of Fort Bliss was the Logan Heights training areas consisting of small permanent huts for officer and enlisted men's quarters, mess halls and latrines and the Beaumont Army Hospital Complex.

Biggs Air Force base was adjacent to Fort Bliss and home for the huge B-36 10-engine propeller and jet powered Peacemaker SAC (Strategic Air Command) bomber. The earth actually shook when that bird flew overhead. Biggs was also a mid-air re-fueling school using the B-29 Super fortress as tanker planes.

The Artillery School had many artillery courses for all the AA weapons 40, 90, and 120 millimeter guns and the 75mm Sky Sweeper integrated gun and fire control weapons then in development. Missile development was in the early stages and top secret and totally unknown to anyone not in the program. New recruits were trained and processed at Logan Heights and sent off to units worldwide, some going directly to advanced schools in Fort Bliss. Students attending these schools were coming and going at all times. This included new students arriving, graduating students leaving, and those students who failed the course.

The student who failed returned to their original units whether they were active duty, RA, NG or ER (Enlisted Army Reserve). Those draftees who were assigned to school after basic training and sent to school at Ft. Bliss faced a more dire consequence. They were pipelined direct to FECOM (Far East Command) and shipped to Japan. At a training center in Japan they were given advanced infantry training, issued an M1 rifle, and soon found themselves as replacements in front line infantry units fighting in Korea. That alone was a good reason to apply themselves at school. If I failed, I would be sent back to C Battery, and probably reduced a grade in rank.

After reporting to the Enlisted Students Detachment and receiving my bedding and foot locker I loaded everything in a push cart and proceeded to my assigned barracks, carried my gear up to the second floor to my bunk and then as instructed, walked the pushcart back to the orderly room. The barracks impressed me with the cleanliness of the floors, covered with linoleum and the latrines were all clean and sparkling. I was assigned to a four-man room with three other Sergeants. The typical barrack layout for the period of WWII and Korea era were two-story wood frame buildings. The first floor had an entrance on one end with a two-man room on each side on the entryway and the open to the barrack. The main entrance was on the side of the building with openings to the latrine, the open barrack and the stairway to the second floor. The utility room with heater and hot water heater was in the rear of the building in back of the latrine. The upstairs floor plan included one two-man room and one four-man room, then the open barrack with a fire escape on one end of the building.

The open barrack was roomy with required distance between each man's cot, hangers for clothing and screened double hung windows over every other cot. In cold weather the barrack was heated and when the hot desert sun beat down, it was hot in the daytime but always cool in the evenings. The latrine offered no privacy at all with open commodes all in a row, sinks and common shower room. It was a busy place in the morning. It was all much more upscale from the barracks in Camp Edwards. There was room for about 80 or 90 men in the barrack. The same barrack normally used double tiered cots which would double the occupancy but, the school barrack offered more comfortable quarters to promote some quiet time to study for the technical artillery courses.

I was getting the feel of order of a well-managed army base at Fort Bliss. I made my bunk G.I. style, filled the foot locker with my clothing and personal items and attached the combination lock I had on my duffel bag to the foot locker. I folded my duffel bag, placed it on a shelf, and placed my uniforms on the clothing rack. Next, with shaving kit in hand, wrapped in a towel and wearing shower shoes, I made my way to the latrine to take a hot shower, shave and wash up after my long journey of the past few days. I put on a comfortable fatigue uniform, sprawled out on my cot and closed my eyes. My impression and mental outlook was all positive. I don't remember any personal contact that day and as chow time arrived I walked the few barracks away to the mess hall.

Only a few soldiers were around as I entered the one-story mess hall building and was again impressed with the cleanliness of everything. The smell of G.I. coffee brewing in the large coffee urn permeated the building. I stepped up to a large milk server and helped myself to a glass of fresh cold milk.

Spread out on the buffet-style serving line was a help-yourself service array of sliced cooked salami and sliced American or cheddar cheese, rows of sliced white bread, salad mixings and condiments. I soon learned that on Sunday, the army served the same cold cut sandwich dinner in all the stateside bases. It was described in vulgar G.I. terminology referring to a horse and that's all I will say. I thought about omitting this but I am portraying my experience and passing it on to the reader.

The army culture in those days was somewhat crude and earthy with plenty of drinking, smoking and language that would shock those from protected backgrounds. These customs and traditions went back for generations as, any veteran who served in the army at that time would agree. When in the company of family or clergy, one must be very careful with their newly acquired vocabulary. "Mom, this is the best %$#@ing meal I've had in months. Gee, sorry about that folks! Many officers advanced themselves through the ranks starting as enlisted men and a common expression at the time was, "You can take the man out of the barracks, but you can't take the barracks out of the man." The U.S. Army of World War II and the Korean War era was definitely not "*Politically Correct.*"

Remember also, these same RA's and NG's were the volunteers who put themselves first on the firing line whenever our nation was threatened. These were the same soldiers who met the better trained and armed hordes of Japanese soldiers who overran them in places like Bataan and Corregidor in the Philippine Islands in World War II. Those few who survived and lived to serve again were held in brutal captivity by the Japanese for over three years. You will meet two of these men later and learn how lightning almost struck them twice. The army of 1951 was basically a man's army. It is true there were WAC units serving an important mission for the military but not in the combat arms. The few WAC's I met at the Fort Bliss NCO club could out cuss and out drink most guys I knew. Cold cuts was on the master menu for Sunday supper and somewhere along the way, the meal received that vulgar G.I. appellation. There will be more to come so get used to it. It just occurred to me that no one I can recall, ever thought about asking those WAC NCO's if they had a name for their Sunday chow?

On Sunday at Ft. Bliss, very few enlisted students ate dinner in the mess hall. For only a few cents bus ride and a short walk across the International Bridge to Juarez, you could dine on filet mignon for $1.25 so, why eat Horse ... well you know what I mean. That first Sunday after chow I strolled around to familiarize myself to my new surroundings and eventually ended up in the PX (Post Exchange) where I indulged myself with some ice cream and meandered back to the barracks.

While lying in my bunk I remember how orderly and well-run everything was. I did not feel a bit lonesome or sad but actually felt relieved and at peace as I drifted off ... I thought I was going to like being a soldier at Fort Bliss.

Reveille call was about 06:30 and the troops assembled in front of the barrack. Beefy Master Sergeant McNieghton, an army reservist attending school, was the assigned barracks Sergeant. Speaking with him is when I first heard about "The Master Artillerymen's Examination." I do not remember any formations or roll calls after that first day and during the entire five months we had only one inspection in ranks when some general inspected the entire Enlisted Student Detachment.

The Army ran the school like a college and it was each student's responsibility to come and go as he pleased. Roll call attendance was verified each morning by the instructors at class and again after midday chow. If you failed the periodic tests, you were simply removed from the school. Each man regardless of rank was responsible to maintain the area around his own space and first three grades were exempt from K.P. which represented about ten percent of the enlisted students.

All anti-aircraft artillery related courses were taught at Bliss and there were many for both officers as well as enlisted men. There was also a combined Army and Air Force cook's school. The mess halls we ate in were actually several-week cook schools where the course of instruction was to teach cooks how to prepare, cook and serve each meal on the Army and Air Force Master menu.

After roll call and some introduction about policy, like each man's responsibility to read the bulletin board daily which is an army SOP (Standard Operational Procedure), we headed for the mess hall. The place was a beehive of activity, the aroma of bacon, sausage, French toast, fresh eggs served any style floated through the air. Add the choice of pancakes, hot toast, oatmeal, every cold cereal you could imagine and fresh fruit. I saw more cantaloupe at Bliss than I ever saw in my life. There was also fruit juice, fresh milk and the strong hot G.I. coffee. You could eat whatever you wished and as much as you wished. We were all amazed at the variety of food. Fort Bliss was looking better every minute.

It was here when I was first introduced to the infamous "S.O.S.," the breakfast specialty that shocked many a big city soldier the first time he saw what it looked like in his mess kit at 07:00 in the morning. The army version is simply chopped beef cooked with chopped onion, some seasoning, and prepared in a creamed sauce poured on top of toast, do I have to spell out the G.I. vernacular of "S.O.S."? Use your imagination! Each service made their own version of this breakfast entre and they all called it "S.O.S." To the Southern and Midwest farm boys it was familiar, their being used to biscuits and gravy but to the typical New York, Boston, Chicago or other big city troopers, it earned the name "S.O.S.," the last "S" standing for "Shingle," that flat piece of wood they nail on a roof which, was actually the Toast. I passed on the "S.O.S." every time but much to my surprise when I finally tasted it, I liked it. I still make it for myself once in a while, much to Lee's chagrin.

Brown up some lean chopped meat and finely chopped onion, add a dash of cayenne pepper, some salt and a spritz of Worcestershire sauce, add some milk to the pan and thicken with corn starch and pour it over some toast... it is very tasty on a gray cold winter morning. I always made it for breakfast when old pal John Zurla visited us many, many years ago. We would all have a good laugh as we saluted "Sargina Davis" and both indulged. Lee would just shake her head and walk away. I have not made it in some time now but there is a smile on my face thinking about it. The army threw away more "S.O.S." than was ever eaten by the troops. Brother John served in the Navy and said the same was true for the Navy version of "S.O.S."

A lasting impression of the Mess Hall shows an overweight Mess Sergeant holding a white cereal bowl full of black coffee in one hand and, a cigarette in the other held between nicotine stained fingers as he taught the student cooks. To assure the students would learn to prepare every meal on the master menu in only a few weeks' time, they simply cooked several items each meal and we at Bliss just ate up the benefit. Our battalion officers who later attended classes at "The Officers Student Detachment" were envious when I told them about our chow.

After breakfast, we assembled in groups depending on the course and walked from the barrack area to the classrooms. There was no marching, we just leisurely strolled up to the class room buildings. The first thirty days of the course was Basic Electronics which came as a real surprise to me. I failed high school math back at Bryant High School and was now facing a real challenge. Much to my surprise, I passed with flying colors and owe it all to the way the army MOI (Methods of Instruction). No one was told when the tests would be given so you just had to be prepared, there was no joking that first thirty days. When the test papers were passed out, I always felt ready.

The first thirty days at Bliss was intense study and concentration and I don't think I wore a class A uniform the entire time, the fatigue uniform was worn at school. Many nights after lights out were spent in the latrine studying my material. I successfully completed the toughest part of the course which was also around the same time as the first pay day and it was then and there I learned a lesson...when to "Fold 'em" or when to "Hold 'em."

After getting paid and returning to the barracks I witnessed a quick transformation from army barrack to gambling parlor, two footlockers were joined together then covered with a G. I. blanket for a quick change to a card table. Cards were produced and one could hear the enticing rattle of poker chips and see the flash of greenbacks. Poker, it was my favorite card game.

The details are a bit fuzzy but I do remember losing a big piece of the entire $130.00 I received for my month's pay. If not for some remaining funds in my footlocker, I would have been broke for the entire month. By mid-month my funds were pretty much depleted and I was ashamed to ask for money from home. For the balance of my time at Bliss I continued to play poker every pay day but I set a limit when I won a given amount I would just get up and quit the game. When I was $20 in the hole I would quit until the next pay day. That never happened because I won every month and knew enough when to pick up my money and move on. Some of the pots were impressive.

The game was dealer's choice but limited to three games, 5 Card Draw Poker, 5 Card Stud Poker and 7 Card Stud poker, no Wild Cards. The stakes, limits and rules of each game were set and never deviated, a no-limit bet and raise was allowed only on the last card when playing Stud Poker and last bet with Draw. With this understanding, we never had a problem in a barrack of about 80 troops with most being poker players. It was not at all like I witnessed at Camp Edwards with the Hell's Kitchen card sharks but, when I played poker, my radar was always on anyway.

A little drama occurred one pay day when I won my biggest pot ever. I bluffed and raised Levin from New Jersey $20 on the last card in a Five Card Stud game. His ace showing the entire hand made him look the winner and his several raises and counter raises built up the pot and his confidence convinced him that he had the winning hand. I quietly went along with the other players as the pot grew. The growing pot enticed all of us to stay in the game. When the last card was dealt, Levin's ace was still the high hand showing and he bet. When it came my turn, I saw the sizable bet he made with confidence I think it was a $5 bet. I saw his bet and raised him $20 by throwing a $20 bill in the pot and looked him straight in the eye with no smile, no expression and the smile on his face quickly faded. If he saw my raise and threw his $20 bill into the pot, I would have to fold and lose. But with his hand scratching his chin and after much consternation Levin just shook his head, folded and said, "I pass." The game was not over yet with still a couple more "hangers on" who might see my raise. I just sat there, took a drag on my cigarette snubbed it out in a butt can, cocked my head and smiled (I might have seen that done in a movie).

The couple remaining players also tossed in their cards as it came their turn to see the $20 raise and fortunately, I had no takers. Hiding my joy and trying not to show any expression whatsoever, I simply scooped up my pot. "Well, show me your cards," quipped Levin. "You had your chance to see my cards for $20 but now, it's too late," I answered. "That's right," the others players agreed. "Ya gotta pay to see the cards...that's the rule." I never told Levin that with his ace showing he actually had me beat and he was always scratching his head in wonder. But we had the rules and we all complied. We never heard the usual "Hey, you can't leave now, your winning all the money." Rule number one was "OK to quit any time." But I do remember playing a couple more hands very, very cautiously and then pulling stakes. I stashed a lot of folding money in the bottom of my foot locker that night.

The only time we broke the rule in our barrack was with Joe Coskey from Baltimore. Joe was 26 years old, one of the oldest and most reluctant of all the draftees. He served in the Merchant Marine from his teenage years and many times while at sea his Mom received draft notices for him which he just ignored. "Mom, they can't find me in mid ocean," was his answer to his Mom. But they did finally catch up with him and after many notices, his Mom took him by the arm before he could ship out again and walked him down to the draft board. New soldier Joe completed basic training and was assigned to attend school at Fort Bliss. Realizing full well what he would face should he fail, he applied himself. With the help of a couple of his classmates in the barrack and the time Joe spent in the latrine studying, he received passing grades.

Joe was a great character with many fine qualities except he could not hold his liquor. He combined drinking with poker and would start betting wildly. We would shut him down for his own good and give him his money the next day when he was sober. The following morning he always sheepishly commented, "You guys are great, thanks."

Joe knew every song you would imagine which he learned during all those long hours at sea with his shipmates. Most songs were sad and lonely tunes about broken hearts and guys in faraway places or on the way to those faraway places saying goodbye to their sweethearts. Two of his favorites were "Lili Marlene," a German soldiers' song from World War One and a popular love song in England in WWII, and "La Paloma" (The Dove). All with similar lyrics and sentiment. Joe taught everyone the English version of "La Paloma" and "Lili Marlene" and we all sang those songs many times in the barracks while sipping a beer and often requested the Spanish "La Paloma" when in Juarez. To this day, whenever I hear those refrains from an old movie I get a little nostalgic.

When I look up in the sky now, Joe, I just know you are entertaining the angels with the strains of "La Paloma" "At eve... ere we left our home for the rolling sea!"

This is a good time to relate my one and only time at K.P. in my entire army service. During that long dry month when I was short on funds, I noticed a message on the bulletin board where a soldier offered money for another soldier to take his K.P. duty. In this case, one of my barracks mates who hailed from either Texas or New Mexico was expecting a family visit on the same Sunday he was assigned to K.P. and I jumped at the opportunity to earn a $10 or $20 bill.

One of the fatigue jackets I bought used for 25 cents at the base salvage depot did not have stripes so I put that on and reported to the RA Mess Sergeant. A big overstuffed redneck with a fat belly and cigarette stained fingers greeted me. He smiled as I walked in to report and said in his Southern drawl, "I've got a special job fo' a Naashunal Gawd SahGint." It's no wonder he recognized me for I often came back for seconds. I followed him outside to the Mess Hall grease pit. It did not surprise me to get the worst job a K.P. could get, and that was to clean the trap that collected all the grease from the kitchen. So, I just rolled up my sleeves and got to work. At the end of the day, that grease pit sparkled. As I left I asked him to check it out and told him, "Hey, Sarge, how's that look now? That was about the worst looking, shitty grease pit I ever saw. My Mess Sergeant in the 773rd would never allow that!" He grinned, flashing his yellowed G.I. false teeth. I grinned back.

That, of course, was at the end of the day of my one and only K.P. duty. Over the course of my five months at Bliss I had many beers with that same old RA mess Sergeant at the NCO club. We had a clique of RA's, NG's and ER's who would go to the Friday night beer fest at the NCO club. A couple of chubby and hardy WAC Sergeants would join us from time to time…I found that many old RA's who gave the worst razzing to the NG's began their army careers as NG's themselves and that RA mess Sergeant was one of them.

The classrooms were in the old original concrete barracks built in the 1920's, they were three-story buildings and the top floor was very hot during the warm months. Someone devised an ingenious water air conditioner to cool that third floor classroom area. After the classroom instruction was concluded, we moved to circuitry labs where we learned all about amplifier tubes and capacitors and how to recharge them and apply them, and learned how to identify the color-coded resistors and other things I have long ago forgotten.

After that first 30 days we finally worked on all the equipment used in a 90mm gun battery. At the outdoor radar park we had some unusual experiences with abnormal radar blips that sped across the PPI scopes (Present Position Indicator) in the SCR-584 radars. Much talk circulated about U.F.O.'s and Texas and New Mexico were centers of activity. We could not be sure if these blips flashing across the scope were real or self-induced by the instructors for a gag or to trouble shoot. The strange radar blips occurred around the same time the sci-fi movie "The Thing from Another World" was shown at the post theater. Later you will read about how Corporal Williams actually met "The Thing from Another World."

One day, which had to be after May 1st and while at the PX, I happened to spot my same 212th Regiment "Pro Patria" crests on someone's shoulder epaulets and further glance revealed none other than Joe Cramer from A Battery. Joe informed me the 773rd was mobilized on May 1st and was now training at Camp Stewart, Georgia, and, he was here to attend school. He told me he was the only enlisted man and a few officers were here also at the Officers Student Detachment.

I was probably the last to be notified of the activation, remember, no emails, no FAX's and no cell phones. My notification had to arrive through channels. Shortly after, I received official word and was sent to Beaumont Army Hospital for my physical examination and some additional immunization shots. None of these details interrupted my classes.

I did not know Cramer that well, only that he was a familiar face on a Monday night, but my eyes lit up when he mentioned he had a car. There was much talk about a nightclub in Sunland, New Mexico, just a few miles from El Paso. So we decided to explore the possibilities and headed out to the Sunland Bar and Dance Hall the following Saturday night.

As the sun faded over the Franklin Mountains, Joe picked me up at my barracks and we drove off. Memory reveals the image of the big "SUNLAND" neon sign glittering a way out there in the distant desert. Often seen in my travels to the various firing ranges in New Mexico and often wondered about. As we got closer, we could hear the honky-tonk country and western music which first came as a shock to this New Yorker when first heard on all the radios. I thought it was terrible until I learned to love it. I was still in the in-between stage of hate and love that May of 1951.

We entered and paid our admission at the door, the place was crawling with guys and gals, mostly guys in either army or air force uniforms or others in civilian clothes wearing cowboy boots and Stetson hats. The music was all country and western and the couples dancing were all bobbing up and down to the tune of Hank Williams singing, "Hey, good lookin, whaaaatcha got cookin' how's about cookin' somethin' up with meee?" That posed a real threat to me. How the hell could a guy with no rhythm even attempt to ask a girl to dance to that music? We went up to the four-deep packed bar and paid for a beer which I nursed as I strolled around leading the way as Cramer covered the rear. It wasn't long before I spotted two very pretty, well dressed and well poised *Texican* girls (Texans of Mexican descent). We got acquainted and proceeded to have a nice time with them. Both were college girls and the one I was attracted to lived in the dormitory at college. She was trying to make a Fred Astaire out of me and got a kick out of my awkwardness on the dance floor. The more I missed a step, the tighter she held me, and I thought maybe I'll work on this "I can't dance routine." I was having a great time but Cramer's girl was not smiling.

Cramer was just a guy I would see at the armory and did not know him that well, I never even had a drink with him before. Something was not right and it was interfering with the progress I was making with my girl. I think she liked me as her eyes twinkled when she made fun of my dancing. I particularly enjoyed the slow dances, the two-step was all I knew and she seemed to fit real well with my arm around her.

Here was a real nice girl to fill my nights while at Fort Bliss instead of the usual rowdy trips to Juarez. We were getting along fine and she was very cuddly and looked into my eyes and said to me, "*Me gustas mucho.*" She giggled at my attempt to use the little Spanish I learned in Bryant High School but it was working. We were already making plans to get a cab to a park near her campus and spend some time talking and I could then get an inexpensive bus ride back to Bliss. She said her dormitory was definitely off limits. When she told me she was getting a car from her parents, I was already driving her through the desert with her black hair waving in the breeze and happy to say "*adios*" to Cramer who I now noticed was also not smiling.

I was getting bad vibes from Cramer and did not pay attention to how much he was drinking. He appeared to be getting a little drunk and somewhat belligerent or maybe that was just his personality showing. I don't know what he said to his girl but she wasn't happy and expressed a desire to go home which placed a damper on my amorous desires for the evening. My dark-eyed girl was holding on tight so she did not have to say too much. I got the message.

The plan was for us to split, Joe would drive his girl home and I would take a cab with my girl from Sunland to the park near her dorm in El Paso and then take a bus back to Fort Bliss at my leisure as the buses ran all night. It may have been MacArthur Park where they had of all things alligators living in an enclosed pool and across from the Fort Bliss bus stop. I was glad to get rid of Cramer but apparently his girl did not want to be alone in the car with him so that further complicated things... we all had to leave together. Thanks, Cramer!!!

We all left and Joe went for the car: it was a two-door so I opened the door and folded the passenger seat so my girl could climb in the rear as I followed. Joe remained in his seat as his girl climbed in the front passenger seat. She directed Joe to her home in a modest neighborhood in El Paso with small single family homes. When we got there, it was still only about 11:00 PM and some neighbors were sitting outside as we pulled up to the girl's house. We would drop off Cramer's girl and continue on to MacArthur Park and then say "*adios*" to Cramer. I was thinking we would sit up front so we could direct Joe to the park. Cramer would drop me off with my Senorita and then we would finally get rid of him. Didn't happen.

As his girl was about to exit the car Cramer made a grab for her and she pushed him away as she opened the door to get out. I saw Cramer raise his right leg and in a flash he kicked her out of the car onto the ground. She cried out to her girlfriend who was just as shocked as I was, so I pushed up the front seat and eased her out of the car just as a few bystanders started walking to the car to see if anything was wrong. As they approached, my girl warned with her eyes that it was time for me to say goodnight. "Cramer, put this car in first gear and let's get the hell out of here," as I jumped into the front seat. Guys like Cramer were the reason some of the locals hated some G.I.'s...yes, he was a Hell's Kitchen son and also a S.O.B.

In a trail of dust, I could see the street was full of dark-eyed guys and *"No mas bonita senoritas."* I don't recall the dialog on the way back to Fort Bliss. When we approached a popular bar just outside of Bliss, Cramer wanted to stop for a beer. My response is now totally forgotten and don't recall the dialog and don't recall even talking to Cramer or even seeing him again or if he even finished his course, whatever it was. Once C Battery was deployed in Brooklyn and then Korea, we no longer had any further contact with any of the other batteries in the battalion, and I never had the opportunity to go back to "Sunland."

Many other adventurous events occurred while at Fort Bliss in the environs of El Paso, some in Juarez, others in White Sands and in the mountains of Ruidoso, New Mexico. Some involved females, some about the life as a soldier in Fort Bliss and one about a practical joke that went haywire. But, the reason for my being there was never lost and it paved the way for me to gain the technical training I needed to be an effective and knowledgeable Fire Control Platoon Sergeant in the 773rd.

The Thing from Another World

The sci-fi thriller *The Thing* was featured in the Fort Bliss post theater during the spring of 1951. It was a blockbuster film and still an interesting and exciting film to watch today. It featured a monster of deadly proportions, excellent sound track and a claustrophobic setting in an isolated scientific base in the Arctic. It was a great hit for the time in all the basics, story, action, music and thrills. Probably every G I. in Fort Bliss saw the movie at the base theater. It played at about the same time U.F.O. activity in the New Mexico desert was at a fever pitch and we in air defense were in some ways involved. At the radar park, many of us personally experienced displays on the radar P.P.I. scope that were indeed abnormal. Everyone tried to guess whether it was real or just "instructor's fun." Those instructors were quite creative but, this time I did not see any instructors grinning in the background. Most of us were uncertain.

After watching *The Thing* at the post theater, we continued talking about the drama in our barracks and a group of us were found after lights out in the latrine where the lights remain on all night. We were all swapping stories about the possibility of life in outer space and discussing whether the U.F.O. stories were true or false when, in walked Corporal Williams who was attending a radar repair course. When Williams was finished with his business and on the way upstairs to his bunk we asked, "Hey Williams, what do you think about the possibility?" "No way, man...I'm just sorry I saw that damn movie. It still gives me the chills" or something to that effect. With that Williams said "Goodnight" and stepped upstairs to his bunk right at the head of the stairs and across from my four-man room.

Hmmmmm, we all thought, maybe Williams will get a closer look at the *"The Thing."* Barracks pranks are as old as armies themselves and have been a place for mischief for many decades. At any rate, the plan unfolded. Williams would be meeting *"The Thing"* in person tonight!

We covertly regrouped in my four-man room and I put on my helmet liner and then a white towel placed over the helmet liner with two holes cut out to see through, the eyes of the towel darkened with burnt cork. In 1951 corks were plentiful. I put on Dell Orto's extra-large rain coat and extra-large black leather G.I. gloves. The towel on the oversized head was tucked under the rain coat collar. In the dark, it resembled James Arness' grotesque head in the movie.

Dell Orto was a northern California lumber jack six feet tall and I was lifted to sit on Dell Orto's broad shoulders. The rain coat was draped over Dell Orto making him appear almost nine feet tall and *"The Thing"* had to duck between the roof rafters.

Many in the barrack saw the movie that night so scouts went out to silently alert conspirators to start making the scary sounds of the music so important in keeping the movie audiences on edge. With some help from accomplices Dell Orto and I stooped over to exit my room, "*The Thing*" moved closer to poor Williams' bunk. I was glad to have the helmet liner on because my head did bump into a rafter. To add some drama, a scene was recreated when the monster, slammed open a door which made every soldier in the theater jump and the women scream.

Someone slammed open the door to the four-man room right outside Williams' bunk which was the cue for the conspirators to start the eerie music as the gag unfolded. "*The Thing*" hovered over Williams and looked about nine feet tall and quite authentic in the darkened barrack. Through the eye holes in the towel I saw Williams turn on his side and then turned again on the other side and turn again, this time with eyes wide open. With panic in his eyes and bellowing a screech, Williams seemed to just jump up as if propelled by a spring and flew through the opened window above his bunk, ripping the screen, and now found himself clinging to the eave overhang under the window. The gag backfired, and now both jokesters were more frightened than Williams. We jumped out of the disguise after seeing the joke boomerang and swiftly grabbed poor Williams by his feet preventing him from falling off the narrow ledge.

The lights were flicked on and guys were forming around Williams' bunk. Williams now fully awakened realized the dream that became a reality was now after all only a joke. Instead of his slugging me and cussing me and Dell Orto whom he now recognized, Williams just sat upright on his bunk and said, "You guys scared the shit out of me," and everyone was apologetic. I cried out "Go ahead Williams, take a poke at me, it was my idea. Go ahead, I deserve it." Williams just sat there shaking his head and repeating, "Man, I don't want to hit anyone, I'm just glad it was only a fucking joke." We pranksters were all very relieved that Williams did not fall off the eave which could have resulted in tragedy. I do not recall if the screen was ever repaired...Williams always kept that window closed.

With all the commotion the barracks Sergeant came upstairs and inquired, "Everything OK here?" "Yeah Sarge it's OK." "Alright then, put the lights out and hit the sack." Even the roving fire guard came in to check on things. The barracks were again dark and silent with more, "Sorry about that, man" to Williams and then a couple conspirators started quietly humming the music again until they also had enough fun for one evening.

There were no more pranks for some time until Ahern's quart size can of orange juice exploded on a torrid summer day after sitting in the hot sun all day in the overheated second floor of the barracks. Guys yelled "Foul joke, bad joke, foul!" as they saw the juice splattered all over Ahern's uniforms later realizing it was an accident of nature. Other canned goods were now stored in foot lockers and out of the direct rays of the sun.

Next to Ahern's cot lived a soldier named Randy whom everyone complained he never took a shower nor washed his clothes. He was asked many times to wash and groom himself which he just ignored until he was given a warning…"Either you do it or we will." He scoffed and told a few of the guys to do something to themselves that was physically impossible for them to do.

Soooo…one quiet Sunday morning I heard a loud scream coming from outside my door and ran out to see Randy being carried downstairs head first and fully clothed and with others carrying his duffel bag down to the latrine. He was forced into the shower, clothes and all, and out came the coarse G.I. scrubbing brushes with the harsh yellow G I. soap and Randy was given the infamous "G.I. shower," along with all his dirty clothes and duffel bag. Randy became "Mr. Clean" from that time onward.

Today, army quarters offer some privacy compared with the barrack system of WWII and Korea where you did your business together, showered together, shaved and brushed your teeth together, and at chow time you ate together. Even when you closed your eyes you still had no privacy. You just had to get used to it or your army time could be hell time.

If someone goosed you, you had better stand fast for if it was known you were goosey you could expect a prod in the butt at every assembly and in the army of that time you were on line for everything. God help those Goosey!!!

Enter Sergeant Sarenson, from a California Guard outfit. Now, Sergeant Sarenson was a small framed guy with a bad leg from a childhood accident. He had a very slight limp and if his outfit was called, he could have been medically discharged. I never knew if his unit was called but I would bet that he would hide his limp to make sure he went with his outfit. Sarenson was in the guard for a number of years and was in my same Fire Control class, he was a pretty savvy Fire Control NCO. He helped a lot of us to better understand the X, Y and H factor in solving the AAA problem that I cannot at this late date even remember.

He was also goosey, if someone placed a ruler, pencil or finger within a foot of his ass, he would jump. Was he taken advantage of? Yes he was but only once! He was also a martial arts expert. He would grab your finger as fast as a rattlesnake strike and in seconds you would be crawling in the Texas sand pleading with him to release your finger. The more you squirmed the more it hurt. It didn't make any difference to him if you were six feet and 200 pounds of muscle, you were at his mercy.

He went through the gamut and became an untouchable. He was not a rounder and joined us only once or twice on our many trips to Juarez. He occupied one of the two-man rooms on the first floor. He had been to school at Bliss for many courses and was able to swing a private room not because he was unsociable but because his hobby was leather working and he had all his tools with him. You could always hear him tap, tap, tapping making a basket weave pattern on wet leather with his stainless steel tools. So you can understand why he roomed alone He showed me how to make a beautiful hand tooled leather holster with basket weave pattern for a Colt Peacemaker pistol along with others who also made custom belts, holsters and wallets for themselves or gifts for family with Sarenson's expert instruction.

It was always a great scene to watch as new guys came and went and tried to goose him only to find themselves sprawled out on the ground and pleading to be released as the pain increased with every wriggle. They just met Sarenson, that frail little guy whom they found could strike like lightning.

Sparky Watts (real name withheld) was another goosey guy but he lived a little hell at Bliss. I never got too close to him after as my partner in the circuitry lab, he created an explosion that christened him with the name "Sparky Watts." He scared the hell out of me and everyone nearby. We were learning about something and I have forgotten exactly how it happened but I was next to him when something exploded. After that I got myself a new partner and never went near him again. If I saw Sparky coming, I went the other way. He even cleared the latrine when he came in where you were surrounded by water but no one took any chances.

My new lab mate was a draftee named Ed Wence who created "Sparky Watts" and even wrote the song about him that of course Sparky hated. I only remember the catchy phrase, it went something like "Sparky Watts from Podunk Junction, forgot to make a Selsyn Function" or something like that. I forgot the lyrics and recall it was clever and funny to everyone...except Sparky.

Everywhere Sparky went, sparks and flames soon followed. To further complicate his life, he was also goosey. Just watching him on the chow line fending off attacks from all angles made you feel sorry for him.

RA Corporal West was from an RA 90mm outfit near Washington D. C. and always tried to challenge me about Fire Control knowledge. I always held my own and we became good friends who tried to outsmart each other. He was one of our group who traveled to Ruidoso, New Mexico with Dell Orto behind the wheel of his 1950 Buick.

On the way back, we stopped off at White Sands to see the brilliant pure white gypsum deposits that appear to have been neatly dumped by thousands of trucks in even mounds in the New Mexico desert. The Texas and New Mexico deserts are quite awesome and all the cars had canvas water bags hanging from the front of the car. You do not want to be caught in that desert without water. A water trailer always accompanied the troops whenever training in the desert and an eye was always on the lookout for rattlesnakes. My pal John Zurla was struck by a rattlesnake on one of his many tours at Fort Bliss and it was a harrowing experience for him.

I am sure the area is much more civilized today but back in 1951 the area showed no sign of man. This was close to the Trinity site where the first atomic bomb was tested and the area was still closed off until the radioactivity was claimed to be fully dissipated in 1953.

One weekend with West and Dell Orto in the mountains of Ruidoso, New Mexico, we checked into a motel crowded with girls from some university in New Mexico and we were the only guys there. Ruidoso was a skier's delight in winter and also had a famous race track which we never saw, we were distracted that weekend by other more earthly diversions. But I do remember the area was beautiful and green compared to the desert around El Paso and Fort Bliss.

We had some excitement in Juarez one night right after pay day when all the Logan Heights recruits got paid and went to Juarez for the first time. Pay day was not the time to go to Juarez because that's when all the trouble occurred with all the recruits out of control due to the effect of alcohol and the brothels. Back at the armory before I left, the older vets advised "buy the Juarez cops a beer and make them your friend as soon as you go to Juarez." It paid off one night in the Lago Blanco Bar off the main drag.

We never went to Juarez that close to pay day because Juarez became a zoo, we even called it "Juar Zoo." A few of us decided to go to the Manhattan Club on the main street for legitimate drinks and a nice Marimba Band and no unescorted females allowed. From there we would cross the street to La Florida Club for a steak dinner. A great grilled sirloin steak cooked to order, potatoes, delicious Mexican rolls and coffee all for .75 cents with a filet mignon costing $1.25. It was good meat and clean and was a hit with everyone who went to Juarez whether they were in the service at Bliss or Biggs air base or simply a *turista*. Remember, it was in 1951 when a new Ford cost $1,500.

After dinner, someone suggested we go to the Lago Blanco, the only place in Pig Alley that served an honest drink but you would have to fight off the girls. So, just for laughs, off we went. The dives along Pig Alley were all crowded with recruits from Logan Heights. I mentioned to pal Bob Cavan, a Sergeant from a Savannah, Georgia Guard unit, that we may not want to linger too long for I smelled trouble with the crowds of partying and rowdy recruits. The Lago Blanco was bristling with activity. The first thing we all did was to remove our little overseas caps soldiers wear and I am sure you have seen the hats I refer to. The reason was because to promote their wares, the girls, yes, the prostitutes, who worked at these bars would grab a hat and run upstairs calling "Ondelay (come) thee rrroom" or they would nag you with "You buy me drreenk." The drinks were overpriced and only colored water from which they received a percentage. "You buy me drreenk," they curtly asked. "*No Dinero*," you answered. "Oh you cheapee skate," they would call you. This was a saying we all used back at Bliss when asked for a loan from anything from a pencil to a ten dollar bill. When you declined, you were called "cheapee skate." We ordered a Carta Blanca unopened and opened it ourselves at the bar and never put that drink down.

As we were observing the foolishness, a young private approached us and pointed to the balcony above at a *senorita* and told us "Sarge, that girl just took my hat and put it in her panties and ran upstairs with it. If I don't get my hat back, me and my buddies are going to tear this joint apart." We told him that would be a very bad move and to cool off and we will talk to the Mamacita and she will get your hat back...which she did!

At about the same time, one of the cops we knew pushed his way through the crowd to our group of four Sergeants and said "Come on Sarge, much trouble here tonight, you follow me," as he escorted us through the growing mob of unruly recruits, opening his advance with the aid of his baton. He led us to a back alley over a drainage ditch and pointed to the back way to the main drag and advised us to go back to camp. "Much trouble tonight." We took his advice and proceeded to the main street, turned left and quick timed it to the bridge while making sure our hats and ties were on properly and that we did not appear to be drunk. We crossed the International Bridge to our side of the border in El Paso. No one in our group of Sergeants were John Wayne, Burt Lancaster or Lee Marvin who would have gladly torn the joint apart with the recruits, we were real life sergeants and real life soldiers and got our asses the hell out of there thanks to *El Amigo La Policia.*

A little aside about the attire of the Juarez policeman in

1951. First, his uniform was khaki colored and usually TW (Tropical Worsted) material like U.S. army officers were accustomed to wear in those days. I only remember a few who wore hats, their countenance was always very stern with a "don't mess with me" look. The image of shiny badges and belt buckles is there with my most prominent recall being the array of side arms carried on their waist in fancy tooled leather holsters. No two were alike. Most outstanding was the carved ivory or fancy Mexican silver grips on the *pistola,* mostly large .45 caliber military autos either U. S. Colts or Spanish copies.

My very first trip to Juarez one Saturday was a memorable day. I crossed the border by walking over the International Bridge and along with other *turistas,* I probably tossed a few pennies over the bridge to small Mexican kids who scrambled for them. The Rio Grande River was quite low at that point and was just a trickle as I remember it.

It was interesting to stroll down the main drag, passing all the legitimate bars, restaurants and tourist shops. I remember passing La Florida Club, the best restaurant in town where I was to enjoy dining on many steak dinners. I walked all the way down to the end of the main street and saw what appeared to be an open air market off to my left so I roamed that way just exploring, observing, and listening. It was my first time out of the U.S.A. and I kept my radar on but as I leisurely walked around I noticed how friendly and non-threatening all the people seemed to be.

I was the only G.I. around and people seemed surprised to see me approaching alone. The open market had stalls offering for sale food, clothing, pottery, colorful displays of paper and real flowers, and an abundant assortment of other wares. I would catch sight of an occasional tourist and the sounds were all interspersed with the sounds of Mexican music which I liked very much. I did not hear a single Hank Williams song and that was a relief. The Mexican music was great, I liked the sound and although I could not understand all the words, I liked the tempo. Everyone seemed to be smiling and I felt very much at ease.

As I ventured further, I could see a few blocks ahead a large mass of people gathering in front of an old building a couple stories high with wrought iron balconies and adornments. A closer look showed that it was a hotel and it seemed like something out of an old Western movie. The closer I came, the louder and clearer I could hear the words of the crowd as they repeated, "Pay Dro," "Pay Dro," I looked up in the direction the crowd was looking and a man and some pretty *senoritas* stepped out onto the balcony. I asked a *senorita* in my Bryant High Spanish, "*Que paso?*" what was happening? This girl just looked at me in amazement that I did not realize who I was looking at. She just pointed her finger at the group on the balcony and cried out, "Pedro Infante," whom I learned was the Leonardo DiCaprio of Mexican cinema. He was at that time the heart throb of every Mexican *senorita* as well as all the *senora's*. Sure enough, on the way back I spotted a big life-sized movie poster and there he was in full color, Pedro Infante himself.

On the walk back and crossing the main street to the other side, there was a quieter and less populated area with rows of small adobe one-story buildings. They had various signs in front and one that read "Cantina." Out of curiosity I stepped inside the cantina and was momentarily distracted by the dimly lit atmosphere compared to the bright sunlight outside. My radar quickly upgraded from "Search" to "Track," only to be reassured I was among *amigos*.

A half dozen or so older Mexican men all dressed in working men or farmers clothing with straw hats were smiling my way. It seemed they noticed my Sergeant stripes of three up and one down. "Sargento," "Bueno," I heard. I smiled back and ordered a bottle of *cerveza* while watching the bartender opening it in clear sight. I sipped and responded to the favorable impression I seemed to have made and relaxed my guard. After lighting a cigarette, I offered one or two which were accepted with a smile and a "*Gracias*" and "*Bueno,*" and more smiles. I soon realized these people were hard working and simple people as I sipped some more of my *cerveza*. I noticed their hard-looking hands as those of a working man who did a hard day's work. Their hands were much like my Grandpa Cavallo's hands who was a laborer and always had a smile of contentment on his face. These men gave me a reminder of my own hard-working people.

At first I was puzzled by their drinks and the ritual of a quick lick on the hand between thumb joint and fore finger followed by a dash of salt on the damp spot which they brought to their lips. At the same time, they picked up a piece of what looked like a lime and squeezed the juice in the mouth followed by a swig from a colorless liquid I found out was tequila. They must have noticed my wonder when one of the men raised his glass and said "Tequila" and offered me a drink. "*Si, si, bueno*," his *compadre*s called out. Now how could I refuse without insulting my new friends so I answered using my finest Spanish accent and replied ... OKAY !

Smiling faces watched as I was shown, "monkey see, monkey do" fashion. With left hand between thumb and forefinger pick up a piece of lime, lick the skin above the lime and shake on some salt. Lick the salt, squeeze the juice of the lime in my mouth and then with the right hand swig the tequila in one shot. "*Caramba*" I thought to myself, that tequila is potent!

I'll stay with the *cerveza* and we all laughed. "*Bueno, bueno*," was all I heard as I tried to cover up my gagging from the tequila, but I am sure they noticed my big Irish ears getting red. That Mexican lime which I was corrected was a *limone*, the sweetest lemon or lime I ever tasted. Since, that time I had many *limones* squeezed in my Bloody Mary's when I traveled to Mexico on business many years later. The Mexican *limones* made the best Bloody Mary's which we have not had since 1968, our last trip to The Villa Vera Racquet Club, a high-end resort frequented by Presidents and Princes in Acapulco where we usually un-winded after a hectic business trip to Mexico City.

I only drink Virgin Mary's now, which I haven't had for some time and I think I'm due. An ice filled glass of tomato juice, a splash of Worcestershire Sauce, a generous squeeze of fresh lime juice and a dash of tabasco...I don't use ground black pepper any more but powdered white pepper helps and of course you cannot beat the tasty Mexican *limone* I now see in some food stores. A stalk of cold fresh celery to stir in makes a tasty treat. Now for the sounds of some good Mexican music.

The image leaves me as I waved a*dios* to my new friends, names long ago lost. I walked out into the still bright sunshine and blinked my eyes a few times to adjust to the warm sun light. I liked Old Mexico and the Mexican people I met there.

The day ended with a delicious steak dinner at La Florida Club and a bus ride back to Bliss. The whole day's outing cost me only a few dollars. I can still hear the sounds and music of marimba bands, the guitars and the brass. That sound dissipates as I get closer to Fort Bliss and the sounds now echoed by Hank Williams crying out "Yorrr cheeeatin' ho'art will amake me blueeew." Shhhh, I don't want to say anything bad about Hank Williams, don't want to cause a riot in Fort Bliss. God forbid if you spoke any ill words about Hank Williams or his music but... I liked the Mexican music better.

I enjoyed Juarez and the people I met along the way. I realized that in the U.S.A., a young girl with no education, experience or talents has vast employment opportunities as long as she wants to work. Not so for the underclass in Mexico in 1951. Young girls desiring or needing employment had only one choice unless they had an influential friend and that was the Lago Blanco or other such places. There were no McDonald's or Burger Kings or Kelly Girls or Gal Fridays where they could earn a weekly paycheck. I realized at an early age how fortunate I was to be an American and still feel the same today.

I liked being a soldier at Fort Bliss. I even liked the idea of just being a soldier. Would it last, I wondered. This was only school and the real army life awaited me at Camp Stewart, I decided to take one day at a time and just wait and see.

Many instructors at Bliss recently served in Korea and with the war now in its second year they rotated back to the states. Some were posted at Bliss as instructors or to the Logan Heights Recruit Training areas. The Artillery School was considered to be a choice assignment for these returning Officers and NCO's. They were dedicated to passing on as much knowledge as they could, both technical as well as anecdotal, to prepare those of us who one day might serve in Korea. Their advice was remembered.

The days moved on and we were approaching the completion of the course. Heeding advice from older RA's, I opted to travel home per diem for my furlough before reporting for duty at Camp Stewart, Georgia. This would put some dollars in my pocket as I prepared for my journey home.

I played basketball at a post gym near the Beaumont Army Hospital Complex and found that there was a bulletin board with notices for those traveling per diem. One caught my eye, "Opening for one traveling to New York City by car and share expenses." It was posted by a Medic at Beaumont Army Hospital who was traveling to Manhattan in a 1949 Ford and seeking paying travel companions. The deal was made and I would be traveling east with two MP's and a medic. The first traveler was to be dropped off in Washington, Pennsylvania, at the western part of the state and the three remaining to continue on to NYC.

Our class assembled for the simple graduating exercises and the class picture and we received our diplomas for successful completion of the course. I turned in my bedding and picked up my travel orders and money. Then I made my way to Beaumont Hospital to meet my travel companions. We loaded the 1949 two-door Ford Sedan with two foot lockers and four duffel bags. Seated in front was the driver and an MP in the passenger seat and two of us sat in the rear. Off we rolled as we said *adios* to Fort Bliss and believe it or not, I did notice the sun setting in the west as we turned our backs on El Paso.

As the Eastern sky darkened in front of us we traveled over the Franklin Mountains and headed northeast towards Oklahoma. I think we traveled on Route 66 for part of the way. We were alerted to keep an eye out for deer as it grew darker and watched a few Texas mule deer staring at us off in the distance.

To save time, we all agreed to stop only to refuel, eat and relieve ourselves at one pit stop at a time. This was in September 1951 before the interstate complex of super highways. All the roads were still the old Blue Highways and secondary roads up through Texas, Oklahoma, Arkansas, Missouri, Illinois, Indiana, Ohio and then to finally stop in Washington, Pennsylvania in the western part of the state. One soldier departed taking with him his duffel bag and foot locker which lightened the load. We all stretched our legs before driving on the first interstate in the nation, the new Pennsylvania Turnpike.

The Pennsylvania Turnpike was a dream compared to all those old highways and hastened our trip to my home in Woodside in good old New York. Total time from Fort Bliss to home was 47 and one half hours. It was good to be home for a while.

Anecdotes of the Trip

Two memories stand out. One was a quick gas stop someplace in Arkansas or Missouri at a dreary old gas station with a big EATS sign outside. The building was a clapboard shack someone called home and business. A shriveled little old lady walked out and acknowledged the drivers request to "fill her up." The nod of her head acknowledging the drivers request and her quick scrutiny of four disheveled looking soldiers was noted by us. She pumped the gas, the driver paid and the lady disappeared inside. To save time we decided to stop here to eat, hit the bathroom, and then be on our way. We walked in and sat at the lunch counters only four stools and looked through the pass-through window to the kitchen and called out "we want some burgers." Out walked this same little underfed gray haired lady now wearing an apron. She eyed us narrowly confirming our far from well-groomed appearance, we probably didn't smell that good either being cramped up in the car for hours.

She suspiciously and politely took our orders "Four burgers with onion and four coffees." She looked over her shoulder and called out through the pass-through window in a clear and commanding voice, "Four burgers with onion." She quickly poured out and served four coffees and disappeared into the kitchen. The next thing we heard was the sound of hamburgers sizzling on the grill and some noise coming from the kitchen. We stretched our necks and spotted this same old gal frying up the burgers and putting them on platters while placing the plates on the pass-through window. She then reappeared to pick up the burgers and placed them on the counter in front of us.

Satisfied that she fooled us into thinking she was not alone, she seemed pleased we didn't want anything else. We passed on the apple pie that looked old and stale, then paid the tab as we proceeded on our way. On the way out I sneaked a glance back and caught her with a smile of relief on her wrinkled little face.

This poor old soul was probably terrified by being caught all alone when four guys came in looking like desperados so she wanted to give the impression she was not alone. Maybe she still remembered when villains like Machine Gun Kelly and Bonnie and Clyde terrorized the back country.

Susie's Three-Eyed Cow

Along the roadside in Ohio farm country, we saw a series of signs that read, "See Susie's Three-Eyed Cow," "Amazing Three-Eyed Cow," "Only 4 Miles to Susie's Three-Eyed Cow," "Turn right at next arrow to Three-Eyed Cow." The driver looked in the rear view mirror smiled and said, "Well what do you guys want to do?" "Yeah," we all agreed, "let's do it."

The driver turned right at the next arrow and we drove for what seemed an awfully long time, everyone looking at his watch. "What the hell, we came this far let's go all the way." Down the road we continued as the road ran out of pavement and became a dirt road. The driver seemed to be gripping the steering wheel tighter and everyone was silent. Finally we arrived at a decrepit rundown frame house with a small shed and a big captivating sign, "Home of Susie's Three-Eyed Cow." Out walked a cute little girl wearing a clean neat dress with a frilly apron who identified herself as Susie. She did not bat an eye at our appearance as she rattled the tin can in her dainty little hand and announced "Twenty-five cents apiece pleeeeease," which we acknowledged as we all heard the clank of our four quarters fall into the can.

We then followed her into a stinky barn and there right in front of us was a filthy disgusting looking cow with crooked horns and a big bump or wart right between her two eyes. Susie proclaimed, "Now isn't that an amazing sight!" and escorted us back to our car where she politely curtsied and offered, "Thank you sirs and have a good day." We all jumped back in the car and laughed like hell as the driver quickly revved up and made a screeching "U" turn to get back on the road in the least amount of time. "Conned by a twelve year old girl." "Ha, ha, ha, she was no twelve year old, she spoke like an adult. She was a 20-year old midget!" "Ha, ha, ha," we all chuckled. "A @#$%ing 20 year old midget."

"Well I'm glad we stopped or we would be thinking about the three-eyed cow all the way home," the driver chuckled. We wondered how many quarters little Susie deposited in that tin can. I wonder who coached Susie with her presentation. Her old man was probably inside peeking out the window and watching four more boobs taking the bait. Or her midget husband was watching and laughing all the while. We will never know!!!

A Tragic Anecdote

"B-29 Tanker down at Fort Bliss" read the head line. We saw it happen one Sunday morning. A few of us lingered in the mess hall one Sunday morning drinking coffee while the mess Sergeant was directing the K.P.'s when we all heard the roar of an airplane overhead sounding much closer than normal. We all ran outside and saw the plane crash land in an open field a little ways from the mess hall.

We ran along the road without getting too close and there was a B-29 flattened and smoking as airmen scrambled out of the plane to escape the wreck. A school bus was hit but it was only a glance and thank God the kids on the way to Sunday school were all safe. Crowds started to gather as Base Fire equipment was rushing to the scene. One of the fire trucks got too close and was itself engulfed in flames.

"Is it a tanker?" a woman in the crowd asked and with that reminder the crowd eased back expecting to see more flames reach out and maybe even an explosion. It was a tanker and it just took off from Biggs when it went down with a belly full of jet fuel for a five-day tanker re-fueling mission. To our horror, as the fire intensified a car stopped next to us and two young women jumped out identifying their husband's plane. "Is it his plane?" she asked her friend, "Oh my God it is," she cried as her friend caressed her. "Count how many got out!" someone else yelled. I forgot the count but we did see several and counted them but one was still missing and we later learned he died in the crash. .

There was no explosion, just violent flames and the fire crews extinguished all of the flames before any further casualties occurred. The firemen did not leave until the smoking remains of the plane and fire truck was saturated with foam.

No one felt like a Florida Club steak that night and we cancelled plans for the Mega-Musical show that Sunday at the Guadalajara Club in Juarez. They performed a gala Spanish and Mexican musical at the Guadalajara Club that was a fantastic spectacle.

This may be a tasteless time to comment about the five-day re-fueling missions but there was a club in the area where some Air Force wives would go during their husband's "Five day mission." The club offered them a chance to relax, have a few drinks, listen to some music, and get away from the kids for a while and, who knows what may happen. There was always a friend to baby sit and one could repay in the same currency!

This was part of life at Fort Bliss in 1951 and not that I went there often because wheels were necessary to even get there. But the few times I did go, I never once saw that girl from my earlier train ride to El Paso. I do not remember the name of the club and it may even have been in New Mexico.

The next posting would be at Camp Stewart, Georgia.

Leaving Fort Bliss, Public Domain via Wikipedia Commons

Fort Bliss Some Sundays

Most soldiers missed breakfast on a Sunday and slept in after a Saturday night of "Hooting with the Owls" and the next day unable to "Soar with the Eagles" and…just waited to be rescued by Joe Staunton after he returned from church.

Joe Staunton, which is the closest I can guess was the correct spelling of his name, was an older, serious and religious soldier living on the second floor of the barracks. Joe went to mass every Sunday morning and did some volunteer work in the chaplain's office. He was highly regarded by all and we tried to keep it clean when Joe was around. Most of us admired Joe.

After church, Joe would stop off to buy cans of soda and assorted fruit juices with plenty of tomato juice in the mix and bags of ice. He was in charge of the second floor kitty which we all chipped in to provide "Staunt" with the necessary funds to buy restoratives. All the barracks had a couple large metal garbage cans called simply, G.I. cans. The guys scrubbed them clean so Joe could fill one up with the cans of refreshments and plenty of ice. A rule was laid down that no radios were played on Sunday mornings until after a certain hour so as not to disturb the late risers.

I see the image of a G.I. can at the head of the stairs right outside my room packed with drinks of all kinds for all to treat themselves with. I can still see the beads of moisture accumulating on the outside of the metal G.I. can and dripping on the inlaid linoleum floor which was always easy to clean up later.

After a can or two of ice cold tomato juice, which was always my favorite, a shower and shave was next. A group of us would elect to go for brunch and if a thought for a trip to Juarez was planned where uniforms were required, we would climb into freshly laundered and starched khaki's. If not, then a T-shirt or sport shirt and slacks would be the uniform of the day. At that time only the genuine cowboys wore Jeans and, only "Levi's" would do.

I was issued two sets of khakis before I left for Bliss but found that was not enough to always keep a couple clean freshly laundered and starched uniforms on my clothes hanger. It was not long before I discovered the Salvage Warehouse all the RA's used. You could purchase new khaki trousers and shirts for a few dollars each at the Post Quartermaster store or, you could buy the same used and laundered clothing for only a few cents each like, 25 cents for a shirt or trousers at the Salvage Warehouse. So, I bought a few extra fatigue and khaki uniforms to maintain a clean wardrobe for only a couple dollars.

A quick trip to the post tailor to sew closed the khaki shirt breast pockets to lay flat, take in a little on the side and the sleeves, and for a few dollars you had a nicely tailored wardrobe. Green recruits arrived at Bliss with new baggy khakis and left as sharp soldiers in their tailored and starched uniforms. It was only a few cents to take in the sides of a shirt and to tailor the trouser length. Where I live, a tailor gets about twenty five bucks to just do the trouser length. Back then my $130 a month went a long way.

Around noon several of us would walk to the bus stop or go by car if available for a ride to our favorite restaurant for brunch. We would occupy a couple of tables and indulge in a spread of breakfast goodies. We started with hot coffee served by a smiling and pretty Texas waitress. Followed by half a cantaloupe, orange juice, eggs over medium... hmmm...this Sunday make it three eggs over medium. I never liked my egg whites runny. Sausage, home fries, grits, biscuits and maybe even a hot cake or two. A lot of chatter of G.I. lingo and sharing the camaraderie many of us old veterans remember of our younger days as soldiers. Yes, we probably all smoked cigarettes at a time when you could innocently and ignorantly enjoy a cigarette before we knew how much damage smoking did to our bodies.

We were a diverse group...any and all were invited. It was always "Hey, anyone ready for breakfast?" and a group would gather outside the barracks. The group usually included Cavan, Wence, Dell Orto, West, Rodriguez, Dixie Anderson, Levin, Comsky; sometimes even Staunton and Sarenson would join the party. Both Staunton and Dell Orto had wheels. Even with the war raging in Korea, I don't recall any talk at all about it. There were plenty of jokes and storytelling about girls from home and local girls, and as long as Staunt was not around... the senoritas in Old

Mexico we all said no to and maybe about some the guys may have even said, "*Si, Si.*"

We all knew school days would not last forever so we took every chance we could to enjoy the moment. That hit home towards the end when we were instructed by more and more officers and NCOs returning from service in Korea. Although no one talked about it, we all started thinking a little more seriously about what the future had in store for us.

"More coffee boys?" the waitress asked. "Hell yes and keep it coming. And how about some pecan ring cake with vanilla icing to go along with the coffee." "Hey Dell Orto, you got a light? My Zippo is outta gas." In those days, every G.I. had a Zippo lighter whether he smoked or not. Especially if he spent time in the field where G.I. gasoline was a perfect fuel for a Zippo. I still have mine that has been bone dry for years and it still has a do-it-yourself fix to the hinge I made in Korea out of a piece of commo wire.

Once we graduated from our course we all went our separate ways. The only one I ever saw again was Cavan who lived in Savannah, Georgia. He invited me to his home for dinner when I was at Camp Stewart and I think his outfit was soon after called to active duty. When in Korea, I ran into Major Dugan the Fort Bliss radar park commander and the RA First Sergeant who checked me in at Fort Bliss that first day I reported there.

Just writing about those Sunday brunches followed by gallons of coffee has me splashing an Alka Seltzer in a cold glass of water with beads of moisture running down the side of the glass. Burp!!

The 10 engine B-36 Bomber miniaturizes the 4 engine B-29 Super fortress. With 6 pusher propeller piston engines plus 4 jet engines and a wing span of 230 feet, it was the largest piston engine plane ever built. When the B-36 flew overhead the entire ground shook and all heads were raised to look at this awesome aircraft. Unfortunately, the B-36 was proven unreliable and became obsolete and replaced with all jet bombers. *US Air Force Photograph*

FORT BLISS, 1951

Gallagher and Wence, he named Sparky Watts and also wrote the song. He steered clear of Sparky also.

L to R standing: Cheapee Skate - forgot his name but guys stopped lending him anymore money, Schonian, a good hearted trooper from Baltimore, Wence. Bottom: me and a soldier kneeling next to me name forgotten.

159

White Sands New Mexico pure white Gypsum. Largest surface deposit of Gypsum in the world. Dell Orto in black shirt owned the 1950 Buick which, was our wheels taking us to distant vistas while at Fort Bliss. CPL West posing on all fours. Me on my back wearing my new Gaucho styled G.I. Brown shoes with buckles visible in the photo. Tongues hanging out and dying of thirst with water and snacks only a few feet away in the Buick. A park ranger took our picture. Probably, the same weekend we checked into a motel in Ruidoso with young colleges girls everywhere and we three the only guys around the swimming pool…and even the life guard was a girl. West and Dell Orto thought little about scuffing their shoes while I was so careful to protect the shine on my new Gauchos… I always was a bit of a Dude!

THE ARTILLERY SCHOOL
ANTIAIRCRAFT AND GUIDED MISSILES BRANCH
Fort Bliss, Texas

TRANSCRIPT OF GRADES
of
SERGEANT VINCENT G. GALLAGHER

Who attended the following course
at this installation:

FIRE CONTROL ELECTRICIAN (GUN) COURSE NO. 54 - Inclusive dates - 29 Mar 51 - 31 Aug

SUBJECT	GRADE	WEIGHT	HRS IN ATTENDANCE
Methods of Instruction	85	1	35
Basic Electronics	77	6	315
Remote Control	84	5	112
Radar	96	1	39
Fuze Setters	87	2	35
Directors	90	10	213
Power Plants	82	1	35
Multiple MG M15	90	1	35

Final Grade   85.5
Final Rating   Excellent
Relative Standing   19 in class of 29

*Only grades of SATISFACTORY AND UNSATISFACTORY given in these
subjects.

Passing grade for all subjects: 70 percent.

FOR THE COMMANDANT:

Edward B Cramey

EDWARD B. CRAMEY
Major, AGC
Registrar

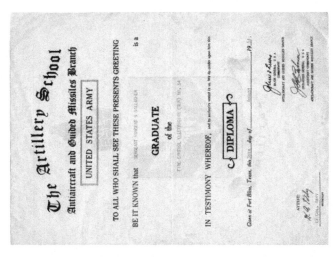

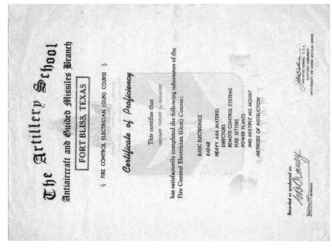

162

FIRE CONTROL ELECTRICIAN (GUN) COURSE NO. 54

PARTING SHOTS

Artillery School Enlisted Student Detachment, Fort Bliss,
Texas June 1951. Surprise barracks inspection by General and
Madame MacRidgewayHower accompanied by Aide De
Chump Colonel Irving Intheway. ATTEN-HUT. Oh it's only
Ehben, Gallagher and Levin ...AT EASE!

The Juarez Patrol fortifying themselves with the Manhattan
Clubs fifteen cent drinks before facing the determined
Senoritas at the Lago Bianco.

164

Pranks and the Pranksters

There was always time for a practical joke for those with a good sense of humor. They also knew the time would come when they would be the target. For those who could not take a joke, especially those who thought it was funny when someone else was the victim, army life could be challenging.

While on the artillery range, a new recruit was told, "Ask Sergeant Barker we need 25 more feet of firing line." The recruit might be sent off to ask several others before realizing he was on the "Firing Line."

Gun Commander tells Private McGann "We need the 'Cannon Report' before we can O&S the 90's." McGann is sent all over that firing range to get the 'Cannon Report' until, he hears the first loud report of a 90 firing...he grasps he's been had.

Some were more creative, after June of 1950 as National Guard units all over the country were being alerted for mobilization. Our Supply Sergeant was activated several times before the 773rd was actually called...telegram and all! It was fun pulling pranks on him because he always got mad but, laughed the loudest when the joke was on someone else.

One evening John Zurla and I chatted outside the armory in White Plains, NY after an officers meeting. He noticed Captain Manning parked his 1958 Chevrolet right where we were talking, on the corner by the mail box. John knew I drove the same year Chevrolet. He said "Give me your car keys a minute." He opened the locked door of Manning's Chevy and we drove it across the street and parked in open view in front of a bank...walked back to the corner and waited for Manning.

We chuckled as we waited to see Manning's reaction. John told me many General Motors cars at that time would accept keys from other models and this was indeed so.

Manning soon walked out of the armory then, down the steps to mail some items in the mail box where he thought his car was parked. He stopped short, looked a little surprised and with a quick, "Hi," to John and I, he walked past us and continued down the street. He stopped short and without a comment, turned around and dashed right past us back to the armory, taking the stairs two at time. We waited to see how this was to play out when he came out again dashing down the steps.

Expecting him to say "OK you jokers, now where is my car?" Or just stop for a second and just glance across the street and see his car in plain view. Instead, he exclaimed, "Some son of a bitch stole my car," and before we could calm him down, he followed with, "I just called the White Plain Police and they are on the way!" Zurla looked at me, I looked at him, and we both scrambled to our own cars.

When the police saw his car parked across the street Manning said the police chewed him out for wasting their time and of course, Manning guessed who the real car thieves were. He promised to get even with the both of us and we were on alert for a while. He soon forgot about it but he always told the story with a relish about how Zurla and Gallagher stole his car.

The American Legion had a bar next to the armory and the battalion officers would congregate from time to time to celebrate any occasion. Captain Kelly always planned these revelries and this became a venue for many pranks. I showed up one night with harmless capsules of potassium permanganate, a product Urologists used as a dye to scan a patient's urinary tract during the bygone days of ancient fluoroscopes. Potassium permanganate had only one side-effect which, was to discolor the urine blue for a day or two. Any guy taking a pee without knowledge of the dye would be quite shocked to look down and see the blue streak.

About four officers were involved with this prank. I had to be sure I had enough time to take apart the gelatin capsule and covertly pour its contents of crystals into the brown colored bottle of beer. Captain Kelly was the chosen victim. My cohorts would distract Kelly every time I attempted to strike until I finally slipped all the crystals into his beer bottle. One tiny crystal stuck on Kelly's lip and turned blue but was washed down with his next sip of beer much to the relief of the Pranksters. The evening came to an end and we all headed for home to soon forget the evening's events.

The following week at the officers meeting, knowing, that I was a pharmaceutical salesman and perhaps a little suspicious, Kelly asked me about blue urine. I referred him to Captain Curtis who was the battalion Medical Officer. I forgot about the antic of the previous week and grabbed Captain Curtis to clue him in so Kelly would realize it was just a prank and that he did not think it was a souvenir he may have picked up while serving in the Far East. Curtis laughed when I told him and said he saw that trick many times at medical school. "I'll assure him it was harmless."

Kelly may have had some suspicions but never mentioned it to me. He was an unwilling target for a lot of jokes which he just "poo-pooed" and made like he was above this childishness displayed by some of the less mature officers whom he said..."Acted like adolescents." This attitude placed a "T" for Target right on his pate. "I'm the Senior Captain in the battalion and have no time for this nonsense," he remarked. During camp tour at Fort Hancock, on the New Jersey shore, Captain D'Amico while surf fishing one night found a box turtle on the side of the road. He painted white Captains bars on the turtle's shell along with, "Senior Captain" and placed the turtle in the officer's latrine near the showers. Every AM all the officers were greeted by the friendly turtle slowly ambulating throughout the latrine. Some active officers from the Nike unit quickly caught on and would call, "Atten hut" and salute the slowly pacing little reptile. Some brought lettuce and other goodies for the turtle and we noticed someone added, "773 AA" printed over the Captain bars. At the end of camp tour, D'Amico returned the turtle to his home pond where the turtle would live out his life as...the 773rd AA Senior Captain.

At annual weapons qualification weekend at Camp Smith, Kelly always occupied a two-man tent in private and close to the officer's shower and latrine. His job as the battalion Adjutant the leading staff officer, was an administrative function separate from the line officers' duties. Most administrative men in the army were reserved as opposed to the battery officers who were more outgoing or more mischievous by nature.

Zurla arrived that weekend with three inch salute fire crackers he bought in Alabama when attending Army flight school. We waited for Kelly knowing he would usually wait until later so he could have the shower room to himself with no one rushing him.

We sneaked around to the rear of the shower room and to the window which we purposely left open. We heard the shower running and Zurla lit and tossed a salute in through the window and we both took off as we heard the loud bang. That not being enough, Zurla said. "Let's see if he is still in the shower." He was, so I tip toed into the shower room while Kelly was still leisurely showering and attempted to slip a salute closer to the shower. As I stooped to place the sizzling fire cracker I was startled by an explosive right behind me as I saw Zurla running away back to our tent. The SOB placed a salute right in back of me.

OK, I thought… war is declared. I'll get that @#$%ing Zurla but I will wait until his guard is down. I warned him, "John, I'm in no hurry but…it's coming. Only you will never know when, until it happens." I continued, "Yes, yes that was very clever John, but you know I can be very creative myself!" He slept with one eye opened that night and I would catch him checking his gear and bunk and being on a Red Alert or as we called it now in the Nike program "Alpha Status" - the highest level of alert.

I was in no hurry and kept Zurla on "Alpha Status", for a long time. This was at Fall Weapons Qualification so I waited until next summer camp tour. He was on edge a long, long time. We had plenty of drinks together during that time and I always saw him check his drinks by smelling or close scrutiny expecting my reprisal at any moment. He of course knew I was a pharmaceutical salesman and had plenty of savvy and access to various chemicals, laxatives, and dyes that could cause all kinds of mischief. He even thought for a while that I forgot about it and began to relax. So I just let it sit.

We camp toured at Fort Hancock New Jersey and shared a two man room at the BOQ (Bachelor Officer Quarters). My plan was already formed and I was ready to strike.

One morning I awoke very early in total silence as my

buddy was still sleeping soundly. The night before he placed his freshly starched khaki's neatly hanging with his collar brass all polished with silver first lieutenant bar on right side and brass crossed cannons with missile on left side ready to wear this AM. With needle and thread readied I sewed together the uniform, first the shirt and then the pants. Watching for any movement I saw my buddy was still fast asleep so, I continued sewing together several of his pants and shirts lined up on his cloths rack just like we did to Supply SGT Joe Caruana many times back at Camp Stewart. I was going to hide his highly polished low quarter shoes but did not want to push my luck. I put away the evidence of needle and thread, grabbed my shaving kit and a towel and rushed to the latrine to shower and shave, dashing back I got dressed and was on the way to the mess hall when John aroused. I commented, "Man I'm starved...see ya in the mess hall." John stretched as I ran out... You can bet that I was now on "Alpha Status."

John tried but was caught in the act because he was just not sneaky enough to get me in such close quarters with no accomplices. But old sly Quidone got me all the time. He would sneak into my room unnoticed when I was fast asleep, place his portable record player under my cot with a "Mexican Brass from the Bull Ring" record and a timer set to go off just before reveille at max volume to blast me out of bed. He caught me so many times that I finally absconded with his record player and put it in Lieutenant Gilburd's car trunk. Gilburd was a very serious and capable officer who always maintained proper military decorum but only too happy to participate covertly as an accomplice. He never had to worry about being a target because no one ever would suspect he was involved in any pranks. I would not dare put the record player in John's car because that is the first place Quidone would look.

I trained with a counterpart Fire Control officer, an RA West Pointer ready to participate in any BOQ capers. He told me about a joke played at jump school in Fort Benning, Georgia. They prepared a fully clothed and equipped weighted dummy to accompany a group for a parachute jump and placed a certain officer's number on the dummy. The jumpers all jump in sequence and are all hooked up to a static line before they jump which remains attached to the plane. When they jump the static line automatically opens the chute. They also have a reserve chute just in case. With no static line hookup to the chute, it never opened and the fully clothed dummy plummeted to the ground with a thud. I guess the old mischief makers in the 773rd were not all that bad after all.

Chapter 5

Camp Stewart, Georgia

Another National Guard unit answers the call. The 773rd was alerted in April 1951 to begin active service on May 1st for a period of two years, which I am sure did not come as a surprise to anyone. I was already at school in Fort Bliss and was the last to know for I had no contact with anyone from the unit, no cell phone and no email. National Guard Infantry Divisions were already called along with hundreds of regimental and battalion sized artillery and other combat arms and service units beginning in 1950 with 700 NG units sent to Korea.

In this narrative, I mention about the men who marched out of the armory during wartime and some of my comrades who marched out twice to go to war, once in 1941 and again in 1951. I personally never marched out with the outfit to go to war as I was already on active service since March of 1951. I missed the large and impressive ceremony at the armory for the men and their wives or girlfriends. This occurred the evening before they marched out to the same rail head in the West 40's to take a troop train south to Camp Stewart, Georgia. This was the very same rail head and route the 212th took to Camp Stewart back in 1941.

Camp Stewart was opened as a training base in 1940 and was an antiaircraft artillery training center in World War II and the Korean War because of the expansive artillery firing ranges and impact areas.

Today, Camp Stewart is now Fort Stewart a permanent major training center for Infantry, Artillery and Armor units with vastly expanded modern facilities to support troop training and the military families. When the 773rd was there, it was still a tent city no different from Second World War days.

I remember arriving at Stewart in a taxi I took from the Savannah Railroad station and do not recall anything about the ride there. My memory re-awakened when approaching the main gate which was nothing more than a little wooden shack with no actual gate, just a simple sign stating "Camp Stewart" and an arrow pointing down a tarmac road. The two M.P.'s looked tired and would definitely not pass inspection at Fort Bliss.

'The surroundings were in the middle of nowhere in a wet and swampy area with drainage ditches alongside the road. I compared the clean dry desert air at Fort Bliss to my new environment. This was not an inviting impression but, there was no use looking back now.

Directly in front of the entrance to Camp Stewart was a grassy circle and placed in the middle for all to see was a totally wrecked automobile. Next to the wreck was a sign displaying a skull and crossbones and showing the number of traffic deaths at Camp Stewart. "Drive Safely" was printed in large block letters for everyone to take notice.

The M.P.'s checked my orders and waved us through. The cab driver observed the 25 MPH speed limit and proceeded slowly. I observed my new wet location of the Eastern Georgia tidal area and soon realized why Camp Stewart earned the nickname "Swamp Stewart." There were no mountain ranges, just the flat terrain interspersed with clumps of white pine trees, scrub oak and marsh grasses.

During World War II, additional resources were required to accommodate the thousands of German and Italian prisoners of war captured during the fighting in North Africa. The prisoners actually built a good deal of the improvements at the facility and lived very well there and were even paid for their labor. The German and Italian POW's lived better and were fed better at Camp Stewart than they were while serving in their own armies in Europe and Africa.

Stewart was also the first base for the Woman's Aviation Service Pilots (WASPS). These were the female pilots who actually flew the planes that towed the Aerial AA target sleeves then in use. It was shortly after that time when the army decided it was safer to develop the Radio Controlled Aerial Targets (RCATS). I wonder what prompted the army to make that decision. Maybe that's where the rumors originated. The 212th trained at Camp Stewart in 1941 along with thousands of other

AAA soldiers. I can only assume the stories of AA guns shooting down and/or damaging tow planes were all too true and witnessed by hundreds of soldiers, some very possibly from our own unit. Maybe even Major Kraus saw these accidents and was determined to avoid them.

The WASPS also flew ferry flights of warplanes across the Atlantic to Europe as well as ferrying warplanes to the West Coast for shipment to the Pacific Theater. I believe the WASP's finally received their much deserved Government recognition for their very important service to the nation in World War II.

It was dusk and I noticed a smoky haze permeate the atmosphere around Camp Stewart. One could detect the smell of fumes...someone was burning something. I glanced at my watch and noticed some black specks of soot already on my shirt cuff and wrist. Who the hell is burning trash I thought? We briefly passed through an area with small white painted wooden buildings, one marked Post Headquarters, others with Post Infirmary, Chaplain, and PX. It all seemed to me to be so small and rustic. It was somewhat oppressive because behind all these buildings were dense Pine Barrens that one could not see beyond and no mountains as reference points. I thought to myself this will be a difficult area to orient oneself when training in the field.

We drove down a road leading to the troop's quarters and as far as the eye could see were row upon row of O.D. (Olive Drab) colored squad tents. Camp Stewart was indeed a tent city with no permanent barracks. Projecting through the roofs of the tents were metal chimneys emitting a grayish black smoke that told me it was soft coal burning in the stoves at Camp Stewart and giving off that smell of something burning. The black soot settled on everything. Oh well, I thought I was in the real army now so I might as well get used to it and smile anyway. "Lovely view, isn't it, cabbie?" I said, trying to smile. The driver belly laughed and said, "Oh, Ya all get used to it" in his slow Southern drawl.

Finally, up ahead, we saw a sign that read "C Battery, 773rd AAA Gun BN 90mm" on a red artillery colored sign with yellow writing. I paid the cabbie, grabbed my duffel bag and walked to a small white wooden frame building marked "Orderly Room." I entered what contained the Battery Commander's (BC) office, the First Sergeant's desk and the Battery Clerk's desk with his typewriter. Stepping inside the empty office I saw a closed door with a sign that spelled out "Supply Room." "Hey, anyone home?" I called as the supply room door opened and pal Max Ries walked out.

At first I did not recognize him. The last time I saw Max was before I left for Fort Bliss. "Hey Vin, how the hell are you, we were expecting you. Welcome to "Swamp Stewart," hope you enjoy your stay." I noticed my buddy was covered with that soot and that it pretty much covered everything in the office. Max who was always well dressed and well-groomed looked like he could use a shower and he blended in with the environment. Would I ever get used to this place, I wondered.

Max was on CQ (charge of quarters) duty and flashed his sly smile as he welcomed me. He told me I will not have to pick up any bedding because a couple of the guys made up my cot for me and placed my foot locker at the foot of my bunk. How nice of them! A little warning light started to blink "alert" in the back of my mind. Max surprised me when he said I was to share the first tent at the head of the battery street with the other top Sergeants: First Sergeant Bill Mauro, Gun Platoon Sergeant Bill Barker, Supply Sergeant Joe Caruana and Motor Sergeant John Zurla.

Max congratulated me and showed me a copy of the order promoting me to SFC (Sergeant First Class) and Fire Control Platoon Sergeant. "The battery sure as hell needs you," he exclaimed. Old Mr. Nicoletti was right about those promotion opportunities by volunteering to take the Fire Control course. I just didn't think they would come so fast and hoped I would not let the battery down.

I followed Max as he led me to my new quarters at the head of the battery street. Street! What a joke that was, it was nothing more than a patch of sand. "Watch out you don't step in any cow shit," Max warned. "Cow shit ... are you kidding me?" "Hell no, the cows are all over the place here." I soon learned about the Georgia "Open Range Laws." Cattle were permitted to graze on federal government land anywhere in the state of Georgia. I wondered how many of those auto accidents were caused by cows.

When we entered the tent I immediately smelled the G.I. preservative odor that every soldier who ever lived under army canvas will remember. The tent was the standard 12-man squad tent then in use by the army. It was kind of dark with only two 40-watt bare bulbs hanging from wires which, provided the only source of light.

After being greeted by the NCOs' I had not seen for many months and handshakes all around followed by congratulations confirming my promotion. It was for real and not something Max engineered to greet me with, having access to the orderly room and the typewriter.

First Soldier Mauro said he will give me an update tomorrow AM. With that, Max showed me where the latrine was at the end of the battery street and returned to his duty as battery C.Q. The Charge of Quarters is an NCO duty like an all-night watchman guarding the orderly room and supply room and to alert the battery in case of fire or emergency.

The latrine was a one-story concrete block building with wash basins, urinals, commodes and showers. I think the latrines were the only buildings in camp that were not wood frame structures. To the rear of the latrine was the thickly overgrown marshland of scrub oak and pine trees typical to the southern Georgia terrain. Who the hell picked this location for an army base I wondered. I turned on the corroded faucets in the shower as they gurgled before pouring out lukewarm water. Camp Stewart was recently re-opened to accommodate the new and growing army. The plumbing had remained dormant since World War II.

After my shower and returning to my tent, I checked my bunk to make sure the legs on one end were not slightly folded so the cot would collapse when I climbed in. I remembered Max's sly smile! Instead, as I tried to slip in between the sheets I realized when making my bunk Max double short-sheeted me and to add to the humor someone put dry crunchy corn flakes between my set of clean sheets. Even though the joke was on me I laughed along with

175

everyone else as I planned my reprisal. I knew some of my Sergeant buddies were accomplices here.

There were more welcomes to "Swamp Stewart" from some other troopers including my buddy newly promoted Sergeant First Class (SFC) Frank Mistretta, the battery Machine Gun Section leader. I cleaned out the corn flakes, remade my bunk, cuddled up between the sheets, closed my eyes, and drifted off to a contented sleep with no more doubts in my mind about myself or "Swamp Stewart!" I was back home in Charlie Battery and glad to be here. I was going to like soldiering at Stewart also.

"Speed March!" "Speed March!" "Rise and Shine!" "Speed March!" "Off your ass and on your feet!" someone yelled. "Fatigue pants, boots and T-shirts!" "Speed March!" "Let's go, let's go Sergeants!" urged First Sergeant Mauro.

"What the hell time is it?" I asked, "Time to get up for a Speed March" "What the hell is a Speed March?" I asked again. "You'll see, let's go," I heard someone yell as the Sergeants were all hastily getting into their pants and boots. I heard someone yell out "Oh shit, not again." I jumped into my fatigue pants, combat boots, T-shirt topped off with my fatigue hat and ran outside in the half dark with a glance down on the sand for cow shit and, sure enough I could hear a couple troopers exclaim in the pre-dawn, "Those fucking cows." I guess someone connected with some cow dropping as I noticed a couple of cows lazily moseying away from the swiftly forming soldiers of C Battery.

Sergeant Mauro called the roll as I stood in front of the Fire Control Platoon acknowledging friendly faces and observing the stare of the new guys whom I was to get to know. Sergeant Klopfer the Range Section Leader and acting Fire Control Platoon Sergeant did not look too happy as he said hello. Sergeant Gerald Backer the Radar Section Leader gave me a hearty welcome with a handshake and a broad smile which was Gerry's trademark.

First Sergeant Mauro called the roll and snappy "Yo's" were heard after each man's name was called. If absent the section leader would yell out, "On sick call" or "On K. P." or yes, we had one man AWOL, in the gun platoon. The First Sergeant reported,

"Sir, C Battery all present or accounted for," as he saluted and the Battery CO returned the salute.

The Battery Commander First Lieutenant George Byrnes formed the battery in a column and led the Speed March with the command to double time. Master Sergeant Barker in his commanding voice yelled a double time cadence count soon followed by C Battery sounding off with him, with a little sing song lyric more nasty than military. We all sounded off and I quickly picked up the simple lyric. It had plenty of X-rated words.

At the age of 19 and in good physical shape, I thought it was invigorating to be up and running as I saw the sun rise breaking through the pine trees. The darkened sky seem to take on a gray and then blue color opening up the window of my first morning in Camp Stewart, "Joe Ja." The battery picked up the pace as more off color lyrics spiced up the speed march. Even Supply Sergeant Caruana had a smile on his face as he picked up the step. The sun was now peeking through the scrub oak. Yeah, I thought to myself, this is the real army now. I liked it and I liked being an SFC. No one except my Astoria friends Max Ries and Bob Dema knew I was only 19 and not the 21 recorded in my file.

Not everyone was enthralled with the Speed March as we rounded the bend and ran down the home stretch approaching our battery area. Barker still sounding off the cadence. He was of medium height with a big voice and in good physical shape. He stood tall in front of his platoon and was a damn good Gun Platoon Sergeant of about 70 men. I felt good leading in front of my platoon of 30 men with a few familiar faces calling out to say hello. I knew those new men were watching closely to see what kind of a soldier their new platoon Sergeant was. So, I had to make sure to keep up the stride in front of them. Even with all the easy living at Fort Bliss, I was able to move out with my men in the Fire Control Platoon. Although, on that final lap I did feel winded but still kept up the pace in front of my platoon. I was glad to have such good leg muscles which is now about the only muscles I still have.

Lieutenant Byrnes, a big framed man, seemed to puff a little and Lieutenant O'Rahilly, a slim man still pranced with head

177

held high and breathing easily with a smile showing he was right in his element. Some of the older warrant officers who drank and smoked too much started to lag a bit. Mess Sergeant Davis was in the mess hall supervising breakfast and I never saw him ever attend a Speed March and they were frequent. The old timer knew all the angles. Davis was a classic. It is interesting to relate again that Sergeant Davis was among those who departed the armory and arrived at Camp Stewart back in 1941, so this was kind of a bleak homecoming for all those vets who now Speed marched down these same roads again only now, they were ten years older and ten years broader. "Sagina Davis" always had a reason for not joining in the fun!

Some of the older guys huffed and puffed trailing the battery. My age was in my favor and I felt great! I never had powerful upper body strength but riding my bike all over Queens County as a kid gave me the strong leg muscles I needed to take me wherever I had to go in my army life. Top Sergeant Mauro, a non-smoker who only drank an occasional beer, was in great shape.

I noticed how Charlie Battery had grown and matured and how impressed I was with the soldiers in the battery. With many new faces of draftees who completed basic training and advanced basic and were now training as artillerymen. We also had a number of Paratroop Jump School dropouts from Fort Benning, Georgia, and not a bit ashamed to have dropped out of such demanding training. They benefited from their special training and for whatever the reason found themselves in Charlie Battery. They were all good soldiers who added a dimension that showed the NG's how to look and act like a soldier and be proud of his uniform. They brought a lot of good habits to the unit. These men all volunteered for Jump School and most of them were draftees and their presence had a very positive effect on the battery, several were in the Fire Control Platoon.

As we trained I soon learned I had excellent soldiers in my platoon, mostly draftees who were a credit to their uniform. I was proud of every one of them as we advanced in our training. About one third of my platoon were black soldiers who came to C Battery during the disbanding of the all black units which was accomplished, by President Truman and benefitted the now fully integrated U.S. military. Good job, Harry.

Every morning the battery is assembled at one end of the battery area and lined up in a long line with arms extended for "Police Call." Simply, to clean the area. The troops are spread out in a straight line with section leaders spaced a row or two in the rear to be sure everyone picks up anything that "does not grow." The object is to pick up everything from cigarette butts to candy wrappers or any other refuse. The order to "move out" is given by the NCO in charge and the troops scan the ground and bend to pick up every morsel of litter on the ground. It's no big deal and done for ages in the military. Any old vet remembers bending over and hearing some NCO yelling out "All I want to see is elbows and assholes, now move out." Any G.I. who thought he was above that menial task would have a tough time in the army. It also stressed to the troops who smoked to "Field Strip" their cigarette butts by tearing them apart rather than tossing them and then have to pick them up at Police Call and it stuck. This of course was way before filter tips on cigarettes. Charlie Battery did this chore every morning and the NCO in charge was rotated among the top two graders SFC's and Master Sergeants.

During Police Call, the remaining top Sergeants collected in the mess hall to drink coffee and harass Sergeant Davis. "This Messa Hall is not open 'til I say so." "Hey Davis," the First Sergeant asked, "How come I didn't see you in the last Speed March?" "Ima too busy in the kitch, we got the green cooks." "Ha ha ha," we all laughed. "You know all the angles, Davis." "This coffee tastes lousy, what the hell did you do to it, Davis?" "You no lika the coffee here, go see what it's like in D Baddery, get the hell outta my kitch brudder." It went on and on but Davis always had an answer. If any old NCO's read this I am sure a smile will come across their faces the same as mine.

The BN S-3 (Operations and Training officer) scheduled these marches secretly and well in advance. We had many before we left Camp Stewart. They were only announced to the troops on the morning of the march. Even when it rained, it made no

179

difference, ponchos or raincoats and helmet liners were added to the uniform. The battery officers were given some advance notice so they would know enough to get a good night's sleep the night before. Hopefully, they had enough sense to turn in early, rather than the embarrassment of arriving in the wee hours of the morning with a hangover and then face a Speed March.

That first morning I met all the men in the Fire Control Platoon consisting of two sections, the Radar and the Range Sections. The platoon had about 30 men evenly divided between the two sections. Sergeant Gerald Backer, an original NG from the Upper East Side of Manhattan, was the radar section leader. His father owned a kosher butcher shop in New York City and I remembered him as a tall well-fed man who filled out his uniform and was always eager to do a good job. He always took his training seriously and it paid for him now as the battery's Chief Radar Operator (CRO) and Radar Section Leader. He knew his job and did it well. C Battery's SCR-584 Radar was his baby and he knew how to cross-train his operators so that each man could do the other's job. He was a respected and respectful section leader but not the sharpest soldier. Seeing him at Camp Stewart was a little shocking as we shook hands in greeting. Backer lost a lot of weight at Camp Stewart and his uniform just hung on his lanky frame. He explained and even apologized to me for the weight loss.

Because Camp Stewart was newly re-opened and not receiving rations to match the Army and Air Force Master Menu, the men in the battalion were not eating that well at Camp Stewart. Local pork was on the menu several times a week and plenty of ham and bacon served in the mess halls. This was fine for those not of the Jewish faith but, Backer missed too many meals because of his religious beliefs; he could not eat pork. After a sparse diet and working in the hot humid Eastern Georgia climate, Backer suffered. Glancing over my shoulder during the speed marches, I noticed the strain in Backer's face but he still led his section. I had a lot of respect for Backer. I noticed Joe Zurla, John's younger brother, bugging Backer every chance he had. Good natured pranks were acceptable but Joe, a real bright guy, just poured it on a little too heavy with Backer. Backer was not as combative as Davis and just took it.

From the time the battalion arrived until the end of August rations were under par and everyone complained including the mess Sergeants. Finally, the supply system caught up to Camp Stewart shortly after I returned. I missed the worst part of the training in the hot humid summer months with plenty of snakes, spiders and other critters making a G.I.'s life miserable in "Swamp Stewart." When Stewart was finally on the Master Menu, everyone was happy about the improvement but, the chow was not as good as it was at Fort Bliss.

SFC Klopfer was Captain Klopfer's son from the old 12th Regiment State Guard. He joined C Battery some time ago and was a good soldier. He caught on to the operation of the M-9 Director and did an excellent job. He was now the Director Section leader and acting Fire Control Platoon Sergeant. He did not seem too happy to see me and I guess rightly so. As M-9 Director Section leader, he would have been next in line and a natural for eventual promotion to Platoon Sergeant. He was no doubt disappointed that the Platoon Sergeant position was held for me and I was more surprised than anyone was. I had some work to do. They were all good men and it didn't take long to get everyone working as a team.

When the battalion arrived at Stewart, the first course of training was basic infantry training for the entire unit. Regardless of specialty, the first priority was to train as an infantry soldier and then later learn to be an artilleryman. First Sergeant Mauro always said, "We are soldiers first." So I needed to go through all the basic training I missed while at Fort Bliss.

Battalion Adjutant Captain Kelly called my battery CO and asked to have me report to him at once. "Well Sergeant Gallagher, we all hope you learned a lot at Fort Bliss because C Battery really needs you." "Good morning, Captain Kelly," followed by a smart salute which he returned. That is just a part of military courtesy. I'm not saluting a man, I'm saluting the rank and the military tradition I respect. Some guys had a tough time with that. I never did.

"We have to get your records up to date having missed some training while vacationing at Fort Bliss." All the artillerymen knew about Fort Bliss and Juarez, and Kelly thought himself a very clever and very witty person. Actually he was but always with that "I'm smiling AT you, not WITH you" look on his face.

"I think we are in luck," he said. After Kelly checked with the various ranges and programs he discovered a group of ROTC (Reserve Officers Training Corps) new Second Lieutenants were in Camp Stewart for basic training. He told me I could join them through the courses I missed while at Fort Bliss. That was just fine I thought, and it even sounded like fun.

Kelly was a positive thinker as long as I knew him and if he just put aside trying to be clever and witty, he would have avoided the many pranks that were played on him by his fellow officers. Which, to me at that time were totally unknown. Hell, I did not have an inkling of an idea that in about five years' me and buddy John Zurla would be Kelly's major protagonists. There was a world of experiences facing all of us at that early date of 1951 before the time when we three would be officers serving together in the 773rd.

Kelly attached me to this group of about 100 new Second Lieutenants and we took the same basic course together. These new Second Lieutenants were badly needed and most would soon be leading Infantry Platoons in front line units in Korea. The casualty rate for new Second Lieutenants assigned to lead an infantry platoon was indeed very high and replacements were always needed.

"Captain Kelly, sign me up as soon as possible, sir." When I said "Sir" I meant it; it's all in each man's mental outlook. Too many G.I.'s resented the "chicken shit" which only made their service time tougher. I just laughed it off under my breath and went on.

Remember, "Do it now and bitch about it later." "Salute it if it walks," say "Yes Sir" or say "No Sir," then just walk away and "Faa get about it," advised First Soldier Bill Mauro with his Nu Yawk inflection.

182

I spent the next few weeks getting my record up to date as I crawled under the live machine gun fire at night. "Not to worry," exclaimed the NCO in charge when addressing us at the course. "It's too cold for the snakes to be out so just be sure to keep your heads down in the sand under the wire and just follow the boots of the man in front of you." "OK," I thought, one more thing to check off the list! This was followed by jumping and running through the obstacle course without getting my new Corcoran boots too wet and then barely, and I mean just barely, getting my ass over an eight foot high wall. I told you my upper body strength was lacking, I could never climb up that rope in the Bryant High School gym more than a couple feet while I watched guys climbing with their feet straight out in front of them and with arm over arm climb straight up to the top ... man, that's something I could never do.

I had some fun at the grenade and small arms courses because the NCO's running them said I would not have to wait for the ROTC bunch and they would check me out. I tossed many hand grenades, fired hundreds of rounds of .45 caliber ammo in the M-3 sub-machine gun, .45 auto pistol and shot the .30 caliber Browning machine gun.

Corcoran jump boots were introduced by paratroop soldiers to the troops in C Battery and purchased for a modest amount. They were accepted regulation by the army at the time. They had a rigid-tipped I think steel tipped toe and well-made and extremely comfortable boots, more so than the standard issue combat boots. They took a keen shine and the Jump School guys taught the men how to build up a layer of polish that would take a quick shine and keep the boots fairly waterproof at the same time. I had two pair from then on a work pair and a dress pair with inside zippers for quick on and off. Up to that period they were the most comfortable boots I ever wore ... great ankle support and perfect for Speed Marches!

Now, with my basics completed, I returned to applying what I had learned at Fort Bliss and had to adapt to actual field use, no longer in a controlled school environment. I was in charge of two sections and needed to combine them to one Fire Control

Platoon with each man knowing his job as well as the other jobs in his section.

I left the Radar Section operation in complete control of Sergeant Backer who did a fine job in training his radar men and had little time for jokes. I learned that was just his personality. It prepared me for the similar personality of SFC Warren Burns, the RA radar section leader who would be joining the platoon for deployment to Korea, there must be something in the psyche of those radar men. It was somewhat of an introverted job anyhow, squinting into a PPI scope in a darkened radar van interior and keeping the radar well-tuned with constant and meticulous adjustments. Backer and his men were like a team of diagnosticians: "What was that glitch on the scope?" "Why was it there?" "Let us pull out the magnetron relay panel and see if it's the PPI driver adjustment." "Could moisture have affected the Servo motor adjustment we made yesterday?" "Yes, yes, pull that servo panel on the antenna base and check it out," quipped Backer...followed by, "Get out the TM's (Tech Manuals). "Find a target to track to verify," answered Corporal Osterwich. I left this radar crew alone. Hunter Air Force Base was nearby so there were always planes flying within the range of the radar.

Better to steer clear; as long as the radar was operational, I did not butt in. C Battery rarely needed the battalion radar mechanics to help get the radar back in operation. Backer also served as our Battery Radar Mechanic which we never really had until we went to Korea. "Sergeant Backer, have your men get up a little earlier so they can shave before head count in the morning." "Oh, yes, yes, Sergeant Gallagher, I will be sure to see to it." How the hell do you tell a guy like that, "By the way, Backer, you know you can get your khakis and fatigues washed and starched by the post laundry for only a few cents each." "Yes, yes, Sergeant Gallagher, I know and my men use the post laundry but I find the starch makes my uniforms too uncomfortable." "OK, OK, Backer. Keep the radar door closed when brass are in the area." "Yes, yes, Sergeant Gallagher." Gerry Backer was a great asset to Charlie Battery as long as he served with us.

The last time I saw Backer was in the mid 1960's. I was in Pharmaceutical sales and Lee was with me one afternoon while in my territory on the Upper East Side of Manhattan. This was Backer's neighborhood and we ran into him. I can still see him half-bending his tall and once again filled out frame to shake my little sweetheart Lee's hand and that familiar smile as he said, "Yes, yes, well how do you do, Mrs. Gallagher?" There the image vanishes. I do not remember Backer ever saying no to anyone.

Backer's only complaint as a soldier was his run in with Joe Zurla when O&S'ing and other functional duties. Zurla liked to harass Backer, it was just his way. I told Joe to ease up on Backer and Joe smiled "Oh hell, it's just in fun." "I didn't realize he was so sensitive," and Joe was smart enough to take it easier with Backer.

Technical knowledge of the equipment which, for its time was sophisticated and highly specialized, required an intelligent soldier to quickly learn and understand its operation. But it wasn't only knowing your specific job, it was the ability to work and function as a team that was most important. This was now my platoon and I saw right away that I had some great guys who needed to know the team was Charlie Battery. At the same time, I had to earn the respect of my men and that took more than just wearing the stripes and having the title.

Now the nucleus of the battery was still mainly the original NG's from New York but most of the men in the battery were draftees and some RA's. The first of the many calls for replacements to FECOM were already happening and many of the original NG's were already pipelined to Korea or put on notice by the time I reported back to Charlie Battery.

The battery lost two of the best officers we had, Lieutenants Byrnes and O'Rahilly, followed by Captain Kelly, Mr. Nicholetti, Sergeants Calvano, Scalfani, Meyer, and Privates Robinson, Quinn and Davids. Motor Section leader SFC John Zurla was now on notice. I would guess that fifty percent of the original NG officers and men were pipelined to Korea during our stay at Camp Stewart, most of whom were in the Gun platoon,

Commo section or motor section. No Fire Control personnel were pipelined.

Master Sergeant Bill Barker, the Gun Platoon Sergeant, was a great NCO and a great soldier. He was a marine vet who joined the 773rd back in 1948. He is remembered for his big voice and as an effective drill Sergeant. He taught Charlie Battery's out of step troopers how to step off smartly and keep in step to his cadence count and marching ditties that he learned in the Marine Corp.

One evening just before Zurla's departure to FECOM, we went to the NCO Club for a few beers. When we returned to our tent, all the Sergeants were fast asleep. Sure enough, there was Barker asleep lying on his back with heels together, toes apart at a 45 degree angle, both his arms held straight along his body sleeping at "Attention." Sergeant Bill Mauro told me and Zurla about the way Barker slept and at first we thought it was just a joke. Mauro also told me and Zurla that all Mauro had to do to waken Barker was just clap his hands and Barker would jump right out of bed. Comical, we thought, when we decided to electrocute Barker, who had a thing about electricity!

Zurla produced a length of harmless rope which we taped to an electric extension cord. "OK Gallagher, you attach the hot end of the wire to Barker's metal cot frame and I will plug the other end into the light socket," Zurla spoke in a not too quiet a whisper. He continued, "When he awakes and touches the metal frame he will get a real jolt of electricity." We saw no expression on Barker's face, just his easy-paced breathing. So again we repeated it, this time in a little bit louder whisper: "Attach the wire to his bed, etc. etc. etc." Still no rise from Barker. Now in an even louder whisper we again repeated, "Attach the hot end of the wire, etc. etc. etc." We noticed Barker blink a little and just as I was holding back a laugh, he sat up straight in his cot saying something to the effect of "Don't plug the wire in" just as John slapped both hands together making a sharp crack just like the instructors did at Fort Bliss to keep us on our toes when troubleshooting hot circuitry. No longer able to hold back my laughter I collapsed laughing when Top Kick Mauro yelled out "You guys better shut up and go to sleep ... we may have a Speed March tomorrow morning."

The next day Zurla left for FECOM so I had to keep on red alert awaiting Barker's counter attack; you never knew when it was coming. Thinking back, I believe it was really good training to keep us NCO's on our toes. Of course, any pranks against First Sergeant Mauro was strictly and definitely off limits.

I found out Barker put the corn flakes in my sack that first night so at chow that morning the top Sergeants had a good laugh at Barker's expense. "Don't screw with the master, Barker," as I pointed my finger at him like a lightning rod and BUZZZZED. "At ease Gallagher, don't you think I knew it was a fucking rope?" Barker was planning something, he was a great guy but not particularly creative. I noticed a few nights later one end of my cots legs were slightly bent waiting for me to collapse the bed when I sat down. I checked to make sure my shined Corcoran boots were not in the way and would not get scratched as I sat down on my cot and acted real annoyed and surprised when it collapsed. Barker and Caruana laughed like hell. I did not think this was only a diversion before he struck with the real prank but natural curiosity still kept me on silent alarm.

The course of training kept the 773rd out in the field almost constantly. Much of my time was spent on the advance detail accompanied by Barker. We were busy finding the coordinates on the map then, staking out my Fire Control equipment and Barker's four 90's and four quad mount .50 caliber machine guns, we worked as a team. When the battery arrived, we were busy directing the placement of the equipment and of course Davis was firing up his field kitchen in the bed of a deuce and a half.

As long as we still had our Fordham educated ROTC Lieutenant O'Rahilly, my job was easier. He was well-qualified, competent and well respected as an officer but unfortunately we lost him to FECOM. I was stuck with a platoon leader who would just walk away when the topography map and compass came out and disappeared completely when I set up the Aiming Circle (AC) tripod. I always saw Barker chuckling and shaking his head back and forth when I tried to explain the Aiming Circle to this new Lieutenant.

All the men in my platoon were only too eager to help explain to anyone new exactly what we were doing. Unfortunately, for our new lieutenant, it went in one ear and out the next. If he had any brains he would have applied himself and learned. All he had to say was, "Show me how to level and orient the aiming circle" and I would have been happy to show him and would have welcomed his help and made him an expert on the aiming circle. That is how I learned how to use the aiming circle by asking and then, doing it myself.

One thing I never learned to do was adjust the Azimuth Servo on the radar antenna mount when back sighting. At Fort Bliss the radars were already emplaced and O&S'd. When recently returned from Bliss I was not a bit ashamed to ask Corporal Osterwich a draftee from St. Louis, who adjusted the azimuth servo daily. He was more than happy to show me and that's how you learned by having a knowledgeable person show you and then doing it yourself.

During this stage of our training, the army introduced the Aggressor Force. This was a new concept in virtual combat training recently developed by the U.S. Army and gleaned from the experiences and failures in Korea. This special unit was led and staffed by recent Korean War returnees and helped prepare troops for duty in Korea. They were an eager beaver group of professional soldiers, expert in guerilla warfare and diversionary tactics with a main mission to destroy the artillery battery. Some of these troopers seen at the PX had the Ranger strip above their Third Army shoulder patch.

They were given a distinctive helmet and insignia and made to look as foreign as possible. They were expert at attacking and disappearing in the vast swamplands only to be waiting for the advanced party at the next new battery position. I will say it was kind of eerie to be alone in the bush setting up the Aiming Circle with the small advance party, always looking over our shoulders expecting to see the distinctive helmet atop an Aggressor peeking at us from behind a clump of palmetto palm and swamp grass. It

188

kept us all on alert, as opposed to the many times when, already staked out and waiting for the battery to arrive, we were just sitting around smoking and skylarking. Now we were all more thoughtful about what we were doing and a lot of this impacted us and served us well in Korea. Training at Stewart was now more intense and we were all much more serious about our training.

The surrounding area of tideland Georgia was in the middle of a thick white pine tree barren which attracted a *Piney* culture. For generations, the *Pineys* tapped the pine trees and established a cabin industry manufacturing turpentine. The soldiers would see a *Piney* driving an old beat up truck or walking alone carrying bags of supplies. They just ignored the soldiers and went on their way. They were quite mysterious and kept pretty much to themselves never seen in the company with those outside their own culture. While in the field and on many advanced detail training patrols, we would come upon a ramshackle cabin. Further inspection hinted that the shack may still be occupied. Still, I do not remember at any time ever seeing any occupants. One enticing myth was that these shacks were inhabited by scantily clad and lonely, sex-starved *Piney* women just waiting behind those half-opened doors for a soldier to enter ...that was never verified!

While writing this narrative and reliving the past, I think about these swampy Aggressors from the Georgia Pine Barrens. A smile appears on my face as I think about a secluded *Piney Shack* in the middle of nowhere with the door slightly opened.

The foliage in the outback areas of the reservation were overgrown from that humid climate making the Topographic maps sometimes obsolete. We had to reopen washed out trails and roads that appeared on the map but were no longer still there. In order to do this, we had to rely on the farm boys from the South who were in our battery. "Alabam'," was, you guessed right, an Alabama farmer. His real name is totally lost to me but his image is still there. He could start any motor in the battery no matter how wet in Georgia and no matter how cold in Korea. He drove the battalion bulldozer to dig the hole to conceal the radar in Korea and in Georgia, cut through the overgrown trails to make a corduroy road in the marsh land.

Building corduroy roads is a task soldiers accomplished going back to ancient times. Simply cutting down trees and cutting them trail wide and then placed on the ground next to each other they provided the traction for any wheel either ancient or modern. Somewhere along the way we discovered Primer Cord and the method to safely use the detonators. The cord looked like thin rope and came in coils. Attach a detonator then a quick wrap around a tree and a "Fire in the hole" warning shout for all onlookers to duck and a tree came down ready to be cut up or blown up to the correct sized lengths. I tried with SFC Phil Sayers, one of our gun commanders, to chop down a pine tree with the axe but gave up and instead used the primer cord. After that, all the axes were placed back on their racks on the vehicles.

Gun Commander Cruz was the most proficient "Cords Man." A Louisianan from New Orleans and miles from any farm, Cruz was the explosive expert in the battery and also one of the Jump School dropouts. His favorite subject was Cajun cookin'. This tall, impressive extrovert was well liked and respected by all, especially the guys in his gun crew. Cruz AKA "El Gato," also the name of his 90, was the first to suggest wrapping the primer cord and felling the tree in seconds instead of using the axe. This was before chain saws became popular. All the NCO's volunteered to blow up the trees and fortunately no one was ever hurt.

Every gun commander was seen with primer cord and detonators, ready to make corduroy roads even when we didn't need them to cross streams. I blew up a few trees myself but El Gato and his gun crew always made the best roads.

While in the field a driver may be ordered to drive back to Camp Stewart on a detail. If, he passed by a shrimp shack he would just park in the rear to blend in with the scenery and treat himself to a tasty meal and a cold drink. All army vehicles had their ID's stenciled in white paint on both bumpers. The Battery Commanders Jeep was marked "3A 773AA" "C1" denoting, 3rd Army, 773rd Antiaircraft Artillery Battalion C Battery Vehicle Number 1.

Fun in Jacksonville, Florida

In 1951 Camp Stewart was isolated from many diversions readily available at other bases. The nearest city of Savannah was 40 miles away, accessible only for those with a car or those who could afford an expensive taxi ride. Buses served the area but not for an evening's pass because it was just too far from Savannah. The only place to go was Hinesville, a tiny hamlet with scant diversion. Camp Stewart in the fall/winter of 1951-52 was a grim place. I remember an occasional softball game but sometime the field was even too wet for a ball game.

For a Saturday night fling, a soldier dressed in a class "A" uniform which in summer meant khakis with a tie. He walked to Hinesville, had a basket of shrimp, a couple of beers and that was about it for all ranks. Even the nearest Midway Diner required a car because it was too long a walk to get there from camp.

I am sure that Hinesville, Georgia, is a vibrant community today and Fort Stewart, being a major permanent base, is now a very decent installation with many services and diversions for the troops and their families. But my memory of 1951 Hinesville is very uninviting, just a couple of worn down old gray faded pine wood structures. One was a bar room always overflowing with guys in army uniforms, and another was a smaller structure, again a worn-out gray pinewood store selling military uniforms and accoutrements. The other was the same bare wood construction where there was always a line of hungry customers waiting to buy, for only a dollar, fried shrimp or fried chicken baskets overflowing with delicious Hush Puppies. That is also the very first time I can remember seeing food served in a basket.

I have an old pay card somewhere among my mementos. My pay at the time as an SFC with four years longevity was $160 a month and no place to spend it. Although I recall seeing army training film I do not remember ever going to a proper movie while at Stewart and do not believe there was even a post theater which is normally found on all army posts. The troops only diversion was the Post Exchange (PX) or a walk to Hinesville, to stand on a line for a shrimp basket, stand on another line for a beer at the beer hall and then walk back to the tent city. The walk all the way back to your tent would again perk up your appetite and then you must wait until dawn for breakfast.

Davis was the only one I remember who had a car and he lived off post with an old girlfriend from 1941 and he came and went as he pleased. There was a definite lack of presence of any pretty sweet-smelling females and this was noticed by all the G.I.'s. The few local girls who worked in Hinesville were under close protection by their Pa's and big brothers who drove pickup trucks all with guns hanging in the back window. We heard stories about soldiers climbing out bedroom windows with their pants and boots in their hands as a jealous hubby was aiming his shotgun at them. This actually happened to someone I knew, name withheld. He had to scramble out the bedroom window to the G.I. vehicle parked in the rear of the shack and make a hasty retreat back to camp hoping the shooter couldn't read the unit identification on the rear bumper.

Sergeant First Class Frank Mistretta was one of my buddies since 1948 and we planned to get a weekend pass to get away from all the soldiers and hitch-hike our way to Jacksonville, Florida. Over 100 miles away, Jacksonville was a sailor town where my brother John had a few liberties. This gave us the idea that maybe an army uniform would be a novelty to the girls there. We made our plans and were off to highway 17. This was ages before interstate I-95 cut its way between Maine and Florida. We hitched rides many times before at summer camp on Cape Cod and felt confident we could do it again in Georgia. Most of the way was on the bus route anyway so we could always catch a bus. In those days and in that area the bus would stop anyplace for anyone who had the fare.

The first leg was still on blue highways in Georgia so with tooth brush, razor and weekend passes in our pockets we were off. One ride let us out someplace at a crossroad to nowhere so we just walked and hitched as we went along. Looking down the road, we viewed an oncoming vehicle coming our way which became a pickup truck and rapidly approaching. We were getting ready to jump in the back as it got closer and slowed down. We noticed what looked like a friendly group of young teens in the back of the pickup and thought it would stop to pick us up. Instead, it just revved up the engine and in a cloud of dust it swerved almost hitting us. The pickup went on its way with all the teens laughing and shouting profanities at us. To make matters worse the bastards hauled firecrackers at us as they sped by.

With no further excitement, we were let out of a car near the Jacksonville Greyhound bus terminal. We thanked the driver and went into the terminal washroom to clean off the grime of the road and refresh ourselves. We both got a boot shine. We did notice the complete absence of any army uniforms which made us feel better already.

It being our first time in Jacksonville, we walked down the main street and passed a movie house with *The Steel Helmet* in black and white lettering on the marquee. We later found out the movie was about G.I.'s fighting in Korea. We stopped into an inviting bar for a sandwich and a beer. When we entered, we were startled to see the bar full of sailors drinking and eating, cigarette smoke circling up to the ceiling and the juke box blaring. As we entered, the talking seemed to stop and all eyes were upon us. We thought for an instant we would have to fight our way out of this sailors' bar that we were invading in our army khakis.

I forgot what we ate but remember the beers as they came fast and furious and the sailors did not let us pay for anything. There were plenty of smiles and those sailors made us feel like heroes. Apparently, they all saw the matinee of *The Steel Helmet* and could not help enough to steer us to Jacksonville Beach where they said the girls will love us. With smiles of thanks we finally said "so long" to the friendly sailors and made our way to Jacksonville Beach.

We did meet a couple of girls who were on the beach bathing and could not help but notice their cute shapes in their bathing suits. They smelled so nice with suntan lotion and perfume and we felt good about our decision to come to Jacksonville. We spent the entire day with them. Later that evening, they invited us to stay overnight in their small apartment. Except for maybe a squeeze and a few hugs and kisses I don't remember going any further. They cooked dinner for us and I think we bought the food.

I remember a lot of laughs and smiles on everyone's faces and I don't recall anything beyond a happy time with those two young and pretty southern girls. The trip back to camp is still dim in my memory and I seem to remember taking a bus and then a taxi back to camp to be sure we would make reveille Monday morning. I don't remember a Speed March that Monday morning but even if there was, we both would still be smiling. Memories fade about our plans for return trips to Jacksonville because of an unforeseen set of circumstances.

A Trip to Savannah

After buddy Frank Mistretta and I discovered the sweet diversion of Jacksonville Beach, Supply Sergeant Joe Caruana went home to Woodside on a special short leave to purchase a new 1951 Black Ford Victoria two-door hardtop. When he arrived back at camp after an all-night drive from New York City, Joe was excited to show us his new car. We all admired the shiny new Ford and couldn't wait to take a ride in the car. Joe said he would be happy to take a trip to Savannah that evening for a nice dinner and a few drinks and hustled into his supply room to catch up on some paper work that supply Sergeants always had that were requisitions and inventory related.

First Sergeant Mauro and I were invited to accompany him and we were quite excited about the prospect. It was a Saturday and I polished my collar brass and my brass buckle and put a nice shine on my low quarter shoes. I thought about what I was going to order for dinner that evening. As evening approached, the three of us stepped into Joe's car that still had that fresh new car smell and we were on our way to Savannah.

Joe told us about how great it was to drive all the way from New York in his new car and the prospects of now having wheels to take us away from camp from time to time was exciting. Joe said he was fine to drive anywhere at any time. Plans for weekend passes were discussed for trips to Tybee and Jekyll Islands and other barrier islands we all heard about from the southern boys.

We three enjoyed the luxurious ride in the auto industry's first two-door hardtop. The ride on Route 17 was an interesting but not breathtaking trip through tideland Georgia, meandering through swampy tidewater terrain with water on either side of the road almost all the way to Savannah. In Savannah, we had a couple of beers and a sumptuous meal we all thoroughly enjoyed at an upbeat Savannah restaurant. I had a steak dinner and Bill and Joe had a seafood dinner being in the heart of the Southeastern seafood area.

The dinners we three Sergeants enjoyed were a far cry from the chow Davis had to serve in his mess hall. We strolled around town and an image survives showing First Sergeant Bill Mauro asking Joe if he was OK to drive back after being up all night? His answer was "Hell yes, I like night driving" he assured us and, was looking forward to the drive back to camp.

First Sergeant Mauro sat in the back and I sat in the front next to the driver as Joe settled down behind the wheel. Somewhere along the way Bill dozed off in the back seat and I slumped in the front seat and also fell asleep. The driver finally succumbed to his driving odyssey and fell asleep while still at the wheel.

As he slept, the car sideswiped an oncoming trailer truck loaded with grapefruit. The Ford swerved to the right off the road and into the tideland swamp water. I remember being poked by someone shouting "Get out, get out," and noticed my uniform from the waist down was wet and I was sitting in a pool of water, the car was turned on its side halfway in the water. It seemed strange to see Joe now looking down at me with a wild look on his face and yelling, "Open the door!" Not being able to open the door enough to climb out, I turned to Joe and urged him to push open his door and climb out as fast as possible. In the back seat, Mauro was also shouting to the driver to open his door and move out.

Joe finally opened his door as both passengers pushed him out and we all climbed up the bank not knowing if the car would burst into flames and maybe even explode. It all seemed unreal and dream-like as our brains started piecing the events together realizing we just had a serious accident. As we three scrambled up the embankment, we saw the road was already aglow with flares.

To avoid a head-on collision which probably would have killed the three of us, the driver turned sharply to his right and the rig jack-knifed and both trailer and truck overturned with grapefruit scattered all over Route 17. Looking down at the totally wrecked new 1951 Ford Victoria half submerged in swamp water verified in an instantly reawakened brain that we were in a wreck. I do not remember any pain until Joe looked at me and frantically shouted something like "Your face, Vinny are you OK?" I touched my face and noticed my hand was bloody. Glancing down, I saw blood stains all over my khaki uniform shirt confirming my injury. The pain still somewhat vague, the shock started to set in after seeing the blood and feeling the throbbing pain now becoming more acute. I remember seeing Bill and Joe talking to whom I first thought were Georgia State Police. They were instead speaking to the local Sheriff and his deputy.

There standing on the shoulder of the road was the typical southern sheriff often portrayed in the movies as fat, tobacco chewing, slovenly attired and wearing a crushed sweat-stained Stetson hat. There he was, straight out of a grade-B movie, standing right in front of us. His badge was pinned on an opened loose fitting jacket, his fat belly hanging over his pistol belt. Standing next to the sheriff was a more orderly looking, soft spoken and what proved to be a more compassionate deputy. The sheriff asked to see all the soldiers' I.D.'s and drivers' licenses and discovering all three were Yankees from New York, and some with even foreign-sounding names and worst of all, "Eye'talian names." "Wut kanda naaames is Mau-ro and Caru-aana?"

When it was determined that Joe was the driver, the sheriff charged him with reckless driving. He then asked how much money we had. If memory serves, the balance of forty or fifty dollars after the evening's festivities was all we three soldiers could show. The sheriff's comment was "Wall that's agonna be the fine fur reckless drivin', you boys are lucky to still be a-walkin'."

Without any written warrant, the sheriff simply took the cash, turned his head to spit the juice from his cud of chewing

196

tobacco and put the money in his pocket. All the while the Top Sergeant requested the sheriff to radio for some medical assistance for "this injured soldier." The Sheriff's comment was, "Midway Diner is about a mile down the road, he's still a-walkin' ain't he?" Hearing that comment, I proceeded to walk down Route 17 facing the traffic now building up and headlights shining in my eyes and, barely making out the lights of the diner in the distance. I heard a horn behind me and turned to see the deputy slowly driving my way. "Hop in soldier, I'll drive you to the diner."

When we arrived at the diner, I thanked the deputy and exited the car. By this time, it was almost dawn and my mouth ached. The waitresses all screamed as I entered the diner and they saw the bloody mess. I went into some additional shock when I saw myself in the mirrors with blood all over my pants and shirt. "I must throw this uniform away," was the only thought I can remember at the time. Someone called Camp Stewart and my next image found me sitting in a vehicle, the pain worsening as the M.P.'s hastily drove through the early morning fog of tideland Georgia and back to Camp Stewart.

After some cursory patching up the only damage was some loss of blood, two broken teeth and a mouth wound and I was returned to C Battery by the M.P.'s. No x-rays or any additional treatment is remembered. The medics did give me some medication to relieve the pain.

I have no recall about how Joe and Bill ever got back to camp. I do remember the First Sergeant was unhurt but Joe's left foot was injured and later healed. From that day on, the Supply Sergeant was known by all the troops in C Battery as "Grapefruit Caruana," a title he hated.

Lucky for me, the medical officer for the 773rd was Lieutenant Bernard Josephson, a New York City dentist who accompanied the battalion to Camp Stewart serving as the Medical Officer. Josephson took some x-rays, treated the wound, and administered some pain medication. My wounds healed just fine. Josephson thankfully had excellent dental skills and fitted me with caps for my two broken teeth. He did an excellent job because they lasted all through my service in the States and Korea. The temporary caps were finally replaced with permanent caps by a civilian dentist in 1954.

Joe was pretty sorry for what happened and told me if I needed anything to just ask him. Joe was a good friend and drove me many times to West 62nd for Monday night drill. Joe lived on 63rd Street in Woodside and I lived on 59th. I assured him I was fine and after Doc Josephson patched me up with two new teeth, I told Joe not to worry. I know he felt terrible both about the car and my injury.

Two images stand out in my memory. First, remembering when reporting back to C Battery from Fort Bliss and approaching Camp Stewart's main gate, I saw on display in front of the M.P. booth a totally wrecked automobile. The vehicle was wearing a warning sign about safe driving and a skull and crossbones indicating a death had occurred and a number showing the number of accidents and fatalities on the roads to and from Camp Stewart.

Memory Two was to later see the totally wrecked Black Ford Victoria there at the very same spot with the indentation of my upper front teeth plainly marked on the unpadded metal dashboard of the car. This was of course before seat belts, padded dash boards and air bags. There was a number on the sign for the number of accidents but this time no skull and crossbones.

It took me many years later to realize how the three of us were blessed and touched by the Lord to have survived that crash. I believe the prayers of my Mother and Father who loved the Lord and loved me were answered that night along Route 17 in Georgia.

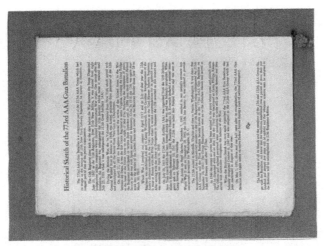

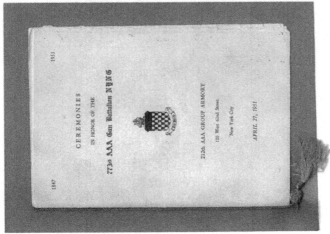

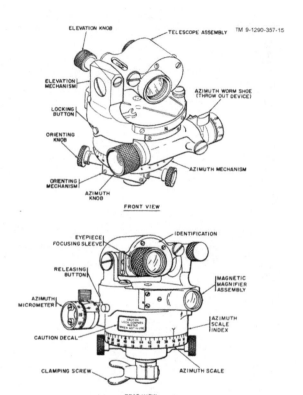

M1 Aiming Circle
(US Army Training Manual TM 9-1200-357-15)

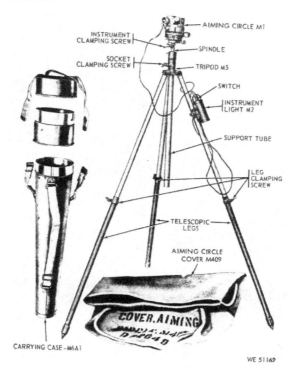

TM 9-1290-357-15

M1 Aiming Circle Tripod and Carrying Case
(US Army Training Manual TM 9-1290-357-15)

On Army Field Forces Maneuvers as storm clouds gathered remember "The Rain Makers." We were O&S'ing with Osterwich adjusting Azimuth Servo and Zurla back sighted Radar with the Tracking Head. Army Photog asked me to grab the phone and jump in to balance the shot. We finished just in time as the clouds burst and we ducked into the radar van. You can tell my SFC stripes were brand new.

SIGNAL CORP RADAR   SCR584
Wikipedia Public Domain

Phonetic Alphabet Used Prior to 1956

A ABLE	J JIG	S SUGAR
B BAKER	K KING	T TARE
C CHARLIE	L LOVE	U UNCLE
D DOG	M MIKE	V VICTOR
E EASY	N NAN	W WILLIAM
F FOX	O OBOE	X XRAY
G GEORGE	P PETER	Y YOKE
H HOW	Q QUEEN	Z ZEBRA
I ITEM	R ROGER	- DASH

Phonetic Alphabet Effective 1956
for all NATO Nations

Letter	Word	Pronunciation
A	ALFA	AL FAH
B	BRAVO	BRAH VOH
C	CHARLIE	CHAR LEE (or) SHAR LEE
D	DELTA	DELL TAH
E	ECHO	ECK OH
F	FOXTROT	FOKS TROT
G	GOLF	GOLF
H	HOTEL	HOH TELL
I	INDIA	IN DEE AH
J	JULIETT	JEW LEE ETT
K	KILO	KEY LOW
L	LIMA	LEE MAH
M	MIKE	MIKE
N	NOVEMBER	NO VEM BER
O	OSCAR	OSS CAH
P	PAPA	PAH PAH
Q	QUEBEC	KEH BECK
R	ROMEO	ROW ME OH
S	SIERRA	SEE AIR RAH
T	TANGO	TANG GO
U	UNIFORM	YOU NEE FORM (or) OO NEE FORM
V	VICTOR	VIK TAH
W	WHISKEY	WISS KEY
X	XRAY	ECKS RAY
Y	YANKEE	YANG KEY
Z	ZULU	ZOO LOO

The Aggressor Forces training continued into the 1960's. For realism the Army provided more elaborate foreign looking uniforms and insignias and aggressors were re-named Trigonists with an insignia of a green pyramid on a white background. *Photo Courtesy Rickey Robertson Collection*

When in the field scouting a new battery location, we had our eyes open and it seemed those alien-looking helmets would pop up behind every palmetto bush. I think it did help to keep everyone focused on the training. The aggressor forces were increased and the army found the training worthwhile.

205

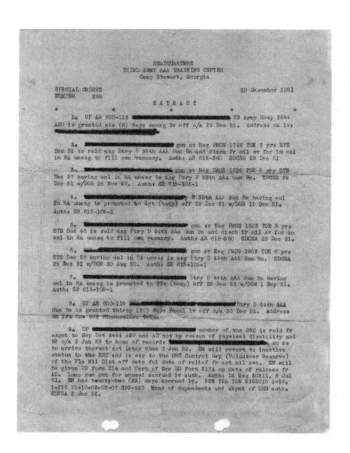

3rd Army Special Order

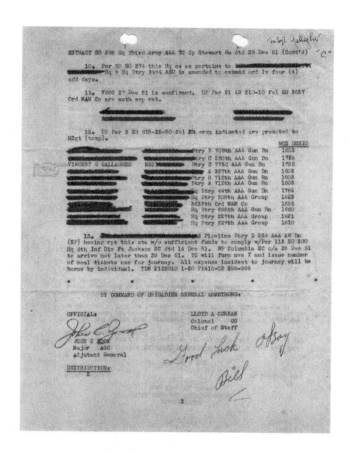

EXTRACT SO 268 Hq Third Army AAA TC Cp Stewart Ga dtd 28 Dec 51 (Cont'd) "C"

10. Par 60 SO 274 this Hq es as pertains to ~~XXXXXXXXXXXXXXXXXXXXXX~~ ~~XXXXXXXX~~ Hq & Hq Btry 3444 ASU is amended to extend ord lv four (4) add days.

11. VOCG 27 Dec 51 is confirmed. UP Par 21 AR 210-10 fol EM 3637 Ord MAM Co are auth sep rat.

~~XXXXXXXXXXXXXXXXX~~   ~~XXXXXXXXXXXXXXXX~~
                                        ~~XXXXXXXXXXXXX~~

12. UP Par 3 SR 615-25-50 fol EM men indicated are promoted to MSgt (temp).

			MOS DESIG
~~XXXXXXXXXX~~	~~XXXXXXXX~~ Btry B 708th AAA Gun Bn		1603
~~XXXXXXXX~~	~~XXXX~~ Btry C 260th AAA Gun Bn		1725
VINCENT G GALLAGHER	602 ~~XXXX~~ Btry C 773d AAA Gun Bn		1725
~~XXXXXXXXX~~	~~XXXXXXXXXXX~~ A 337th AAA Gun Bn		1603
~~XXXXXXXXX~~	~~XXXXXXXXXXX~~ Btry B 712th AAA Gun Bn		1603
~~XXXXXXXXX~~	~~XXXXXXXXXXX~~ Btry A 712th AAA Gun Bn		1603
~~XXXXXXXXX~~	~~XXXXXXXXXX~~ Hq Btry 44th AAA Gun Bn		1784
~~XXXXXXXXX~~	~~XXXXXXXXXX~~ Hq Btry 206th AAA Group		1823
~~XXXXXXXXX~~	~~XXXXXXX~~ 3637th Ord MAM Co		1585
~~XXXXXXXXX~~	~~XXXXXXXXXX~~ Hq Btry 698th AAA Gun Bn		1660
~~XXXXXXXXX~~	~~XXXXXXXXXX~~ Hq Btry 227th AAA Group		1621
~~XXXXXXXXX~~	~~XXXXXXXXXX~~ Hq Btry 227th AAA Group		1610

13. ~~XXXXXXXXXXXXXXXXXXXXXXXX~~ S Pipeline Btry D 23d AAA AW Bn (SP) having rpt this sta w/o sufficient funds to comply w/Par 113 SO 300 Hq 8th Inf Div Ft Jackson SC dtd 14 Dec 51. WP Columbia SC o/a 28 Dec 51 to arrive not later than 29 Dec 51. TC will furn nec T and issue number of meal tickets nec for journey. All expense incident to journey will be borne by individual. TDN 2122010 1-20 P1410-02 395-999

* * * * * *

BY COMMAND OF BRIGADIER GENERAL ARMSTRONG:

OFFICIAL: LLOYD A CORRAN
                                         Colonel   GS
                                         Chief of Staff
JOHN C KOOK
Major   AGC
Adjutant General

DISTRIBUTION:
E

2

Promoted to Master Sergeant

RCAT aided by built-in parachute. Upon concussion from the exploding artillery the engines would stop and the parachute deployed. Ground crews operated the RCAT by remote control while in flight. The retrieval personnel were positioned out of harm's way in either boats on water or trucks on land and then stand off until it was safe to retrieve the RCAT for repair and reuse.

Chapter 6

Fort Hamilton, Brooklyn

My memories of Camp Stewart seem to just fade away and I don't remember too much about those closing days except a few highlights. Towards the completion of our Field Forces maneuvers, an announcement came down from 3rd Army Headquarters that the Master Artilleryman's examination was offered and I took the test at Camp Stewart headquarters. I arrived at a room with numerous older Sergeants First Class smoking and twisting their hats as they appeared nervous about taking the test. It was not that important to me. I went into the classroom, sat down, took the lengthy exam, turned in my papers, and went back to C Battery. Some time passed and an order was given to me by Master Sergeant Bill Barker who was acting First Sergeant. The order verified my new rank of Master Sergeant and I received a copy of the order noting Bill Barker's best wishes.

The 90's and all the heavy equipment were already placed on flatcars and headed north. We turned in all our vehicles Jeeps, ¾ ton and 2 ½ ton trucks and were told we would be receiving all new army vehicles with heaters and automatic transmissions when we arrived at our new destination. The battalion was keeping the tracked CAT prime movers to tow the 90's.

We now had to fill in the remaining time. The Battalion S-3 training and operations section created training classes right out of the basic FM's (Field Manuals) and then sent monitors out with clipboards to check to make sure all of the battery's complied.

My recall brings me back to the Fire Control Platoon of about 30 men seated in front of me on a grassy patch of ground with their backs towards the sun. With army approved lesson plan in my hands and a few troopers standing by as a demonstration team. Standing to the rear was my Assistant Instructor, holding a copy of the lesson plan. I would share this duty between my two section chiefs, Sergeant Backer and Sergeant First Class Klopfer who also helped prepare the daily lesson plan.

These classes were held a distance from the battery area so a monitor could observe but not necessarily walk all the way out to get a closer look. The lesson plans were prepared to conform with the army MOI (Methods of Instruction)...Introduction, Presentation, Explanation, Demonstration, Application, Discussion and Critique. I faced east, the Assistant Instructor faced west and my demo team would be posted to observe other critical points of the compass. This was necessary to cover the approach of any monitor to give the instructor a timely alert. Satisfied all points were covered, I opened with, "OK, Raise your hand first to be recognized and then ask your question. No shouting out questions. Animal, Vegetable or Mineral. Go ahead, Fenenwald, it was your turn yesterday." This was after all the training and maneuvers were successfully completed and the army just had to fill the empty hours so, why not make it fun and entertaining. It seemed all of Charlie Battery's Fire Control Platoon enjoyed Twenty Questions rather than hearing me expound about redundant topics they already knew.

If any of my "lookouts" spotted someone heading our way, I had plenty of time to order a Demonstrator standing by to go through the motions as I explained using a pointer. "Boy! Charlie Battery Fire Control Platoon is really on the ball" or so it would seem from 100 yards away. No need to walk all the way out to check thought the monitor, making notations on the checklist and besides, it is getting close to chow time anyway and that would be a long walk back to the Battalion mess hall." Sergeant Backer would ask me, "Why do you always hold our classes so far away from the battery area?" "Isn't it obvious to you, Sergeant Backer?" "Oh, yes, yes, now I get it!"

We passed all the army field forces tests for our proficiency in antiaircraft artillery firing, direct fire and field artillery firing and we would soon be saying goodbye to Camp Stewart. The troops boarded a troop train but, some privileged Officers and NCO's were allowed to travel by car and that is how I left Camp Stewart. With the Battery Commander, my platoon leader and the First Sergeant. We all shared driving my Lieutenants car overnight and arrived in Fort Hamilton, Brooklyn the following evening.

The only memory I have of that trip was the continuous sound of, "Animal, Vegetable or Mineral" from my favorite brain game, Twenty Questions. It started off after we became bored looking at the view along Route 17 as we drove through the tidelands of Georgia and South Carolina. Remember, there was no I-95 Interstate Highway in those days and we thought Twenty Questions would keep everyone awake. By the time we arrived in Brooklyn, we covered subjects from Davis's girlfriend to the chicken back a K.P. Private put in Master Sergeant Barker's mess kit after removing the big juicy breast, when he saw it was his platoon Sergeant to, the cartoon of Miss Swamp Stewart, to the beauty at the Shrimp Shack, to the crown of thorns on Jesus' head…that is one I guessed. I can't tell you how many hours I spent with Lee and our boys John and Vincent playing that favorite game. I'm still ready, anyone want to play? "Animal, Vegetable or Mineral!" I'll even let you go first.

The ride to Brooklyn and Fort Hamilton was non-stop. On arrival, we were met and directed to battery headquarters and barracks in the old 1920's era coast artillery dated wooden barracks... The period barracks were luxurious compared to the tent city of Camp Stewart. We were in for another pleasant surprise when we ate in the Fort Hamilton enlisted personnel mess hall. It was cafeteria style with seating at comfortable four-person tables. We all chuckled seeing Sergeant Davis in the mess hall all dressed up in a cook's white uniform. He didn't look so happy taking orders from a wiry young second lieutenant mess officer and there was no smoking allowed while wearing that white cooks uniform. "Geez, Davis" cried Barker the Gun Platoon Sergeant, "You look just like a Medic in them whites. I thought for a minute ya gonna give us a *Short Arm Inspection.*" If you cannot guess what that inspection might be, ask someone.

Fort Hamilton was a country club army post that was unfamiliar to those of us in the 773rd. The grounds were maintained park-like, avenues of beautiful country-style private homes with steps leading to white wrap around porches. These homes were surrounded by flowered shrubs and stately shade trees that blocked out the nearby commerce of Brooklyn. Neat little black and white signs were posted on the lawn in front of each home: "Colonel J. Jones," "Major B. Bailey," "Lieutenant Colonel J. Johns," and so on. These charming homes were provided by the army for all the top brass and their families while working at First Army Headquarters in New York City. Shhh...no rowdies and no cussing and you better get used to saluting anything that walked. Was this wise to put the 773rd within eyesight and earshot of this special high-level post with all this desk-bound brass? Man, you better have the proper uniform on when you went to chow and your brass better be polished. We would soon find out how well the 773rd fit in here and it wouldn't take very long.

The mission for the battalion was to join the network of many air defense artillery units deployed throughout the metropolitan New York City area. These units were all part of the USARADCOM (US Army Air Defense Command) and NORAD (North American Air Defense Command). This was in conjunction with the US Air Force Tactical wing of interceptor planes, the early warning Navy picket ships and the DEW line, the arctic early warning radar defense shared with Canada. War with the Soviet Union against the western powers was considered a likely possibility and a first strike air attack on North America was expected over the North Pole, the shortest distance from Russia. For once, the U.S. was prepared with our military together with all our western allies on alert throughout the world.

Each firing battery was assigned a gun site position in a metropolitan area with the least amount of interference with normal day to day activity within a given community. Two batteries were sent to the boondocks of Staten Island, this was before the later building boom on the island when there was still plenty of wide open spaces and even wooded areas. Another battery was sent to Canarsie in Brooklyn along the Belt Parkway, hidden by the marsh grass. This left Headquarters and C Battery with the prime location to remain in Fort Hamilton.

Our battery enjoyed all the conveniences, including warm clean barracks with plenty of hot water to enjoy a daily shower and shave. There was great chow and all the benefits of diversion were offered to the troops both on and off post. We were happy campers and Charlie Battery set up on ground right in Fort Hamilton and only a short dash from our barracks whenever air alerts were sounded.

The site was also directly across from the nurses' and WAC quarters and far enough away to respect the women's privacy, or so the desk-bound planners at Fort Hamilton thought. They were never in an artillery outfit equipped with high power telescopes on all the equipment.

I did not know the guys were getting an eyeful every day but I noticed soldiers lingering on the tracking head, and I walked over with an inquisitive look on my face. Recently promoted Sergeant Joe Zurla now, M-9 Director range section leader ordered, "Kinzer, let Sergeant Gallagher look through the elevation scope." Instead I simply looked through the azimuth scope. To my surprise, I saw brassieres and panties. I checked the Azimuth scope orientation reference point written on the side of the tracking head and saw printed in block letters for quick reference, "Azimuth Green Flag Post XXXX Mils." The flag post was directly over the women's bathroom window. I smiled at Joe Zurla and told him to change the orienting point. "I don't care what the guys track on the scopes but, orienting every morning and putting it in writing is just too obvious." All the guys laughed and said, "Yeah…it is too obvious." We did not think anyone did anything terribly wrong.

I did not know about the 90's and when I told Barker about the eyeful the Fire Control men were getting he said, "Son of a bitch, I knew it didn't look right," as we both walked over to talk to his gun commanders and checked each gun's azimuth orienting point to see for ourselves. Barker yelled, "Don't you think someone would notice the four 90's pointing at the female bathroom every morning?" "Change the orienting point now and point it at something on the other side of the Belt Parkway, and away from the nurse's quarters. Then remove the scopes and put them back in their storage boxes." "Gallagher, I hope this don't screw us up here. This is good duty at Hamilton."

Even on 24/7 alert the guys could go to the PX to get some refreshment, do a little shopping, borrow a book from the post library, play various sports, it was a great post with several movie houses all within a short bus ride from Fort Hamilton. The NCO Club was high end and all the faces here were happy ones. Passes on a rotational basis allowed the men to dress in a Class "A" uniform and take a short walk to Fourth Avenue just outside the main gate, with plenty of good places to eat and many friendly taverns and neighborhood bars with local folks happy to chat and enjoy a drink with a soldier. After all, Fort Hamilton was a good neighbor to the locals and a profitable one for the businesses. Also, in almost every direction the troopers looked, they were surrounded by attractive females returning the men's smiles.

We heard plenty of stories about the barren, isolated gun sites where A, B and D Batteries were living and I visited them myself. I was glad to be driven back to Fort Hamilton. They spent 24/7 in field uniforms on site with only a shower truck to Hamilton each night to take a few men at a time to take showers. There was no other place for the men to go.

Let me introduce Private First Class White Elk to you. This of course is not his real name but it is close enough and you will meet the real soldier. He was a regular army volunteer from the Southwest and his family lived on an Indian reservation. He was a gunner in the Quad mount machine gun section and back at Camp Stewart, every target in his gun sight was hit when firing at the range. His uniform was always neat and clean and he was very well liked and respected in the machine gun section. His boss, my pal Sergeant First Class Mistretta, always spoke very highly of him. White Elk had only one shortcoming. He liked his beer a little too much.

Back at Stewart on every pay day, he dressed in his Class A uniform with his brass well-polished and walked out to Hinesville to enjoy his chicken or shrimp baskets with his buddies in the machine gun section. They would all go next door to the bar for drinks and White Elk would have to stay until he had his fill. His buddies would urge him to return with them but, he said he was fine and would see them later. The next morning, White Elk would be standing tall at reveille so they learned there was no need for concern about their comrade. At Stewart, the M.P.'s got to know White Elk and would give him a ride back to camp and more than once he would sleep it off at the guard house. He would get up the next A.M. and the M. P.'s would simply give him a ride back to Charlie Battery. This gave him plenty of time to change into the proper field uniform and smartly answer with a strong "YO" when his name was called at head count. He was one of the best soldiers in the battery. During training at Stewart, he never gave anyone trouble. He performed his duties honorably as a soldier and all his periodic reports on his record showed "Performance as a Soldier, Excellent." In Stewart, White Elk made Soldier of the Month many times but, the most frequent winner was my Astoria pal PFC Bob Dema, one of the sharpest soldiers in the battery.

During my service ending in the sixties I saw alcoholism in the army across the range of age, race and rank. Sadly, the Army neglected this sickness by just ignoring and accepting it.

The first pay day at Fort Hamilton, PFC White Elk dressed in his Class A uniform and proceeded to the many taverns, cafes and bars along Fourth Avenue just outside the Fort Hamilton main gate. My memory is now focused on the court martial charges which read.

"PFC White Elk walked through the front gate on his return to Fort Hamilton at 23:00 hours," quoting the M.P. on duty at the gate. The M.P. further said, "PFC White Elk said hello to me and I said hello back." The M.P. continued by stating, "PFC White Elk was properly dressed and did not seem to be drunk." That was all the M.P. had to say about him. To get to his barrack located at the rear of Fort Hamilton and close to the old coast artillery gun placements near the Belt Parkway, White Elk would have to pass in front of the entire row of homes of the high-ranking officers.

He apparently entered one of these homes without permission, walked upstairs to the second floor and found the bathroom. The Colonel's wife followed with her statement, "I was awakened by some noises and thought I heard water running in the bathroom so I got out of bed and went into the bathroom. There, lying in the bathtub totally naked, was PFC White Elk fast asleep with the water still running almost to overflow. His clothing was thrown all over the bathroom floor. I turned off the water faucet and my husband called the M.P.'s."

The last time I saw White Elk was in Korea where he was serving in an M-19 Twin 40 mm self-propelled unit. I remember his smile when I told him the battery followed him here to Korea. He asked about his old section leader SFC Frank Mistretta and I told him Mistretta was transferred just before the battalion left for the Far East and he was not with us. "Hey, White Elk, have you been drinking?" I asked. "No Sarge, I don't think I will ever drink anymore." He was bundled up in a winter parka so I couldn't see if he made Corporal which I hoped he had. "*Sayonara*, White Elk," I said as I jumped into my jeep and heard him call out "See you, Sarge!" I also hoped he was true to his word about not having anything more to drink.

Within only days of White Elk's departure, a few of us sergeants went out to Fourth Avenue one evening for a few beers. It was just after both SFC Caruana and First Sergeant Mauro were notified of a transfer. They were relieved from duty and just waiting for their orders. Caruana's replacement, RA Sergeant First Class Van Ness, just returned from duty in Germany and was already at C Battery. Master Sergeant Barker joined us and off we went to have a drink to say goodbye to Caruana and Mauro and to welcome Van Ness to the battery. We returned at a reasonable hour and stopped off at the latrine before hitting the sack. I looked in the big wash sink and floating in a tub full of water was a pair of combat boots. Caruana laughed when he saw them until he noticed that his name code was written on the inside lining. "Some son of a bitch put my boots in the laundry tub," Joe shouted.

My clothing and gear code was G-4XXX, denoting the first initial of my last name and the last four digits of my serial number. Every soldier's clothing had his code on the inside trouser waist bands, shirt collars and on all clothing and gear.

Caruana was wild with anger. I told him to just take his boots out of the sink and put them on the floor under his cot to dry. He was leaving in only a few more days and his duty in C Battery was over. The announcement was made the next morning that if the guilty party did not turn himself in, the entire battery would be ordered on a forced march with full field packs and weapons after chow at 18:00 hours (6 P.M.). We Sergeants spoke to Caruana and he stubbornly insisted, "Bullshit, I want to know who did it." Unfortunately, the Battery Commander did not exercise good leadership judgment and allowed this episode to escalate out of control.

At 18:00 hours (6 P.M.), C Battery lined up in front of the barracks in full field uniform, steel helmets, field packs, with their weapons at "Sling Arms." Not a smile was found on any soldier's face. Sergeant Caruana and the battery officers and warrant officers were all locked in a meeting in the orderly room while the battery waited outside hoping that the march would be cancelled at the last minute. Barker went into the orderly room and swiftly returned with a look of gloom on his face.

Master Sergeant Barker stood in front of the battery and commanded first, with the preparatory command, "Batry...Atten," followed by the command of execution "Hut," and a hundred heels clicked together. Next, "Ri it, fa-hace." "Forward, harch, hut, toop, threep, four, hut, toop, threep, four," in his loud bass voice. The Battery smartly marched off with Barker leading followed by the guidon bearer carrying the red artillery guidon flowing in the breeze with yellow lettering "C" above and "773rd" below the crossed cannon artillery emblem. We didn't have to advertise, everyone knew who we were. The cadence broke the calm silence of this quiet army post as windows were opened and doors flung aside and all eyes were on these olive-drab artillery troops marching on the road along the beautifully groomed lawns and promenades. I hoped Barker would not follow with "cadence count" and the battery would call out loud and clear. This I thought seemed out of place in this tranquil army post but he did and C Battery counted cadence loud and clear. At least Barker knew enough to keep silent with his off-color marching ditties. I had a bad feeling about this forced march as every man stepped off smartly as Barker had drilled us in Stewart and no one that I could see looked happy.

I'm sure some spectators wished they never saw the 773rd, no one uttered a word and there were no sounds from the crowd of service personnel and their families. Doors slammed shut as we passed the beautiful homes along Officers' Row, one of which had recently been invaded by White Elk who only wanted to take a bath – this innocent soldier thought with his alcohol saturated brain.

The images stop there and I don't remember ever seeing or talking to Caruana until years later when I ran into him along Broadway in Woodside. He kept on looking at my newly capped front teeth!

Soon after the incident with White Elk and C Battery's forced march, a new location was selected for C Battery on Bay 46th Street and Cropsey Avenue. This was in a neat well-groomed middle class residential area a short drive from Fort Hamilton and a shorter drive to Coney Island. The advance party of Lieutenant White and Sergeants Barker and Gallagher located an empty lot that was once a city park bordering the Belt Parkway. I leveled and oriented the aiming circle with proper declination correction while Barker staked out the 90's. The battery soon rolled in as we quickly emplaced, leveled, oriented and synchronized the radar, tracking head and the 90's. The commo section reeled out wire and hooked up a field telephone at each station. When ready, each station checked in with the battery commander stationed in the radar van. Of course, no settling rounds were fired. It was a tight fit and the four quad mounts had to be placed on 2 ½'s and parked outside the area one quad, right next to someone's back yard. We reported in by radio to report the battery was operational and we were back in the air defense radio loop monitoring incoming "Time and Line" checks and responding affirmatively.

If one were to drive by car from our site on the Belt Parkway through the Brooklyn Battery Tunnel to Manhattan, it would have taken you to the middle of 42nd Street and Times Square in about 25 minutes. Even that close to the bright lights and excitement of one of the world's largest and most vibrant cities, Charlie Battery was right back sleeping on folding cots in sleeping bags under canvas squad tents. We were back standing on the chow line with mess kits in hand as the cooks dished out Sergeant Davis's chow, drinking chemically treated water from Lister Bags, washing and shaving out of a steel helmet. We were living exactly as we would be later on in Korea. The only noise at night was the constant buzz of traffic along the Belt Parkway. Many noticed the Manhattan night was never totally dark as it was back in Camp Stewart only illuminated by trillions upon trillions of stars.

There always is a good side to every reversal in life and right across the street from the Battery was a little Italian store offering home cooking just like any Italian Grandma would make. This would introduce both the Black and the White Southern boys and the Hispanics from the southwest to Braciola, Lasagna, Veal cutlet Parmigiana, Eggplant Parmigiana and made Brooklyn Italians out of all of them. Instead of Red Man tobacco juice dripping down some of their cheeks, you would now see tomato sauce splattered all across their field uniforms. "Hey Alabam', how do you like them sausages and peppers?" "They's jist fine, ah likes 'em reeeel fine."

A high percentage of troops had to be on site at all times to keep the battery fully operational. Dress uniforms and foot lockers were still in our barracks back at Fort Hamilton, where we had hopes of someday returning.

A shower truck was sent to Hamilton after chow every evening with about twelve troopers rotated to take showers and stop off at the PX and drive them back at about 10 PM. Davis went to battalion every day in the mess section 2 ½ ton truck for rations towing the water tank trailer to be refilled with drinking water. He would also take the outgoing mail and return with the day's incoming mail.

Mail Call was always a highlight of the day as each man sat down with a little bit of home in his hands and devoured the words. It was even more important when the G.I. was in a strange and unfriendly land thousands of miles away from his loved ones.

My Uncle Louie Cavallo lived with his family not too far from our site and one Sunday evening on the way home from Grandma Cavallo's house, he brought me a large piece of Grandpa Cavallo's birthday cake. PFC Odom, a Southern soldier on guard duty, detained my uncle at the wire gate until I came up to greet my uncle. Uncle Louie was an infantryman in WWII in France and I showed him around the gun site. He told me that it smelled familiar, recalling the smell of G.I. canvas. Uncle Louie wished me luck and I thanked him for the cake which I shared with some of the guys including PFC Odom. Odom was a good old boy, a tall lanky cowboy who traveled with his guitar and kept his buddies in the Motor Section entertained as long as they liked Hank Williams music. It was around this time that I slowly started to like country and western music myself.

The next image is around St. Patrick's Day 1952. A few short blocks down Cropsey Avenue was a small neighborhood bar discovered by First Sergeant Legard. He said to me one evening, "Gallagher, you are an Irishman, so come along with me I have a surprise for you." "Okay Sarge, what is it?" He motioned for me to follow him off the site as we walked to the bar on Cropsey Avenue. We were treated to and surprised to see...Green Beer in honor of "Saint Patty's Day." Apparently, Legard made friends easily and we had a nice time at that friendly neighborhood bar with the locals who showed us respect while we were still wearing our not too clean field uniforms, probably reminding many of them of their own service in World War II.

Legard was a career man with many years of service and was a quiet and efficient NCO. He knew his job without being loud and overbearing. I would annoy Barker's with, "Old Legard gets the job done without making a lot of noise." This was sure to get his goat! Barker and I were the best of friends but this was our favorite pastime but, never in front of the troops. At this time we were actually too busy with battery duties to even think about pranks against each other. We went on alert when the air alarm went off and sometimes we did track real "Bogeys" in the PPI scope and the Director sent fire data to the guns until cleared as "Friendly." The gun crews never knew this while the Azimuth and Elevation Clock setters were matching dials waiting to hear the word, "AUTO" and the crews standing by with a chain of live ammo ready to hear one word, "FIRE."

The best Lee and I can remember, it was around this time when we first met. This was around the time Battalion Sergeant Major Taylor announced to the batteries the army's special offer to the National Guard and Army Reserve top two grade Sergeants First Class and Master Sergeants, an enticing offer. If they re-enlisted in the Regular Army for three years, they would keep their rank and the rank would be made permanent. Most wartime NCO promotions were temporary.

This occurred the Thursday before my Sunday blind date with Lee. We three Sergeants agreed to re-enlist, Barker, Davis and Gallagher. Our First Sergeant Legard was happy to send our three names to battalion at Fort Hamilton. I felt good about it because I had already been talking to Lieutenant White about OCS (Officer Candidate School) and, he told me it would be wise when I am ready for OCS to go as an RA Sergeant.

Around that same time Max Ries told me his fiancé would be visiting her girlfriend who lived only minutes away from our gun site. He asked if I could get him a pass and go on a blind date with him. "Sure Max," I said, thinking that it would be a nice break to clean up and get away for a few hours myself. I made the arrangements with his boss Barker and Top Kick Legard to give Max a pass. This was easy because Max had a great reputation in the battery and they readily agreed.

As a top two grade NCO, I had a permanent Armed Forces Liberty Pass which will be significant a little later in this memoir. With his pass in hand, we got a ride to Fort Hamilton, showered and shaved. It felt good stepping into a freshly starched class A Khaki uniform. Max had his late 1940's black Chevy still parked at Hamilton, so we bundled our boots and field clothes in the trunk of his car to be available upon our return to the site. He was excited and happy to see his girl who he had not seen since his Christmas furlough. He was glad to be stationed so close to home and his girlfriend.

I remember driving through an Italian and Jewish neighborhood with Catholic churches on one corner and synagogues on the next. We passed kosher butcher shops and delis, and Italian restaurants and pizza parlors on many streets. The one and two family homes interspersed with apartment buildings were all neat and well maintained. I was totally unfamiliar with this neighborhood in Brooklyn known as Bensonhurst.

Acting as Max's co-pilot, we passed the intersection of 75st Street, when I told him we had a few more blocks to go and we made a right turn off 19th Avenue onto 71st Street and parked in front of Lee's home.

We saw Max's girl Angie standing and smiling in the open doorway. It was the first time I ever saw her and she was a very pretty girl. She and Max made an attractive couple, I thought. We walked up the stairs and Angie invited us in and led the way to a comfortable nicely furnished living room and offered us a seat.

Max and his girl were all smiles and happy to be together and, another young lady was sitting in the living room named Grace who was Lee's next door neighbor. This was very nice to sit in such a soft easy chair and thought it would be great to just sit back and enjoy a cigarette and a beer. Then, Lee walked in wearing a white tightly tailored sweater with gold threads emphasizing her full bosom and slim waistline. She also had on a black velvet flaring ballerina skirt and black patent leather high heel shoes. Her black page boy hair style framed the prettiest face I ever remember seeing. I think I stood up to say hello but the only thing I am absolutely sure of happening was that I fell in love at first sight and wanted to spend the rest of my life with this adorable sophisticated young lady named Leboria Theresa Reres. Her voice sounded like music to my ears.

I no longer felt in charge even though I outranked everyone in the room. The next image is slightly blurred as we walked out and I do recall opening the door and following her into the back seat of the car. We buzzed off and I felt quite awkward next to this sweet-smelling precious looking girl. I was even a little afraid of her or afraid I may say something stupid or do something dumb.

Where did my confidence flee to, I wondered? I never felt this way about a girl before. The image blurs and I do not recall who made the decision to go to the Pizza King in Laurelton, Long Island. Max was trendy and had probably taken Angela there before. I remember entering the restaurant and hearing loud music blaring: I was hoping for a slow song when I saw all the couples dancing. We sat at a round table and the girls were smiling – maybe, I thought, at my awkwardness. Someone ordered a pitcher of beer and a large pizza ... maybe it was even me, I don't remember. Max put some change in the juke box and he and Angie danced to lively music.

The next slow song I finally held Lee in my arms. I touched her so lightly as though she were made of glass. I never went out with such a beautiful girl who enchanted me so much. Max fed the juke box and danced with his girl, both very good dancers. Again, I was out of my element and the next slow dance I held Lee a little closer but felt like putting both my arms around her and just holding her in my arms for a while. But instead, I stiffly held her at a respectful distance and did the best I could to remember my one and only two step. She smelled so nice.

The evening seemed to race by and on the drive back my confidence was restored. I tried to start a conversation several times but she seemed aloof to me. "Could I see you again?" I asked. "Well, I am really very busy, I work full time at Lever Brothers in their new all glass building on Park Avenue and I attend Brooklyn College evenings and I am soooo veeery busy." "What nights do you go to school?" I asked. "Monday, Wednesday and Friday" she continued "So...now you can see how busy I really am" she said. "What are the hours?" I queried. "From 7 to 9 PM...a real full schedule," she answered. "Great," I said, "I'll pick you up tomorrow night at 9 PM in front of Brooklyn College and drive you home." She would have to think real quickly to get out of that offer. I do not remember what she said or even if she said anything at all. Maybe I won the first round.

Lee does not remember nor do I recall the balance of that evening because I was working out in my mind how I would get home to get my Dad's car and put this complicated operation into action the next day. The only thing remembered was going over the plan with Max and needing his cooperation. It would mean another pass for him to see his girl so he was in and yes, he would drive me to my home in Woodside and meet me there later that evening so I could return my Dad's car and he would drive us both back to the site. We pulled up near the gun site on Cropsey Avenue and he found a parking spot.

I needed to deal with the intricate logistics. First, I needed a pass for Max for Monday night to drive me home to Woodside.

Barker would grant that, he was Max's boss and I had some pull in the Battery. I was sure Legard would go along with everything.

Now, as long as we did not have an alert upgrade, the pathway was open. Max would drive me home I would change into civilian clothes, borrow my Dad's new 1951 Ford sedan and be on my way to Brooklyn College.

One important step needed to be taken. I just agreed to re-up for three more years and Lieutenant Smedley must be told first thing Monday about my change of mind. So far, I had not signed any papers nor did I raise my right hand yet to be sworn in! It takes a brave man to change his mind I thought ... I was not going to re-enlist.

The first thing Monday morning, I saw Smedley and told him I changed my mind. His comment was "That is between you and the Sergeant Major." Great, I thought, I could take care of Taylor and I had not signed any papers. I ran across the street to the Italian Deli and called my Dad. "Dad, I just have to borrow the car tonight, please do not say no." "OK son," he must have felt the urgency in my voice. "Great, thanks Dad."

The request to report to battalion with Barker and Davis to sign our re-enlistment papers and raise our right hand to be sworn in is still a little dim. At any rate, that was not an issue for I was waiting patiently for 5 PM and hoping no emergency upgrade in alert status would defeat my plan.

With breakfast completed, I checked with my two section leaders and told Joe Zurla he was in charge of the platoon tonight he gave me a "Thumbs up" and said all the equipment was fully operational. I checked the battery commo section and heard the time and line checks were coming in by phone and radio and everything was still normal so now it was just waiting it out.

"Hey Max, let's be ready to roll out of here at exactly 17:00 hours (5 P.M.)." "You bet," he answered. This was ages before cell phones and pagers. Once off the site we were free and clear. At 5 P.M. Max pulled his car up to the wire gate and I climbed in.

Images fade as I now find myself in my old bedroom and peeling off my field uniform and Corcoran boots. I jumped into the shower, shaved, splashed on some Old Spice after shave, pulled on clean underwear and looked in my closet. I pulled out a pair of light blue gabardine slacks with a 17-inch peg on the cuff, a linen blue and gray sport shirt with yellow stripe across the chest and stepped into a pair of blue suede square-toed shoes. This was the style back in high school in 1950.

Remembered by both Lee and I are the two brick columns in front of Brooklyn College where she would be waiting for me. I located coordinates using compass and topo maps in the middle of a Georgia swamp and the Texas desert so I had no problem finding Brooklyn College. I did stop for a beer to settle my nerves which was not a good idea. But as I mentioned before, "You can take the man out of the barracks but"…well you know the rest!

I arrived in plenty of time to find the two brick columns. It grew darker as it approached 9:00 PM and I had already circled the spot several times and…there she was! Lee was standing in between the two columns in a smart-looking bluish tweedy business suit with a belt drawn tight around her waist and blue high-heeled shoes. She was carrying her school books and her pocketbook. My heart skipped a couple beats as I pulled up in front of the columns right on time. I got out, opened the passenger door for her, and she climbed in placing her books and purse on the Fords bench car seat next to me. I jumped back in and instead of taking her directions to turn down some avenue to Bensonhurst, I drove on to the Belt Parkway. She said "Where are you going?" "Oh, I just thought we would take the scenic drive" or something to that effect. Lee smiled and seemed to just sit back and relax for it had been a long day for her also. I peeked at her perfect profile, her eyes half closed as the breeze flowed off the water through her hair. "I think she commented about how nice the car was and I told her that my dad just bought the car about six months ago. I wasn't a bit nervous now with Lee sitting next to me. I felt in my mind and heart she would someday be my wife.

We made small talk and drove past the Floyd Bennett Field cut off. Up ahead was a gas station that had a pass-through to the other side of the Belt Parkway to a parking area at Plum Beach. I never took a girl there before because I did not have a car or a local girl to take there. I remembered the cutoff because I passed it several times when visiting the Canarsie Beach gun site. Remember… "The small details."

I drove through and parked among a few other cars. Stopping the car and turning off the ignition, I turned to Lee, looked in her eyes and said "I love you and want to marry you." I think she said "You are crazy," but she did not say no. I think she smiled and I made sure I did not touch her. I just wanted to get that message across to her. It felt good because that was my mission of the day. With that accomplished, I drove her directly to her home where, I would visit her until the end of August. By that time, we were both in love with each other as we are to this day. I am writing this today, on our 62nd anniversary. We will dine tonight at the Desmond Hotel in Malvern, PA where we had our joyous 50th anniversary party in November, 2003.

The Cropsey Avenue site proved too small and we moved to a new site off the Belt Parkway at the base of the Mill Basin Bridge. Access was off Flatbush Avenue where "Alabam" cut a road through the marsh grass with the battalion bulldozer. A tideland sandy beach ran through the site and the troops could take a swim and freshen up during high tide.

Lee's busy schedule did not leave her much time for dating and I could not neglect my own responsibilities. She agreed we see each other on a Friday or Saturday night for only a couple hours. I would hop on the shower truck and direct it to Lee's house and arrange for the truck to pick me up on the way back. Lee's house was on the way to Fort Hamilton so it was no inconvenience for the troopers.

Lee's brother Tony did not like the idea of the cumbersome 2 ½ ton truck rounding the corner of 19th Avenue and 71st Street with a dozen G.I.'s gaping at all the females. After dropping me off at Lee's house, the truck would roar off and continue down the street under everyone's startled gaze and return again at 10:00 P.M. to pick me up

I took my showers on rotation at Hamilton like everyone else during the week to save my weekends to see Lee. Like millions of other field soldiers, I learned how to keep my body clean by washing out of a steel helmet. Mess Sergeant Davis usually provided warm water for the troops to use for washing and shaving. He was an old soldier and knew how important it was to the troops to have a little luxury like warm water. Even so, he always bragged, "Charlie Baddery a buncha sissies, when I have no hot water, I shave with cold water and sometimes I dry shave with no water...I was the REAL field solga!" as he puffed away on his cigar.

During our time together, Lee and I would sit on her front stoop sometimes, her neighbor Grace and her fiancé Vic would join us. Vic was a Sergeant in the Air National Guard at Floyd Bennett Air Field quite close to the C Battery Site which, made conversation easy. They remained our cherished friends for many years.

Our romance was making very slow progress during March and April and was interrupted by my receiving orders to attend a special 30 day class at Fort Bliss on a new fire control system and I left on May 1st. It was a long time before I actually kissed Lee but when I came back from Fort Bliss the courtship took on a serious turn and it was around that time she told me she loved me and the world according to this unpolished soldier from Woodside was wonderful. This took place on the Staten Island Ferry one night when we took a cab to the Brooklyn Ferry Terminal. We picked a seat on deck and watched the lights of New York City as we cuddled up and I kissed her for the very first time, which was to be followed by over 60 years of more kisses. She told me that night she loved me.

Before we received orders for the Far East, C Battery had some drama back at the Mill Basin gun site. Corporal Brewer which, is not his real name, was an RA recently returned from duty in Korea and on a gun crew. His wife was living in Manhattan when he was notified she was seriously ill. With a few minute ride from the site to public transportation he would be home in less than an hour. He asked for an overnight pass to see his wife. A reasonable request and easily afforded but, terribly handled by the gun platoon leaders.

This problem was thrust on me one morning when I went on duty as acting First Sergeant. Legard was re-assigned and in the interim, until we had a new first Sergeant, I shared the job with the Gun Platoon Sergeant. It being my day on duty, I reported to the Command Post tent to a new officer I was just getting to know. The Lieutenant told me, "Did you hear about last night, my life was threatened by CPL Brewer?" "No sir, what happened?" The lieutenant told me that last night the Battery Commander was away when Brewer entered the command post tent demanding a pass and a ride to public transportation. One word led to the next and Brewer lost control. All the time Battery Clerk Pizzo was in the C.P. tent cleaning several machetes that were starting to rust from exposure to the salt water environment. The supply Sergeant had given Pizzo that job to do in his spare time.

Pizzo said, "In a flash, Brewer grabbed a machete, made some threatening remarks and gestures and ran off the site, with machete in hand." The lieutenant added, "Gallagher, get a detail to get him back here before he hurts anyone." I had some dealings with Brewer who came to us with a clean record and I was surprised to hear he became as unhinged as the lieutenant and Pizzo said he was." The lieutenant followed with "The last we heard, Brewer was seen walking on the road in the marshes." I saw the gun platoon Sergeant and said, "Let's go out and see if we can talk him in before he hurts someone or someone shoots him for seeing a wild looking guy running around with a machete in his hand." Sergeant Quidone replied, "Didn't the lieutenant tell you Brewer threatened to kill me also." "I told him I could not give him a pass and only an officer could do that and, he threatened me." "OK, get me a couple of Brewer's closest friends who know him and want to help bring him back," was my next best option.

The two men from Brewer's gun crew reported and one said, "I knew he was gonna do something like this," the other followed with, "The problem with his wife has got Brewer crazy, he asked his section leader and officer for an overnight pass a couple days ago and he was refused. I don't know why the hell he couldn't get off the site for a couple hours anyone can do his job."

Our mission was to bring him back peacefully if possible. "Let's try to talk him in and get the machete from him." I told them, "I don't want you two armed, I will have my carbine and ammo out of sight in the jeep." "If he gives us any trouble we will just leave him in the dust and let the M.P.'s deal with him." "Let's try to find him first."

We drove up to the point he was last seen by the water truck and his crew mates started calling him. First the guys called and after a few minutes I yelled out, "Brewer, this is Sergeant Gallagher, don't let this get out of hand. Just come on back with us and hand over the machete. Have some chow and as soon as the B.C. arrives we will you sit down with him and see if he can give you a pass. An apology for your threats and your actions may put everyone at ease." Silence... so I called out even louder, "You don't want to screw up your good record," and more calls from his friends. "Brewer, think about it come on back to the battery or you will be on your own to deal with the Fort Hamilton M.P.'s." "Lieutenant Smedley is a fair man and I am sure he will work with you. Keep your record clear."

We advanced slowly as we drove along the sandy road surrounded by marsh grass growing five feet high restricting the visibility, all the while yelling encouragement to Brewer. One man looked to the right and one looked left as I eyeballed the back trail. We yelled out as we drove and would stop to call again, wait a moment, and then drive on.

The cross street at the end of the road was ahead a few hundred yards and a few yards off to the side we saw the tall marsh grass separate and saw poor Brewer all dirty and scratched by the grass, staring wide-eyed at us. He still had the machete in his right hand, "Come on Brewer, give me the machete handle first and hop in the jeep and let's get you some chow." With a nod of his head and a shrug of his shoulders his whole body seemed to surrender as he handed over the blade and climbed in the jeep. "I just gotta get home for a day," he spoke with tears in his eyes and his face smeared with dirt. "Let's go back" I told the driver.

We drove back to the site and went directly to the mess tent. I told Davis to fix him up with something to eat. "Hey Brew, sit down over here I make you some eggs, how you want," as he ordered a cook to give Brewer some water and coffee. Brewer looked up at me and cracked a sad smile and his image disappears from my memory.

I felt bad for Brewer. A platoon Sergeant's responsibility is the training, readiness and welfare of the men in his platoon. I would have handled the situation differently. Quidone was a good NCO and probably didn't realize the urgency here. Maybe Barker would have handled the incident differently. I looked at the bright sunshine and blue sky and thought today could have been a nice day. The tide was up at Mill Basin and the water looked inviting. All the off-duty men were enjoying a swim and I could have been splashing around in that water if it was not for the problem with Brewer.

My job done, I returned to the Command Post. The lieutenant peeked out the C.P. tent and I gave the machete to Pizzo. "Lieutenant, Brewer needs a pass to see his wife so as soon as the battery commander gets here let's bring him up to date." I do not recall if Brewer received any charges or if any action was taken against him. You never knew when these experiences would fall right in your lap.

M-33 School

In the beginning of May, I received orders to join Lieutenant White and we both left Fort Hamilton for a 30-day course at Fort Bliss on the new M-33 intergraded Fire Control System. The M-33 was extreme cutting edge technology and represented the finest of Bell Telephone and Western Electric's technical expertise. All 90mm and 120mm gun units in the U.S.A. and the 90mm units overseas sent their Fire Control Platoon Officers and Sergeants to this 30 day course of instruction at Fort Bliss. The M-33 repairmen were then attending an extended course at Bliss. This was unusual to have officers and enlisted men in the same class but the army wanted to get this new equipment into the hands of AA troops world-wide as soon as possible to meet the demands of the rapidly advancing aircraft capabilities.

The system was much advanced and improved over the 1940's era M-9 Director and SCR-584 Gun Laying Radar. This new system was designed to destroy the new faster jet aircraft that flew at higher altitudes. The M-33 placed our country again out front in Anti-Aircraft Artillery technology. The M-33 had two radars, an acquisition (ACQ) surveillance radar that continually rotated to search for targets and a narrow beam highly accurate tracking radar (TRK) to track the target once it was acquired. Integrated in the radar van were all the components for the director. The range of operation was extended and the accuracy and ease of operation much advanced. The course covered basic introduction to the system's components, then learning how to emplace and march order the system, and finally actual operation in the field by the team members.

At school, the teams were made up of about a dozen or so men representing a normal operational crew and included both officers and enlisted men in the same crew. So, this was different and interesting, it also encouraged the rascally inclined practical jokers an opportunity for some laughs. Of course, sometimes the joke explodes on the joker.

Lieutenant White attended the same course but we were not on the same crew team, giving me a little more freedom. I had fun at Bliss with some other NCO's who had a similar sense of humor... which was too bad for our new classmate Lieutenant Carter.

The image opens with placing my gear in a second floor four man room similar to my first tour at Bliss, then changing into a field uniform and walking back to the supply room to get my foot locker. When I exited the barrack, there directly in front of me was a push cart which I grabbed thinking someone left it there without taking the trouble to walk it back to the supply room. As I was pushing the cart a tall burly and older Master Sergeant yelled out that it was his "@#$&ing cart" and "Hands off!" I looked at him curiously and he did not look happy. A few nasties were exchanged and I walked back to the orderly room as he tried to keep up with me pushing his @#$&ing cart!

Once at the supply room, I was issued my foot locker and looked around for a cart and none were available. At the same time the Master Sergeant was loading his foot locker on his @#$&ing

cart. He looked at me and I at him and we both doubled up laughing as I tossed my foot locker on top of his and he laughed as he yelled out, "I'll push it half way and then you can take over," as we chuckled on the way back to the barrack. "I'm Peterson," "I'm Gallagher," and introductions were now complete. We were on the same team and those 30 days were interesting and with the welcomed relief from normal troop duty, was the most fun time I had in the service. No responsibility, just picking on a certain dumb lieutenant team member and learning about this new Fire Control equipment.

I was assigned to the same four man room as Peterson and his buddy Sergeant First Class Bevins whom he knew from previous service. I forget where their units were located but both were regular army soldiers and served together in the Philippines in World War II where they were both captured by the Japanese. They survived the Bataan Death March and spent the remainder of the war as prisoners of war. The fourth man was also an RA Sergeant First Class from a 90mm unit in the Chicago area.

During the 30 days with them, I learned more about their experiences that I will share with you. Bevins was on a "Hell Ship" which was attacked by the Allies but arrived safely in Japan where he was put to work in a coal mine. He had a nasty circular scar about the size of a silver dollar on his forehead from being beaten. Bevins told us his life was saved by an older Japanese civilian supervisor in the mines who secretly gave him food and clothing at the risk of his own life.

I remember Bevins telling us when the Americans arrived to liberate him, he and the other prisoners thought they were Russian because of the new-style U.S. helmet and the M1 rifle. When he was captured in the Philippines, the army was still wearing the old WWI tin hat style helmet and using the bolt action Springfield rifles. The prisoners did not at first recognize the newly clad and armed G.I.'s.

Peterson spent his time in the Philippines in prison camps. He was a big man and was put to work in various outdoor heavy manual labor jobs, which also resulted in his being better fed than most prisoners. He claimed that was the reason for his survival. He said if they were working with only a couple low-ranking Japanese guards, they were given food and on occasion the guards shared cigarettes with them. But if the guards were caught, everyone was beaten including the guards. I mentioned about almost being struck by lightning twice and can tell you what was meant by that.

After WWII and now repatriated, both Peterson and Bevins remained in the army. When the Korean War broke out, they were both assigned to the same unit stationed in Japan. They were among the first of the U.S. soldiers sent to Korea. The enemy was so overpowering in arms and manpower that Peterson and Bevins's unit was surrounded facing capture once more. This time, the North Korean People's Army were not taking prisoners but were instead executing the retreating South Korean ROK forces as well as the Americans. Peterson and Bevins swore they would not be taken again.

They were among the rapidly retreating forces heading south to the Port of Pusan for possible evacuation back to Japan. They saw an opportunity to commandeer a 2 ½ ton truck and make a beeline along the one and only road they thought still open to Pusan. They came close to being captured again but bypassed a roadblock and narrowly made it to Pusan. "No, no, not again this time," they yelled and made it to safety. Those prisoners taken were later found on the battle field with hands tied behind their back with American G.I. telephone wire and shot in the head execution style. Some police action!

Sunday would usually end with a steak dinner at the Florida Club and then Mexican music and entertainment at the Guadalajara Club. True, we would also go on occasion to have some laughs with the *senoritas*. Once again, when asked, "Come thee room" and then refused, "No Dinero." we were all accused of being a "Cheapee Skate." Further infuriating the *senoritas* was the display of so many stripes and still "No Dinero!" So, we were "Double Cheapee Skates."

I do not recall anyone being drunk, disorderly or obnoxious. We were just a few NCO's relieved of every day responsibility and just having fun living for the moment knowing at the end of the 30 days we would be back at our full-time jobs.

The Guadalajara put on a fantastic show of powerful Mexican and Spanish music with many singers and dancers. Later in life I did business in Mexico City and entertained on a corporate expense account with no expenses spared. I visited many clubs and none compared when it came to pure talent, with The Guadalajara Club in Juarez in old Mexico.

Some diversion was afforded to both Officers and NCO's by picking on Lieutenant Carter (not his real name), an officer who proved that he lacked any common sense. When one of us was emplacing the equipment and had to move a particularly heavy piece, we always asked him for help as he was a big strong man. We gave him the heavy end to lift. He had trouble learning and understanding exactly what we were all there for. This was his first time in Fort Bliss and everyone was reminded or I should say warned about being very careful to observe all the laws in Mexico and to steer clear of any trouble with the Juarez police. This Lieutenant did have a run in with the Mexican police and spent a night in the Juarez jail for which he took a lot of teasing from the Sergeants as well as his fellow officers.

The next image is clear in my mind, after we completed the course, Lieutenant Carter looked me straight in the eye and said, "I hope we don't meet again, Sergeant Gallagher." I don't recall how I responded but probably just shrugged it off. It was destined for us to cross paths again only this time, he was my boss!

When I returned to Brooklyn, my relationship with Lee became more serious and I wanted to see her every chance I could. During the week, I took the shower truck to and from her home. By that time, her Mom Jean sent me back to the site with a bag full of veal cutlet sandwiches, other Italian specialties and, of course, Italian pastry from Alba's Pastry Shop on 18th Avenue.

My stripes got me off the site on weekends, and I was able to get Max a weekend pass once in a while. Max kept his car parked within a short jeep ride from the sight along with several of the other men in C Battery who had cars. He would drive me to my home so I could borrow my dad's car. I took Lee to meet my folks and remember taking her to lunch at a fancy Italian restaurant in

Corona and then going to see my parents. All I wanted in those days was to be with Lee.

We were on high alert status in those days and that meant a high percentage of personnel had to be on site 24/7. As soon as the alert status was relaxed, I got away to see my girl and ticked away the day's until my active duty time was fulfilled the following year on May 1st, 1953. This was interrupted one morning that summer when we heard a startling announcement that came without any warning.

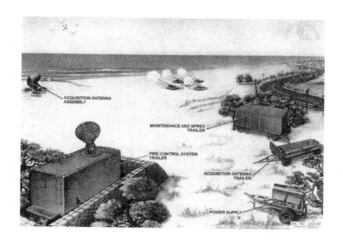

In 1953, the M-33 became standard issue to US Army and National Guard Anti-Aircraft Artillery units serving in Army Air Defense Command USA-RADCOM).

(Pictures from US ARMY Training Manual TM-9-6092-1-1)

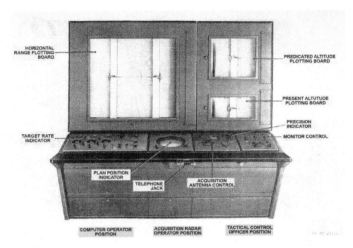

Tactical Control Console: monitoring the targets' present position. Rate of speed and showing predicted position on moving charts. Ready to give order to fire the four guns.

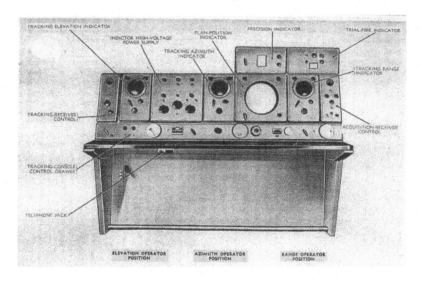

Tracking Console: Tracking present position of target and awaiting orders to transfer the target from the Acquisition Radar to Tracking Radar to Lock-On and track selected target

M33 TM 3.jpg (JPEG Image, 800 × 997 pixels) - Scaled (74%)   http://www.usarmygermany.com/Units/Air Defense/M33 TM 3.jpg

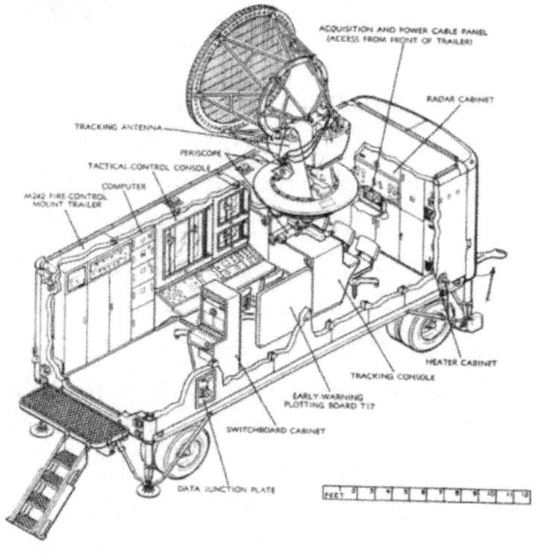

RA PD 233159

Figure 4. Fire-control-system trailer—plan view.

1 of 1   11/6/2014 10:35 AM

View of the M-33 Integrated Fire Control System with controls for two radars - the Acquisition Radar and the Track Radar plus the Fire Control Director and communication system all in one van. Capabilities were increased to destroy all known aircraft at the time and designed to quickly train Fire Control personnel for a quick and familiar transition from AA Artillery to the Nike-Ajax Missile system then under development.

(Pictures from U.S.Army Training Manual TM-9-6092-1-1

Goodbye to Brooklyn

One August morning at reveille and while still stationed at the gun site in Mill Basin, we received an important announcement from the Battery Commander. We knew something important was up as everyone was ordered off their equipment and told to assemble in front of the Command Post tent.

"The 773rd has been relieved of any further duty with USARADCOM and the battalion has been ordered to report back to Fort Hamilton with all personnel and equipment to process for deployment to FECOM (Far East Command)." Wow, what a shocker that was. Heads spun around in wonder. "Can this be real or a very bad joke?" some thought. Apparently, Smedley got the message. "Men, this is for real we're going somewhere in the Far East! The Battery Clerk will post a list on the bulletin board with the names of all personnel who will go with the unit. If your name is not on the list, you will be reassigned elsewhere until your term of enlistment expires. Now, let's have breakfast." The First Sergeant called out, "Battery, dis ... missed."

One trooper yelled out, "I knew this couldn't last...we're going to Korea." That was the first rumor. "No way, its Okinawa, I knew it all the time." "Negative, I just got it from PFC Rooney who works at battalion S-2 (Intelligence). He told me he heard if the Russians attack, it will be in Japan and that's where we're going." " And so it went as the rumor mills worked on overtime! I was too busy to even stop and think about where we were going, we had to mark the equipment in white stencil in specific places. Not only on our radar and the director trailer but also on every cable, junction box, trailer, 90mm gun mount, quad mount and all miscellaneous gear we would be taking with us. We marked equipment with the travel code "9205B" until we saw it in our sleep.

The troops would be traveling by troop ship from the Staten Island Army Port of Debarkation. The equipment would be going by freighter to meet us at our new location wherever that might be. We were ordered to turn in all our new jeeps, ¾ ton and 2 ½ ton trucks. We were told this was because the spare parts at our destination were still those parts used in the WWII model vehicles which would be issued to us on arrival.

Some guys were all smiles when they learned they were re-assigned elsewhere. At the same time, new people were reporting almost daily. The combat strength for a 90mm AA unit was 150 men per firing battery plus 200 men in Headquarters and Headquarters battery. So the new strength would be 800 men compared to the 550 we had at the time. That meant the 773rd would need to add 250 new men to give the battalion a full deck. How many would be wild cards in that deck, we had no way of telling. More than a few would be problems for the 773rd including both officers and enlisted men.

We received our added manpower and replacements from all sources, one being regular army units only too glad to finally get rid of some of their problems. It sounds dumb but that is exactly how it played out. Most of the problems were alcohol related. I received one of these soldiers in my platoon whom you will hear more about later and a battery officer causing serious trouble.

Our First Sergeant was already reassigned. So, that left me as acting First Sergeant. One morning as I was having a cup of coffee in the orderly room with Battery Clerk Pizzo, we noticed someone approaching the front door. The sun was shining through the door and I saw the silhouette of a tall lanky man walking with an unusual but familiar gait. One arm holding something the other hanging down the palm facing to the rear. "Oh no," I thought, "Could it be?" Sure enough, opening the door and entering Charlie Battery's orderly room was none other than Lieutenant Carter, my former class mate from Fort Bliss M-33 School. Surprised and with mouth agape I saluted him as he proclaimed, "Well, we meet again, Sergeant Gallagher," as he slammed down his orders on the clerk's desk.

Special Order #??????? . 1/LT Joseph Carter Serial # 0? ??? ??? Assigned C Btry, 773rd AAA Gun BN, Fire Control Platoon Leader MOS 1725. (MOS 1725 Fire Control Chief … the same as mine)

"Welcome to Charlie Battery," I said, waiting for him to return my salute. Here was the guy who spent a night in the Juarez jail, could not keep himself out of trouble, and took chiding from officer and NCO alike for all his foolishness. I do not recall any further contact with Carter until after we landed in Korea.

We welcomed more new officers and men as the battery strength grew to the required 150 men. This included our new First Sergeant Master Sergeant Kolody, a regular who served in an M.P. unit in WWII. He was an excellent soldier and a sane and sober NCO. In Korea, he was the last man in the battery on the chow line. I greatly respected him for many reasons and he was a good influence for this young National Guard Master Sergeant. The realization of overseas deployment with the possibility of going into combat renewed my interest and actions to be the best NCO I could be. A new dimension was added to my responsibility for the 30 or so men in the Fire Control Platoon.

Already having an Armed Forces Liberty Pass with no time limits, I pretty much came and went as I pleased with no more 24-hour alert. I was able to see Lee almost every evening.

I burned up the roads between Fort Hamilton, Bensonhurst and Woodside in my Dad's 1951 Ford until the day finally came when the 773rd left for distant shores. I was stopped for speeding a few times on the Belt Parkway and actually got three speeding tickets during that time. I just smiled at the policemen and tossed away the tickets when he left.

When I returned from overseas, my Mom gave me her familiar stern look and handed me all the reminder notices she received from the Motor Vehicle Bureau. Wisely, she never mentioned them in her letters to me while I was still overseas. But when I did return she said, "Take care of these speeding tickets; do it now and then bitch about it later." Two of Mom's sons were in the service and plenty of friends, neighbors and family also served so she was familiar with the G.I. lingo. I think the tickets were about 15 dollars each, so I appeared at court wearing my uniform but the stripes and ribbons didn't mean a damn thing to the judge. I paid the $45 and heeded the judges warning to drive carefully. At that time, the speed limit on the Belt Parkway was 25 or 35 MPH if my memory is correct.

The clock ticked away very fast and the last night was a sad one for all of us. Over the years, this memory has lasted for me and Lee and we always have a smile of thankfulness as we look back. Now at 84, as I write this part about two 20-year-olds caressing and kissing each other goodbye for what may be the last time, I choke up thinking about those who never did come back home. They would never again hold their sweethearts in their arms nor would they ever again see the smiles of joy in their loved ones faces nor feel the warmth of their embrace. Instead, those families would spend a lifetime grieving for the loss of their soldier. In my heart and mind, the real heroes are those who never returned and those bearing the mutilations and amputations to their bodies from the horrors of war. Again, thank you Lord for sparing me those scars.

All the equipment marked 9205B was now on the way to Korea, the actual destination unknown to us at the time. My duffel bag was packed and placed on my cot with my weapon, webbing and helmet liner. For the next couple of days we were all in limbo. I dashed off to Lee's house those last few days until the day finally arrived for us to say goodbye.

The night before I left, we took the subway to Woodside so I could say goodbye to my Mom and Dad and only have a vague memory of brothers Jim, John and sister-in-law Helen and niece Caroline. My folks drove us back to the train station on 61st Street and Roosevelt Avenue because my dad was totally unfamiliar with Bensonhurst and not sure about traveling there at night. So we said our goodbyes and Lee and I ran up the stairs to the station.

Before the train arrived, I had a flash of memory about my Uncle Louie missing in action in WWII and of my cousin Vincent killed in action in Burma. My thought swiftly flashed to my folks whom may never see their son again. With that in mind, I took Lee by the arm and we ran downstairs just as the car was driving away. "Come on Dad, drive us to Flatbush Avenue and you can jump right back on the Belt Parkway to Queens." We all smiled and before we knew it we were saying our goodbyes again as Lee and I both saw the '51 Ford disappear in the dark. I get a little lump in my throat as I think about what my Mom and Dad must have been thinking as they drove away.

We caught a cab on busy Flatbush Avenue and lingered on Lee's front stoop where we gave each other our farewell kisses. It was not easy letting her go that night and it will always be in my mind. Lee remembers that last night just as I described it. As soon as the cab sped to Fort Hamilton all my thoughts were now back to C Battery. I don't remember tears on anyone's face.

Early the next morning, buses pulled up to the barracks as the battalion loaded all 800 soldiers for the short ride to the Brooklyn-Staten Island Ferry Terminal. It was awkward sitting on a bus seat while aboard the ferry and feeling the soft roll of the ferry cruising across New York Harbor. "Oh man, don't let me get seasick now." I thought as I glanced around at many disturbed faces probably feeling the same sensation. A few deep breaths and I felt fine. The troops all seemed to relax and just settle back to a buzz of nervous chatter.

The next memory I have is of looking at the back of the soldier's boots in front of me as C Battery marched up the ship's gangway, weapons slung over the right shoulder and duffel bags over the left. A vague image and maybe even just the reminder after years of hearing Lee's cousin Red Perrone who worked on the Army docks and saying he saw me and called out my name. Maybe I heard Red or maybe it's just a suggestive thought but no doubt about the First Army Band playing all those songs I heard played by the 12th Regiment Band back in 1947. The strains of "So Long It's Been Good to Know Ya" could be heard as the troopship *C. C. Ballou* steamed out of Upper New York Bay through the Narrows and headed out to the Atlantic Ocean, steering a southern course.

The thoughts of all the troops in the 773rd were concentrated on what the future may bring, what new sights, sounds and challenges were awaiting us. Our loved ones remained at home to endure the worry and fear for their soldier's safety, just as generations of loved ones have done throughout all our wars.

Picture taken just before I went overseas. We were sad and saw each other every day until I boarded the troop ship.

In front of Lee's home winter 1953. She knew how to pack a snowball. The first winter in our home in Baldwin in 1960 we had a late night snow storm and we decided to go out and play in the snow. Lee proved her aim when she bounced a snowball off my head and war was declared. After I raised the white flag and squeezed and kissed her we found we were locked out in the cold with no keys while, our two little boys were fast asleep upstairs. I had to break a basement window to gain entry.

This picture taken for her cousins wedding party in September 1952 soon after I left for Korea. Worry showed in her eyes.

Someone took this picture in the rear of Lee's home. I left for Korea the next day.

The Armed Forces Liberty Pass

When looking at old mementos I found this piece of evidence contradicting the established premise that Lee did not give me her phone number that first blind date. As I thumbed my way through my old records and curios I accidentally dropped the Liberty Pass and it landed flip side up. There it is, in Lee's own handwriting using her eyebrow pencil, she signed her signature *Lee*...office phone number *Murray Hill 8-6000*...and extension *Ext 227*...She must have liked me a little to give me her office phone number or maybe, she just felt sorry for this pitiful soldier who drank too much beer, smoked too many cigarettes and was so forlorn to have the desire to re-enlist in the regular army for three more years...Lee still keeps me guessing about this.

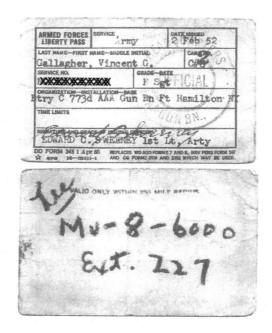

Chapter 7

Aboard the USS C. C. Ballou

Most soldiers' memories of their life aboard a troopship during the WWII and the Korean War was very harsh. My first impression when settling in aboard the troopship *C. C. Ballou* was quite different.

The *Ballou* had many decks with the highest above the water line being "A" Deck. This was Officer Country with the Officers Mess, showers and latrines (called heads in the navy) and rows of semi-private cabins. The next deck below was "B" Deck, where large meeting and classroom-sized compartments for training lectures were located.

The next deck below was "C" Deck which was the entry deck for boarding and contained compartments on both sides of the ship for six men. Each compartment had a single port hole facing the sea and a private entry door in the inner passageway. At the end of the passageway was a large open shower room and head for the use of the "C" deck personnel. On the Ballou these cabins were reserved for each battery's top two grade NCO's and one cabin, for the battalion's five First Sergeants and the Battalion Sergeant Major Taylor. I never lived in the ships below deck troop compartment until I returned from Korea when it seemed half the troops were top grade NCO's.

Our six man compartment on the left or Port Side of "C" Deck was shared with Gun Platoon Master Sergeant Quidone, Sergeants First Class, Mess Davis, Supply Van Ness, Radar Burns and Motor Nebbia. We were all quite comfortable; although crowded, it was luxurious compared to the troop compartments. The cabin measured about 8 feet wide and about 14 feet long. Upon entering the compartment, the six bunks (three high) were on the right wall or properly called bulkhead, and on the left a little table to write on and some folding chairs were placed for convenience. A porthole was located on the outside bulkhead looking out at the sea, allowing some fresh air and light to enter which added to the comfort in the close quarters.

248

A short walk out the door and a few cabins down the passageway led to a walkway to take you to the Port or Starboard side the C Deck railing. We spent considerable time on the 38 day voyage gazing over that railing, counting the flying fish, and observing the fluorescence of the waves in the starlit evenings. That is, if we were not playing Monopoly, Twenty Questions or reading.

We six NCO's did not play any poker not knowing what challenges may lie ahead in the future we wanted to keep things simple. I don't remember any discussions about where we were going, what the future might hold for us or any talk about the war raging in Korea. For some reason we thought our destination was Okinawa or Japan and I do not recall why these locales were even mentioned. Burns, Van Ness and Davis all traveled by troopship in World War II and attested to the fact that we were living more comfortably than they ever had. Davis told us he was on 12 different troopships and that is why he knew his way around while on the *Ballou*.

Over the two top bunks, a transom ran directly overhead cutting down considerably on the space for the unfortunates stuck with those two top bunks. Davis was one of them because as soon as we entered the compartment, we each tossed our carbine and duffel bag on our selected bunk. I quickly grabbed a middle one. Quidone was left with a top bunk, transom and all, and the other three bunks were taken by Van Ness, Burns and Nebbia.

Davis missed out on selecting his bunk because the five Mess Sergeants had to report for a meeting with the Battalion S-4 Supply Officer. Davis with all his girth had to squeeze into that other top bunk.

All the enlisted troops ate in the large mess compartment and we had the best chow we ever had in the service. We were not sure if we would be the only troops aboard for the whole trip but thought it would be great if that were true. It wasn't, we were about to have plenty of company. The capacity of the *Ballou* was almost 4,000 troops with a crew numbering over 300 men. It took several days to arrive at our first stop in San Juan, Puerto Rico. We had wonderful breakfasts, less remembered lunches, great roast turkey and roast beef dinners.

The first sight of Puerto Rico was when it was only a purple gray silhouette in the distance that became the Morro Castle at the harbor of San Juan. About a thousand troops from the Regular Army 65th Regimental Combat Team (RCT) comprised of Puerto Rican U.S. Army troops boarded. The buzz included a rumor that we would be getting off the *Ballou* to have a cold beer in San Juan.

The image jumps to marching in a column of batteries in the hot humid Puerto Rican sun about a mile or so to drink a warm beer and then marching all the way back to the ship.

That night, the mess hall was much more crowded with the additional 1,000 men from the RCT. The chow was good but not as good as the first few days. All the mess Sergeants were now supervising cooking the chow for the army troops. There was a small contingent of U.S. Navy Warrant Officers quartered on "C" deck and we got to know a career warrant officer and would talk with him from time to time. He was a laid-back sort of man with a very boring job in administration of some type. We were now heading towards Panama and it was hot, humid and becoming more tropical. Cartagena, Colombia, was to be the next stop.

As the *Ballou* approached Cartagena, I happened to be reading a period historic novel about the British Navy in the 18th Century. The author described approaching Cartagena and you could tell he was there to do research because of the accuracy in which he described the harbor. The day was beautiful, sunny and tropical, and we were all on deck taking in the vista of this historic fortified harbor with roots going back to the 1500's. How much gold, silver and other treasures were shipped out of this harbor to Spain in the 16th century was hard to imagine. This plunder was taken at sword point by Spain at great cost of blood and sweat of the native people. The high tech weapon of mass destruction at that time was the Spanish Toledo steel sword blade. Firearms were an accessory to those cold steel blades that killed thousands of the local indigenous people in South and Central America and the Caribbean Islands.

We were on the port side, away from the dock side so we had a full view of the harbor and all the activities related to the docking of a major vessel. Following the *Ballou* into her berth at the dock were numerous dugout canoes with local natives peddling their wares. These natives were a mixture of blood of the original native Indians, the Spanish *Conquistadores* who invaded in the 1500's, and the black slaves brought in from Africa over a span of 300 years.

These locals paddling alongside the docked vessel offered rum, wood carvings, various native curios and, much to Davis' interest, alligator jumbo-sized women's purses. "Hey, I gonna buy that purse for my sister, that's worth a hundra dollas back home." With that Davis started bargaining with one of the natives for "How much!"

The drill was the native would hold over his head an article and call out the cost. Bargaining would ensue until the price was agreed upon. Then, the native would toss a rock up to the buyer several decks above the canoe. The rock was tied to a rope on one end and a basket on the other. The buyer would pull the basket up with the aid of the rope and place the necessary money in the basket using the rock to keep the bills from blowing away and then lower the basket down to the native while still holding on to the rope end also tied to the basket. The native would take the money, count it and if correct, place the article in the basket to be retrieved by the buyer. This process continued throughout the day as goods were exchanged for cash including rum and other merchandise.

Well, old Davis in his usual obnoxious manner while bartering and verbally abusing the poor native finally agreed upon a price. "My sister will love this bag," Davis grinned at us. As he placed the required amount minus a few dollars less than agreed upon, he lowered the basket. When the native counted the money, some heated comments were passed back and forth and with one swift yank, the native pulled the rope out of Davis' hand.

The native immediately grabbed his paddle and proceeded to swiftly leave the scene while still clutching Davis's money in his hand. We all thought Davis was going to jump right overboard after the native as he yelled, "I'm gonna catch you brudder, you somana bitch!"

There were five of us who witnessed this event and three of us were in contact with each other for another ten years. All agreed we witnessed a priceless piece of "773rd Comedy." There were no smart phones back then to record it. I cannot even guess how many times this has been told around the 773rd as Davis fumed. Even years after he left the 773rd to pursue his career in the Regular Army the story was still a classic.

We were watching the *Ballou* take on board a full brigade of Colombian infantry soldiers maybe 3000 total. Someone also noticed huge straw sacks maybe six feet by six feet being loaded into the *Ballou*'s cargo hold. Some sacks were marked "*arroz*" and others "*frijoles*." My high school Spanish told me it was rice and beans and spelled out to us hungry G.I.'s, no more turkey and roast beef dinners for the troops.

For the balance of the trip through the Panama Canal, the Eastern Pacific to Honolulu, the Western Pacific to Japan and finally continuing on to Korea, it was beans and rice and more beans and rice, and then a change of menu to rice and beans and more rice and beans, and I mean every bloody day.

The predominant number of Latin American soldiers aboard thrived on this diet while most of us in the 773rd ate it grudgingly. Ironically, realizing the nutritional value of this combination of beans and rice, I now cook very tasty combinations of this healthy food. Our own Hispanic troopers walked around with smiles on their faces. We did get a good supply of fresh fruit with plenty of oranges and the welcomed eggs for breakfast, both the fresh as long as they lasted and then, powdered eggs and hashed brown potatoes a welcomed change.

We had some melodrama in Panama between the Puerto Ricans and the Colombians. It was ugly and we had no clue about how much hatred there was at that time between these two Hispanic peoples. The Puerto Rican troops were waving their bayonets at the Colombians as they were climbing up the gangway boarding the ship.

The Ballou Stops Off in Panama

We sailed out of Cartagena with quite a bit of fanfare given to the departing Colombian troops by their government. Davis was still out to get the native who scammed him and life aboard the *Ballou* was back to the dull routine for the 773rd. I had a few classes to give but we on "C" deck, with the one exception of Lew Davis, were pretty much excluded from troop duty during the voyage. We made some visits to see our men to inspect the quarters, showers and latrines, we found them to be clean and well maintained.

I forget how long it took to arrive in Panama, which found us waiting our turn to pass through the canal. But, I do recall the battalion Sergeant Major Taylor arranging a trip to the U. S. Navy Chief Petty Officer's Club for food and drinks for all the first two graders. The *Ballou* was moored at the dock and I remember walking along a lovely walkway through neat lawns and palm tree shaded lanes to get to the Club. We had a welcomed dinner and drinks and were treated very well by the Navy people. It was pay as you go and it was a real treat and a great break from the dull routine and worsening diet aboard ship.

The troops were allowed on the pier for some refreshment, a cool beer and a chance to stretch their legs. That relaxation turned into a combat zone when the Puerto Rican Regimental Combat Team mixed with the Colombian Infantry Brigade.

We Sergeants were all relaxed as we sipped our drinks and watched the sun go down in that tropical setting. Sometime later a Navy Chief Petty Officer approached our table to report a riot exploded on the dock between the Colombian and the Puerto Rican troops who were all allowed off the ship. Once they mingled it soon turned into a free for all and local troops and M.P. units were called out to control the riot and get the men back aboard the *Ballou*.

The 773rd had a very high Hispanic presence and many of our troops were from Puerto Rico and others with families from many Latin American nations as well. Many hailed from the Southwestern states of Texas, Arizona and New Mexico. We never had any problems and never witnessed such violence. All the troops from Puerto Rico and Colombia were ordered to turn in their weapons and bayonets for storage until we arrived at our destination.

Traveling through the Panama Canal was an interesting experience. They would confine a ship in one of the locks while tons of water poured into the locks to raise the vessel to the level of the next body of water. The ship would then proceed on the lakes through the valleys. Like everything else, it became repetitive and we soon went below for chow and back to our compartment to play some more Monopoly. This is when Davis would bitch about our game of Monopoly and how it bothered his daytime sleeping. "Boardwalk, Park Place, Railroad! I have to sleep I go on duty in a couple hours." You could imagine the response from the real estate magnates playing Monopoly to Davis's plea for quiet.

Next Stop: Honolulu

The longest and most boring part of the voyage was the leg from Panama City on the Pacific side of the Panama Canal to Honolulu, Hawaii, a distance of over 4,000 miles. The daily routine is now quite lost to this aging soldier's memory. Compared to the voyages in the early part of the Second World War, when Japanese submarines were sinking our ships in these same waters, we could not but reflect upon our good fortune to be traveling in 1952 and not 1942.

Again, when the destination was in sight it was only a purple blue haze in the distance. What springs up in my memory bank is seeing the Aloha Tower as the *Ballou* approached the dock in the Port of Honolulu. The image also reveals Hawaiian beauties in low-slung grass skirts dancing the hula on an elevated stage right at "C" deck eye level and staring at smooth skinned tanned gyrating hips and belly buttons which aroused the desire in all of us.

This was to be my one and only trip to Hawaii. I am happy to have seen the beautiful tropical scenery in 1952. Any modern photos show the same location now with high-rise hotels obscuring the beaches, palm trees and natural beauty of the Island.

I remember dressing in a fresh khaki uniform and joining my comrades for an army bus ride through the busy downtown area and along the coast to Waikiki Beach and the Royal Hawaiian Hotel with Diamond Head looming off in the distance. I think the 773rd were the only soldiers allowed ashore and I still give many thanks to our Colonel who planned this break for his 800 grateful troops.

I have a vague memory of a new soldier with the last name beginning with a "K" among a few casual Hawaiian draftees reporting to the 773rd. He was assigned to my platoon and I remember meeting his parents as I was boarding the bus and promised them I would take care of him. I do not recall how this occurred but a good platoon Sergeant's job is to look out for his men so, I made the promise I knew that I could and would keep. He was a troubled soldier and was sent home sometime after we arrived in Korea.

This is now a good opportunity to introduce you to regular army Corporal Harris who was a cook in C Battery. Harris was very tall - well over six feet. For the short time I knew him, I remember him as a good soldier wearing a broad grin and well-liked by all. Even his grouchy boss Davis spoke well of him. Harris was a black trooper from the South and his problem was his size.

Corporal Harris reported to C Battery just before we left from Brooklyn. He had limited boots and clothing because the quartermaster could not find his proper sizes. He was told that once he arrived overseas he would be properly outfitted. He had high hopes when we heard our next stop was to be Japan where he was sent to the Eighth Army Quartermaster and returned to the ship and told he would be outfitted in Korea. When we arrived in Korea, he was told no boots his size were available so he was ordered to return to the states and never went any further north than Pusan.

In the picture section, you will see him posing with two Colombia soldiers. I'm sure that broad grin remained on his face all the way back home to the ZI (Zone of Interior), as his orders read. He proudly showed everyone his orders to prove this was not his decision as he exclaimed, "Hell, I volunteered for the Far East, I was hoping to get combat pay if I went to Korea!"

On Pass in Yokohama

The *Ballou* entered the busy port of Yokohama at the same time a rumor floated that the 773rd was not debarking here and that we would remain onboard. We were later informed that we would be free every night with passes, with the understanding that we must return to the ship every evening by 10 or 11 P.M. All of the other troops debarked for processing and by this time we all knew our final destination would be Korea.

I buddied up with Burns, my radar section chief, and remember walking down the gangplank to the dock. Burns, a veteran of the fighting against the Japanese in the Pacific, had considerable hatred for the "Japs." Walking along the dock and approaching the gate, we saw a number of little Japanese children selling red artificial poppies. These poppies were similar to those sold in the states on Armistice Day in commemoration of the many American troops killed in World War One.

Many Soldiers were buried in the Military Cemetery in Flanders Field in Belgium and other military cemeteries in Europe. The poppy was among the only flowers that would grow on those war-torn fields and a poem was written by a Canadian Artillery officer who lost his friend in a battle there. "In Flanders Fields" was written by Major John McCrae to honor his friend Lieutenant Alexis Helmer killed in action. Both were in the same Canadian Artillery unit. The profits for the sale of these similar poppies were supposedly for the Japanese veterans of World War II or just pocketed to scam money from the thousands passing through these gates.

You could imagine Burns comments when he saw this so we just walked away from the kids. I smiled at them and they smiled back but Burns just stared right through them mumbling something about the "Those %$@&%$@'Japs." It was in mid-morning so our first stop was a restaurant to have some ham and eggs. Now I have mentioned back in those bygone days I did not eat fresh fish. The smell of fish permeated the atmosphere even while still at sea and approaching the harbor in Yokohama. When the cute Japanese waitress placed my plate before me I only picked because the ham and eggs even smelled like fish to me. "What's wrong, Gallagher, I thought you were dreaming about ham and eggs?" Burns asked in his Tennessee drawl. "They just smell and taste like fish," I said as I picked through the food. The twinkle in the pretty Japanese waitress's eyes took our mind off food and after paying and leaving the restaurant, I asked Burns, "You still hate all the Japs?"

We continued taking in the sights and sounds. We found a small hotel, bar, restaurant or what can be better described as a quaint Japanese Inn. On first entering, we had to take off our shoes as we were greeted by an attractive mature Japanese woman, impeccably coiffed and dressed. She greeted us like we were royalty rather than two G.I.'s in a strange land. We stepped up to the raised entry way and was shown to a small bar presided over by a clean cut, articulate Japanese man, probably in his 30's. We ordered a Japanese beer and sat down on a small bar stool and not the floor mats the Japanese usually sat on.

The atmosphere was very relaxing and some soft oriental music was playing in the background. After a couple of drinks, the barkeep who was actually the owner, engaged us in conversation. Of all things, the subject became "Where were you during the war?" The barkeep noticed some World War II ribbons on Burns uniform; after seven years of occupation, the Japanese were all very familiar with the American service uniform and decorations.

"Oh man!" I thought to myself, not knowing how Burns would react to this topic. I wondered whether we will have to leave this nice little Inn. But, Burns was a pretty serious and responsible person and politely exchanged some experiences with this new Japanese acquaintance, who as it turned out told us he was a former Japanese Artillery officer. These two former enemies swapped stories about their personal experiences in opposing armies.

The drinks were now flowing and I saw a complete change in Burns who was now relaxed; he and the former Japanese Army officer were talking like long lost pals. The owner called a few of his pretty female staff to perform some songs and dances for us. The strains of "China Night" and other songs I can no longer remember filled the air and it became like a house party. Even straight-laced Southern boy Burns and "No Rhythm" Gallagher were dancing with these lovely Japanese girls to a song I recall about "Coal Men." Maybe some old vets who served in Japan with the occupation forces would remember the songs and dance. As we were dancing, I smelled steak broiling on the grill and this time it did not smell like fish. It was the most delicious steak I ever had.

It was a great break for me and Burns. The owner asked us if we would like to go to bed with one of his lovely young ladies and we could choose whomever we wished. But we noticed it was approaching the hour when we would have to return to the ship.

As we were leaving all the women waved "*sayonara*" to us as we put on our shoes and hoofed it back to the *Ballou*. "You come back tomorrow," they all called out. The little raised entrance we entered hours before and greeted by a mature somber-faced woman was now crowded with Japanese girls and women waving at us and beckoning for us to come back. Burns no longer hated the "Japs," and the interaction between the two former enemies added another dimension to my first visit to Japan. The Japanese are a cultured and physically clean people, the typical Japanese bathes daily. They love good food and drink, and enjoy themselves. We both felt good as we hastened through the darkened neighborhood heading for the lights of downtown Yokohama and the *C.C. Ballou* for our final journey to Korea.

Remembered by every serviceman sailing in these waters was the smell flowing from the Korean peninsula and one that would only get stronger the closer one got to the mainland. For ages, the Koreans and other Asian farms used night soil...human waste to fertilize their crops. Our forces were warned not to drink any water not boiled first or treated with chemical purification tablets nor eat any uncooked food. Once inland and up country, the

258

western nostril became accustomed to the smell and after a while we no longer noticed it.

The battalion marched to a rail head where we were unceremoniously directed to a somewhat decrepit troop train with an aging steam engine, huffing and puffing, waiting for the 773rd to board.

The C. C. Ballou and M.L. Hersey were built to identical specifications at Kaiser Ship Yard in Richmond, California during World War II. The A. W. Greeley is also a sister ship. *USNS General A.W. Greeley by US Navy Public Domain via Wikipedia Commons.*

Sister ship General C.G. Morton sails under Golden Gate Bridge same as Hersey did April 1953. Four thousand G.I.'s were on deck laughing and yelling thankful to be back in the United States. *USS General Morton AP-138 by US Navy Public Domain, via Wikipedia Commons*

Front row L to R
SGT Cruz,
Gallagher.
Second row L to R
SGT Price, SFC
Burns.
Followed by 150
thirsty Charlie
Battery troopers.

Cartoon from C.C. Ballou newspaper

PASSING THRU THE PANAMA CANAL

A day long journey through the Lakes and Locks of the Panama Canal. Odd to see a ship coming around the mountain and heading our way.

Notice how high we are on C deck looking across the lock looking at another ship setting lower in the water. Interesting for a time but became redundant as the day progressed.

L to R: Supply SFC Van Ness, Gallagher and M/SGT Gun Platoon SGT Tom Quidone.

I am quite sure this Door to Door Salesman was the same guy who took off with Davis's money.

Motor SFC Ralph Nebbia laughed for a week while SGT
Davis bitched about his alligator purse.

Not too much attention was paid to the Sergeants on C deck
after the disagreement Davis had with the alligator bag
salesman.

SFC Warren Burns tagged and packed as we enter Pusan
Harbor. Koje-Do Island POW Compound in background. We
had to get used to the Night Soil aroma drifting off the land.

SFC Lew Davis did not realize at the time he would be awake
all night on the train ride north trying to get his big frame
comfortable for a few winks of sleep.

CPL Harris next to two Columbian Infantrymen. He was happy to debark in Korea, hoping to get outfitted and proceed north with the battery. He was ordered back to the states because they could not find his proper boot sizes.

Supply canoes kept the traders well stocked. I do not know if any of these natives had "The Curse of Lew Davis" on their heads.

Extracts from C.C. Ballou newspaper produced by the troops.

All I remember is looking at the boots in front of me as I
climbed up the gangway to C deck.

These drills did not concern us as we sailed such calm and
friendly waters. We made up for it on the way back from
Japan when the sea engulfed the troop ship in a violent storm
in the Western Pacific.

A little language barrier among the Latin American troopers going native when they had K.P.

I did not notice this picture back in 1952 nor did I pray in those days. This jumped out at me now and made me thankful for the prayers of my parents and my sweetheart Lee.

Chapter 8

Korea - September 1952

The Train Ride North

The battalion boarded this old train a relic of Japan's colonial days and sat on uncomfortable wooden slatted bench seats to begin the overnight journey north. We knew our Battery Commander Lieutenant Smedley and Platoon Leader Lieutenant Carter but did not know some of our new officers and warrant officers. So, I will describe the new battery executive officer for you. My first image of him was on the long train ride north. His name was ... well, let's just call him LTNYBLUE because he claimed to be a New York City detective in civilian life.

I see him standing in the swaying car wearing his soft fatigue hat with a First Lieutenant's single silver bar attached. His police revolver in a shoulder holster. I would guess he already had a few drinks of an adult beverage. This was not an encouraging sight to see for me and my men. The next image of him comes when I was jarred awake by pistol shots and Lieutenant LTNYBLUE was returning to our car and mumbling something while holstering his pistol. "Anything up, Lieutenant?" I asked as a couple of us faced the lieutenant who now could not hide his drunkenness from us. He gave no reply, just a nod of his head as he sat down in his seat. "I'd better keep an eye on this guy," I thought, as the long night wore on.

We all squirmed looking for that comfortable spot for a few winks but it never came. Mumbles were heard of "This fucking train," and other complaints but the worst case was the big oversized Davis trying to get comfortable. Some doubled up to give a whole seat to Davis. He was, after all, older, bigger, and heavier, we saw he was in pain as he uttered a few classic Davis comments about the Koreans and their lousy "railroad." Dawn finally arrived and it was time to get off the train. "When the hell do we eat," was a familiar bellow from the troops.

269

The image fades and opens to a neat row of tents, cots and sleeping bags were issued to us and then we ate chow in a big mess tent with a sign, "Welcome to the 45th Infantry Division." We had no idea or even an interest in where we were; food and comfort reigned on our list of priorities at the time. After a month of rice and beans on the troop ship, the 45th laid out some great chow for us. That evening we heard automatic fire coming from somewhere in the dark distance which perked up everyone until it subsided. But, I just rolled over cuddled up in the comfort of my sleeping bag. This was much more restful than the night before trying to get comfortable on that hard wooden bench seat and keeping an eye on a drunken lieutenant.

The next memory I have is being ordered NCO in charge of a detail only because my platoon leader Lieutenant Carter was assigned officer in charge. The detail included 25 2 ½ ton trucks each with a driver and an assistant driver to form a convoy to drive to point "A" and load some cargo, and to deliver it to point "B." That was at the battalion assembly area where we re-connected with our heavy equipment marked 9205B.

When I asked Lieutenant Carter about the estimated distance and time to complete the detail he said he did not know. "Do you have the strip maps?" I asked. Again, "No," he answered with a blank expression. I found the NCO in charge of the motor pool and asked him for details. He said "Yeah"... I told that dumb lieutenant where to get the strip maps, didn't he tell you?"

The motor Sergeant was in the process of having the tires checked and the 25 trucks and the jeep re-fueled. I found G-3 and received the strip maps for each driver and an estimate of time on the road, time to load, drive to the assembly area unload and return to the 45th motor pool. It was to be a long day so I found Division G-4 Supply and ordered rations for three meals for 50 drivers and assistants and 3 for Carter our driver and myself. Lieutenant Carter did not think of one single thing about this detail, he was like this as long as I knew him.

270

I appointed one senior driver as my assistant and gave him a copy of the list of men on the detail and had him line up the drivers and march them to the division G-4 supply. I supervised as each man received his rations and a combat issue of ammo for their weapons, .45 caliber 30 round magazines for the M3 Grease Gun and .30 caliber 15 round magazines for the M1 Carbines. Each man received 90 rounds of ammo.

When we marched back to the trucks, I told the men to load a magazine in their weapon but not to crank one into the chamber because we would have time for that if necessary and to make sure the weapons safety was on. The drivers all followed my word and looked serious and attentive. Training was over and this could become real for I had no idea nor did my Leader even ask about security on our trip. Fortunately, I was told we would be traveling in secure areas in the daytime. Take no chances Gallagher," Sergeant Haldane Irwin warned me. "I've been here before and know these bastards." Irwin's warning stayed with me until I left Korea.

"Gallagher, what's this all about...RATIONS and AMMUNITION?" I just looked at Carter gave him a strip map and jumped in the back seat of the Jeep. "It's all yours, Lieutenant. I have your ammo issue and rations. Did you bring a canteen of water?" No answer. We pulled out of the 45th motor pool in front of the convoy now led by the lieutenant. He directed the driver to make the first turn in the wrong direction. The driver just shook his head and glanced at me with a serious look in his face. I also saw him touch his grease gun making sure the loaded magazine was properly in place. The lieutenant glanced over his right shoulder trying to read a road side written in Korean characters. "Lieutenant," I asked, "Take a look at the map, sir, I think we are going in the wrong direction." "You did enough, Gallagher," he sarcastically replied. "Screw you," I mumbled under my breath. What a start for my first day in Korea. To myself I thought "Maybe if I just ignore him, he will go away?" Believe it or not he did go away. Sometime after he applied for a transfer to another battery and we were happy to see him go. Apparently, he was not welcomed into any of the other batteries in the battalion and finally landed in a Twin 40mm outfit where no one knew him … good riddance. We later learned he was in the same 40mm unit White Elk was in.

The next image is seeing a group of M.P. officers and NCO's cussing out Lieutenant Carter for blocking the road and ordered him to turn his convoy of 25 trucks and one Jeep around in a 180 degree U-Turn. We were blocking the MSR (Main Supply Route). This was the main road for carrying rations, drinking water, ammo, replacements and medical supplies to the front lines and the evacuation of the more seriously wounded and sick soldiers.

Without realizing it he was leading this convoy directly to the front lines and this was the closest I ever came to the 38th parallel that I knew of. We could hear automatic fire as well as artillery fire only much louder this time than the previous evenings.

I do not recall who the Jeep driver was, for he was not a C Battery man. But I could see his serious demeanor as his head turned towards me when maneuvering his Jeep at the head of the convoy in this huge "Mother of all U-turns."

As the convoy rolled, the driver was looking at me for confirmation of any turns the lieutenant ordered. Carter was at least wise enough to give me the strip map. With the mission accomplished and spared any small talk between the NCO and the Officer in charge, we all returned unscathed and kept the leftover rations; I don't remember if they were "K's" or "C's." But remember, they all had a pack of four cigarettes.

With help from a couple corporals, we made sure each man's weapon was cleared before I gave up my job as NCO in charge. We did notice some carbines and grease guns already had a round in the chamber. Probably when the men heard we were getting closer to the sound of fire, they followed their instincts.

The convoy detail was over so the next stop was the 45th's great mess where we all sat down for hot chow. So ended our days with this famous National Guard Thunderbird Infantry Division from the Southwest.

(45th Division Patch)

K-55 and So-Jung-Ni

The Battalion moved to an assembly area on a muddy plain somewhere near Seoul. We set up squad tents and Davis set up his kitchen and prepared and served the troops canned beef stew that first night. I remember going into the mess tent for some coffee and saw the cooks opening up big cans of beef stew. We spent a few days there while each battery was collecting their equipment, guns, radar and all the equipment sent from the states. We received the full complement of tents and mess equipment followed by motor transport, 2 ½ ton trucks, ¾ ton trucks and Jeeps together with cargo trailers for all the vehicles. These were indeed the older WWII vehicles to replace those new models we left behind in Brooklyn. The CAT's were sent with all the equipment and material we had coded 9205B in Brooklyn.

One morning, the officers and Platoon Sergeants had a meeting in the CP tent and we heard about our mission as the air defense for a new jet fighter base code named K-55 somewhere south along the MSR (Main Supply Route). We received strip maps and Topo's from the battalion S-3 and studied them to see exactly where we were going.

The destination was on a hill east of Osan in a little hamlet known as So-Jung-ni which we later discovered was no more than a few thatched roof huts on an ox cart trail.

Headquarters Staff and Headquarters Battery was to be stationed along with one firing battery at the airbase still under construction. When we arrived there the base runways were already built and operational, F-80 jet fighters were flying from K-55 and soon joined by the latest F-86 Saber Jets. All the while, Quonset huts were being built for the quarters and ancillary buildings for all the Air Force personnel.

The 773rd's remaining firing batteries were positioned some distance from the air base, with C Battery located the most distant and most isolated from K-55. Army and Air Force higher commands were not taking any chances in defending against any air threat to the new air base and the valuable jet fighters.

Meanwhile with all the construction at K-55 the enemy had plenty of time to assess the threat this new airbase was to them and all eyes were on C Battery as we emplaced our air defenses. Another unknown to us at the time was the threat of a guerilla ground attack from the foot hills east and northeast of Charlie Battery's position. These foothills had ox cart trails winding into the mountainous terrain to the north allowing a path for infiltration. This probably still goes on at this late date between two nations who are only honoring a "Cease Fire," violated many times by the itchy trigger fingers of the arrogant North Koreans over the past 60 plus years.

When the 773rd entered those hills and ridges, we did not see any forest with mature trees and wondered why. The reason for this lack of old forest was because Koreans continued to cut down the readily accessible immature trees with their basic hand tools. This was done to provide the necessary and only source of fuel to heat their homes and cook their food. This was done either by burning the raw immature wood or converting it to charcoal, resulting in the hills barren of any mature trees. In our time in Korea, one could always smell the wood smoke or charcoal burning in the villages.

The homes were small structures by our standards, made with wood wattle and covered with a mixture of adobe like rice straw and mud. The roofs were all thatched with rice straw. The stove, a built-in affair, was outside the house adjoining the few inch raised hollowed out area under the house. When the cooking fire was lit, the heat was naturally drawn under the house keeping the dried mud floors warm. The family slept on straw mats right on the warm floor and this kept them cozy and protected from the severe Korean winters.

I checked online and viewed a Korean TV show called *Arirang*, a popular Korean song well remembered by Korean War vets. A show I watched just happened to be about the restoration of the Korean forests over the past 60 years following the war. Those same treeless ridges and mountains are now beautifully green with mature trees.

The song "Arirang" is the most popular song in South Korea, a beautiful and nostalgic tune many of us remember with a little sentiment of our own for these hard-working industrious people. The song signifies the hardship the Koreans have suffered only to make them into the strong and resilient people they are today. (To listen to the song, go online to "Korean War Memorial, Arirang" or facebook.com). The song has a haunting melody.

Those tiny mountain villages sheltered organized guerilla forces supposedly cleared by ROK (Republic of Korea) forces. They were located in such out of the way and inaccessible areas that were cleared today and as soon as the ROK forces left were re-occupied. The locals made no complaints because of their fear of retaliation from these ruthless irregular forces. This is intelligence we were not informed about when we were sent to recon, stake out and, occupy our position in So-Jung-Ni.

Battery Executive Office LTNYBLUE, who was also the gun platoon leader, led the recon party to locate and stake out our new home at So-Jung-Ni. The party included the gun platoon Sergeant, the fire control platoon officer and Sergeant, a couple of Jeep drivers and the battery gun mechanic Max Ries driving his ¾ ton truck with a few gun platoon men riding shotgun. I think Bob Dema was also with us.

With eyes wide open and all our senses alerted, the small party moved out. We were issued googles to protect our "wide open" eyes from the grit and grime of the dusty road.

We passed strange and exotic sites unfamiliar to North Americans. Graves were seen along the way and we learned the more ancient graves were shaped like a womb and many with phallic symbol stone markers common to ancient burial sites throughout Asia. We were not there to study Korean archaeology but simply took in all the sites of this turbulent land which appeared strange to our Western eyes. We were ordered to show the greatest respect for all Korean graves during our service there.

The villages we drove through all showed signs of the devastation war brings to the innocent civilians and we also noticed the happy faces smiling at us when the people saw the white star on the side of our vehicles showing we were Americans.

The American G.I. was a symbol of peace, freedom and a full belly to many war-torn innocents throughout the world. I only wish more Americans realized this as we veterans do who, have served as witness to the suffering of those ill-fated masses.

If the Korean civilians liked you, you were called "Numba One" If the Koreans do not like a person, that person is, "Numba Ten." If they really didn't like you, the males used the phrase "Numba Hucking Ten." They had a problem pronouncing the letter"F." Of course, if they liked you a lot you were "Numba Hucking ONE"…this lingo was soon copied by the G.I.'s.

Christian missionary signs were seen and many leper colony signs were passed on the way. Korea was a Japanese colony for many years but the influence of Christianity dominated Korea. I later learned that the Korean peninsula was home to the largest Christian population in Asia. The early Christian missionaries living throughout Asia sent their teen-aged children to the largest Christian high school in Asia in Pyongyang, now the capitol of the godless North Korean communist dictatorship.

This time I did not have to arrange for any strip maps, rations, water or ammo, these details were efficiently taken care of by our own people. Instead of giving the responsibility to the fire control platoon officer where it belonged, I was given full guardianship of the M1A1 Aiming Circle which was needed to orient the battery. It lived under my cot while I was in Korea. My platoon lieutenant was seated next to the driver and I don't recall hearing a word from him as I was all eyes taking in all the scenery or likely spots for an ambush. "Keep alert, Gallagher," I was again reminded.

LTNYBLUE approached me when I was setting up the aiming circle: "Gallagher, I never had a chance to handle the aiming circle. When you have some time let's go over that with me." "Sure, any time, sir." He was a quick learner; it's too bad alcohol was to be his downfall. The lieutenant was an efficient and responsible officer when he was sober.

Nothing stood out on that ride except miles and miles of thatched roofed huts and vistas of rice paddies and Korean civilians tending their ox carts. As we drove through the villages, we saw multitudes of little black-haired kids with inquisitive eyes staring at us. We were to learn that many of these cute little smiling waifs would steal anything they could get their hands on.

Apparently, LTNYBLUE knew his business with Topo map, strip map and compass: he led us to our destination with no wrong turns. We arrived on a barren hill in the middle of nowhere where Charlie Battery set up our new home. We all jumped out of the vehicles and proceeded to stake out the battery.

We did notice some curious local eyes upon us but we were many miles from the front lines and thought nothing of the inquisitive eyes as we continued our business. "I wonder how many of them are on our side," I remember overhearing one of the guys.

We were soon followed by the battery and all of the equipment was hastily emplaced, leveled and O & S'd. Settling rounds were fired as we reported by radio to 10th Group that we were operational not in voice, but using the code for "Operational." "Nudge Charlie to Talon One"..."Nudge" what a code name for the 773rd...why not "Raptor," "Hawk," or "Kite" but, we were stuck with "Nudge" by the RA's from 10th Group ....the Finks!!

The perimeter defense was organized with guards around the clock and barbed wire was set up to encircle our entire position while squad tents started going up. My job was to make sure all the fire control equipment was emplaced, oriented and synchronized and the guns back-sighted. A command post (CP) tent was set as headquarters and home to the First Sergeant, Supply Sergeant and the battery clerk.

I remember those first nights sleeping on such hilly terrain and waking in the morning with my legs from the knees down half off my cot from slipping downhill. "Gallagher, we should dig slit trenches, we have no protection if we're hit. These lieutenants should know better," SFC Burns spit out in his Tennessee drawl. Fire Control dug fox holes for protection from an enemy that could rake us with an automatic weapon. Lieutenant Carter asked me if that was necessary. I just looked at him, turned around, and walked away!

The battery was soon kicking back and feeling more relaxed and safer in our position. We started hiring some mess help and a few "house boys." Ours was Kim, the most common name in Korea. He was fitted out in G.I. clothes, all too big for him but he did not mind at all. His mom was hired as an on-site wash women and I must admit she was quite an attractive woman, probably in her 30's.

All Sergeants had a secondary function along with their main job. Sergeant Joe Zurla was made Laundry NCO in addition to his fire control duties. I was assigned perimeter defense NCO and rodent control NCO. I made a large drawing of our ground defense perimeter within the barbed wire showing the placement of the .50 caliber ground mount machine guns for effective crossfire and each section's position when the ground alert was sounded. This diagram was placed in the CP tent. The ground alert warning was an empty 90 mm brass shell case dangling from a wire attached to a wood mount. A couple hits with an accompanying iron bar and the gong sounded a ground alert. The air alert was simply turning on the siren in one of the CATS. All simple and very effective.

The radar and the M-9 Director were both humming. "Any equipment problems?" "Negative," was the return answer which was a relief to hear after an ocean voyage of nine thousand miles. Our old 1940's radar and director were still doing their duty. Our experienced RA radar chief and his excellent crew were responsible for this because the radar was the biggest concern, being the most prone to breakdowns.

The call was heard to "Take Ten...Light 'em up if you got 'em," as Charlie Battery kicked back for a break. "When's chow?" was heard again now on that hill in So-Jung-Ni... "Chow is ready when I say it's ready," scowled Davis with his usual reply!

Charlie Battery ate late that night and in shifts but Davis was now showing his experience without a comment as he hustled his cooks and kept the chow hot for all sections as mess kits were heard rattling. He was a pain in the ass but nevertheless a damn good soldier and a damn good Mess Sergeant. He did it like he was there before, which he was. Many people who never actually met

Davis knew about him and he never knew how much of a legend he would become.

The last two men to eat that night were Master Sergeants Kolody and Gallagher. I never thought "Bucking the Chow Line" a good leadership move. Kolody was always on duty, always in uniform wearing his web belt with two loaded ammo clips in his ammo pouch, and his first aid packet. I remember he even walked around with his canteen full of water. At that time, weapons were carried by some or within easy reach. Kolody was a loner and the only soldier I remember who kept a diary. I would have followed that guy anywhere. We had a lot of real good troopers in Charlie Battery both with and without stripes on their arms.

The first time the "Air Alert" was sounded every man hit his assigned position and we searched for the incoming target with no idea what we would encounter. We were told the enemy used small low flying aircraft that would duck in and out of the mountain passes. This would protect them from the radar locking on long enough to send data to the director and transmit firing data to the guns. This was more of an observation by the enemy to test our air defenses and harass the men who had to remain awake and on duty. When all the AA units in the area fired the sky was lit up like the Fourth of July with tracer and high-exploding ordnance but, no enemy planes were ever destroyed. These flights were christened "Bed Check Charlie" and happened all the time and we were always ready for them. Which, probably discouraged the enemy from sending their medium bombers south.

We did have ground attack alerts. The only time I can recall a fire fight occurring was early during our deployment, when the motor section troops were hit from the foot hills on their exposed position from the southeast and, returned fire with small arms and a single ground mount .50 caliber machine gun. It occurred at night and I was awakened by the sound of the .50 caliber and small arms fire. I thought it was a dream at first but the platoon got moving to our ground alert positions and soon the firing ceased. My NCO's always thought the sight of that Quad Mount .50 caliber machine gun discouraged any threat to our sector of the defense perimeter.

Maybe that's the reason I had it put there after all … we were the nerve center of the battery!

Motor Section Chief Sergeant First Class Ralph Nebbia reacted swiftly when the attack took place. He ordered his motor section of about 15 soldiers to take the pre-planned defensive positions and fire in the direction of the incoming fire exactly as we were trained on maneuvers in Camp Stewart when the aggressors attacked our artillery position. The attackers did not hang around too long but the attack kept us all on alert waiting for a stronger attack which never came but, the battery was ready for it. We were by now well trained thanks to those "Swampy Aggressors" back in Camp Stewart.

Ralph was a good man and an original Guard volunteer from the group of Hell's Kitchen guys from Manhattan's West Side. Ralph always stood tall in my eyes for all of the years I knew him and served with him, from 1948 to 1962. After many years of no contact, I met with several of my now aging comrades in Florida in 2005. The names and memories flowed back. I got Nebbia's phone number and called him only to be sadly told by his wife that I was too late, Ralph had passed away only a short time before. She said he would have been happy to speak to me and so would I have been very happy to have said hello to Sergeant First Class Ralph Nebbia.

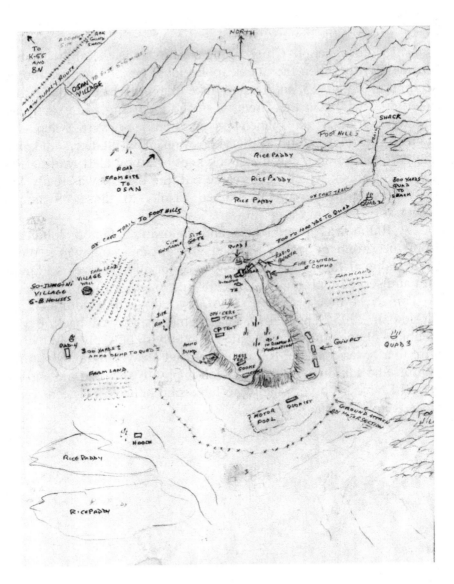

So-Jung-Ni Site Plan

New Platoon Leader

Charlie Battery was busy doing what the Army referred to as "Improvement of Position." First, all the guns and equipment had to be dug in and sandbagged and this is where Alabam' was kept busy, digging the large hole for the radar with the bulldozer after he leveled the crest of our hill. Everyone was busy filling sand bags and this was between all the other duties of providing security for our site and keeping all the battery equipment running smoothly.

During all the hustle and bustle of the battery activities, our new Platoon Leader First Lieutenant Haber showed up one morning to meet his new platoon. He was much shorter than Carter and did not command much of a military presence but, I knew not to judge a book by its cover. Haber was a well-trained and knowledgeable ROTC officer even though he pranced around with his nose sticking out of his fur-lined parka hood as the days grew colder. Maybe we were all jealous of his winter parka and Mickey Mouse boots. Those insulated boots would have prevented frostbite to many soldiers and marines during the first Korean winter in those frozen ridges swarming with thousands of Chinese Communists forces.

Our new lieutenant had an embarrassing event occur when he accidentally slipped and fell into the radar hole before the hole was properly railed off. He could have been badly injured if he had fallen all the way to the bottom but between his bulky parka and a sloppy side wall he was saved. We did have to help him climb out. Once he was all recovered, he just stamped his feet brushed off the dirt, stood before us and we all laughed like hell WITH him. He was a good platoon leader and I think this episode showed his spunk to the platoon. He took over all the trial shot problems (TSP) Carter did not know how to do. That, put me standing on the radar roof to do his TSP's with one eye on the radar elbow scope and my other eye on a Tech' Manual. Lieutenant O'Rahilly gave me enough pointers about TSP's to actually run the problem myself. Today, I may feel sorry for my treatment of Carter but, we were there to do a job and everyone had to do his share… Hooray for

Lieutenant Haber... a very capable Fire Control Officer and Platoon Leader.

With the approach of winter, the battery was busy assembling the Quonset huts that went up rather quickly once the troopers got the hang of it. They were heated by two diesel oil heaters also used to warm shave water and cook with, offering a warm and snug harbor for Charlie Battery that third Korean winter. Each hut housed about 20 soldiers and I occupied a corner with a wooden crate to serve as a wash stand.

In the meantime, our tents were still comfortable even though we set up on such hilly terrain. The weather was still warm during the day and we could air out the tents and seal them up for the cooler nights. We slept on folding canvas cots with air mattresses and sleeping bags. We were very well fed from Davis's mess tent except if on a patrol or a trip away from the battery when "K" or "C" rations were on the menu. Thanksgiving dinner at Charlie Battery included roast turkey with all the trimmings. Of course, it was all in the open where we ate all our meals regardless of the weather. It was not until the following March when the battery enjoyed the luxury of a Quonset hut mess hall.

Yes, we could run to our tents but that was on the other side of the gun site and if it was snowing, your meal was decorated with big white snowflakes. I don't recall this being much of a nuisance but do remember how well we were fed in Korea. Scrambled dehydrated eggs and thick country sausages was always a welcome breakfast, washed down with Davis' strong dark G. I. coffee; Yeah, it was better than the other batteries' watered down coffee. He had some kind of a deal to get more coffee so he could make it darker and tastier. "You no lika my coffee here, go drink it someplace else, Brudder." Davis often bellowed.

Time was spent away from the site on trips to some observation areas and field artillery FDC's (Fire Direction Centers), in places up north. Lieutenant Haber was in charge and I rode in the back seat of that Jeep and appreciated and respected his leadership. We were gone overnight on several occasions, one time, when my overcoat was stolen with my wool and leather gloves and another, when I "Midnight Requisitioned" a brand new pair of insulated Mickey Mouse Boots. We were always on the alert, only this time not against a creative practical joker but to look out for an enemy encounter around the next hilltop. I never had the gunsight on my carbine aimed at an enemy and only the good Lord knows if I was ever a target.

While at the Eighth Army PX located in an office building in Seoul originally built by the Japanese, I spotted a German made Kodak Retina IIA 35mm camera on a shelf for $35.00 and bought it. I was with Haber and the Jeep driver Willets and remember having a couple hamburgers which were the first we had since leaving the states. I finally acquired my .45 automatic by then and carried it in a shoulder holster concealed. This possibility of capture was in the back of my mind probably from talks with Peterson and Bevins back at Fort Bliss. It popped up on those lonely roads with my platoon leader and driver which urged me to keep alert and probably was the reason I carried the .45 concealed. Odd what protective and false security we invent for ourselves when we have to. I was always on red alert whenever off that gun site in So-Jung-Ni and heeded the advice of the more experienced RA's Sergeant's Burns and Irwin.

Back on the site I played with my new camera and was helped by a trooper who had some photography knowledge and took some interesting pictures, some of which accompany this narrative. My favorite were photos of the tough but good natured South Korean farmers and their families.

Soda crackers were somewhat of a high demand item in our battery. Everyone would grab some extra at every opportunity and they were always available to us. When we noshed our personal goodies in the evening, it was always nice to have some crackers to go along with the pepperoni or salamis the guys got from loved ones at home. Suddenly, Soda Crackers became scarce as Davis growled… "No more Cracks."

I liked to keep a few small cans of Libby's tuna fish and cans of those salty black olives that I would buy at the K-55 PX. Anyone from the platoon going to K-55 would take orders. But, most goodies came from home and I cannot tell you the joy those packages brought to every soldier.

My Mom sent me her oatmeal cookies and my Dad used his ingenuity to send me spirits not available to us in Korea. He would cut an unsliced oval loaf of fresh Jewish rye bread in half, hollow out the inside to rest a pint sized glass bottle of brandy or whiskey, and then tape up the entire loaf making a well-wrapped and boxed shock-proof package. It came in handy that winter and his thoughtfulness kept me well supplied to warm my insides and share with others. Lee kept me in stock with hard salami and provolone cheese. I also liked the little tins of salty Italian anchovy filets Mom sent from home. I can still hear Burns Southern drawl, "Gallagher, how can you eat them rotten Eye-Talian sardines?"

Davis had important contacts, one with a Marine Reserve Air unit flying the single seat attack plane, the Douglas Sky Raider. The marines had huge quantities of canned beer stacked in an oversized Quonset building and how they procured the beer was a mystery to us but an excellent source. The Sky raider pilots were both officers and flying Sergeants from WWII. They were an interesting group and we watched planes landing with battle damage after missions north to support our troops.

One day before Davis left in his 2 ½ ton truck to ride to battalion to pick up rations, water and mail he said, "Gahlic, today you go to battalion with me and ride shotgun so, it's just you and me OK," I knew Davis was implicating me with something but, what the hell I was young and curious and happy to visit the Air Force PX at K-55 to restock my supply and take orders for the men in my platoon. On the way to K-55, Davis confessed "Hey Gahlic, I stop off to see my friend, OK?" "You are driving, it's OK with me." I guessed who the friend might be and did not think it was the Christian pastor at the orphanage where we sent food from time to time.

Davis stopped at a thatched roof hut and said "Come on say hello for just a minute," as we both hopped out and entered the one-room hut. Now I was expecting an old haggard looking unwashed Korean lady but was shocked to see this attractive young Korean woman. She was quite different from his chubby loves back in Ludiwici, Georgia. She was smiling as she put her arms around Davis and gave him a big hug. Davis was all smiles himself and acted like a teenager on his first date. "This is my girla friend, Gahlic," he said as I looked approvingly at her at the same time, my eyes zeroed in on the wall shelf stacked with boxes of G.I. soda crackers. Now, I knew why such restraint when passing out soda crackers and his usual comment, "No more cracks" to the troops.

Lew Davis was never married that I knew about and the only relative he ever mentioned was his sister. He got Charlie Battery beer, extra coffee, plenty of chow and also seasonings and cheeses from an Italian medical unit he also connected with. But he was tough to work for and a lot of guys hated him and bitched about the food just to get him mad.

The Culture and Settling In

One morning we watched a new shack being built in plain view just outside the perimeter of our position. It seemed to go up in only a few days and that is when we were introduced to the Asian "Pull Saw." The cut with the pull stroke rather than our push stroke. The Koreans did wonders with their basic and ancient tools. Several heavily made-up young girls arrived and moved into the shack and it was no secret to anyone what their business was.

One of our CeeWO's (Chief Warrant Officer), let's call him Mr. Henwood as all Warrant Officers were addressed as "Mr.", was sent by the battery commander to put up a sign on the door that said, "OFF LIMITS." The girls immediately tore down the sign every time he tried to hang it up. It looked more like a game and it also proved CWO Henwood was no stranger to these "Happy Hookers." Every time we mentioned it to Henwood his face turned red. The women laundry workers in C battery were very disdainful towards the prostitutes who set up shop in their back yard and shook their fingers at the G.I.'s they saw frequent the shack. "Yu Numba ten" they scolded. "Baby G.I. Numba one, he no go there."

The Korean culture emphasized that the family was the center of life. As in most Asian cultures, the elders were all venerated by the younger generations. A strong faith in God and a dedicated work ethic helped the Koreans coming to our shores in the 1950's succeed with little or nothing. With the support of the extended family, they found the American Dream in just one generation.

In Philadelphia during the late 1960's, it seemed that the Koreans had a street business on every corner in Center City. The family succeeded by chipping in to buy a used beat up old van and the men got up at 3:00 AM every morning rain or shine. The men would drive to the Philadelphia market to purchase produce or anything else they could sell at their family street corner stands.

How did they do it when most could not even speak English? They learned some English from contact with G.I.'s during the war and the kids and the women it seemed learned English quicker than their men did. Once in the USA, their children were not disadvantaged at school, they learned to speak English without an accent, went to college, and were later employed as professionals.

The Korean "Papa-san" was the head of the family and tended the oxen. He worked the rice patties and the fields, went off into the foot hills with an empty "A" frame on his back and returned loaded with fire wood. The "Momma-san" maintained the house, washed the clothes, cooked the food, hauled the water and cared for the children. As soon as the kids could walk, they were assigned simple chores. The women would be seen in the field harvesting the big white "Daikon" radish, an essential for the dish of "KimChi." During rice harvest, the entire family worked to provide a supply of rice for the cold winter months ahead. Those little Korean kids I saw were happy little tykes with runny noses and all sewn up in a winter outfit with a slit between the legs to just squat, to do their duty at anyplace at any time. There were no baths houses in the Korea that I saw.

The man's hands were a dead giveaway to show who the man really was. The man who worked the land had hands that were hardened, gnarled, and dirty proving he spent his life from childhood on doing manual labor. Hands were something I always noticed to help distinguish honest farmers from perhaps guerilla officers. Unlike those of the local honest hard workers, officers had smooth hands. "Take a good look at their hands," warned RA Commo Chief Irwin. Again, I was fortunate to have great guys to serve with in Korea and I always thought the 773rd was a lucky outfit for me.

The favorite hand tool of the Korean farmer was a very sharp hand scythe which was used for dozens of chores. One use I never witnessed but telephone lineman Rankin watched as a young Korean lad tossed his scythe at a pheasant and killed it on the spot. Another accoutrement of the Korean farmer's kit was a brass-bowled, long stem pipe either tucked into his waist band or in his hand while smoking it with tobacco. I do not recall any suggestion whatsoever about drug use of either smoked or used in any way. The Koreans enjoyed their own locally brewed rice spirits which, I never sampled. I did witness however, the effect it had on those Koreans who drank too much of it. I was satisfied with the supply of beer we had in C Battery and the spirits my Dad sent to me from home.

Among the warnings to the troops was the reminder to avoid any water not first sterilized by boiling or eating any raw food. Definitely avoid any Korean made spirits like"Marilyn Monroe Whiskey' or "Lucky Strike Whiskey" or any other label reminding a G.I. of home.

"House boys" were common in Korea. The guys would chip in a little every week and our fire control house boy Kim would clean our boots and shine them using commo wire, an ingenious method I saw first in Korea. He swept up the dirt floor in the tents and later the plywood wood floors in the Quonset hut. After a while, we put our steel helmets aside and everyone had a wash basin bought cheaply in a Korean market made from forming beer cans into a nice round wash basin. The Koreans were expert in fabricating useful items from the things we normally would throw away. They never disposed of anything that could be made into something useful. I had a bigger wash basin which was originally a big round cookie tin full of cookies sent to me by my neighbor Marty O'Grady's grandmother at Christmas time.

We had barriers and never ate Korean food although, discounting their lack of hygiene, the Korean diet was very nutritious. Whole grain unprocessed rice was the stable. Fresh vegetables with very little meat. Dried fish or squid was eaten to provide the necessary protein. Hot pepper, garlic and pickling added some spirit to their food. I took a picture of a Korean woman tending to her long rice noodles drying on racks which I just found among my mementos. Remember, Marco Polo is thought to have introduced pasta to Southern Europe back in the 13th century when he returned from Cathay (China). I don't remember ever seeing a fat Korean because they had a healthy diet and they had to walk every place they went. I do remember our house boy Kim getting sick after eating our high calorie, high salt, high sugar and high fat content food from Davis's mess tent. But, the chocolate was always welcomed and enjoyed by the Korean kids.

The men in C battery donated some money and food to an orphanage which I visited and while there, met the director who spoke English. I noticed a group of little Korean kids attending school and took a picture of them. One little girl reminded me of my pretty future sister-in-law Vincenza (Vinnie) Reres whom at the time was a little older than the young Korean child. There were many more orphans we saw in Korea who were less fortunate and did not have the connection to any support group. They had to take care of themselves. As I write this narrative I now wonder about them and how they fared in life.

I guess my Irish sentimentality shows when I think about Christmas Eve 1952. The snow was falling gently on C Battery when our motor section delivered a group of about 20 Korean orphans from the Christian orphanage to our site. The young children were about 10 years old. They started singing lively and popular Christmas carols in their native tongue and then again in English. An image shows them singing "Jingle Bells" in English with a Korean accent which brought smiles to every G.I.'s face.

It's a good thing that the sky darkened as they sang the

finale with "Silent Night" this time, their young voices articulating in perfect English that everyone could understand. The children, now slowly walking away towards the trucks, were holding each other's hands because the intensified snow fall made the ground slippery. You could hear above the sound of the wind the sweet refrain of their voices as they sang, *"Silent Night...Ho-ly Night...All is Calm...All is Bright."*

The soldier's shift of their feet and a swift wipe away of a tear showed every man I saw was touched by that evening. I don't remember anyone wishing anyone else a "Merry Christmas."

"Saber jet down," came over the radio from battalion one night in mid-winter and we were called in the middle of a snow storm to help search for the pilot who crashed his F-86 jet in the foothills on his approach to K-55. The battery spread out over the snowy frozen terrain, walking through high snow drifts piled up by the winds which howled down from the northern latitudes.

We covered as much ground as possible without seeing anything and the visibility dropped to almost zero as I led my men back to the site where we could just walk right over the barbed wire with the snow drifts so deep. I do not remember if the wreckage was found or if the pilot survived.

On a bitter cold evening that winter in February, 1953 I celebrated my 21st birthday. Of course, I could not make a big deal about it because the army thought I was 23 years old. But I did get off the site to have some drinks at an unofficial air force NCO club just outside K-55. It was nothing more than a shack with a little handmade bar and a G.I. issue diesel oil stove to warm the shanty. But, it served all the top brands of legitimate spirits from the states covertly smuggled in by pilots flying to and from Japan...Very Hush-Hush. Maybe the reason it was never raided was because the officer pilots didn't want anyone to know how the booze got to Korea.

Four of us, the two Commo Sergeant's, the Supply Sergeant and the birthday boy indulged in some serious drinking and we all got plastered that night. My Astoria pal Bob Dema told me he got off the site one night to go to the same "Night Spot" and was surprised by some small arms fire that quickly sobered up everyone. I had my .45 on me and we had a couple M-3 grease guns with us and the supply Sergeant borrowed Sergeant Cruz's personal .45 which gave us a sense of protection. But by the time we drove back, if attacked we would not have made it. One must be 21 to vote in those days and I do remember thinking to my inebriated self, I was now a man and old enough to vote.

What stands out very clearly is our black assistant commo Sergeant now loosened up by the alcohol and saying, "You guys are treating me like one of your own" with tears in his eyes. He was formerly in an all-black unit before the integration of our military. I never thought about the hurt some blacks feel about their treatment because of color and remembered those "Whites Only" signs in St. Louis. If I were black, that certainly would hurt me, especially if I were in uniform serving my country.

That night, the carousing Sergeants answered him using the accepted army vernacular with, "God damn it, we are all wearing the same fucking uniform and are in the same fucking army and no one gives a shit about the color of anyone's fucking skin." I still remember those words even though we were all pretty drunk and, it was the first and last time I was so drunk. My recall of the evening is clear at times and also blurry, but the idea that now I could vote seemed to remain among my private thoughts. I don't remember who got behind the wheel of the Jeep to return to the site: it may even have been me. Nor do I remember the sign or the countersign but, whoever was on guard duty opened the wire gate to let four drunken Sergeants back on the site that cold frozen evening.

About the noisiest times were when Joe and his pinochle players were engrossed in that serious game I could never understand. My favorite was always "poker." Dealer's choice with no wild cards and a quarter maximum bet. We had paper script money and used 30 caliber carbine, 30-06 M1 and .45 auto cartridges as chips until someone came up with a set of real poker chips. I insisted and was supported by my two section leaders the game should be a fun low stakes game to avoid problems in the platoon.

A black trooper in my platoon, radar operator Corporal Pappy S. was an older RA from St. Louis and somewhat reserved. Pappy also suffered an occasional petit mal seizure and asked that no one mention it to the officers because he wanted to stay in the army. He never drank anything stronger than a Coke. He was called off the site one day on a detail and returned to C battery with two overcoats, the one he was wearing, and another one for me. "Hey, who the hell put his overcoat on my cot," I yelled. In the army, you did not put your clothing on someone else's bunk, just in case your body was carrying things that crawled. "That IS your overcoat," Pappy S. answered and smiled. I tried it on and it fit fine so I wrote in indelible ink on the inside collar G-4XXX. "Thanks Pappy, I sure in hell can use it."

Back home months later, I took a short cut through the Bed-Stuy section of Brooklyn on my way home from Lee's house. I stopped at a gas station and to my surprise I saw the Assistant Commo Sergeant now wearing civilian clothing. I gave him a big and loud "Hey XXXXX, how the hell are you." He made no comment but jumped in his car, waved and drove off. His reaction stayed with me and it is still there.

Years later when Lee and I owned our Gal/Man Friday temporary help business in Philadelphia, our main office was in Center City with five other offices in the nearby suburbs. We were staffed with employees of all races. Most of our people in Center City were black, given the large black population in Philadelphia. Whenever we were strolling down Chestnut Street and met any of our Temps, we were always greeted with a warm "Hi, Mrs. G.," followed by a little hug for Lee and a "Hey, how ya doin' Mr. G." We walked back to our office feeling very proud of our team.

PFC Henley and LTNYBLUE

My Dad John was a man who enjoyed a drink but always in moderation. He preached to his sons about how the abuse of alcohol affected friends and family and his warning remained with us. I had early experience with happy alcoholics among our neighbors and friends including our tenant Billy O'Malley.

As a young JBA sailor, I met at the Merchant Marine offices in Manhattan some mean hombres who were not happy drunks but nasty drunks and when I later joined the Guard, I met more mean drunks who could not handle alcohol. I watched myself because I had a taste for it and as I grew older, found that I also had a capacity for it of which I became well aware. Later in life, I just quit hard liquor and cigarettes completely and never looked back.

During my time in the service both in the Guard and on active duty, I saw many alcoholics who should have been put in the hospital and treated. The U.S. Army had a closed eye policy to the drinking problem that was ignored for too many years.

When ordered to Korea, our ranks were filled by many RA's from AA gun units in the area and these units were cleaning house. One man reported to the platoon whom I thought was too old to be a PFC. I will call him PFC Henley. He was about 5'6" and slightly built with close cropped salt and pepper hair. He got along with the men in the platoon and did his job. Henley's section leader Sergeant Joe Zurla, and I felt that Henley was a good man. I did notice an outline on the sleeves of his faded field uniform where chevrons once were sewn.

He approached me one afternoon after lunch and asked to have a word alone with me. "Sure Henley, what's on your mind," I asked. "I want you to know that I am an RA with ten years' experience and was the Fire Control Platoon Sergeant until a recent disagreement with my battery commander who busted me to PFC."

He said he would prove to me that he was qualified to be the Fire Control Electrician, which rated Sergeant Stripes, and so far that specialty in the platoon was still vacant. He took that same Fire Control course in Fort Bliss that I took years before I did.

294

"Thanks Henley for your confidence and offer to help," I answered and added "I did not know where we are going but I know every man, myself included must do his job as an important member of the team." With that said, we both went back to work. He would be treated equally as all the men were. If we still did not have a Fire Control Electrician and if Henley proved he was as good as he said he was, I would ask his section leader Zurla's opinion. If he agreed, I would get him promoted to corporal. If Henley continued to do a good job, I would recommend him for promotion to Sergeant. I found out he had a wife and children at home and if he was doing the job why not pay him for it?

I was never told why he was busted but not too many weeks in Korea revealed the reason was that he was an alcoholic and a sick one. His commander was cleaning house. Henley should have been sent to an army hospital to be treated for alcoholism and not sent to Korea with the 773rd.

The brothel "Hooch," just outside our perimeter was declared, "Off Limits" but, was doing a thriving business. We were still in tents and I was living in the Director Section tent pitched on the slope of a hill. I was stretched out relaxing writing a letter or reading by candle light. At about 9 P.M. LTNYBLUE entered our tent and surprised us with his presence. "At Ease Men, where is Sergeant Zurla?" He asked…"Here Sir" as Joe snapped a quick salute as he rose from his bunk. "Are all you men accounted for?" The LT asked. As we both looked around in the dimly lit squad tent, we noticed Henley's cot was empty and one other man was on guard duty. Caught off guard Zurla exclaimed, "No Sir," both of us wondering, "Where the hell is Henley?" We were unaware the battery commander was at a meeting at the airbase leaving LTNYBLUE in charge.

It was obvious to all that the lieutenant had been drinking when he ordered me and Zurla to meet him at the motor pool and "be quick about it" followed by "bring your weapons." With a surprised look at each other, we obeyed the lieutenant's order, still quite ignorant of what the evening events would hold. Later that night and after the drama that took place, both Joe and I were given a large ruled pad and told…no, we were ordered by First Sergeant

Kolody, to record in detail the entire evening's events. Kolody told us, "Before you hit the sack, write down everything you witnessed tonight and I mean every detail you saw and heard from the time you first saw LTNYBLUE. Then time and date it, print your names, sign it and bring it directly to me regardless of the hour." Kolody slept in the CP tent a few tents down the slope from us. His previous service in the Military Police was underscored that night.

LTNYBLUE knew Henley was drunk and at the hooch and we later found out both were there earlier that evening. The lieutenant ordered PFC Archuleta to drive us all to the hooch. We all jumped in the jeep and the lieutenant signaled the guard to open the wire gate to let us pass and we were on the way. What the hell was next? We had no idea.

Most men had no desire to be off the site after dark, but some could not control the urge to go to the hooch drunk or sober. Yes, some guys did get drunk and some guys did pay the prostitutes as soldiers have done since biblical times. Yes, some guards gave their buddies the countersign so they could easily get back on the site when challenged by the sentries.

And yes, an edgy guard on a dark night would not hesitate to shoot while carrying his loaded weapon with a round already in the chamber. All he had to do was click off the safety with his trigger finger and shoot realizing, his life could be on the line. How many times this happened when an innocent but drunken G.I. was the victim no one knows. We had many close calls caused by the effects of alcohol. Only those who experienced guard duty on a dark, cold and lonely post in harm's way could understand this. Some did fire at a real or imagined something lurking around in the dark making real or imagined noises and, it was not unusual to hear shots at night. .

On an ink dark evening, the sentry will challenge any sound with "Halt," and then follow with the "Sign," a secret word selected for that day. He expects to hear the secret word for the day's "Countersign," and will if still doubtful demand, "advance to be recognized." If the guard is satisfied, he allows entry and no further discussion is necessary. If on that same ink dark evening, when the sentry challenges and orders "Halt," and gives the "Sign" and there is no response, the most likely next sound will be Bam,,,Bam...Bam...discussion ended!

Upon arrival at the hooch, Archuleta was ordered to stay with the jeep. "What the hell is going on, Sarge? Is the lieutenant crazy?" "Sit tight," I think I said to the driver and probably did not have to tell him to keep his eyes open as Joe and I followed the officer into the hooch.

PFC Archuleta was in Charlie battery from the training at Camp Stewart and our posting in Brooklyn. He was a wise and well trained soldier that everyone could depend upon. He gripped his carbine at the ready port and crouched behind the jeep to take some cover. You could tell his entire being was on high alert. The worst feeling in a tight spot is not knowing what may happen next.

As I entered the hooch, I spotted Henley in his shorts with his skinny bare legs showing. Apparently both he and the lieutenant had designs on the same frightened girl. A disagreement about the girl took place between the officer and the enlisted man and a scuffle followed. The lieutenant, quite a bit taller and much heavier than Henley, threw the first punch. Henley followed up with a punch that sent the booze crazed lieutenant on the floor. With a confused expression on his face, the lieutenant looked up at Henley's section leader Zurla and ordered him to shoot Henley. Joe looked at me in amazement and we both moved quickly. Joe passed his carbine to me as I grabbed the lieutenant's carbine on the mat and dashed out to give the weapons to Archuleta. Joe was always a quick thinker.

"What's going on?" Archuleta asked as he stood alone in the cold air shivering with his weapon ready. He was wearing only his field shirt and in the rush he had not grabbed his field jacket. I told him, "I'm bringing out Zurla and Henley and getting our asses back to the site. If the lieutenant won't come, screw him...we're getting the hell out of here." I may have been more descriptive than using "screw" but its close enough. Zurla and I collected Henley and his clothes and stormed out of the hooch. We left the drunken officer just where he was, now sitting on the mat fondling the girl and drinking from a bottle of homemade Korean whiskey, the stuff we were all warned not to drink.

We heard what sounded like muffled or distant shots as we ran to the jeep and the driver "revved up" the engine. "Come on, come on," Archuleta called out. I heard subdued shots and thought they may have come from the lieutenant's revolver. The door of the hut suddenly burst open and the lieutenant stumbled out as we all made a run for the jeep.   Poor Henley, still drunk, didn't know what the hell was happening. Zurla and I tossed Henley in the jeep partially clothed and Archuleta gave that Jeep wings as his foot mashed down on the gas pedal.

We were met at the wire gate by the Sergeant of the guard and First Sergeant Kolody. The lieutenants said, "You saw him hit me first, right?" He was the executive officer and the officer of the day. With the battery commander away, LTNYBLUE should never have left the gun site: he should have ordered another officer or warrant officer the duty to collect Henley or, more wisely, just did nothing. Guys were always sneaking off the site to visit the girls. He had other things on his booze befuddled mind. Hitting an enlisted man was another breach of military law. Each infraction alone could bring serious charges against him.

As Henley's Section Leader and Platoon Sergeant, we obeyed Kolody's orders and wrote down every incident that we saw and heard that bizarre evening. Satisfied we did not omit anything, we delivered our narratives to Kolody. "The crazy-son-of-a bitch could have gotten us all killed, I hope they hang him," ranted Archuleta. That's when Kolody ordered me and Zurla to the CP tent and instructed us to document the evenings events while still fresh in our mind.

The battery commander returned from battalion in the early pre-dawn hours. He could be heard by many as he raged at LTNYBLUE. "You are restricted to your cot until I hear from battalion about what I should do with you, you crazy drunken bastard," Smedley screamed. I never heard Smedley in such a frenzy.

Some of the guys who were not up to speed about the night's drama asked, "What the hell is Lieutenant Smedley yelling about?" By breakfast time, the entire battery knew about poor Henley and the drunken Executive Officer. By mid-morning, LTNYBLUE was on his way to battalion, nothing more was heard about the incident and we never saw him again. We turned in Henley's carbine to the supply sergeant and word reached us that Henley was serving time in the Eighth Army stockade in Pusan called, "The Big Eight".

That was my last memory of Henley until March 1953 when Zurla and I received orders sending us south to be processed home. Once in Pusan, we asked where the "The Big Eight" was located. I am glad we did not have to go inside the prison compound for it was as depressing a sight as one could imagine. But we were able to speak to Henley from the other side of the prison fence.

We asked if we could do anything for him, He said he didn't want us to do anything and that there was nothing anyone could do for him anyway. He was sad and defeated and appeared smaller than we remembered him. He also appeared much older. A vague image remains of us passing some script (money) to him and that ends the very sad account of PFC Henley and LTNYBLUE.

New Captain and Up Close with the Enemy

One morning at breakfast, we saw a new officer wearing captain's bars and discovered we now had a new Battery Commander named Captain Martin. First Lieutenant Smedley had to take a back seat as Executive Officer, the job formerly held by LTNYBLUE.

The new battery commander ordered an officer and NCO meeting. We all found some space in the CP tent and Captain Martin introduced himself and told us he was an army reserve officer on the "Ready List" and was surprised to find himself back in uniform and in Korea. He smiled when he said "I did not know I was that ready!"

Apparently, he served in WWII in the artillery branch although not in a 90mm gun unit. "So, I'll have to learn about your equipment." He followed with, "I will need the help and cooperation of every man here to fulfill our mission." He said he will be roaming around the site and will get a chance to meet everyone to become more familiar with the battery.

We all felt his introduction was fair, honest, to the point and very well stated. Sure, we would help our new captain to learn about a 90mm AA battery; after all, he was not there to operate the equipment but to learn the tactics and lead the "Charlie Battery Team." Too many officers came in knowing nothing and afraid to admit it and lacked the confidence to even ask for help. We all felt good about Captain Martin.

The Captain spent his full day circulating around the gun site asking officers questions, NCO's and the men. Each day, he learned about us as we got to know him a little better. He was a well-seasoned officer. Lieutenant Smedley did look a little let down and thought that maybe the Colonel held him responsible for Lieutenant LTNYBLUE's disgracing the battalion.

It seemed to us that the new commander held more meetings than Smedley had. We were told about every Intelligence report that came in from 10th Group dealing with guerilla activity and air buildup of twin engine medium bombers across the Yalu River. We were kept on our toes and responded quickly to air and

300

ground alerts, both real and false alarms. We were ready.

This was in the fall and sometime before the frigid snow and winds whipped through the mountains from the north. Commo Section Lineman PFC Rankin wanted to go pheasant hunting. The thousands of beautiful ring neck pheasants that grow wild in the Dakotas and those nurtured by each state's Fish and Game Departments were all native to Asia and brought to North America many years ago.

Attracted to the rice and grain fields, the wild ring neck pheasant population was abundant. So Rankin got permission from his section leader Irwin to try his luck in the dried up rice paddies and rolling hills to the east of our site. He would be accompanied by his buddy in that Quad Mount crew to our Northeast and both pals would spend an afternoon away from the site.

Rankin grabbed a couple of candy bars and filled his canteen with water, slung his carbine on his shoulder and was off pheasant hunting. Here in the states, it is illegal to hunt pheasant with a single projectile weapon, one must use a shotgun with shells loaded with many small lead BB like projectiles. Rankin was a good shot and would try for a head shot so as not to damage too much meat.

The commo section radio bunker was in the fire control area where I spent many B. S. sessions in the radio bunker with commo chief Irwin and his assistant, together with my two section chiefs Burns and Zurla, we had many lively discussions. The bunker was cool in the warm weather and warm in the winter with the help of a diesel oil heater. We would just sip a beer and swap personal stories while listening to the radio reports and some word from the other batteries.

Sometime later Rankin returned with a plump pheasant and told us he saw a new hut that was not there before and it had a radio antenna partially hidden. I told Irwin "we should report that to Martin… That's looking right at us Irwin." "Yeah, let's go," he answered.

The captain ordered me to form a patrol and check it out immediately and, "Let me know what you see." "Take no unnecessary risks, information is all I want from your patrol. Only

301

use your weapons if necessary. Clearing those hills is not our job, that, is the ROK army's job and our mission is right here in case of air attack." The Captain made this very clear to us as we hustled back to pick our men.

We selected Rankin, Robinson, Willets and "Baby GI" his real name is now totally lost because that is what everyone called him. He was nicknamed by the Korean laundry ladies because to them he had a baby face. You know, nicknames stick for better or worse. Sergeant Cruz was "El Gato," and Baby GI was Baby GI and he was stuck with it. It didn't seem to bother him because all the Korean women thought he was good looking. I won't dare tell you what the troops nicknamed Mess Sergeant Lew Davis!

Our weapons were Carbines and M-3 Grease guns and were carried locked and loaded with a round in the chamber. Both the carbine and M-3's had two magazines taped together for quick reloading if necessary. We did not have any hand grenades which would have been a welcomed addition for our small party. No need for any maps or compass, it was right out in those hills in front of our position. Irwin called the Quad Mount Chief across the rice paddies to give him the word about our mission.

"Yeah, yeah I know about the antenna Captain Martin told us to watch you guys." "We will keep an eye on the patrol and keep the Quad running just in case." The Quad mount was powered by a small Briggs and Stratton gasoline motor. "If I see you guys hit the dirt, we will fire over your heads to give you a chance to get off that trail." That was very reassuring as we walked across the fields and rice paddies and entered the ox cart trail on the way to where Rankin saw the hut.

Little villages were in those mountains connected by the Ox cart trail and when the ROK troops made forays into the area, the guerillas vanished and when the ROK's left, the guerillas returned. This is the way guerillas operated in all wars, by intimidating the locals.

We crossed the open area in front of the position through some dried up rice paddies. All the while we were under observation from the Quad Mount crew off to our right and as we advanced. It gave us a sense of security knowing the Quad crew was there looking over our shoulders.

It was a bright sunny day with perfect visibility for us...and no doubt eyes were on our recon party from two directions. The twisted trail was all up hill and our tail man would glance at our back trail to make sure we were still in sight of the Quad mount. There were only six of us and lightly armed at that.

We climbed up the hill and saw the hut but not a soul was in sight. I halted the patrol and conversed with Irwin after noticing a swale sloping downhill behind the hut which could hide any number of men. I passed the word to the patrol to keep an eye open but did not have to...they were alert and ready.

It seemed a while but it probably was only seconds when we saw one man coming up over the swale and another stepping out of the hut. The man climbing up the swale had the appearance of the average typical Korean farmer. He was not smiling and looked frightened. The one stepping out of the hut was also dressed in native garb but he was much cleaner and just did not seem to fit in. His hair was neatly groomed and he appeared to be much younger than the other man. Neither one had anything in their hands. Irwin ordered the younger man by calling out "Eedie Wah," and motioned with his hand to "Come Here!" The man responded with a nod of his head smiled and slowly approached Irwin. Irwin was not smiling. This was Irwin's second tour in Korea and I was glad to have him with us.

Irwin glanced at me as we both noticed the younger man's hands. Maybe it was my imagination but I felt the Korean caught on. His hands were spotless and smooth, not dirty and gnarled the way all of the honest farmer's hands were. All our senses were on edge making us ready for anything.

Irwin spoke a little Korean and inquired about radio antenna in Korean, English and animated hand language. The man answered "Havo no." He knew why we were here, I guessed. I passed him as I went to enter and inspect the hut. "Radio, antenna?" was asked again with some charade-like hand motions. "Havo no," was again the answer as I passed him and took a closer look at his hands and overall appearance as I carefully entered the hut. No one was inside and I did not see any sign of any radio equipment. The inside did not look like it was lived in which added to my suspicion. On the way out I glanced inside the honey bucket waste and saw it was unused; that confirmed our suspicions, this was an observation post to keep an eye on us and report what they saw.

I asked Rankin to show me where he saw the antenna. Rankin pointed out the spot on the hut and saw recently patched up holes in the mud finish. I looked at the younger man's face as he just smiled at me showing his white teeth.

Irwin mumbled, "This guy is a God damned officer and I would bet on it." The other older man just stood frozen in place and had fear written all over the typically expressionless Asian face. We did not know how many more might be concealed behind the swale and along that trail.

Feeling we had accomplished our mission, I said to Irwin "Let's get back to the battery and give Martin our report." Irwin replied, "You bet, let's go." I followed with "Baby G. I. move out, me and Irwin will cover the rear. If you hear any fire, hit the dirt and get some cover," I told the men. "Willets, you follow Baby G. I. and Rankin. Robinson, you hang back with me and Irwin," I ordered...all answered me with an affirmative. We were ready to hit the dirt for any cover and start shooting, knowing the Quad mount would fire over our heads to keep the enemy busy while we made our retreat.

No one doubted we were face to face with our enemy and we would never know how many if any more were actually hidden by that swale. Nor did we know if they would fire at us in broad daylight. Probably every man on that patrol had these same thoughts flashing through his mind as we slowly eased back down that trail and crossed the rice paddies back to the site.

We saw the quad still trained on the trail and probably other eyes were on that Quad mount also. No shots were fired. Before setting out, I had been told to observe, report and only fire if necessary. I did as I was ordered and was not looking for any medals or casualties, the entire patrol was glad to be back without incident. The mountain ranges in South Korea have been avenues of transit directly up to North Korea and probably still in use today by trouble makers from the north. This intrigue has been going on for over 60 years and no one can see the light at the end of the tunnel. Only now, the mischief-makers may have nuclear weapons and the means to deliver them.

Captain Martin took our report and he notified higher headquarters. We never saw any ROK Army troops enter into those foothills from our position but did hear some sporadic small arms firing coming from the area. Captain Martin guessed the ROK forces knew of a more covertly approach to attack the guerillas rather than hitting them in a frontal assault on that ox cart trail. We knew what he meant because we all felt boxed in on that narrow trail ourselves.

The South Koreans have been fighting the same enemy for years and American combat troops have been standing guard next to the Republic of Korea Army on the 38th parallel for sixty-plus years. So far this has discouraged the North from making any more adventurous dashes across the border and an uneasy cease-fire peace has been preserved. We now wonder… "How long will peace last in that troubled and divided peninsula?"

Going Home

The winter of 1952-53 found Charlie Battery, snug in our heated Quonsets and well fed by Davis. When duties took me off site it gave me an opportunity to see how other G.I.'s lived. With snow drifts in the fields there was not much thought about any possibility for a ground attack but we were still wary of those foothills to our northeast and remained ready. The battery performed daily checks on the equipment and continued the daily routines of roll call, sick call, guard duty and K.P. followed by the highlight of the day, "Mail Call." Plenty of packages arrived from home and were shared with buddies. Along with samples from my men's packages, my Mom's oatmeal cookies were enjoyed by the platoon. Brandy from Dad with his unique and thoughtful "Rye Bread" packaging added a treat to Davis's G.I. coffee on cold mornings.

The troops still lived in the open and spent little time in the Quonsets until the end of the day. The gun crews manned the 90's out in freezing weather along with the machine gun crews and tracking head crew at all hours. "Bed Check Charlie" was still flying, all bundled up in enemy winter garb. Still, there were no winter parkas and insulated boots for Charlie battery. I can't help reflecting now about the battalion S-4 (Supply Officer) who failed in his duty. We never saw him nor anyone from battalion except a few times that winter and those we saw were wearing parkas and insulated boots.

As the weather warmed up, some troops were sent on five-day "R & R" (Rest and Recuperation) to Japan. The remainder of the original NG's started to rotate back to the states with replacements arriving almost daily. I did not take advantage of R&R but sent men from my platoon who still had many more months to serve in Korea before they were rotated back to the states. One morning, my replacement reported he was an RA SFC named Partridge. I could now kick back and take it easy until my orders came in sending me south. About that same time, another RA SFC Katsaros reported to take over Joe Zurla's Director Section. Burns, my radar chief, still had time to serve before he was replaced and sent back home to continue his army career.

The platoon threw a going away party for me and Zurla. We ate up all the goodies the guys chipped in for, including a stash of Davis's "cracks" pilfered from the mess tent right after Davis left. We also put a pretty good hole in the platoon's beer supply that night.

I remember SFC Partridge had a few smiles but did not seem too happy an NCO. He may have been pre-occupied with other matters that I was not aware of. But, Zurla's replacement SFC Katsaros was right at home in the platoon and just as mischievous as most. He laughed all night and was always ready for a laugh at anyone's expense including his own. He was a regular guy who knew when to soldier and be serious and when to kick back and just take ten. My CRO (Chief Radar Operator) Burns did not have the same sense of humor most of us had but he seemed to be enjoying himself until his caricature was unveiled.

PFC Angelo Torres, was a talented artist capable of caricaturizing anyone. He could pick out and then accentuate a comical feature on anyone and create a cartoon of that person. His talents were recognized by MAD magazine where he later enjoyed a long and successful career as an artist. That night, on a large piece of drawing paper, I was portrayed wearing a huge moustache, much exaggerated from the one I grew when first in Korea and then, ruined when trimming by candle light and then sadly shaved it off.

Atop my head sat a toy-sized helmet with master Sergeant stripes and my big ears sticking out from under. A toy gun was slung over my shoulder. Sticking out the rear pocket was a pint bottle marked "XXXX" whiskey...I guess they all knew about my Dad's parcels. On my feet were an oversized up-to-my-knee's and unlaced pair of Corcoran jump boots and in my hand a pennant inscribed, "Keep Alert...Charlie Battery Fire Control." I took one look at that piece of art and doubled over laughing joined by all the guys in my...no, not mine anymore but, SFC Partridge's platoon.

When the laughter died down, Zurla glanced at me and kind of rolled his eyes to say, "What's next?" Joe was shown with a smirk on his face wearing an oversized fatigue jacket with sleeves hanging over his hands together with upside down Sergeant Stripes. In his arm was an ancient tome with rabbit-eared pages sticking out in all directions with the title stating, "I KNOW IT ALL, written by Joe Zurla." Joe didn't know it all, but he was a bright guy, ready to take any side in a debate with a sneer that could try any authority figure's patience. But like his older brother John, he was an excellent soldier and one you could always count on. With all his mischief-making Joe was a damn good soldier and section leader whom I was proud to serve with and...he WAS smarter than most.

By this time, my glance at Burns caught a not-too-happy expression on his face because this RA did not think the proceedings were all that funny. Torres placed Burns' caricature on the display easel and the guys howled. Burns thought Torres went a little too far. But, I thought it was right on target.

Everyone knew Burns spent years in the Pacific in WWII in the field with no facilities. The troopers who did not practice good hygiene in those hot and humid climates suffered all kinds of skin problems and rashes for not washing themselves whenever they could. Burns preached this to the guys in the platoon; most listened to him and fared well but some did not.

At that particular time, we had not showered since we left the *C. C. Ballou* some six months before and, that had been a salt water shower. The wise ones listened to experience and kept their bodies, all parts, clean whenever possible. During the latter part of our deployment, we had it much easier than many others during that third and last Korean winter.

Burns took a lot of kidding from the guys in the radar section about washing: "Hey Sarge, are ya gonna give us swimming lessons next?" An image of a little yellow rubber duckie is there in my memory, sitting in Burn's empty steel helmet. I may even have been the one who put it there. Or maybe it was in Torres's artwork but it is there nonetheless. Maybe even one of the quiet guys in the radar section may have written home for one and it may have even been Corporal Pappy S. He always looked innocent but laughing inside at all the antics some of which I'm sure he participated in. . . .

Another idiosyncratic quirk about SFC Warren Burns - his wife and kids back home never knew he was in Korea. One day I noticed him putting stamps on a letter, "Hey Burns, we don't pay postage here in Korea." "My wife and kids think I'm in Japan and send me stamps," he answered with a smile. Remember, no email, no internet, and one could get lost in those days even in the army! Quirky, yes, that is the word I was looking for to describe Burns. He was a great soldier and great Radar Chief and looked after his troopers but he was ... quirky! I guess we all possess some quirks of our own.

The Fire Control and Commo Quonsets huts did not stink like some of the other huts did that early spring when the doors were now open after being kept closed against the cold. Burns made sure the doors were opened cold or not, just to let some fresh air circulate and, sleeping bags were hung outside to air as long as it did not snow. Kudos to Burns because he led the way with his years of practical experience and, as his younger and less experienced boss, I listened to what he had to say. Torres dropped the veil on Burns picture taking his moonlight bath in a huge oversized steel helmet ... I tried not to laugh but I just could not hold back and doubled up laughing. Burns wore a crooked half grin. Then, he too laughed like hell.

There was Burns sitting in his bathtub-sized steel helmet with water up to his neck, two skinny knees sticking up above the rim of the helmet and with scrubbing brush in hand scrubbing his own back ... water splashing in all directions, hair standing on end. Burns chin was hanging on the rim of the helmet Popeye-style. Burns did have a slight protruding jut in his chin which Torres' keen eye caught and exaggerated. SFC stripes were tattooed on his bare arm that was hanging over the rim of the helmet. Torres caught the expression on Burns face exactly as he did on mine and Zurlas so well that anyone at a glance would recognize each one of us. Amazing the way Torres told the story in his drawings...a superbly talented artist.

I don't know if Torres kept his portfolio of C Battery because he made caricatures of every officer and NCO who came and went and kept the platoon in stitches. He never showed these pictures to anyone else that I knew of, other than the Fire Control Platoon. He made caricatures of Colonel Slavin and, of course, battalion executive officer Major "Fangs" Kraus who would have had Torres hog-tied and boiled in oil if he ever saw the pictures Torres drew of him, "fangs and all!"

Torres art brought a little relief and some laughs for a lot of guys missing home and their loved ones. The RA's and NG's were all volunteers but, the draftees without a choice, were torn from civilian life. They were now walking a cold and lonely guard post with weapon in hand asking themselves, "What the hell am I doing here?" PFC Torres brought more than he realized to the soldiers in Charlie Battery Fire Control.

From time to time, a small USO troupe would appear at the air base to entertain the troops and most of my platoon attended on a rotational basis. The shows usually played for a couple days. I went to see a barely known accordion player and a totally unknown G.I. singer/impersonator act.

The singer was tall and manly looking, and he imitated all of the famous and popular male singers of the 1950's. Which, he did quite well accompanied by the talented accordion player. He closed the act with a serious note about our service in Korea and how much our families worried about us. He announced. "I took singing lessons as a child and my Mom always wanted me to become a serious singer. So, I wish to sing the next song in my natural voice and dedicate the song to all our Moms back home who worry about us every day while we serve here in Korea."

The audience was silent and serious as the accordion player provided a heart-warming chord. This impersonator stood in front of a double Quonset hut filled with soldiers and airmen and belted out an aria from a popular opera in a perfect female soprano voice that had everyone collapsing in laughter. I laughed so much that my ribs still hurt when I hit the sack that night. He didn't stop for a second to let us even catch our breath. He just continued the aria, singing every bloody stanza with a serious face and, holding his hands clenched over his heart only causing more laughter. I do not remember his name; he was a soldier serving as an entertainer in the USO. We all commented about how famous he would be some day but, never heard of him again.

I thought the sendoff party was great and briefly felt a little sadness about leaving the outfit and my platoon. I served with great men, brave and true soldiers every one of them: Draftees, RA's, Reservist's and NG's, "All, Samo, Samo" and all "Ichi Bon…Numba Hucking ONE!"

The day soon arrived when Joe and I packed our duffle bags, loaded up with carbines, ammo, webbing, mess kits with full canteens, some C rations, and orders in our hands to "Return to the ZI" (Zone of Interior). Just like the army, they couldn't just say HOME.

The Fire Control Jeep Driver Willets drove us the several miles to the railroad crossing right where my buddy Max was hit by the train. Willets exclaimed…"I sure hope the train gets here this time," as he sneaked a wink at me. Zurla cried out to Willets,

"You mean to tell me the train never arrived for the last guys you drove here?" "Yes Sarge, I had to take them right back to the battery," Willets answered. "I knew it, I knew it, and I get screwed again." Zurla kicked a few innocent rocks when we three looked out in the distance and saw the train approaching. Willets, who was normally a quiet sort of fellow, doubled up laughing out loud.

"Sarge, that's for all the times you played all those jokes on me," "Ha, ha, ha." Willets bent over laughing. I couldn't hold back my laughs as both Joe and I yelled out, "Sayonara Willets," and climbed onto the wheezing and snorting old Korean train.

It seemed that in the army, you were always saying goodbye to guys who played an important role in your life and then you were never to see them again.

We found seats in the same decrepit coach car with the same wooden slatted seats only this time they were not so uncomfortable. I think we had smiles on our faces all the way south to Pusan and never enjoyed C rations more than we did on that train ride, even though they were cold right out of the can. All memories blur as I see both of us laughing and eating our rations. Even the chemically treated water tasted good.

My next image is entering the orderly room of the Replacement Depot called a "Rep'l Depo" and turning in our carbines, ammo and all our field equipment. I made sure I held on to the copy of my Carbine turn-in slip and told Joe to do the same. An old RA told me to be sure to keep it because some of these weapons disappeared at the turn-in point and this could screw up an innocent G.I.'s return home. That carbine was small enough to be disassembled and stashed in a duffel bag. No chances were taken by this young but wiser NG!

The mess hall was always open or so it seemed because after being assigned a bunk, we went right to the mess hall and guys were arriving at all hours. We were there for a few days waiting until enough troops gathered to fill a troop ship to be sent off to Japan for processing home…whoops, I mean return to the ZI!

We visited platoon mate Henley whom I told you about earlier. Now, he was a prisoner in the "Big Eight Stockade." It was a sad event with a lingering impression still in my mind about that RA soldier who should never have been sent to Korea.

While walking through a couple of Quonset huts to take a short cut to the mess hall we were attracted to the gambling right in the open with G.I. script money floating all around. I watched as Joe stopped at a few blackjack games and quickly picked up his winnings and moved on. I soon joined him and can still hear the losers yelling, "Hey, you can't just win and leave," as we chuckled and moved on from game to game. We both stuffed a lot of script into our pockets that day.

The day finally arrived when we boarded a bus, rode to the pier and embarked on the troopship *USS General M. L. Hersey*, a sister ship to the *Ballou*. I have no images about the short trip from Pusan to Kyushu the southernmost island of Japan. But, I do remember the exotic scenery on the bus ride from the dock to Camp Mower, an army base in Sasebo on the grounds of a former Japanese Naval base.

We did not realize at the time we were only 56 air miles from Nagasaki and that Sasebo was a secondary target for an atomic bomb that day in 1945.

Sasebo, USS M.L. Hersey

We debarked not knowing where we were and boarded buses. We were intrigued by the scenery from the docks to Camp Mower. The terrain looked like a painting with perfectly formed precipitous pyramid-shaped mountains with many trees and colorful flowers in abundance, matched with carefully contoured and terraced rice paddies...silhouettes of men and oxen. The farm land looked like it was right out of a painting and totally unworldly.

The next memory focuses on a large gymnasium-like room with high ceilings while we stood in place, each man holding his duffle bag. The groups consisted of about 100 men each going through the same drill in prison-like precision. A PA system announced, "Place your duffle bags and belongings directly in front of you and make a right face." We complied. "First rank step off, forward march." Each column following one after the other in chain gang fashion and moving fast as the cadence picked up. Every man in step, and moving closer and closer to the aroma of food cooking.

I see a tray in one hand and a mug in the other and I could hear a buzz of happy chatter accompanied by the sound of sizzling noises and the exclamation, "Oh my God it's a steak." I placed my tray within easy reach of a food server dressed in a spotless white cook's uniform. He dropped a big sirloin steak on my tray. I just gaped at the size of the steak when someone said, "Move along" just as someone else dropped a heaping serving spoon full of mashed potatoes and another poured brown gravy on my taters to which veggies and salad were added. Another voice repeated "Keep moving along, men ... there's plenty for all and seconds if you want." Things start to blur but I remember the smiling gleeful faces sitting at a long table and seeing my tray laden with all this food and I even remember a quart of fresh cold milk. The milk was the first to go down the hatch because it was the first fresh milk I had since I left the States.

What a great day, we thought. But we hadn't seen anything yet! All the troops ate their fill and stepped outside to an open area for a smoke and to form in small cliques. "Hey, where in New York do you come from?" Asked Zurla, "Brooklyn," answered a guy who turned out to be Joe Greco. "Hey Louie, this guy is from Manhattan," Joe Greco yelled at Louie Clementi also from Brooklyn. "You from New Yawk, too?" A congregation of New Yorkers, whoops, New Yawkas, all assembled around Joe Greco, the most talkative and funniest. Clusters of like-minded soldiers from all over the country joined in small gatherings.

"Group XXX report to building number XXX at XX: 00 hours," the PA system cried out as white helmeted soldiers directed us to our proper locations swift and precision like and we found ourselves back in that first building standing at that same spot with our gear untouched. The PA ordered loud and clear, "Remove all your clothing and place them on your belongings and face right and march off in file, be sure to remove all underwear and socks." We were led to a shower room and given soap as we

313

stepped under a hot shower, the first time in six months for me as I scrubbed away all the Korean grime. I can't tell you in words how good that hot shower felt. We filed out as clean fresh towels were thrown at us as we dried, continuing along the fast-moving assembly line and were issued in quick succession first underwear and then socks, slipping them on as we moved along. Next came fatigue pants, jackets, OD pants and jacket, khaki shirts, ties, belts, boots, field jacket and overcoats. We exited the assembly line and were led to our quarters. Here we all dressed in new fatigue uniforms and overcoats, feeling the joy to be really clean again; wearing fresh new clothing made everyone feel great.

Outside we joined our sectional cliques to be entertained by Joe Greco, "MMMMMM how eez ova there in Korea?" imitating the expected questions his Italian Grandpa in Brooklyn would ask. He had every guy asking each other, "Mmmmm, how eez ova there in Korea?"

Lots of laughs were enjoyed by all. There were no Corporals or Sergeants, just G.I.'s on the way home to family and sweethearts. We did not then, as I do now, have any thought for those 37,000 killed in the Korean War who would never again see their sweethearts and families and would never ever feel the warmth of their embrace. Along with those killed in action are the 92,000 wounded who returned home with horrible injuries to their maimed bodies, with amputations and trauma that may hurt for a lifetime. This was a time of joy for the lucky ones returning in one piece with only the memories of their experiences to remind them of their time in Korea.

Afterwards, we carried our shirts and jackets to a bevy of Japanese tailors to alter our new uniforms and sew on the required chevrons and patches and to receive our authorized ribbons, again in assembly line manner.

We walked into Camp Mower dirty, hungry, tired, confused, and perhaps a little apprehensive. We now sat down in our new barracks with cots, mattresses, mattress covers, sheets, pillow and pillow cases and two freshly cleaned G.I. wool blankets. Don't ask me how long it took from dirty G.I. to clean, shaven and smartly dressed soldiers. It just flashed through my memory bank at 150 miles an hour.

I went into town on pass and bought some gifts, a decorative tea cup set for my Grandma Cavallo, which now sits in our China Closet and some jewelry for my Mom and an enameled jewelry box and picture album and some ear rings for Lee. I also bought Lee a silk kimono and silk pajamas. "What size you say," in broken English the Japanese sales girl asked me. "Samo, Samo your size," I gestured to the diminutive lady. When Lee tried on the kimono we could wrap it around both of us and it sat in our closet for 63 years until we looked at it the other day and marveled at the still bright gold thread work. It was used as the background for this book cover. I also have a hazy memory of sending my 12-year-old brother Jimmy a flashy and popular jacket with an Asian dragon on the back and sent by G.I.'s in the thousands to kid brothers back home. I have a picture of him proudly wearing it. Lee looked cute and cuddly wearing her Japanese pajamas on our honeymoon.

Boarding the *Hersey* was a cat and mouse game as 4,000 guys crammed aboard. I noticed many top two graders being pulled out of the line and heard some Sergeants saying to a lieutenant, "Yes sir, yes sir." That could only mean one thing, "details." Sure enough, as much as I tried to hide my stripes a lieutenant did pull me out of the line of troops streaming down into the deep belly of that troop ship. He assigned me Compartment First Sergeant. "Yes sir, lieutenant," I thought to myself. I know how to play that game after seeing a Master Sergeant mopping up a passageway. "What's up, Sarge," I asked him. "I posted a dozen names for a cleanup detail on the bulletin board and no one showed up," he said while he pushed his mop. I simply said, "Oh," and went on my way.

That evening, I posted the names not of privates who would not show up but names, ranks, serial numbers and ship boarding numbers of five Sergeants hoping at least one would show up. The next A.M. two Sergeants out of the five names I posted showed up. Whew, I wiped my forehead and passed on to them the lieutenant's orders and gave them the roster of names for the couple hundred men in the compartment. "There must be at least 50 Sergeants there on the list," I told them. They didn't need a hint, they played the same game I did and after that first A.M., they never touched a mop again. I would see them from time to time topside on deck, as they smiled and gave me an OK hand signal. The compartment was cleaned and that's all that mattered. I don't know why I kept it, but I still have that bulletin board notice among my mementos.

I went on deck and joined the audience around Joe Greco. "Hey Joe, mmmmmm...how eez ova there?" as he proceeded to keep everyone amused telling us what we already knew about Korea or even some things we never heard about but created by Joe, only now with an Italian accent like his Grandpa.

My journey on the *Ballou* was like a luxury cruise compared to the trip on the *Hersey*. I slept in the claustrophobic hold that I only remained in for the few hours to sleep. Awakening early in the morning I dashed off to the mess hall ate, hit the latrine... no, "The Head"...then disappeared among the troops on deck. That lieutenant never found me although I did see him snooping around the deck probably looking for me or some other shifty Sergeants. I remembered him because he wore his air medal and Army wings on his fatigue jacket so I can only assume he was an Army aviator or artillery observer who flew in a light unarmed single engine observation plane, a pretty hazardous job in Korea in those days.

That first night aboard the *Hersey* I was tucked into my confining canvas bunk when, in the wee hours of the morning, I dreamed about hearing someone pounding the side of the ship with a giant sledge hammer trying to get in. I was alarmed to wake up and realize it was not a dream because someone or something was pounding the side of the ship only it was not a hammer. It was a raging typhoon. "All military personal must remain in their bunks until the storm abates," the PA warned. "All water tight-compartment doors have been secured, all army personnel must remain in their bunks." "All hatches are secured. No Army personnel allowed topside." Oh man, that was not reassuring as we were now locked in this steel chamber below the water line.

"Hey Joe, how do you feel?" "How the hell do you think I feel, you think this tub will sink? Did you see all that rust on deck?" he said. You could sense the tension. I am somewhat claustrophobic, more so now than at that age, but I definitely felt it that night. If I never heard the announcement about locking the water tight doors and hatches, I would have been fine. A claustrophobic has got to have a way out! Remember, I was stuck head first in a darkened tunnel as a kid for I don't remember how long. It may well be the reason I love the wide open spaces so much.

"Why did they lock all the fucking doors?" someone yelled out. That didn't make me feel any better. You could feel the unrest of the troops and the pounding on the side of the ship which elevated everyone's concern. Then, in the darkened compartment, Joe Greco yelled out "Mmmmm, Hey Clementi I ask you, how eez ova there in Korea?" That broke the ice and those of us familiar with the saying just broke out laughing. "Hey Gallic, how ees ova there?" The pounding seemed to finally rock us all off to sleep.

The PA blasted as the *Hersey*'s Skipper awakened us with a much welcomed, "This is the Captain speaking, the mess hall is now open and we recommend all hands report for breakfast before going topside." I jumped out of my bunk and when landing on deck I felt a little dizzy. I tossed on some clothes and went straight to the mess hall where I grabbed a few hard boiled eggs and placed them in my pockets, gulped down some orange juice, drank some black coffee with a good helping of sugar, and ate my dry toast on the fly as I climbed the stairs two at a time anxious to get out on deck and out in the open air.

The sky was overcast and the water gray as I peeled an egg and tossed the shell overboard. Just as soon as I ate the egg, I started to feel better and the cool fresh air cleared my head. I saw guys with their heads hanging over the side of the railing retching painfully with the dry heaves. I told many guys to go to the mess hall and get some hard boiled eggs and dry toast and force it down with juice and coffee; some did and came back on deck with a smile. The wind in my face and the open air raised my spirits, and I probably lit up a cigarette with my old faithful Zippo lighter. I still

317

have the Zippo among my mementos and it is still wearing the makeshift repair to the hinge I made in Korea with a piece of commo wire.

The word must have gotten around as the G.I.'s started to accumulate on the open deck with much better countenances now that they had something to eat. I looked up from the frothing sea as Louie Clementi approached me looking terrible. "Hey Louie, have a hard-boiled egg," as I handed it to him, Louie took one look at the egg and dashed to the railing. Joe Greco showed up and took Louie down to the mess hall. "I'll get him fixed up," he said as he took Louie by the arm helping him to the gangway. Joe Zurla was the next to come on deck and he had already eaten some breakfast and said, "I've been on many deep sea fishing trips out of Sheepshead Bay and never get seasick." "Did you have some chow?" I asked. "Yeah," he said, as he showed me his pockets full of hard boiled eggs. Joe knew how to take care of himself just like all his pals did from the West Side Hell's Kitchen fraternity.

I think it took us 18 days to cross the western Pacific from Japan and sail into San Francisco Bay. It was about 6:00 AM and I had already had my breakfast which was of all things, believe it or not, 18-day-old fried liver. Most of us settled for some toast and coffee. I don't know nor could I imagine what the hell the navy did with 4,000 servings of 18-day-old fried liver nor could I figure out who the hell decided to serve it for breakfast that last morning as we sailed under the Golden Gate Bridge.

Off to the right we saw a pier and a beige colored building with a U.S. Army sign and the American flag flying at full staff in the breeze. It looked wonderful to me. We heard a band and saw a woman dressed in a fur coat singing into a microphone. I do not recall her name or the tune. San Francisco meant nothing to me other than I was now that much closer to Brooklyn.

We debarked and transferred to a smaller vessel, then being shipped across San Francisco Bay to some inland waterway and marched to an Army post. Many years later, I did locate the post in Marin County but that is now lost to me.

From 1963 to 1979, I traveled to San Francisco dozens of times on business with Lee accompanying me on most of those trips. John and Vincent joined us on a surprise trip to California in 1968. When on one of those trips, Lee and I took the boat ride in San Francisco Bay and sailed under the Golden Gate Bridge out to some seal rocks. On the ride back, I reflected on my trip aboard the *M. L. Hersey.* I looked to my right and spotted the very same beige colored building on the Army pier. There was no fried liver that A.M, I had my favorite Saint Francis Hotel breakfast: a fresh fruit compote, eggs benedict, coffee and of course starting off with Mimosa cocktails. Lee probably had very dry scrambled eggs with toast but we both enjoyed our fresh California orange juice and champagne mimosa cocktails and, we still do!! And it does not have to be California O. J., Florida O.J. will do just fine.

My memory of the stay at that army base in Marin County is still vague and we may not have even slept there. We ate some chow and then formed into groups of about 30-man parties. We were bused directly to Oakland Airport. I don't see any familiar faces except Joe Zurla. We were next led to an old WWII twin engine Curtis C-46 cargo plane. Instead of the familiar dull O. D. paint job, it was now wearing bright colors and some unknown airline name painted on the fuselage.

We were now on our last leg of the journey home as we climbed aboard the C-46 and were seated, waiting for the plane to take off and fly us east. It did not happen that day.

"Fasten your seat belts" was announced as the plane's engines roared loudly and the plane started to move. After a short taxi another announcement informed us, "We are returning to the terminal." Apparently, mechanical problems were detected and the flight was cancelled; we were told that we would be flying out the first thing in the morning. We would be spending an evening in Oakland. Some of the guys were excited about going to San Francisco. That night I looked out the window of my hotel room at the bright lights of San Francisco in the distance and had no desire to go there. I just wanted to go home to see my girl.

We boarded the plane again the next day and hooked up our seat belts as the plane rolled down the runway and lifted off, climbing out over the water which provided a good view of the San

Francisco skyline. This was a special thrill for me for it was my very first flight.

We hop-scotched across the country because the plane had to make many refueling stops all the way from Oakland California to North Philadelphia Airport. This is when we experienced flying in a non-pressurized aircraft. Each time we landed, the pressure hurt our ears as we lost altitude and approached the field. The crew told us to swallow hard and yawn but it didn't seem to help. The flight was an overnight trip and after multiple landings and take offs, it was getting tiresome for all of us. I noticed at a few airports the all new four engine luxury aircraft the Lockheed Constellation with its distinctive Tri-Tail. I thought it must be great to fly in one of those beautiful pressurized-cabin airplanes. In later years, I flew on all the various aircraft jet powered and propeller driven from single engine bush planes in Alaska to the giant Boeing 747 and everything in between. But I never did fly in a Lockheed Constellation.

Finally, the pilot announced we would soon be landing at the North Philadelphia Airport. I do not recall how many hours it took to fly coast to coast in that twin engine former cargo plane. Some of these vintage C-46's are still in use today having had many engine changes but still flying the same aging air frames built in the early 1940's.

When we landed, a bus took us directly to Camp Kilmer, New Jersey, for processing and it was a quick transition from soldier to civilian. A group of us hired a cab to drive to Manhattan and then I took a cab from Manhattan to Woodside. The ride with the guys is pretty much forgotten but the ride alone in that cab to Woodside is imprinted in my deepest memory, filled with emotion, doubt and for some strange reason, a little remorse. I could not understand this new feeling of uneasiness.

The cabbie was talkative and I was pensive. I think I would have preferred to be returning to Lee alone and then get used to being home. I never discussed my feelings about that evening to anyone. When the cab pulled up to my home and I saw a sign over my front door, "Welcome Home Vinny." Why did my folks have to put up a sign?" I asked myself. The cabbie announced, "Well, here we are, soldier." I heard his words and froze for a moment, my confidence vanishing for a brief instant as I paid him. Then I grabbed my duffle bag, eagerly ran up the stairs and opened the door. All uncertainty disappeared when I saw Lee. I dropped my duffle and with both arms caressed Lee and then my Mom and I joined everyone smiling and laughing. I was home, my army days were over.

I noticed Lee had lost a lot of weight but looked so pretty to me I just wanted to hold her in my arms. My Dad John and Mom Nellie are seen in my memory as smiling and happy. I don't know how many novenas my Mom must have prayed for me but now she looked happy. Brother John looked closely at my ribbons as he commented, "We hoped you weren't hiding something from us." "No John, I was way behind the front lines. I am all in one piece and happy to be home."

In about two weeks' time, I was back working and planning our wedding with Lee. She was starting to fill out a little now that I was home. I did not realize until I got home how much she worried and prayed for me. We were never in the same room together when I was not holding her in my arms. As I write this I am looking over my shoulder at her still pretty profile and I am thankful she waited for me and kept me.

The Forgotten War

President Harry Truman was reluctant to name the attack by North Korea upon its neighbor South Korea a war. Early on he simply called it a "Police Action," causing disparity between the President and those in the military especially those facing the enemy. Today all government references use the term "Korean Conflict." Our military suffered consequences because of this lack of commitment on the part of the President to send the necessary combat assets of men and material to win and then get out of Korea. Perhaps if we did that the entire Korean peninsula could be today, a peaceful productive nation. And, we would not need 25,000 American forces holding the front line with our ally South

Korea and peace would prevail in the Far East with no threat of nuclear annihilation that now exists.

Fifteen UN member nations sent combat troops and five more sent non-combat units to Korea during the war from June 1950 to July 1953. The Republic of Korea awarded a Korean War Service Medal to all the UN member troops serving in Korea during that time. This award was refused by the United States because the President did not agree it was a war which may tarnish his legacy. 50 years later, all the surviving Korean War veterans were awarded the Korean War Service Medal in 2003 then referred to as a 50th year commemorative medal. Those 37,000 American families who lost their loved ones in Korea had a hard time agreeing with President Truman that it was not a war. And those 37,000 heroes are as good as forgotten except by their bereaved loved ones and those of us still alive and proud to have served with them and thankful to have survived.

There is no doubt the attack on South Korea was a bloody war that killed millions of military and civilians on both sides on that divided peninsula. There are a few conflicting theories as to why the invasion even took place at that specific time. One theory focuses on the speech made before the National Press Club in January 1950 by Secretary of State Dean Acheson. He proclaimed the defense perimeter of the United States would not extend beyond Japan, the Philippines and the Ryukyu Islands. This implied that the United States would not defend South Korea if attacked. This announcement gave a green light to North Korea, and encouraged China and Russia to help North Korea without the risk of U.S. intervention. Less than six months after that speech was made, The People's Republic of Korea armed forces pounced on their neighbor in the south. With, Russian and Chinese weaponry and with Russian advisors/combat troops among the invading army and air force.

In five short years following the end of World War II in 1945, President Truman drastically reduced the United States from the strongest military in the world to a dangerously weaker and less combat ready force by 1950 which again, caught our nation totally unprepared for a war.

In May 1951 General Omar Bradley appointed in 1949 by President Harry Truman to be our Joint Chief of Staff, gave the following message to congress: "The wrong WAR, in the wrong place, at the wrong time, with the wrong enemy." General Bradley had no problem calling it a war.

American troops went to Korea with a handful of hand grenades and an M1 rifle. Light infantry weapons were all they possessed to face hordes of North Korean troops armed with Russian and Chinese automatic weapons, Russian Artillery, Russian T-34 tanks and Russian TU-2 bombers and Yak fighters.

Right next to my bunk in Korea was a stored and folded 3.5 inch bazooka rocket launcher each platoon was issued and never had to be used. It is too bad the U.S. troops did not have the 3.5 inch early on but defense cutbacks sent American soldiers under-gunned into Korea with the smaller 2.26" Bazooka rocket launchers that were obsolete in World War II. To make matters worse, when fired the troops found the rocket ammo was old and defective and just bounced off the Russian T-34 Tanks. It was a disaster to allow this drastic reduction in our military when only five years earlier our military saved the world from dictatorship. It was later admitted and proven that active Russian combat troops were in that first wave of tanks and aircraft. The history is readily available and easily accessible there for anyone to read about if at all interested.

The North's Peoples Republic of Korea now has over 9,000,000 active, reserve and paramilitary and is one of the largest military in the world. The South's Republic of Korea has 625,000 active and 2,900,000 in reserve. We know how dangerous North Korea is today with Nuclear weapons and working on the means to deliver warheads to North America. Maybe Truman should have listened to MacArthur and gave him enough assets to win the Korean War while we had the manpower and weaponry in the field to be victorious. It is a wishful thought that the entire Peninsula could today be a peaceful democracy and productive society, not one torn apart by freedom and plenty in the south and oppression and starvation in the north. The only well fed North Koreans are among the leaders and not the masses. Photos of the third generation Leader Kim-Jung-Un shows he is even chubbier than his well-fed father and grandfather while the masses are still underfed and undernourished. North Korea survives today with help from Communist China, Russia and Iran.

A total of 1,700,000 Americas served in the Korea War between June 1950 and July 1953. Most were draftees: here is a list of only the U.S. Infantry Divisions engaged on the ground.

1st Cavalry Div. RA	24th Infantry Div. RA
2nd Infantry Div. RA	25th Infantry Div. RA
3rd Infantry Div. RA	40th Infantry Div. NG
7th Infantry Div. RA	45th Infantry Div. NG
1st Marine Div.	

Visit the Korean War Project, www.Koreanwar.org, to see an accurate list of every American military unit serving in Korea during the three year war. You can even check on comments by veterans and their families. 700 National Guard units served in Korea during the war.

A Tribute to Max Ries

Max had not slept for 36 hours when this picture was taken after delivering the MJB to Charlie Battery.

Three pals from Queens L to R Bob Dema, Vin Gallagher and Max Ries. My two pals thanked me for talking them into joining the 773rd that first morning in Korea.

Max's duty as the Artillery Gun Mechanic was an important job in the battery and a technical position calling for the rank of Sergeant. The Artillery Gun Mechanic was responsible for keeping the four 90mm AA guns fully operational and properly maintained at the battery level. Not unlike your own automobile requiring periodic maintenance even, artillery guns with their numerous systems of hydraulics, recoil buffers, fuse setters and assorted mechanical parts also required routine maintenance.

The Technical Manual (TM) described these battery level checks and the frequency with which they should be done. Each gun also had a log recording the number of rounds fired and how many rounds could be fired before the gun was sent to ordnance for a barrel replacement. The gun was re-barreled, updated and put into inventory for the next user. Every round fired took its toll on the barrel's accuracy.

Max had an interesting job in the battery. If he attended the Artillery School Gun Mechanic course at Fort Bliss, Texas or Fort Sill, Oklahoma, he would have been promoted to Sergeant while at Camp Stewart. He was well on the way to being promoted to corporal but it just never happened. I do not know the reason for the delay and believe it occurred prior to the 773rd deployment to Brooklyn at the conclusion of training in Camp Stewart.

Upon arrival in Brooklyn, changes occurred in the gun platoon when Master Sergeant Bill Barker re-enlisted Regular Army and was transferred and a new platoon Sergeant took his place which added to the oversight. The later order for the battalion to be sent to Korea probably put promotions on the back burner. All the while, Max was preforming the duty with no complaint. I remember being surprised when I reported back to the battery from Fort Bliss and Max met me in the orderly room while serving as the battery C.Q. (Charge of Quarters) an NCO duty and, he was still wearing Private First Class Stripes on his uniform.

In between the required periodic system checks, the Gun Mechanic would be called whenever the gun commander felt something needed attention and would seek the gun mechanic's help. Sometimes, the simple replacement of a worn out gun part was all that was necessary.

If for example at Camp Stewart while in the field, the gun mechanic needed a new part, let's say a new, "M1-A1 Pin, Détente Ordnance Part # 12345," Max prepared the requisition form and had the Battery Commander sign for it and issue Max a pass so he was now on his own. When on the way driving his ¾ ton truck to the Ordnance unit, he may have stopped at a Shrimp Shack. There, he discreetly parked in the rear of the shack while he enjoyed a basket of shrimp, hush puppies and a cold drink. Max had plenty of time on his own and he was always smart enough not to take advantage of his freedom.

The battery commander, the first Sergeant, and the supply and mess Sergeants always had a special detail for Max, he was always there to help. In Korea, this continued with Max spending much time on those roads in Korea alone and in the middle of the night or early AM's on some urgent battery business. Unlike the distractions he had back in the states with a cold beer and hush puppies he had instead, a box of C or K rations, a canteen full of chemically treated water, his carbine with 90 rounds of ammo and a bayonet while towing a trailer loaded with his tools and supplies. Those nights, the old Max smile was no longer there. His only desire was to get to his destination ASAP and return to the safety of the battery. I bet he thought about home and his future wife Angela during those times.

One particular move was when Charlie Battery was called on a fire mission coinciding with some practice somewhere much further north of our permanent position in the foothills of the K-55 Air Base. The battery Fire Control Platoon and the Gun Platoon along with the commo, motor and mess sections march ordered their equipment and joined in a convoy to travel north using Strip Maps to show us the way.

We arrived and set up the equipment only to discover the gun platoon failed to take the MJB (Main Junction Box) which connected the entire firing battery. This piece of equipment was about 24 inches square weighing about 20 pounds. It was a piece of equipment issued to the gun platoon and the responsibility of the gun platoon Sergeant and his officer, the gun platoon leader. This time it was forgotten during the hectic pace of activity when the battery was given the March Order.

When discovered missing late in the day at dusk by his platoon leaders, Max was ordered to drive all the way back to So-Jung-Ni, pick up the MJB and return with it as soon as possible. Without complaint and dedicated to his duty, Max drove the long, arduous and dangerous journey alone to save the day for C Battery. He should have gotten some recognition from his platoon Sergeant and certainly should have been at least promoted to corporal while in Korea.

This oversight was hushed up because no one wanted the battalion commander to know about this carelessness otherwise, someone may have been reduced in rank. In the meantime, the guns were emplaced, the battery O&S'd and settling rounds fired. The Fire Control equipment was energized, checked out and operational while we all waited for Ries to return with the MJB. It didn't happen until well into the cold and dark AM hours. But, no one in battalion knew about it other than Charlie Battery.

I know Max's eyes were wide open and he was on high alert during that grueling drive in the middle of the night in unfamiliar high risk territory. It was one thing to be in a full column with your own battery and draw your courage from the secure feeling of your comrades in arms. It was quite different to be alone at night with only your loaded carbine for company to shore up your nerve. This was typical of Max's war experience in Korea where it seemed these odd and unusual duties would put him at great personal risk. PFC Max Ries was a capable, hardworking and brave soldier in Charlie Battery. One of these extra details brought tragedy to Max.

One cloudy cold morning back at the battery's permanent position, he was ordered to drive some men to the battalion medics at the air base. Again, this was extra duty totally removed from his main job. That ride took him west from our hill several miles to the MSR (Main Supply Route) a graded but unpaved road. I never saw a paved road in Korea other than in Seoul the Capital City.

Arriving on the MSR, he traveled a little north and made a left turn at a railroad crossing and then straight on to the K-55 airbase. When approaching the guard shack, Max waved at the ROK (Republic of Korea) soldier, one of several he recognized from previous trips and the Korean smiled back in recognition. In the dim pre-dawn hour, the Korean guard waved Max on with his passengers showing it was safe to cross the railroad tracks.

Ries made this trip many times and he knew and recognized the Korean guards. Fortunately, his passengers were required to remain at battalion and he took the same route alone to return to the battery for breakfast but he never made it there. I will try to patch together memories of that day.

That morning, Astoria buddy Bob Dema came to the Fire Control area and told me Max was on his way to battalion when he was hit by a train and rushed to a hospital and it was doubtful if he survived. I jumped in a Jeep and recall speeding to the railroad crossing where I saw the remains of his truck and truck parts spread over the tracks with only the chassis and four wheels remaining from his ¾ ton truck.

M.P.'s near the scene who were investigating the accident told me where he was taken and said they did not think he was alive. The guard shack at the crossing was empty and the M.P.'s were asking questions about that. "Where the hell is the ROK guard? Why isn't he here?" I heard an M.P. lieutenant call out.

When the M.P.'s gave me the directions to the hospital, I jumped back in the Jeep and drove off. I stopped at a worn out brick and stone structure probably built by the Japanese during the many years they occupied Korea. An army nurse lieutenant dressed in green fatigues told me where Max was and she passed me on to another nurse who took me directly to his bedside. "Yes, he is alive but critical. He is not awake and you may only stay a minute," the nurse told me. Max's face was all bandaged, red and unrecognizable. Tubes were sticking out hooked up to an assortment of medical devices and he was unconscious. The nurses had a forbidding countenance to their faces and only answered in uncertain terms. They said he "may" be air evacuated out and "if" he survived would go on to Japan. I remember the "if's and "maybe's," and nothing more. They did not sound at all encouraging.

The nurses and doctors were all hustling about with grave expressions on their faces. No one looked like they were having the same fun Alan Alda and the cast would later have on the set of the TV smash hit, "MASH." I watched the show a couple of times but could never appreciate the humor of a hospital setting in Korea. At that hospital I saw soldiers suffering and some hanging on to their young lives by just a hair. It just didn't seem like a venue for comedy to me.

The medical staff I saw and talked to all looked tired with sadness in their eyes as they went about caring for all the guys who were hurting. The soldiers were young men who should have been home having fun. Those patients had blank stares on their faces and most had their eyes closed. One could only wonder what was going through their minds at the time. I remember feeling very uncomfortable there and I wanted to leave as soon as I could. I did not think at that time that Max would survive.

A vague image remains waving my hand and saying "so long" to Max as I looked at him lay there in a coma and thinking to myself, I will never see my pal alive again. The image of that hospital fades when I opened the door to a fresh cold breeze and turned to close the door behind me. When I drove back to the battery, I remember my uniform still smelled from the hospital.

The hospital visit made me feel very depressed and it was the only time I remember feeling actual dread while in Korea. I felt a confusing mixture of elation, sadness and guilt. At the time, I did not really understand these feelings and it bothered me deeply. I was happy that it was not me in one of those hospital beds and maybe hanging on for my life. At the same time, I was so very sad that it was my buddy Max whom, I talked into joining the National Guard in the first place.

Deep in my subconscious I believe I sent some of Max's personal items to his Mom with a letter of some encouragement. I knew Mrs. Ries very well because some of the guys met on a Saturday night at Max and his Mom's apartment on Crescent Street. We would then go around the corner to Bill Tierney's house, across the street from Bob Dema, to decide where we would go for the evening. Maybe to a movie at the Paramount Theater in

Manhattan or the "Burlesque Show" in Union City, New Jersey. This was years before we all were called to serve our country and before we all met our sweethearts.

I also wrote a letter to Lee about Max, I think she still has that letter in our hope chest together with every letter I wrote to her from Korea. I will look for it. The letter was reassuring because I knew she would talk to Max's girlfriend, Angie.

Max was sent to Japan to recover from his injuries and returned home sometime after I did. He and Angie were married in the fall of 1953 around the same time Lee and I were married. Max re-enlisted in the National Guard and worked in the full-time Nike missile on-site program in Spring Valley, New York. It was there he told me the ROK guard who waved him on his return trip from battalion and directly into the path of the oncoming train was, a total stranger he never saw before.

This was investigated by the M.P.'s and it was determined that enemy soldiers dressed in ROK soldiers uniforms were infiltrating the lonely ROK guard posts. Max was belatedly awarded the Purple Heart Medal to join the ranks of over 92,000 American service personnel who were wounded in the Korean War. Max and his wife had five children including twin boys who were all quite young when Max tragically died suddenly at the age of 34, in 1965.

His family today is indeed a beautiful family with grandchildren and great grandchildren all of whom he would be proud. I like to think that Max is looking down at them now with that same familiar smile. Lee and I continue to share our friendship with Max's wife, Angela Mondelli Ries. If any of Maxie's children and grandchildren ever read this tribute, I want them to know he was a fine man, a fine soldier and the best friend a man could have. He was my best buddy.

Eighth Army Shoulder Patch

773rd AA Battalion was assigned to the 10th AA Group in the Eighth United States Army Korea EUSAK. The Eighth Army still serves proudly in the Republic of Korea continuously since 1950.

Sabre Jets overhead

Sabre Jets on the way to MIG Alley

Seoul 1952, Capital Building. Built by Japan in 1911 on site of ancient royal palace grounds. Purposely to erase the memory of the former Korean Kingdom. Japan banned Korean language and customs. Korea destroyed this reminder of oppression in 1995.

Gyeongbokgung Palace originally built in 1395 on royal kingdom grounds destroyed by the Japanese during the partition of Korea ending in 1945. Restored by Korea in honor of their royal history. Notice the same somewhat eroded mountain I saw in 1952. How cleverly Japan tried to hide the past of a subjugated nation. *iStock.com*

Procurement
Specialists
selecting material
to sell to cottage
industrialists.
Any wonder why
they succeeded in
one generation in
the USA.

Korean school children from Osan

Korean Papa–San: strong, hardworking,
resilient…says it all

Famous Korean "A Frame."

House Boy Kim always had a smile and was trustworthy as were most of the Korean civilians working on the site. He was fortunate to live with three generations of his family and it showed in his happy face.

This picture of an orphan tells the story of the innocent victims of the scourge of war.

These people were not looking for a war...the war found
them. This was a spot were bloody fighting took place in
1950. Military age young men were absent from So-Jung-Ni.

Children knew Charlie Battery was good for treats. Before
they were introduced to all the sugars we gave them which
later ruined their wonderful white toothed smiles.

338

Verrone with M1-Rifle and his Machine Gun Section pal both quartered with the Fire Control Platoon. He and Giuliani cooked Italian delicacies on the diesel heater when packages arrived from home.

Washer ladies after a busy day in C Batteries laundry. The fields never saw any mechanized farm machines, those neat smooth furrowed fields were made by a Papa- San and his oxen with a wooden plow.

Pasta, a worldwide favorite, was supposedly introduced to Europe by Marco Polo in the thirteenth century when he returned to Venice from Cathay. This entrepreneur checks her freshly made rice noodles as they air dry.

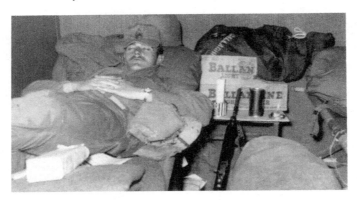

Snoozing after a late night snack. That package of Davis's crackers on my cot were swiped by my Platoon Midnight Requisition Squad from the mess tent. As long as I was implicated, it was all right. An open case of beer was a common site in Charlie Battery. CPL Winstead let his candle burn a little too low. He probably took this picture as evidence of my Cracker Complicity. Food, drink, a warm bunk, a case of beer...not bad eh!

Astoria buddy Bob Dema on lower left probably giving his
Gun Commander SFC Scarborough on right some chafe.

SFC Davis driving to battalion for rations, water and to drop
off and pick up mail. Plus, any other amorous business he may
have???

Bucking the chow line annoyed everyone and some NCO's took advantage of it. I thought it poor leadership judgement to eat before my men did. Top Kick Kolody felt the same way. There he is on-site all day, still wearing his web belt with first aid pack, ammo pouch with two loaded carbine magazines, and his canteen full of water bouncing off his right hip. Me and PFC Archuleta just returned with LT Haber to the site and dumped our weapons and webbing, and hit the chow line much to Kolody's annoyance - he liked being last on the chow line.

Baby G.I. named by Korean washer women after helping dig in and load M2 .50 caliber machine gun. He took his soldiering seriously and always ready to do his duty. Quad mount .50 in fire control area can be seen in top of photo.

342

SFC Farrington one of four of our outstanding gun commanders with some of the G.I.'s in his gun crew of 14 men. Farrington was an RA soldier with years of experience and knowledge which his men benefited from. We had a lot of good troopers in Charlie Battery with, and without stripes on their arms.

This day is remembered when the battalion ambulance and medical officer arrived to escort an officer whom I will not name who had mental troubles. Many of us who knew him felt quite bad, but he probably should not have been here and, booze had nothing to do with it. That's the ammo dump carved out by "Alabam."

343

90mm shell case hangs from scaffold. When struck with metal bar the loud gong alerts battery for ground attack.

All CATS were equipped with sirens which alerted battery for air alert. Sand bagged radio shack partially seen at left.

90 set and ready, Quad Mount on south west side hilltop
of battery before first snow fall.

Same Quad Mount section after first snowfall.

Only picture of SCR-584 Radar in convoy. Battery commander's jeep in front. We are waiting for tail end of convoy to catch up. Ten year old CATS still running thanks to SFC Ralph Nebbia and the star motor section. Every vehicle started this cold A.M.; even SFC. Burns looks cold.

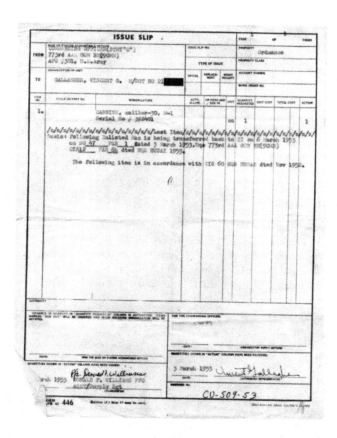

Carbine Turn-in Form

M.L. Hersey at dock in Pusan ready for trip to Sasebo, Japan.
Two unnamed troopers on left plus Joe Greco with shaded face
and his pal Louie Clemente from Brooklyn. Joe Zurla on right. I
don't recall who mentioned about all the rust on the ship.

348

25 MARCH

FOLLOWING MEN REPORT TO
COMPARTMENT 1ST SGT AT 0730hrs
26 MARCH

SGT.
SGT
SGT
SGT
SFC

When I saw that Master Sergeant mopping the deck I knew I had to make a plan. After assigning the compartment First Sergeant Detail to the two SGT's who did show up on March 26th, I spent the rest of the voyage relaxing on deck. The Lieutenant never found me among the masses of guys all dressed in the same green uniform so I just hid in plain sight.

The Air War in Korea

Polikarpov PO-2 Bed Check Charlie

The PO-2 first flew in 1927 and was produced in Russia until 1952. The Korean Peoples Air Force used the PO-2 to probe air defenses of the UN Forces earning the nickname "Bed Check Charlie." The Bi-Plane dropped fragmentation bombs on a U.S. Airbase damaging eleven P-51 Mustang Fighters early in the war. June 1950 a flight of two PO-2's attacked a U.S. Airbase in Suwon scoring hits on an Aviation Engineer Battalion and damaged planes on the runway. No destruction of any PO-2's by AAA fire was ever reported. June 1953 a Marine Douglas Sky Raider shot down a PO-2 the only recorded air victory by a Sky Raider in the Korean War. Incredibly a PO-2 was credited with a jet kill when an F-94 Lockheed Star Fire slowed down and crashed trying to intercept the slow flying PO-2. The plane pictured has Russian Red Star markings but, the PO-s's in Korea wore the Korean Peoples Air Force insignia. *bigstock.com*

U.S. Navy Douglas AD-10-1Q Sky Raider used by Marines and U.S Navy to support ground troops Public Domain via Wikipedia Commons

Vought F4U Corsair Marine ground support aircraft "USMC", by Gery Metzler "CCBY-SA2.0" via Wikipedia Commons

Max Smith (TU-2 at the China Aviation Museum)
Public domain, via Wikipedia Commons

Schlacke-Heiner (TU-2 Public Domain, via Wikipedia Commons

TUPELOV TU-2 twin engine medium bomber showing Soviet
Russian WW II color scheme and Red Star Insignia. This
aircraft was first introduced to the USSR air force in 1942 and
2250 TU-2 aircraft were built during the war. Some were later
sent to the Chinese Communist forces and the North Korean air
force. The plane was used effectively by the communist forces
early in the Korean War but sheltered in air bases in North
Korea for the balance of the war. With a speed of 325 MPH and
an altitude of 29,000 feet it was a formidable weapon carrying a
bomb load of over 3,000 pounds internally with extra bombs
affixed to the wings. Armament consisted of two 20mm
cannons and three machine guns manned by a crew of 5. The
TU-2 were never reported to have crossed the 38th Parallel to
attack our forces while the 773rd served in Korea.

ADVERSARIES

F-86 & Mig-15 by Tim Felce CCBY-SA via Wikipedia Commons

	F-86 Jet USA	Mig-15 North Korea
Length	37 Feet	33 Feet
Wingspan	37 Feet	33 Feet
Weight Empty	10,950 Pounds	8,100 Pounds
Range	785 Miles	700 Miles
Altitude	50,000 Feet	50,000 Feet
Speed	685 MPH	688 MPH
Engine Thrust	5,550 Pounds	6,000 Pounds
Armament	(6) 50 caliber Machine Guns	(2) 23mm Canon Or (1) 37mm Canon

Mig Alley

Chapter 9

Good To Be Back Home

Now back home, I had to find employment to help get me back on track with civilian life and plan our future wedding for the fall of the year. I still had a commitment to the National Guard to complete my second three-year enlistment which would be satisfied in September, only a few short months away.

After returning home, my Mother knew I was troubled, I lost my appetite and something was just not right with me. Mom suggested I see Dr. Gerarty our family doctor who served as an army doctor during WW II. Doc Gerarty checked me out and told me everything was fine and not to be too concerned. He told me it was common among many returning servicemen to feel some guilt to return in one piece and in good health while so many others were not so fortunate and, some were never to return. He mentioned the memories of my cousin Vincent killed in Burma and our many friends and neighbors we both knew who returned from Korea and World War II with terrible wounds.

The doctor continued, "Do not worry, this will not last." He continued, "Many of your own neighbors have felt the same as you do. You did your job and there is nothing to feel guilty about. Your pal Maxie was less fortunate and this was no fault of yours." As I sat there listening to Gerarty I tried to make some sense of what he told me. I did find some relief from these feelings that, I dared not even mention to others.

I did not let my feelings interfere with my desire to find a job to help me to become a civilian again. So in about two weeks I was employed by Household Finance Corporation. It serves no purpose to reflect back in time about what "I should have done" so I will remain on theme. I am thankful for all my blessings and if I had it to do all over again, I would make the same mistakes to assure the same outcome. I have no regrets and have met many men and women shouldering a lifetime of regrets.

My new job was interesting and re-opened the door to civilian life and to gain some business experience. The office manager, Mr. Finnegan, advanced through the ranks and was earning a good living. His two assistants, Ed Agrippa and Chas. Lawrence, both drove new autos, were well dressed and not too many months before Agrippa was out in the field chasing deadbeats in Astoria and Long Island City. I jumped in with eyes wide open and a sense of urgency to succeed. I was partnered with Ed Regan who would soon be an assistant manager.

The names of some people I dealt with may be remembered by some so I will use fictitious names in my narrative. The first was a young Italian chap in his mid-twenties, I will call him Dee. At the time, I thought Dee was just a slow payer who owed money to Household and I had to visit his social club in Long Island City to find him and collect from him. I knew nothing about the mob in those days and simply harassed Dee until I got some money on his account. I noticed his friend's lurking in the background waiting for Dee to just give the word but at the time I was totally ignorant of the threat. I thought he was a nice guy who just didn't pay his bills on time. He was always nice to me and cried about how poor he was and how hard it was for him to get a job. He said his fancy gold wristwatch was a present from his 'Grandma." I look back now and realize he just had fun with a naïve green kid just out of the army pressuring HIM for a payment.

I took their remarks with a grin on my face and never gave much thought to the comments, "What do you expect from an Irishman?" I just shrugged it off when I had money in hand to report back to my boss, Mr. Finnegan. "Real good job, Gallagher," as he referred to Dee and his friends with his favorite comment, "Typical of the area." Meaning, they were Italians, gamblers and worse. Irishman Finnegan never knew I was half Italian.

Being new I got all the problem cases to test me. One was Mrs. Sanchez, a superintendent's young wife who lived in a first floor apartment of a large apartment complex. Her husband passed away suddenly leaving her with two small children and her deceased spouse's loan.

I rang the bell and Mrs. Sanchez came to the door wearing a black dress, her hair a little unkempt and, a couple of tots peeking at me from behind the door. I introduced myself and gave her my shiny new HFC business card and told her I was here to collect on her husband's loan. She answered in a warm Spanish accent, "My husband passed away and I had no knowledge about the loan, I told that to the man who called me from your office."

Legally, she had no responsibility for the debt for it was in her husband's name only. But, he signed a chattel mortgage that pledged his home furnishing as collateral, a technicality the lender held over the borrowers' head. Yes, at times we threatened to take the television set right out from under the eyes of crying children but I don't recall HFC ever doing this. And I had no heart to use these tactics on this attractive and bereaved Spanish woman.

My mission was to get a payment or get her on the phone to speak to my manager. This action was called an "immediate," meaning, I got immediate action on the first call, a plus for my record. So I asked to use her phone and would she talk to my superior. "Yes," she said reacting favorably to my gentleman's approach.

Back in the office Ed Agrippa, the "Bad Cop," instructed me "If they can't pay at least get them to speak to me on the phone." Ed was cast in an excellent role. He had a dark countenance, seldom smiled, and spoke in a threatening monotone

Agrippa could put on an evil aura and tone which he worked on to enhance his tough guy image. His hair was thick and black and grew almost down to his thick dark eyebrows and he had black not brown eyes. Even at 9:00 AM, Agrippa's five o'clock shadow was starting to show. He looked like a gangster right out of a B crime movie...and loved it. He generally had a cigarette dangling from the corner of his mouth.

The office remained open on Friday night so people could make payments and the outside men could track down deadbeats at home or bars...it could get tricky. Management paid for our dinner before we went out and we re-assembled later at the local bar on Broadway and 30th Streets at about 10:00 PM where we all received a morale booster when the boss picked up the bar tab. Ed let his hair down and looked and acted quite normal and turned into a congenial fellow. He smiled and laughed and lost that dark mean countenance. He became a different character completely and he even looked different. Ed Agrippa would have made an excellent actor. It appeared the management trio of Finnegan, Agrippa and Lawrence were all well paid, well dressed and in good spirits which gave me an incentive to do well.

"Hello Mr. Agrippa, I am with Mrs. Sanchez here and she will speak to you." I smiled as I handed the phone to Mrs. Sanchez.

She was calm and explained to Agrippa what she had told me. I could hear Agrippa's voice go up a few decibels and saw Mrs. Sanchez's eyes enflame and then turn hostile as Agrippa started yelling at her. She became so unruffled that her Latin temper took over as she reached for something to throw. Not wanting to be a target I ducked out of the way as she broke down in tears and told me in part Spanish she was sorry and ashamed. I was out of there.

Good job Gallagher, you're off to a good start here, Agrippa told me when I called him from the corner drug store. "What the hell did you say to her Ed? She almost threw an iron at me?" "Only part of the job, Gallagher, you're doing just fine." He continued, "Hold on to the card and I'll send you and Regan back out Friday night."

The outside men met about 5 P.M. for dinner and we set the stage for the "Good Cop, Bad Cop, "routine. It was the same every Friday night only the roles were reversed. But Ed Regan made a much better Bad Cop than I ever did.

We hit the trail and rang Mrs. Sanchez's bell. "Ed, be gentle, she almost threw an iron at me." "OK Vin, you do the talking." Mrs. Sanchez answered our ring with, "I told you I can't pay." but you may come in." As soon as we crossed the threshold, without a word Reagan whipped out a notebook and pen and took inventory of the living room content. "What is he doing?" She asked. Ed looked at me and said, "Mr. Gallagher, shall I explain to Mrs. Sanchez about the Chattel Mortgage?" "Yes, yes by all means, do so," as I listened closely.

"Mrs. Sanchez, the loan is secured by a Chattel mortgage signed by your husband, pledging all home furnishings as security. If we must, we will repossess your property to pay the balance of the loan which is $350." Household Finance had a $500 maximum loan limit. "We would be sorry to have to take such drastic action" Regan continued, "But, if this is the only way we can be repaid for a loan we made in good faith then, we must exercise our legal right."

Regan said all this in a single breath with a serious demeanor on his cherubic face. He followed with, "Mr. Gallagher hoped we would not have to take this action against you but what else can we do?" Regan paused to allow time for his diatribe to settle in Mrs. Sanchez's mind. She said, "I do not have the money to pay off the balance of the loan..."What else can I do?"

"Well, Mrs. Sanchez, your husband agreed to pay $22.50 a month. If the payment continues, we will not be forced to repossess any of your household furnishings or appliances." Total silence...The next one who speaks, loses. Regan looked her straight in the eyes without another word. I just stood there wondering if this is the job I really wanted.

After some seconds ticked by Mrs. Sanchez spoke: "Let me see if I have enough money to make at least a payment," and went into her bedroom while her two children were still watching TV. You can imagine how lousy I felt as Regan winked at me.

Mrs. Sanchez returned with her purse and a twenty-dollar bill in her hand and motioned for Mr. Regan to take it. Looking at me Regan said, "Mr. Gallagher, do you think this will satisfy the home office if Mrs. Sanchez promises to pay $20 a month?" Of course I said, "Yes I do!" Regan turned to Mrs. Sanchez and told her Mr. Gallagher can come by each month to collect the payment if that would be more convenient for her. Regan you bastard, I thought to myself, what are you getting me into here. Out loud I said, "Oh no, no Mr. Regan, I don't think that will be necessary I will take Mrs. Sanchez's word that she will pay $20 a month to pay off the loan and we will change the terms of the loan." We left with the twenty and thanked her for her time.

Once outside, I blasted Regan for trying to get me involved. He laughed and coyly said, "I thought you would like to go back every month...you *habla* don't you?" "I'm engaged to be married" was my reply and this time I was pissed off enough to actually be the Bad Cop!

Finnegan gave me another skip, a woman borrowed from the Astoria office made one payment, and disappeared. Several of the outside men tried running her down and had failed so, Agrippa gave me the card. I knew the neighborhood because all of my Astoria buddies lived within a few blocks of the HFC office. I visited retail stores owned by folks I knew and started asking about her. The local dry cleaner knew her and said she passed by his store every morning on the way to work. "Would you point her out to me one morning?" "Sure, Vin, come in tomorrow morning about 8 AM, I'll have the coffee ready." The next morning, I arrived at the dry cleaner's store with donuts I probably bought from actor Christopher Walken's parent's bakery right across the street from the dry cleaner's store on Broadway. We were sipping our coffee and chatting when the owner pointed her out to me as she passed by and I left in hot pursuit.

I followed her to the elevated line to Queens Plaza where we changed trains to the Lexington Avenue subway. I shadowed her right up to her office in Manhattan and after I waited a while for her to settle down to work, I entered the office and asked to see her. A few seconds passed and she came out to see me with a startled inquisitive look on her face. I smiled as I handed her my card and I thought she would faint on the spot. "Look," I said, "I have to take you to a public phone in the lobby so you can talk to my office to arrange repayment of the loan. Then, I go back to Astoria and you go back to work. If not, management has instructed me to immediately see your employer to arrange garnishment of your salary. It is all very simple you must…make your monthly payments to HFC."

The poor lady was petrified about the thought of my seeing her new boss so she agreed and we both took the elevator to the lobby. "Hi Ed, Miss XXXXX would like to talk to you." I handed her the phone and Gallagher got another "Immediate" and also found a skip.

That day I did not go right back to Astoria I went instead to see Joe at Meridian Employment Agency in midtown Manhattan. His last name is totally lost to memory but he specialized in sales positions. I do not recall how I found him, but I filled out some forms and he said he would find me a sales job in the drug store trade and the fee would be paid by the employer.

Finnegan told Agrippa, "Ed, give the Bacalla card to Gallagher, he seems to be good at finding Skips." Ed gave me some 4 X 6 cards all stapled together and pretty much weather beaten with use; it seemed everyone in the office took a crack at Bacalla but no one found him. I sat down and reviewed the notations going back many months.

I started by making a personal visit to the skip's mother's house in Astoria which was the last known address on record. I rang the bell on the front door of a small single family house and an old frail little Italian lady answered the door and said she was Bacalla's mother. When I showed her my card she invited me into the small sun room as she turned around to close the door to her living room. That was just enough time for me to spot a letter on the small mail table addressed to Mario Bacalla with a return address from a funeral home in Brooklyn which I memorized. Mrs. Bacalla said she did not know where her son was and that he no longer lived at home. But now I had a hot clue and dashed off to a telephone booth and a Brooklyn Yellow Pages.

Following up by visiting the funeral parlor located in the Bedford-Stuyvesant section of Brooklyn, I found that Mr. Bacalla worked there doing pickups for the undertaker and was now working in the kitchen crew of a luxury ocean liner. Some snooping disclosed the name of the line and the ship he worked on. I worked the Bacalla card in between other skips. I found the job challenging and to some extent kind of adventurous, but deep down I knew I wanted to go into sales and start making some real money.

Every morning the half dozen of us "outside men," would go next door to a luncheonette for coffee and to compare notes. We were all familiar with each other's cases and sometimes we would help each other.

One morning at breakfast, one of the guys was reading the *Daily Mirror* and there on the front page was a picture of my man in handcuffs walking down the gangway of an ocean liner with the caption, "FEDS FIND BACALLA." He was arrested after being caught by the Federal agents who were chasing him for more serious activities…narcotics trafficking. "Oh well, Agrippa won't like this, HCF won't get paid on this one" said Dick Finlay.

That spring Lee's folks invited their family jeweler Mr. Schlegel to their home and Lee picked a pretty ½ carat diamond in a platinum setting and we were both happy about the purchase. We looked at engagement rings in a store and were both happy with her choice. I was soon to learn we came from two different ends of the spectrum from "Understatement to Overstatement."

"Where is your ring?" I asked her the following night. "Oh, I can't wear the ring until we have the engagement party" Lee answered.

"Party, what party? We don't need an engagement party, do we?" I thought out loud.

"As a matter of fact, my Dad is taking us to the hall tonight to make the arrangements," Lee stated as I gulped. "Hall? What hall? Who needs a hall? Why not a small restaurant for the immediate family?" Panic slowly set in.

"Don't worry, my folks are going to pay for the party," Lee assured me. "Okay … if that is what you and your folks want, that will be fine with me." I consented with a frown.

Lee's Dad, Andy, was all happy and excited about the big engagement party and the special surprise of the engagement ring Lee's parents were buying for me to wear at the party. He told me this as we drove to Colonial Mansion on Bath Avenue in Bensonhurst. "Pssst, honey, do I have to wear an engagement ring, too?"

Beads of sweat now grew on my brow when I saw a decorated throne on a platform at the far end of this immense ballroom.

"What…what is that throne for?" I inquired. "That is where the future bride and groom will sit in the place of honor at the party," Dad Andy gleefully answered.

Before leaving Lee that evening, I do recall telling her, "OK, I'll go along with the party, if that's what your folks want but I'm not sitting on that throne in front of my family and friends." She just smiled and said she would not sit there either. Her breaking family tradition made my brow feel a little cooler and I loved her even more now.

Once home, I drank my usual quart of ice cold milk and went to bed with visions of thrones, engagement rings for men, big parties, and Colonial Mansion banquet halls...only to awaken in the middle of the night in a cold sweat. "Maybe it's the cold milk you have been drinking every night since you've been home, sonny," Mom Nellie suggested. That was the beginning of my decline from a happy and healthy army fed 160-pound soldier to a 125- pound nervous civilian.

Yes, we had the party for 250 people and it was a big celebration with everyone having a great time except the future bride and groom. Lee felt the same as I did about the throne and it remained empty all during the festivities.

I was getting nervous and Lee was starting to think twice. All I wanted was what I always wanted from the very day I met her was, to spend my life with Lee at my side. I didn't know anything at all about these big engagement parties and elaborate wedding celebrations and the men hugging and kissing each other. I thought I had better pay attention.

I found that they...starting with her Mom and Dad, Brother Tony and Sisters Rose and Vinny... her Grandma Rose, her aunts and uncles, her cousins first, second and removed ...her parents' friends and *paesanos* all embraced me and showered me with love. They did not for a moment hesitant to show it. If Lee loved me, they loved me!!

Lee's parents' wedding picture contained a large assembly of 27 bridesmaids and ushers. Lee's wonderful Mom and Dad enjoyed their large family and close friends and actually had two other couples join them on their honeymoon. Lee and I were both somewhat more private and we continually fit together perfectly for what will be 64 years in November.

During the next few months before our wedding date, I traded in my 1947 Ford coupe for a new 1953 Ford Sedan. We were busy with our wedding plans scheduled for November 1953. Lee later reminded me her great-grand parents Andrew and Vita

Reres were married in Piana Dei Greci in Palermo, Sicily on that very same day in November in, 1873.

We had a beautiful wedding ceremony at Regina Pacis Roman Catholic Church on 65th Street in Brooklyn and my beautiful bride was now finally at my side. I could now hold her as tight as I wished in front of whomever I wished.

Jean and Andrew Reres wedding party. Married July 27th, 1930 at Our Lady of Peace Roman Catholic Church, 522 Carroll Street Brooklyn, New York. Grooms Cousin Lilly Ciaravino was maid of Honor and her husband Carlo Ciaravino was Best Man.

Nellie and John Gallagher wedding party. Married 31st, August 1925 at Saint Columba Roman Catholic Church, 343 West 25th Street, New York City. The groom's brother, Joseph Gallagher, was Best Man and the bride's cousin Rose Graziano was Maid of Honor and later my God Mother who gave me a book on every birthday that I can recall.

We spent our honeymoon evening at the Piccadilly Hotel off Broadway followed, by a blissful week in a cozy private cottage at Split Rock Lodge, in Pennsylvania's Pocono Mountains. We both cuddle up thinking about that long ago time and thank God for our blessings through all these years.

I was happy all the preparations and activities were now over and we could just be together in our snug studio apartment. Lee wanted a pink kitchen and helped with the painting at 147th Street in Flushing. I was still a little nervous about my future.

All the while I was employed by HFC, I was seeking a sales job and landed what I thought a good opportunity. Joe from Meridian Employment Agency called to tell me he found a sales position and arranged an interview. It was a Sales Trainee position with McKesson & Robbins, a national Drug Store and Hospital supply house. They were located on Third Avenue and 181st Street in the East Bronx. Upon successful completion of the one-year training program, I would be assured a commissioned sales territory in Manhattan or the Bronx.

This was in the spring of 1954 and I had one full year at HFC and now I had a better starting salary and benefits, I was hired with two other trainees and when at the sales meetings we could see why we were needed because many of the salesmen were close to retirement age.

I was surprised when asked to show management my service records and discharge papers. Maybe they didn't believe I was a Master Sergeant when looking at my now thin physique. Although originally planned as a one year training program I received a territory in midtown Manhattan after only six months.

Lee was pregnant with John and her salary would soon be ending, so the timing was right. Anything you could buy in a drug store I could get at wholesale prices. It was necessary that I join a union because all non-sales people were unionized.

Our son John Andrew was born in Parsons Hospital on Northern Boulevard in Flushing where another movie director was born some years before him...Martin Scorsese.

We moved out of our little studio apartment in Flushing into a two bedroom apartment in Lee's parent's home in Brooklyn.

Those two years were happy ones surrounded by Lee's loving family who were all very respectful of our privacy. My appetite improved appreciably as we had more dinners cooked by Lee's Mom Jean. I recall the Sunday dinners and the large table set by Lee and her sisters while her Mom cooked all the Italian specialties which I never saw in Woodside on our one and only spaghetti and meatball night. Lee's Mom set the large table with enough food for friends, aunts, uncles and cousins of this big loving Sicilian family.

We furnished the extra rooms and bought our first Television and Stereo sets. Lee enjoyed decorating the Nursery. Even though it was a longer commute to the Bronx, we enjoyed the extra space as our little family grew.

The McKesson trainee program began by working on the top floor tossing around large cases of Kleenex, Kotex and Doeskin tissues with a pretty rugged group of Bronx warehousemen. I spent my Saturday high school years tossing cases of canned goods around at the A& P so my thin frame was already conditioned to this strenuous labor.

Two of the warehouse men were also rodeo riders: one my age and the other somewhat older. I don't remember their names but do recall them showing up for work in bandages from time to time. They were real characters, good guys and apparently good cowboys as well. They were always talking about the cash prizes and the fancy cowboy belt buckles and boots they won for roping and bronco riding contests which they proudly wore to work... all in the Bronx, USA!

The training program moved me downstairs almost a floor at a time to where the long line of baskets traveling on rollers containing the drug store orders were filled. Narcotic products were picked by an older gentleman who was custodian of the narcotics.

I wore my old army khaki's sans shoulder patch and chevrons under my McKesson apron and we all looked the same. On alternate Fridays I wore a suit, shirt and tie to attend the evening sales meeting and paid close attention by listening and observing.

My eagerness to do well resulted in a run-in with Mike the Union Shop Steward. The Manhattan territories received their daily delivery from McKesson quite late in the day and the salesmen voiced many complaints to management. Bob, the manager of the line of rolling order baskets, was always pushing the people to hustle so the deliveries would be made to the stores on time. Mike the shop steward would show up giving the workers a threatening stare and the line would slow down. Mike was pushing for overtime for the workforce. One afternoon I was assisting Skeety, a character who carried his racing form in his apron pocket, and who worked in the aisle containing Eli Lily, Parke Davis, and Smith, Kline and French (Glaxo-Smith Kline) products. I was hopping around speedily picking and filling orders and ignorant of Mike's stares until, I saw his short thick muscular body coming in my direction.

I looked at him and said, "Hi." Without even an acknowledgement of my friendly "Hi," he raged at me. "Who the hell do you think you are making my people look bad?" "What do you mean?" was my reply for I was surprised; I never even spoke to this guy before. "Don't be a wise guy. I know how to take care of wise guys like you." "No, Mike, I don't know what you mean" and I didn't, until I saw Skeety shaking his head no. Mike came at me like the bull he was with his chest puffed out, nostrils flared, and both arms twice the thickness of mine in a fighting posture. I knew an enraged person when I saw one and I wasn't going to let this son of a bitch touch me. I weighed about 125 pounds against his 250 pounds of all beef and no blubber!

Carpenters had been working on the shelving off and on and I spotted a hammer on a shelf that I grabbed and looked straight into Mike's glaring eyes. Mike looked at the hammer in my hand and stopped short. "You are not gonna touch me, Mike," I said. "You want to get me fired, fine, let's go see Mr. Hurley the branch manager right now." The hammer still held firmly in my hand.

Mike stopped short, his entire body deflated, he turned white, turned around and just walked away. I think Skeety took the hammer from my hand. I felt ill and almost threw up I was so rattled from this onslaught by Mike, my dream of becoming a McKesson salesman now in jeopardy. It deeply troubled me to see fear in the eyes of employees who had to obey the dictates of a bully or, lose their job. Can this be really happening in my country only because, I was doing a good day's work? Pay attention, Gallagher!

Mike continued his intimidation of the union members who needed their jobs and had to submit. Until, long after I left McKesson finally closed the Bronx operation. This put all the union members on the unemployment rolls. Everything was moved to the McKesson Queens County facility, a short hop over any one of several bridges and a tunnel to Manhattan and the Bronx. The sales staff all transferred, but, the union workers could not afford to move from the Bronx to Long Island.

During our Friday night sales meetings, we listened to the manufacturers' reps introducing new products and deals, it was an education. The McKesson sales force were a lively bunch and my brain absorbed knowledge at every meeting. I think a senior was ready to retire when my ears perked up when the sales manager, Frank Bloch, said to me, "Well, do you think you're ready?" You bet I was and now I reported for work every day wearing a suit, shirt and tie and headed downtown to call on my customers in mid-town Manhattan.

A lasting impression shows Mr. Eisenstein, a tall white haired and gregarious Hungarian with oversized black horn-rimmed glasses who was always under the spotlight. He owned a drug store on 8th Avenue and 48th or 49th Street. He definitely should have been in show business as he had a wise crack for everyone. If you were thin-skinned, Eisenstein would eat you up alive. He tried with this young skinny Irish *goy* not knowing I was already broken in by serving with the West Side Hell's Kitchen crowd. Many of whom were his very own customers. I could hold my own of course, within respectful limits, with this brash extrovert. Mr. Eisenstein was always on stage in front of his lively audience, particularly, the lunch crowd. He mainly picked on a sheepish looking neighbor appliance repair store owner but when his victim had enough, he would simply say… "Screw you Eisenstein…go back and make some more Tuna Salad."

After taking his abuse a time or two and laughing it off, I asked my Hungarian buddy Bob Partos to give me a catchy Hungarian phrase to impress Mr. Eisenstein with. I should have known better than to ask Bob for a reasonable greeting. I forgot what Bob told me to say and repeated it to Eisenstein the next time I saw him. I still remember Mr. Eisenstein's eyes bulging, his eyeglasses slipping down his nose and staring at me with mouth agape, speechless for the very first time. "No, no, I see now, you don't even know…what you called me…better ask your Hungarian friend to tell you," he exclaimed. With tears of laughter rolling down his cheeks he readjusted his black horn rimmed glasses and said. "Come'er Irishman Gallagher, open your deal book, I have some orders for you."

I shocked him and now McKesson was elevated to be his main supplier and I was no longer the skinny *goy* who got all the *dreck* orders! I cannot even remember what I called him but from that time thereafter I had lunch at his lunch counter as I wrote my order and, "No charge for the entertainment." He would give any popular comedian competition….they had writers. "Mr. E" got his material from the current news and it came natural and fast. When I left that day, he told me to be sure I called my Hungarian friend a $%#@*&^%$ which I do not even recall but Bob Partos laughed and said, "Well I'm glad I helped you get a good customer."

The only time I ever got mad at Frank Bloch was the one day he worked with me in my midtown territory. Driving south on Second Avenue, I slowed down to make a stop before I turned right onto 42nd Street just as the light turned red. "No, no, go right ahead you made the light." Obeying Frank, I turned just as the cop signaled me to pull over and wrote out a nice ticket. I thought Frank would choke on his cigar which by the way, polluted my car. The midtown territory cost me hundreds of dollars a year in parking tickets in those days.

When I sold a large quantity of a particular deal, such as a Dr. West Toothbrush deal, an Evening in Paris fragrance deal or a Julius Schmid Sheik's condom deal, and was anxious to turn in my orders to Frank, he would say, "Do you think you work for Dr. West?" Or, "Big deal what do you want a medal for only doing your job?" He was only doing me a favor by conditioning me for a sales career in Manhattan. He knew the diverse cast of New York City personalities I would be calling on who owned the corner drug stores in Manhattan. This was in those bygone days before the advent of the CVS's, Rite Aid's and Walgreen's. Whom, replaced the colorful Druggist's who owned the neighborhood drug stores in Manhattan where, you could get a damn good freshly made Tuna salad sandwich on rye and a good cup of coffee for less than a buck.

My biggest customer was Hanson's Pharmacy on Broadway and 51st street in the heart of the show district. In addition to the prescription department, Hanson's had a long and very busy lunch counter. One could never know what show business celebrity would be sitting on one of the stools sipping a Coke or a cup of coffee. A popular pharmacy joke in those days was when one pharmacist asked another, "Hey Bernie, what pharmacy school did you learn how to make your tuna salad at, I learned mine at Columbia."

Mr. Hanson was a congenial gentleman, very well-known, well respected and very well-liked. I usually sat at the end of the counter with Hanson and his manager Willie sipping coffee and going over the deals while writing up an impressive order. His location was prime and he sold large quantities of everything. His pharmacy was always busy and McKesson was his prime supplier. He didn't complain about delivery times because he was always well staffed to accept deliveries at any time. I think Hanson's was open all night with walk-thru entrances on Broadway and the other on 7th Avenue.

One day I met Nat King Cole as he was coming out of the barber shop on 7th Avenue right around the corner from Hanson's. It was a thrill to meet him and he gave me a warm smile and greeted me in that famous rich tone of his voice. I saw and rubbed shoulders with many celebrities in my travels but Nat King Cole impressed me the most.

When calling on Hanson's I met affable Pat Brown, the local Wyeth Laboratory salesman. Pat always had a smile on his face and was very well dressed. He would write up his Wyeth order and many times we would have lunch together. He always mentioned to me about how great it was to work for Wyeth. "The next time there is an opening in the Manhattan district, I will let you know" he promised me.

Sure enough, one day Pat was waiting for me to show up at my appointed time at Hanson's. He greeted me with, "My boss wants to meet you." Pat was wearing a gray pinstripe suit in the Brooks Brothers three button natural shoulder style with a white button down oxford shirt and tasteful club tie. By that time, I knew about Brooks Brothers and Pat always looked like he just walked out of their showroom. The older Jewish salesmen at McKesson always claimed that in order to be successful one must "dress British and think Yiddish!" The sales job at McKesson was fun but the costs to drive my car in Manhattan were becoming more and more expensive as parking became a real problem and I found many parking tickets on my windshield.

I met with Pat's boss and yes, here was another well-dressed professional. The interview went perfectly and after some preliminary testing, I was offered the job. To my delight, the position included a $500 a month starting salary (equal to $4,600 today), a new Chevrolet four-door sedan every two years, a book of travel orders to write my own expense check up to $50 every week and all the benefits of that era.

Wyeth was part of the corporate giant American Home Products and one of only a few major pharmaceutical companies not requiring a pharmaceutical degree or at least a college degree to qualify for a sales position. After I started with Wyeth, I registered at Queens College for evening classes under the G. I. Bill. I wanted to continue my education using the credits from N.Y. State University. Sometime later we moved from Brooklyn to Kew Gardens in Queens close to the college. I remember enjoying a couple nights a week attending classes and even had the freedom to leave my territory early to beat the traffic from Manhattan to Queens.

Once the job at Wyeth was confirmed, I gave Frank Bloch two weeks' notice, thanked him for his help, shook his hand and said my goodbyes to all...never know when you may need a reference!

After some training and indoctrination, Wyeth assigned me to a territory on the Upper East Side of Manhattan from 80th Street to 110th Street and from Fifth Avenue to the East River calling on doctors. The territory would be expanded later to include drug stores, some small clinics, a nursing home and Park East Hospital when, I was on salary plus commission and saw real dollars.

I was issued *Gray's Anatomy*, The PDR (*Physicians' Desk Reference*) and numerous other medical literature to help educate me. Wyeth had ongoing training on all their products and we had training meetings all the time that were a blast. We were taught "canned details" to be sure all the important facts about a particular product was told to the doctor until we could put the presentation into our own words without omitting the important facts, including contraindications and side effects.

This opened up a whole new world for me and was very interesting. The only negative was the confines of the territory within some square blocks on Manhattan's Upper East Side. We used tape recorders and did role playing that were recorded for positive criticism which was fun for most of us and informative. To some, it was a challenge. When we were all finally comfortable with being recorded, we had a lot of fun while we were learning.

I called on some of the foremost medical celebrities in the world. Including, Doctor Ramon Castroviejo, a pioneer in corneal transplants with his own hospital fully equipped with the latest in modern medical technology located at 5th Avenue and 91st Street. Doctor Martin Clyman was a Park Avenue reproductive endocrinologist who elevated artificial insemination research into practical application making happy parents of those couples resigned to being childless. Doctor Leon Pordy, a Park Avenue cardiologist, was among the first to apply computer technology to cardiology. I sent my Dad to him for treatment after Dad's concern about his non-fatal palpitation symptoms. These were a few of the most wonderful gentlemen I visited who would listen to my talk about Wyeth products. We would then chat for a while about current events and common interests including an escape from the big city to the Catskill Mountains to clear one's head.

Soon after my hire, I was taken under the wing of manager John Jeffords and his assistant Chuck Barnes, two more "Brooks Brothers" attired professionals. They taught me the pharmaceutical and medical vocabulary so I could understand and talk about Sub-Acute-Bacterial-Endocarditis and Ganglionic Blocking Agents to anyone from a nurse to a Park Avenue specialist without missing a beat.

Next to get me started in the right direction was Bill Howard who had the territory before he was promoted to hospital representative. Bill worked with me for a couple of days to meet some of the most prominent M.D.'s in the territory. After lunch one day, I asked Bill about his Brooks Brothers gray three-button suit. I recently ventured into the Brooks Brothers store and the prices drove me into a hasty retreat.

Bill smiled and said, "I guess no one told you about our custom tailor." Bill picked up the lunch tab and we drove to the Wyeth salesmen's custom tailor shop. It was not on Madison Avenue but downtown on Canal Street. L & L Fabrics, Louie Levy's 100% wool worsted fabric custom made suits in the traditional three button natural shoulder cut, for $37.50 including tailoring and two pair of pants. I bought two and paid a deposit. "So you'll mail me a check already," said the Louie Levy salesman. "Wait, you'll go next door they make the best "Egg Creams." It won't take no time." (Check out NYC Egg Creams on line) "Fredo, quick, quick, you'll do the pants, the sleeves are perfect." We returned to Bill's Chevy with two Louie Levy suits, a banker's gray in a lightweight wool worsted and a charcoal gray in a medium weight. It's been a long, long time since I was a 40 regular!

Wyeth Anecdotes

We were still living in Bensonhurst when I started my new job with Wyeth. Lee and I were both very happy about this move and my previous feelings of uneasiness were now becoming a fading memory. I traveled daily in my new 1956 white and gray four door Chevrolet company car to the Belt Parkway only blocks away from the old Gun Site on Cropsey Avenue, through the Brooklyn Battery Tunnel and up the East River Drive to my territory uptown. Soon after Wyeth introduced a new product that was to double and triple monthly commission checks.

The original product name Milltown Tablets was developed by Wallace Laboratory located in Milltown, New Jersey. It was a formulation named Meprobamate a skeletal muscle relaxant that was tested in anxiety cases and proved to be a soft muscle relaxant as well. It was a non-narcotic, non-habit forming formulation but did require an M.D.'s prescription.

The product hit the headlines, the late night TV shows and took the medical world by storm. A new medical term was added, "Non-Narcotic Tranquilizer."

Meprobamate was licensed to Wyeth who put it on the market as, "Equanil." Wyeth employed 1000 salesmen in the field nationwide. This was years before TV ads were used to promote medical products directly to the consumer. All major pharmaceutical companies employed a full-time sales force calling on doctors all over the country. Their mission was to keep the doctors up-to-date on all the new products, the latest medical studies, on current and new pharmaceutical products and, to provide samples for starting doses for their patients. Hopefully, the result would be written prescriptions.

Wyeth opened the campaign concentrating on psychiatrists nationwide. In Manhattan alone, there were hundreds if not thousands of practicing psychiatrists and psycho-analyst MDs. They were concentrated by the dozens in many apartment buildings. So off we went. The drill was to wait for the 5 minute interval between patients and try to catch the doctor for just a minute or two to give him a few sample packets of Equanil, some recent medical reprints and a small hard bound book titled, "The Philosophy of Insanity," written by a former inmate of the "Glasgow Royal Asylum for Lunatics", in Scotland. We stressed the terms "non-narcotic" and "non-addictive".

The most popular relaxant prescribed at the time was Phenobarbital which was a barbiturate and could be a problem for those prone to addiction. Doctors began prescribing Equanil for their patients and sales skyrocketed.

Wyeth then had a $50 minimum direct order requirement which was tough for the average neighborhood drug store to satisfy so they bought Wyeth products from their supplier like McKesson & Robbins. This put no dollars in the Wyeth salesman's commission account. Once Equanil hit the marketplace, every small corner drug store would order Equanil by the dozen in bottles of 50 tablets which made the $50.00 order requirement easily attainable. That $50.00 in 1956 is the equivalent of about $400.00 today.

Wyeth was making money and so were the Wyeth salesmen. We saved up a down payment on our first home in Baldwin, Long Island thanks to the increased sales commissions. Unfortunately, this prosperity did not last and was interrupted by the investigation of the pharmaceutical industry led by Senator Estes Kefauver.

All the doctor's offices I usually visited were on the first floor level of the apartment buildings on Lexington, Park, Madison and Fifth Avenues. The psychiatrists, however, were all located on the upper floors many with an office in their own apartment.

One psychiatrist was a notable Freudian-educated doctor his name will not be used. His interest was hypnosis and spirituality. The doorman recognized me and directed me to the elevator to the doctor's apartment. I pressed the bell under his name plaque. A distinguished mature gentleman opened the door as I handed him my Wyeth business card. He welcomed me graciously with his European accent and asked me to follow him to his office. His apartment was decorated with modern furniture and gaily colored abstract oil paintings hanging on the walls throughout the apartment. I saw his attractive wife working on an abstract painting so, it was no mystery who the artist was.

The doctor opened the door to his study/office and invited me to sit down as he sat behind his desk. The office was dimly lit with a gaslight era look. Dark carved furniture surrounded by dark wood paneling unlike, the colorful décor of the apartment. A yellowed human skull on a shelf looked down at me. The shelf was cluttered with old leather-bound books and antique medical implements. The dark paneled wall covered with certificates and licenses written in foreign script and English a few, from New York City hospitals. Everything dark, gloomy and busy.

I opened with the standard Wyeth "canned detail" and handed over to him the reprints, samples and the book "Philosophy of Insanity." As I was ready to thank him for his time, he said to me, "You see Mister Gallagher, spirits do exist and are our constant companions." He proclaimed this dramatically as he stared directly into my eyes.

To break his stare I focused on a framed picture as none other than Sigmund Freud himself standing with a young man whom I later learned was this very same doctor. We both smiled as we said our good byes and I thanked him for his time. I took the elevator to the lobby smiled as I saluted the uniformed gold braided doorman and said, "Good afternoon General," as he flipped his finger at me and smiled back!

A real shocker was when Doctor White Carpet invited me into his Park Avenue office/apartment. He greeted me at the door in bare feet and asked me to please remove my shoes and socks before entering. "Don't think for a moment I have you do this to protect my white carpet. Oh, no, no, no, it is for your own peace of mind I do this. Just wait until your tightly constricted feet supporting the weight of your body all day…feel the freedom and peace, of the soft white nap of the carpet against them. See… how good it feels," he said as I followed him into his all white office. I will say this for Doctor White Carpet, it did feel good after walking on the hot pavement of Manhattan's East Side to twinkle my piggies in the soft white nap of his carpet.

There was one Psychiatrist I called on routinely at his office in a townhouse on the East 80's between Park and Lexington Avenues. He wrote quite a few prescriptions which prompted me to keep him on my active list. I would leave literature and samples with his nurse when the doctor was unable to see me.

I would see his prescriptions for Equanil and other products in several local pharmacies. Checking the drug store RX file was a practice we pharmaceutical salesman always did to see what the doctors were actually writing. Only our best friend druggist would open his files to a few favorite salesmen.

This psychiatrist was a relief from the Eastern European trained "Shrinks" and I enjoyed my visits with this American-schooled psychiatrist. We would chat about medication and psychiatry and a favorite topic…trout fishing in the Catskills.

During the "Equanil Campaign," and south of my normal territory, I stepped into a townhouse in the East 60's between Fifth Avenue and Madison Avenues. The black painted wrought iron gate was open and the front door was slightly ajar. I saw the shiny brass plate with the doctor's name engraved next to the door assuring me I was not trespassing where I should not have been so, I rang the bell and entered.

I stepped into a large open foyer tastefully furnished with period chairs and end tables. Freshly cut flowers were placed on a round table in the center of the spacious empty and dimly lit waiting room. The walls were paneled and I did not even see a doorway or hear anything. With the fragrance of the fresh cut flowers, the place gave me the feel of being in a funeral home. I remained a while and just about ready to leave as I turned and, there he was right in back of me. He was dressed in a dark suit, white shirt and dark tie. He was a slim tallish pale gaunt-eyed, cadaverous looking man extending his hand in greeting it felt cold to the touch. I almost jumped out of my new highly polished Florsheim wing tip shoes!!!

I think I hid my fright from him as I extended my hand, "Doctor Morbid?" I asked, as this strange man nodded in agreement, "I am Vincent Gallagher with Wyeth Laboratories and wish to leave with you a sample of Equanil, our new non-narcotic tranquilizer." My thought was to give him a quick rundown on Equanil, leave the sample, reprints, book and scram!!

"Thank you, Mr. Gallagher. Please follow me," he said in a dull tone and a cracked smile from his thin lips. He very politely directed me to a tiny elevator which opened from a panel in the wall and was completely hidden from view. The silence was unsettling…he made absolutely no noise as he moved…I followed him into the elevator and we exited on the next floor. Entering his office, I noticed the black leather couch, impressive mahogany desk and bookcase full of books. Framed Diplomas and honors neatly placed the wall. I noticed there were absolutely no windows at all that I could see and, the constant clamor of Manhattan was totally blocked out, adding to my uneasiness.

My imagination made me wonder how many pharmaceutical salesmen he murdered and how he disposed of their bodies from his inner sanctum here in the East 60's. He invited me in that dull tone to "Please sit down Mr. Gallagher." I stood for a second when he pointed to the chair and not the black leather couch. In a trained and assertive voice, I told him about the new "non-narcotic, non-addictive" tranquilizer Equanil and pointed out the results from the medical reprints I placed on his desk. He was a refined gentleman and smiled a bit more friendly this time. He nodded approval of my presentation and thanked me for the samples and the book. And now, with my pulse quite settled, I was happy to show myself the way out.

Now, glad to be back among the living in the open air of a lovely sunny afternoon on Fifth Avenue, I looked at the inviting flora and thought of the fauna of the Central Park Zoo right here in the middle of Manhattan. So, I took a brief break and treated myself to a nickel bag of peanuts and strolled to visit the monkey house that is, the "Pan Troglodytes" specie (Common Chimpanzee) as opposed to the "Homo Sapiens" specie.

I made it a point to be sure to bring my manager Jeff to see Dr. Morbid the next time he worked with me. I would not tell him about the hidden elevator and would be sure to posture him with his back to that hidden panel.

This campaign lasted until Wyeth was sure that the sales force saw every psychiatrist in Manhattan; there were hundreds in the Upper East Side area alone. The sales meeting at the close of the Psychiatrists Campaign was held at the Elmsford Motel in Westchester County. The twenty or so Louie Levy dressed Wyeth salesmen arrived showing various signs of neurotic and psychotic symptoms. Gus Tuzzolo insisted he was Lucky Luciano and slipped to Andy Barrone and Larry Ruffeli small threatening letters signed with a neatly sketched, "Mano Nera," Black Hand!!

Danny Richter had severe facial tics and Morty Weissman had head shakes. Al Roskoff's silence and blank stares was unsettling for this normally loud outspoken salesman. Even the older, reserved and impeccably groomed Lou Richards showed up with necktie askance, wind-blown hair and a blank expression on his face. Others were swatting at imaginary bees and kicking a make-believe dog like the one the sad patient had in the Scottish Insane Asylum. "Okay, Okay guys ...now let's get down to business," our Manhattan district manager addressed his crowd of lunatics and called the meeting to order.

John Jeffords was a handsome six-footer himself and a grand guy with a great personality and sense of humor. All the wives liked to dance with him at the Christmas parties and I can still see him dancing and smiling with my pretty sweetheart. Another image I have is walking down Park Avenue with him as he would turn around, furiously kicking away the invisible dog always at his heels. Attractive governesses pushing expensive baby carriages looked sideways at this tall, well-dressed man kicking at the air as they hurriedly pushed their precious cargo out of his way. I heard one say in her marked English accent, "My word...is he daft?" She gave us a wide berth.

Hey, there was always time for a laugh and at Wyeth, we had plenty. When I decided to leave Wyeth for more fertile fields, I was saddened to say goodbye to this group of the most affable and professional group of salesmen I was ever to encounter and...I might add...the best dressed salesmen in Manhattan.

Canarsie, Battery A 773rd

One afternoon I was traveling west on the Belt Parkway towards Bensonhurst and passed Canarsie where the A Battery gun site was located before the 773rd went to Korea. As I sped by Canarsie, I spotted a glimpse of a radar antenna that was exposed for a split second. If I were looking the other way, I would never have noticed the antenna. This aroused my curiosity and I turned off at the next exit and went back to exit at Canarsie. I remembered the way through the marshlands because I had gone to that site several times and remembered the dirt road there. Sure enough, in an opening in the tall marsh grass, I approached a high cyclone fence with a locked gate and a red and yellow sign telling me this was, "A Battery, 773rd AAA Gun BN (90mm)." "Well, I'll be damned," I said out loud to myself.

An older soldier approached the gate dressed in an army fatigue uniform with corporal stripes on his arm and wearing the soft peaked fatigue hat. He was carrying a shotgun at sling arms on his shoulder.

The Corporal squinted his eyes because the sun was now setting in the west directly over my shoulders. "Can I help you sir?" the corporal asked with a familiar Brooklyn sound to his voice.

"Yes, Corporal, I was in the 773rd a couple years ago, who is in charge here?" I asked. "Captain Laudati is the Battery Commander of A Battery and the full-time site commander is Lieutenant Zurla," he said. "John Zurla?" I asked in wonder. John was a Master Sergeant the last I heard from him back in 1953.

"Y-Yes, sir," answered the corporal with a slight stutter, the first I noticed, "He is here."

"Tell him Vin Gallagher is here at the gate," I smiled with my reply. The Corporal turned around and in a few minutes he returned with keys in his hand followed by my old buddy, John Zurla, now wearing a First Lieutenant's silver bar on his uniform shirt collar.

"Well it's about time you showed up," burst out Zurla. "We need you in Fire Control, you went to the M-33 School and that is what we now have ... we just got it." Zurla went on to say, "This is Corporal Rosato... Rosato meet our next Fire Control Officer."

"Whoa, not so fast. This is only a social call," I said as the gate was unlocked and I entered. We all shook hands. "I knew you could smile, Corporal, even though you looked so dangerous with that shotgun," and we all laughed.

Sure enough, here was a full battery with four 90's in a Y formation, four neatly placed Quad Mount .50 Caliber Machine Guns all with ammo close at hand and ready. A spanking brand new M-33 Integrated Fire Control system all emplaced with the two radars one, atop the dark OD colored Battery Commanders trailer the other, the bathtub-shaped Acquisition radar, slowly rotating as we talked. It was the tracking radar on the roof of the trailer that caught my eye from the parkway.

"Hey Vin ... how the hell are you? We were just talking about you the other day when this new M-33 was delivered." It was none other than my other old buddy, Sergeant First Class Frank Mistretta.

The site had neat one-story cinder block buildings which included barracks, a BOQ (Bachelor Officers' Quarters), latrines with hot and cold running water, a fully equipped kitchen and mess hall, orderly room, recreation and supply rooms and a large motor pool building for the motor section to service the vehicles out of the weather.

We entered the orderly room through a path of white painted stones and colorful flowers on each side of the path. "That's Smithies' work, one of the full- timers who likes to garden and do landscaping work around the site," John said. The last time I saw this site, there were tents and open latrines and grimy looking G.I.'s from all over the USA, deprived of the luxury of a daily shower right here in New York City.

It was here I learned about the new full time Army/National Guard on-site program. National Guard AAA units together with active Army units manned hundreds of anti-aircraft artillery gun batteries all over the Continental United States with the same mission we had back in 1952 before the unit went to Korea.

This was 1956 during the "Cold War" which was to continue and increase in intensity until the late 1980's when the world heard President Ronald Reagan say to Mikhail Gorbachev the Russian leader of the U.S.S.R., "Tear down this Wall."

At Fort Bliss, the army was in the advanced stage of training troops to soon replace the antiaircraft guns with the new surface-to-air Nike Missile Systems, the actual missiles being manufactured at that very instant in top secret by Douglas Aviation. Of course, this forthcoming missile conversion program was not known to these old pals chatting over a cup of familiar G.I. coffee. Even though, most of the full time AAA people were all cleared for secret and some at that time being processed for top secret clearance...the Nike missiles were hidden from them.

After being caught short so many times our military was now prepared for any assault. Starting with the DEW line early warning radars in the Arctic shared with Canada, England and the USA to, the Allied picket ships and aircraft on 24/7 early alert missions monitoring all air traffic in the Western Hemisphere. All the while, the Regular Army was training in top secret, the forces to man the soon to appear SAM (Surface-to-Air Missile) Nike system. The Nike-Ajax was armed with three high explosive warheads and the Nike-Zeus and Nike-Hercules systems were both armed with high explosive or nuclear warheads to destroy bomber formations or Guided Missiles launched from the USSR.

Our government was determined to maintain a strong defense readiness and did not want to be caught unprepared again. A and B Batteries were both full time 24/7 manned and ready to fire with C and D battery's designated one weekend a month warrior training batteries soldiering right on the two gun sites.

John and I sat down alone in his office and I told him I was perfectly happy with my pharmaceutical sales job and had no desire to become full time. He told me that was fine, that they were all new to the program but the battalion could still use a good Fire Control officer. He told me the Battery Commander Captain Laudati was the only one with any knowledge of the M-33 and Laudati is waiting to return to active duty which, he recently requested. Captain Laudati was a Brown University graduate and was also Fort Bliss trained which assured his acceptance by the army to active duty.

He went on to tell me a Master Sergeant with my record, experience of six years with two years of active service including a tour in Korea plus the two army service schools including one on the M-33 would qualify me for a direct commission. "You have the knowledge we need and the army will repay you by offering you a direct commission to Second Lieutenant." He went on to tell me Colonel Slavin and Major Kraus mentioned my name several times and they would be happy to see me return to the unit.

"Why don't you call Battalion and make an appointment to see the Colonel?" John readily added.

As we were talking, I was feeling more and more at home in these so familiar surroundings and a strange feeling came over me as we talked. Maybe I should return to my lucky outfit and maybe those strange feelings I've had these past few years was because I missed this part of my life.

"Before you go let's go to the mess hall, some of the guys are now on a break," John suggested. "Great, who else will be there?" I asked. John just smiled!

Seated around mess tables were a group of guardsmen, many new and some familiar faces including, Sergeants Frank Mistretta, Scalfani, Forster, Jake Bond, Faust and Mauro. Faces from the old outfit and many new smiling ones offered me a warm welcome. A few quick reminisces and I was all smiles and happy as I shook hands all around.

After this surprising and joyful discourse with my old comrades, I said my goodbyes. Corporal Rosato opened the gate as I drove away in the 1956 gray and white Wyeth Chevy. My mind was overloaded with memories and questions as I drove home to my sweetheart and our now one-year-old baby boy John Andrew, named in honor of his two grandfathers.

"Something wrong, honey?" Lee asked, as we sat in our living room after dinner and rambunctious Baby John was finally fast asleep. "No, no, everything is fine," but she knew something was up.

Sleep did not come easy and I had to tell Lee what was on my mind. Lee could put things on hold but I had to deal with the issues here and now.

"Honey, I may re-enlist in the old outfit and I need to talk to you about it." After bringing her up to speed on the events of the afternoon, she just told me, "Do what you wish but you better think about it first." Why couldn't she just say, "No, I don't want you to do this?" Now I stared at the ceiling for a long, long time before sleep finally came.

"Colonel Slavin, this is Sergeant Gallagher from C Battery." "Hello Gallagher, how are you? The Battalion sure could use you," the Colonel replied. "Fine, thank you, sir, Lieutenant Zurla suggested I call you." The Colonel said, "Can you drop in next Monday night sometime before drill?" "Fine sir, would 7:00 PM be convenient?" The date was set.

After handshakes with Colonel Slavin and Executive Officer Major Kraus, I made a confession. "Colonel, I lied about my age when I joined back in 1947 and want to clear the record."

Slavin laughed and said, "So did I when I joined in the 1930's and so did many others. Sergeant Jake Bond lied when he joined with me back in the 1930's making him older and I found out he just lied again now making himself younger on his last re-enlistment." We all laughed.

The process was to re-enlist for three years with my old rank of Master Sergeant and apply for a direct commission to Second Lieutenant. The colonel assured me with my record and completing two Fire Control Schools at Fort Bliss, the process should move along quickly. "We need officers with your knowledge and experience," he told me.

I didn't have to sleep on it so I gave the colonel my OK and he buzzed the Battalion Adjutant Captain Arthur Kelly to prepare papers for my re-enlistment that very evening. I left the armory as Master Sergeant Vincent G. Gallagher, A Battery's Fire Control Platoon Sergeant just as though I had never left. Only this time, I was now in Able Battery.

Kelly gave me a multiple page medical form for my physical exam. "We can send you to Fort Jay or your own doctor can exam you and fill out the papers."

The commission to Second Lieutenant was approved effective November 20th, 1956. I spent some extra time on site with the M-33 crewmen honing my skills and helping others. I participated in practice alerts when the Air Force coordinated these alerts. Air Force bombers were designated unidentified (Bogey) and then enemy (Bandit) and all AA full time Guard and active army gun sites were staffed and operating all equipment as if an air attack was imminent.

Over the years with Wyeth, my manager never called me to work with him the day after one of the training mission alerts. Wyeth was a division of American Home Products among the major firms to give employees who served in a reserve component the usual two-week paid vacation along with an additional paid two weeks to attend summer training.

An interesting aside involves the emergency pass I was issued for my automobile that had to be attached to the flip side of my sun visor. During an emergency alert this would be displayed to notify the police this driver was on the way to a battle station. I believe all air defense personnel had these passes. When my Wyeth manager noticed it, he was surprised. After that, he no longer poked fun at the popular 1950's ad "You can sleep well tonight, your National Guard is awake" with "Yeah, awake drinking in the local bars." Or, as my buddy Bob Partos would say, "Yeah, they are all awake and hiding out in the fallout shelters in the armories."

The late 1950's and early 1960's were serious times and most Americans had a rude awakening when Kennedy and Khrushchev started waving nuclear swords at each other. The entire world was on edge! Fallout Shelter signs were visible all over New York City and school children nationwide, were given instructions in case of nuclear attack.

In 1957 the two week camp tour we would be firing the 90's with the M-33 system. The battalion convoyed to the artillery range in upstate New York on Lake Ontario. This was to be the last time the 773rd would travel by convoy and the last time we would ever fire the 90mm antiaircraft guns.

Shortly after the unit returned from camp, full time personnel were sent to Fort Bliss to begin missile training. This transition was complete when the full-time Guard soldiers fired the Nikes at ranges in Fort Bliss. The unit took over two Nike-Ajax Sites one in Spring Valley, New York and the other in Lido Beach, Long Island. Headquarters drilled at the Armory in White Plains, N.Y. and, we had a new name, 1st Missile Battalion 212th Artillery, Nike-Ajax.

The biggest disaster occurred in 1958 at the Army Nike-Site in Leonardo, New Jersey, when some civilian technicians and soldiers were working above ground on missiles. While applying some modifications, one of the missiles' three warheads accidentally exploded setting off a chain of explosions from missiles above ground and on-line for these modifications. Several soldiers and civilian technicians were killed on that tragic day.

Hundreds of Nike sites were in service. As the program advanced with the Nike-Hercules and Nike-Zeus, both with nuclear capability and anti-missile defense. The Nike-Ajax sites were occupied by the National Guard full-time units and Hercules and Zeus sites were all manned exclusively by Fort Bliss trained Regular Army units. Nike images can be easily found on line.

I was assigned C Battery Commander and that was fine for me Charlie Battery was my old home.

Armory Dedication Day Picture

Lt. Vincent G. Gallagher
Commanding Officer
Bty 'C' 1st MSL Bn. (Nike-Ajax)
212th Arty.

Lt. Joseph A. Fioriti
Executive Officer
Bty 'C' 1st MSL Bn. (Nike-Ajax)
212th Arty.

Richard J. Henke
Platoon Leader
Bty 'C' 1st MSL Bn. (Nike-Ajax)
212th Arty.

C Battery was stationed at the new armory in Orangeburg near the Spring Valley Nike site in Rockland County, NY. An Armory Opening Day Ceremony was planned and we were required to participate. A program booklet was printed with local ads and some of the unit history and photos. Kraus told me to get a portrait made and have my two officers do the same. The above picture is from that program booklet which I am now unable to find.

It was around that time we were preparing for the annual I.G. (Inspector General) inspection that lasted a few days. To prepare the battery for this inspection, all the officers and top NCO's had to spend time at the armory to get the battery ready for the inspection. The emphasis was on the inventory. Every item from mess kits to weapons to cargo trucks had to be counted and accounted for. It was almost like being on active duty only this was all pay-free. The Army paid for 12 monthly weekend drills, a weapons qualification weekend, and one day for a parade if necessary.

Executive Officer Lieutenant Joseph Fioriti was born in Northern Italy and had a sophisticated and educated Northern Italian accent. Officer Candidate Richard Henke was a serious minded soldier participating in the National Guard Officer Candidate training program. After successful completion of the program, which I think was two years and included extra days training, he would receive a National Guard and Army Reserve commission to 2nd Lieutenant. I left the Guard before Henke got his commission but I am certain he was a credit to the Guard, the unit, his men, and to himself.

Those days, when working in the armory we all brown bagged meals because there was no time or place to run out to eat within the immediate vicinity of the armory with woods and open fields on both sides and beyond. I remember the spinach omelet sandwiches on crusty Italian Bread that Fioriti's wife made for him. After I mentioned that to him, he always had an extra one for me. I met Mrs. Fioriti once and she was as genuine and refined as Fioriti was and quite lovely. I wonder now as I write this narrative what life had in store for those two fine people.

Obeying the Colonel's order, I had my portrait picture taken at a small photography studio next to a little German Ma and Pa luncheonette on Lexington Avenue in the 80's. That was where I sometimes went with my pharmaceutical pals to enjoy great food prepared by the owner and his wife. We all knew the photographer from next door and when she dropped in for coffee from time to time, we always had a few kind words for this attractive older woman.

She quoted me a reasonable price for a portrait and I showed up one morning with my uniform shirt, tie, hat and jacket in a clothing bag. She commented that it was quite a surprise to her for she never associated me with the military and she proceeded to set up the picture, all the while urging me to smile. A few days later, I picked up a print for the booklet. After that day, she was not as friendly towards me as she had been previously but, I thought nothing about this. When Lee saw the picture, she asked me to order a larger one for our home. I thought I might as well because it was the only professional portrait I had in uniform.

When I asked the photographer to make a copy for my home and add a little color to it. She answered, "Oh, I can't, there was a flood in my store and the negative was ruined." Not at all concerned, I simply said something like, "no big deal" and I forgot about it.

One morning, I stopped in the luncheonette after the breakfast crowd and before the lunch crowd and ordered one of their famous German breakfasts. A couple eggs over with German sausage links, home fries and thick dark German rye bread. As the owner poured my coffee and out of earshot from his wife in the kitchen, he spoke softly to me. "You know Wince...zo und zo" shaking his head in the direction of the photographer's store... "Is an odd one. "He told me he overheard his wife talking to her one day and the photographer told his wife how much she hated the military and soldiers. That was why he never told anyone of his neighbors that he served in the German army in World War II. He went on to tell me, "I don't think she had a flood...I think she has a flood in the *Kopf*" pointing to his head. He asked me to keep that to myself just as his cute and chubby wife stepped out of the kitchen. She dried her hands on her apron and gave me a friendly, "Vell, hello Wince. Is Hans taking good care of you?"

When I started traveling for business, I was reassigned from battery duty to a staff job to continue my National Guard service without interruption and drilled closer to home on the Lido Beach Nike Site, on Long Island. I was assigned Battalion Intelligence Officer (S-2) and it was indeed a break from troop duty. The Colonel thought it would give me some time to rethink leaving the guard. Zurla was now a Captain and Site Commander at Lido Beach. It was much easier for me to attend extra "Alpha Status" training. Even though I was the S-2, I was always more interested in Fire Control and, enjoyed the high tension Alpha Status missions.

At around that time, Mutual Funds became popular and I tried my hand at selling them with a slick Italian friend from Astoria. He sold Life Insurance and Mutual funds. It was a concept that attracted me. The requirement was to get an insurance sales license, so I studied the text, took the test, passed it and got my license. I made a few sales within the family, one sale was to my Mom's younger brother who retained the fund. Many years later, my Aunt thanked me for it and so did one of her sons.

One night I earned a $2,500 commission which amazed me (2016 value = $20,000. Who said we have inflation under control?) So...I gave it a whirl and had some fun with my partner Charlie. "Forget about missiles, the @#$%ing Russians, playing soldier and start making some real money," he chided me. We worked together evenings and when I understood the concept of combining funds with life insurance, I worked part time for a while on my own. I learned about life insurance and income protection insurance which resulted in writing my own insurance policy. It had a large whole life death benefit and a rider with a continuing monthly income for Lee until each boy was 18 years old. If I lived a cash balance would accrue with dividends paying the premium. A perfect program and all my self-employed friends bought it. I was thanked over the years and it allowed me to sleep well knowing my family would be cared for. It surprised me about how cavalier some men were about denying their loved ones this important financial security. That year my Wyeth income was less than the year before and I had a taste of making more money.

Mr. W and Beyond

Mr. W. was originally a German national immigrating here in the 1930's. He had a strong work ethic and a brilliant mind and succeeded building his successful packaging business selling fancy closures and glass containers to most fragrance firms. He was a dynamic personality who could lead and inspire as well as demean if necessary to make a subordinate try even harder. He was a natural born leader and had many loyal employees who had been with him for years. In an effort to expand his markets, Mr. W. formed a separate company featuring an array of gift and novelty items for different levels of retail outlets. The new firm did some business but had not achieved any level of mass distribution...that was to be my challenge. So, I gave Wyeth two weeks' notice and joined with "W."

Mr. W. appointed a young CPA named Art who worked with the corporate Comptroller's office to be responsible for the financial end of the business. To oversee the production, assembly, shipping and receiving, he selected a serious young man named Klaus, who grew up in war-torn Germany during World War II. Several other people were transferred from Corporate to work under Klaus and an executive secretary named Betty and a receptionist was added to round out the office staff.

Mr. W. sat down with me and I presented him with my plan to promote the line using Sales Representative firms with a sales force who had a following with the wholesale customer. I told him that he needed a marketing plan to obtain these rep firms in many non-conflicting markets some, he never thought about. There may have been some talk about a percentage of the business for the three young men he assigned to this task but there was nothing in writing. I put more weight on the aspect of making a plan and proving the plan would work. I had the confidence that I could do it and I guess it showed. So, we shook hands and took a chance on each other. The three partners met with Mr. W. and went over the plan, everyone nodded their heads in agreement and, Mr. W. gave his approval.

This was years before the mass information gathering marvel of the internet so, I had to begin my market research phase at the Public Library on 42nd Street and Fifth Avenue in Manhattan. I searched the records to find top sales representative firms with sales forces calling on the beauty supply, high end department store, drug and food wholesalers, fund raisers, health and vitamin trade, military post exchanges, gift catalog, advertising specialty, bar and restaurant, and as many markets where our products could be placed for sale in retail outlets nationwide.

Here was the carrot I looked for along with my two new partners. We were three totally different personalities from divergent backgrounds who got along famously well as a team. We all were hungry for financial reward and had the need to satisfy our desire to succeed in business.

We developed a line of gift products and all contributed to the mix of items. Art priced them profitably, Klaus was responsible for the production, assembly, shipping and overall supervision of the factory employees. The front office staff included Art, Betty and the receptionist to handle all the general office work. All of the staff were from surrounding towns of this south shore Long Island community. Several were from Germany and well known by Mr. W. The presence of these German men and women added a European flavor to the operation.

Step two was to find sales representation in all the individual markets I thought our line would appeal to. This was done while developing the product line with as much help as we could muster and taking suggestions from everyone before including products to the line. At Mr. W's suggestion I took a quick trip to the novelty capitol of America which was at that time, Providence, Rhode Island. I came back with some samples of items we later purchased and ideas for items we could make ourselves.

In brief, the line included a multitude of a variety of accessories for travel or home use for men and women. Fancy sewing kits for sale at Marshall Field in Chicago to a plain kit for sale in the PX for a soldier to sew on a new PFC stripe. An expensive men's leather travel kit to a simple folding tooth brush and compact razor kit to fit in a soldiers pocket that me and my pal Mistretta would have gladly bought at the PX prior to our trip to Jacksonville. Atomizers, pill boxes, Gold Milar travel bags in all sizes and the list was almost unlimited. These products were combined in quantity in attractive deals for display at the "Point of Sale," in retail outlets and offered in pre-package display deals or in bulk.

The product line increased and all suggestions were welcomed and if we could buy it and sell it at a profit or, if Klaus thought we could make it ourselves it resulted in another product for the line. Mr. W took trips to Europe and came back with samples and those we thought would sell were added. I cannot think of a single item that remained on our shelves unsold.

To test the market I called on various local prospects and was met with positive feedback and results...ORDERS!! I contacted my McKesson friends who had opened their own sales rep firm in New York City and we met at their Manhattan offices and showroom to review the line. Their sales force covered the entire Northeastern drug store wholesale trade. I convinced Mr. W. to provide sample kits for this firm and even Art was skeptical about the expense but they all agreed to try it. This concern was put to rest when this sales rep group generated sales to put our firm on the map with orders rolling in from all over the Northeastern states and multiplied with reorders as our line was sold in retail drug stores from Manhattan to Maine.

Introductory letters were sent to the sales rep organizations I selected to personally meet with on my planned sales blitz. Included in the sales letters were color pictures of some of the products and pre-packed deals. Our secretary Betty was attractive and smart. Being somewhat older than the three of us, she got a kick out of how determined we were and she never realized how much help she was to me in my later management years.

Betty helped me with my dictation so I could compose a decent sales letter using the proper King's English which I further developed over the years. "Say it using the least amount of words to get your message across," she advised. She introduced me to the Roget's Thesaurus which I kept at my desk until years later when the Internet revolution made everything quicker and easier.

The response to the direct mail campaign was very positive and visits were scheduled to meet with the sales rep organizations I selected. The itinerary for my first sales trip included a stop in Chicago and the Palmer House. With my future waiting for me out there, I packed a bag and put on a three button natural shoulder suit, a white shirt and club tie with an extra suit and clothing packed in my bag. I spent plenty for Valet Service to assure I looked well-dressed and successful with a fresh shine on my shoes before I met with prospects. I sent pictures to the trade of our people Betty, Klaus, Art, the gals and guys in the back room that helped tell my story. The customer felt he knew that voice on the other end of the phone…it paid off.

My first Jet 707 flight out of Kennedy International Airport was to Chicago's O'Hare, then on to L.A., San Francisco, Portland, Oregon, and Seattle, Washington, then finally returned home through Dallas and Houston, Texas. I was away for about 5 weeks on that first trip to meet and work with the only two existing sales rep firms that our company had while adding others in my travels. In San Francisco, I met with and set up a large nationwide sales rep firm selling to the military Post Exchanges. He introduced me to the extravagances of San Francisco which I shared with Lee on our many visits to that interesting and beautiful city.

Upon my return, we three pioneers were ecstatic but, Mr. W. was more modest in his praise and diligent in his criticism and desire for perfection. He called me one Hollywood morning at 6:00 A.M. when it was 9:00 A.M. on Long Island to tell me I misspelled his name… there were a few confusing Germanic ei'and h's in his surname and, I never misspelled it again! This was typical of his management technique that some hated but after I thought about his criticisms, I benefitted and learned from him. When Lee and I had our own business and a sales person wrote on a prospect profile card, ABC Company. "Mary" in Personnel. That profile was returned to the sales person and then instructed to properly fill out the details with, John Andrews, Personnel Manager and Mary Smith, Assistant Personnel Manager…no shortcuts. Both went on our "Hot List" direct mail campaign in support of our sales force.

Staff meetings were held every morning at the corporate location and all department heads from both firms were present…we three would rotate to attend. Mr. W. would always find someone's error to make as an example in front of everyone so he could say in a sarcastic tone to his German accent "It is pitiful. How in the world did we ever win the war?" The first time I heard him say that, I nearly fell off my chair holding back a smile…but no one dared laugh.

"Pitiful…oh Pitiful" was another favorite of his and often mimicked by the three young partners. Any mistake was soon followed by…"Pitiful…Oh Pitiful. Hopefully, none of Mr. W.'s people were around to report back, I am sure W was kept up to date by those quiet but observant German ladies from his home town or as some thought actually W's relatives. But… after a while they also laughed right along with everyone else.

As I close my eyes, I can see an image of Mr. W. maybe five foot ten or eleven inches tall and trim impeccably dressed in a well-tailored expensive business suit. His bright white shirt with starched collar and classy tie, his shoes highly polished and his gray hair perfectly groomed all indicating his refined taste. Being in the fragrance field he always had a hint of a men's cologne but, only a hint. He is seen, ready to hold and kiss the hand of an elegant woman as any German Count would do on the silver screen. With his continental accent and facade, Mr. W. knew he was a charmer and attention getter. He was not as tough as he acted but he knew he was the center of "his" universe. He had a lovely American wife two lovely teen aged daughters and a brother-in-law who worked in corporate.

Many were awed by him and if his private secretary made a typographical error on the expensive gold embossed corporate letterhead, she would pay a visit to the ladies' room, rip up the letterhead into tiny little pieces and flush it down the toilet bowl. All this to avoid Mr. W's criticism. "Don't you realize how expensive that letterhead is? That is pitiful, my dear please be more careful." Then, he would turn around and have a sumptuous luncheon platter sent in for his office staff, after which he took off to play golf at his country club. As soon as his Lincoln drove away, the entire building seemed to take a deep breath, deflate and relax, including his brother-in-law!

My association with him was a learning process that greatly helped me meet future challenges. Thank you very much, Kurt. I say that now but would never have taken the liberty to ever call him by his first name back then.

As the year ended, orders from eleven markets were coming in fast and furious. Klaus had to hire more help to keep the production line moving. The shipping and receiving department manager asked for more help and every one of us rolled up our sleeves and helped in the shipping department.

At the turn of the New Year, Mr. W. met with the three of us and explained that the initial investment was not fully recovered but the coming year looked promising. Well, let me see what the New Year will bring, I thought to myself. I certainly did my job and so did my partners.

I wanted a two year work record before I left and went along with the program until the spring of 1964. I responded to an ad in the New York Times and landed a higher paying sales job with Beck-Lee Medical, a pioneer in Electro-Cardiology. Travel experience was essential and I logged plenty of travel time in the lower 48 states with Mr. W. After a training period at the home office and manufacturing facility in Chicago, I would be calling on surgical, medical and x-ray dealers in the Northeastern states. I was offered a five figure salary plus commission, a company car - this time one equipped with air-conditioning and all the normal benefits of the 1960's.

The technical schooling and training with electronics in the Guard and the Army came in very handy here. I quickly mastered the operation, maintenance and how to show sales people and medical users the proper function of all the equipment.

I did have to pass a thorough pre-hire test including a day spent taking tests with an industrial psychologist in Manhattan. This included, joining him as his luncheon guest at the Harvard Club. I guess they wanted to check my table manners or to see if I needed a cocktail at 12 noon which I passed on. Later, when I was promoted and hired my replacement, he was put to the same test. I saw the interesting test results which helped us in the selection and management of sales people Lee and I would be hiring for our own business in Philadelphia.

I offered my resignation to Mr. W, thanked him for the opportunity and told him I wished to return to the medical business. I could see a look in his eyes showing some doubt about his management methods in dealing with me. Yes, I was quite different from most and perhaps a little more outspoken and independent than he preferred. I wanted to leave with a hand shake and a smile and felt I was repaid with experience.

My new job was very challenging and rewarding; I was happy in my work to be on my own. I did not need anyone to motivate me or get me up in the mornings to hit the trail and the trail was a long one, all the way from Northern Virginia to Maine.

Lee was my home base administrator who took care of all my correspondence, scheduling, plane and hotel reservations and coordinating our attendance at local and national medical meetings to promote and demonstrate the products. She typed every letter I dictated into my portable tape recorder with a rented IBM Electric typewriter. This was years before home-based business became so popular.

She also accompanied me to all the northeast medical conventions where we set up our booth and displayed and demonstrated the equipment. I invited the local dealer sales people to work the booth so they could follow up on prospects. Lee was a great help and we had fun working the booth together.

It was not a surprise to see the crowds around our display whenever Lee was there. She joined me when we invited key people out for dinner and cocktails at company expense. This trained us for our future roll entertaining important clients when I became sales manager and later marketing director at Medical Electronics and then our own Personnel business in Philadelphia.

The routine when traveling to Washington, D.C. and Northern Virginia area was to spend a week there and then drive up to Philadelphia on the weekend. Lee would arrange for my folks to take care of John and Vincent, then she would pack a bag and take the Amtrak to meet me in Philadelphia for the weekend. We would enjoy our time together and she would take the train back on a Monday morning to New York and I would spend the week in the Philadelphia and Wilmington area. I had several dealers in the area and the vast and important medical facilities always kept my dealers busy. We did not realize at the time that Philadelphia would later reward us with our greatest financial successes.

One weekend in particular stands out for both of us as we think back to those times and give each other a big hug. I would check into a nice hotel or motel and place an expensive bottle of French champagne on ice to await our return to the room. This weekend it was the new trendy City Line Motel and we had nine o'clock dinner reservations in the Tiki Room.

That Friday evening I was anxiously awaiting the 6:20 from New York City to arrive on track 12. I was standing at the head of the stairs so I could immediately spot Lee as she got off the train. It was a full train and people seemed to just pour out but there was no Lee! I did happen to notice a very attractive auburn haired woman wearing sunglasses and wearing a well-tailored dark business suit accentuating her lovely figure.

I may have found myself staring a little too attentively at this beautiful lady as I was scanning for Lee. Then I also spotted this lady was carrying the one suit mate to my two-suiter Samsonite luggage. That's when I realized it was Lee in a new outfit, new hair style and new hair color. "Do you look at all the ladies like that," she coyly asked me, as she slipped her sunglasses half off and smiled. I rushed her to the car and The City Line Motel. I can still hear the "pop" of that champagne cork!! We never did go to the Tiki Room at nine o'clock that night; we ordered room service instead and it was late ...just before room service closed for the evening!

Lee always surprised me and her ideas were mostly warm and cuddly. One cold and snowy early spring Friday evening, after being away all week, I drove the car up the snow covered driveway. In the half- light, I was greeted by of all things...my Daffodil bulbs which I planted last year were now in full bloom. I was astonished to see these flowers blooming in the snow. Until, Lee confessed she bought a couple dozen plastic flowers at The Pink Canary that day to surprise me.

Another Friday evening returning from a week on the road, Lee greeted me wearing a new outfit with wonderful aromas coming from the kitchen and perhaps a different perfume in her hair. As I dropped my suit case, she put her finger to her lips with a "Shhhhhhh'...the boys are fast asleep." Lee's plans included setting the clock ahead so the boys would think it much later and sending them off to bed after a nice dinner. She would then set up our folding card table beautifully covered and set near the fireplace and the stereo set on some soft music. A bottle of champagne was already chilling in the ice bucket and glasses already frosted. Crispy delicious roast duckling was one of Lee's specialties. I felt like a King and, she was my Princess.

Traveling salesmen all compared notes on the best non-tourist restaurants in all the major and some minor cities and towns. I knew where to get the best baked stuffed lobster in downtown Boston, the best crabs and oysters in Baltimore and Washington D.C., the greatest home-made New England clam chowder in Quincy, Massachusetts and super crab cakes without a trace of crab shell at a little hotel in Towson Maryland. Amelio's, a Northern Italian restaurant in San Francisco, Veal Oscar in Frascotti's in Hollywood and La Dolce Vita in Beverly Hills were also favorites. Plus, we knew the best steak houses in Manhattan, Chicago, Kansas City and San Francisco.

I would be remiss not to mention Ramone, the gracious owner of the popular French restaurant "Le Gay Penguin" in White Plains, New York and the famed late night supper club "Piccolo Club" on Second Avenue and 55th Street owned by tough but affable Italian Boxing Champ Saverio Turiello. I spent many early evenings at the Piccolo sitting in a booth doing my daily paper work while waiting for the traffic to subside before venturing over the 59th Street Bridge and home to my young family in Baldwin.

Back in those days, anyone living in the Chicago area could buy prime beef in any butcher shop and supermarket. Today, you no longer see the quality of prime beef of former days. Restaurants in those bygone days employed executive chefs and served expensive cuts of aged prime beef and made their profit on the drinks they served. They could not survive today with customers who have a single glass of wine compared to the gallons of Dry Martini's, Manhattan's, Old Fashions and Whiskey Sours that bar tenders poured back then which multiplied the dinner tab to profitable proportions.

Our bank balance was looking healthier and we both enjoyed the challenges and benefits of my new job. One day, while having lunch at a popular restaurant in Oceanside, Long Island, we ran into buddy John Zurla whom I had not seen since I left the Guard.

John joined us and we brought each other up to date about our lives and John told us he no longer was involved with the Nike on-site program. He had become an army aviator after schooling at Fort Rucker Alabama and flew fixed wing single engine aircraft with the famed 42nd Rainbow Infantry Division, Aviation Battalion. The headquarters were only five minutes from my home in Baldwin.

He told me he had not polished his brass nor put on a green duty uniform with shirt and tie since he became an aviator. He said the one weekend a month drill was a flying weekend and he wore his flight coveralls. He said it was a great break from troop duty with all of the discipline, and spit and polish it required of everyone. He said his recently completed two week camp tour at Fort Drum in upper New York State was pleasant and he spent the time piloting some top brass and a few Artillery forward observers directing artillery fire. After he landed and had chow, the evening was his own to put on a pair of slacks and a sport shirt, then take in a movie, have a few drinks or go out to dinner with his fellow pilots. "I would have become an Army Aviator much earlier in my career had I known how much fun it was," quipped John. All the while, he knew he was firing up my curiosity and interest. Lee did not think it sounded like so much fun.

John was sure to mention that the one weekend a month drill schedule could be flexible. This was sounding better and better to me which resulted in my new MOS "Army Aviator." Yes, I re-enlisted in the National Guard 42nd Infantry Division Aviation Battalion and my pal John Zurla was to be my flight instructor.

"You did what?" Lee exclaimed. "No sweat, honey, I can drill whenever I like it's only one weekend a month and no troop duty like the old days. John will teach me how to fly a single engine airplane...isn't that wonderful!!" Fortunately for us, shortly after I re-enlisted, I was promoted to National Sales Manager by Beck-Lee Medical and we were re-located to the home office in Chicago. My name went back on the inactive Army Reserve Officers list and Lee was happy for me to again say "goodbye" to the National Guard.

I only attended one drill and never even sat in the single engine plane, I would have loved to learn how to fly. I made up for it later by flying as a passenger in several single engine planes flying over the Snowy Range in Wyoming and several flights in DeHaviland Beavers and Otters in Alaska on hunting and fishing trips both wheeled and float planes...it was fun.

I do not know how many aviators were later called to active duty to fly the dangerous skies of Vietnam. Zurla had landed, no pun intended, a job as a pilot with Air America (the CIA Airline) and spent seven years flying dangerous missions in Vietnam and environs.

Over the following years, we kept in touch with the Zurla's and were sadly informed that John lost his battle with pancreatic cancer in 1976 at age 46. Following tradition, his Air American fellow pilots flew an airplane over the Long Island beaches with John's son aboard to empty his Dad's ashes into the wind. If John had lived to tell his story, it would have been much more interesting than mine. John Zurla was the best man, soldier, NCO, Officer and friend in my 29 years of comradeship with him. Those who knew him would all agree with me. Lee and I talk about John as we recall some of our times with the Zurla's and the stories she heard from both me and John about our times together.

Chicago and *fini*

My boss called me to tell me he was coming in from Chicago to attend the 1965 AMA (American Medical Association) annual convention held that year in New York City. He asked me to have breakfast with him at the Mayflower Hotel on Central Park West, just across from the Convention Center on Columbus Circle where we would be exhibiting our equipment. I thought he wanted to coordinate staffing our exhibit booth with our sales force.

"We wish to invite you to take over the National Sales Manager's position which requires relocating your family to Chicago." Like a dream coming true, I awoke to the fact that my hard work was going to pay off this time and I accepted the offer gladly. I excused myself and went to make a phone call. "Hi Hon, put the house on the market we're going to Chicago. We've just been promoted to national sales manager." I had a slight pang of remorse for the sales manager I would be replacing because I did have a great deal of respect for him. Apparently, he did not live up to management's expectations but I was ready.

We arrived in Chicago in September 1965 with John and Vincent then ten and seven years old. Over the years while away on a business trip and as always at the end of each day, I called Lee to check in with her. Usually she would tell me "Oh, everything is just fine at home" and then give me an update on all the bad news when I got back home. The time when, "Vincent fell and had six stiches" or "the Sewer backed up and it will cost $1000 to fix it" or any other home hazards. She never gave me bad news while I was on a business trip…smart lady that she was and still is!

I saw many salesmen who checked on the home front and the wife reported all the day's troubles. "Make that a double," the poor distraught salesman would request from the bartender as he was helpless to do anything about the bad news except worry. Lee did that to me only one time when she told me that a letter arrived that day in the mail. It was addressed to First Lieutenant Vincent G. Gallagher and mentioned active duty. "Is that something you requested?" "No, are you kidding me?" I replied. "It's all in the envelope with something about missiles and air defense," she continued. "It looked so important I just had to open it." "Yeah," I said, "I requested active duty back in 1959 but was turned down and now they call me, six years later?"

We both kept this under our hat until I did some investigation. If this recall had happened a few years earlier, I would have gone gladly.

A chance meeting with a Master Sergeant at an Army Reserve Center on Chicago's west side proved those old NCO's had all the answers. After checking my records of service he said, "Hell no, you didn't even keep up your retirement credits and served six years as an enlisted man and six more years as an officer in an active reserve unit and are eligible now, for an honorable discharge. That last re-enlistment in the 42nd Division Aviation Battalion probably caused some confusion. My official Honorable Discharge from the Army of the United States was received dated, October 6th, 1966.

With a slight pang of remorse that quickly passed, I continued in my corporate career with buckets of good experience under my belt. The position required extensive travel throughout the USA, Canada and Mexico. It was a welcome challenge and the family was at home in a new luxury garden apartment complex with great neighbors and a beautiful swimming pool we all enjoyed. The village of Arlington Heights was a little like Baldwin, Long Island, and we felt we were in for the long haul and would soon be buying a home there.

The next few years were jammed with challenges, adventures, frustrations and enjoyment. I had a top notch professional sales force calling on all the medical, surgical and X-ray dealers nationwide. Canada represented a sizable share of our business and was my personal responsibility. We had an older and faithful dealer in Eastern Canada and my efforts helped to create a new relationship with the Stevens Company, the largest and most dynamic medical firm in all of Canada. They employed a large sales force with offices extending across Canada from Quebec to the beautiful city of Vancouver, British Columbia on Canada's West Coast. I remember looking out those extra-large oval windows of the Air Canada Vickers Viscount and Vanguard turbo-propeller air liners which gave such great views on daytime flights and night landings. But Air Canada was not the most punctual airline to fly on back in the 1960's.

Somewhere along the way we were acquired by a Fortune 500 corporation with product lines and facilities in many industries and a desire to burst into the medical electronics market. And believe me, they bought the best company to achieve their aims with a built-in sales force and hundreds of dealers anxiously awaiting new products to sell. I saw greenbacks dangling right before my eyes. Our product line would become part of the Scientific Instruments Division. It proved to be a cumbersome union. The division made huge customized mass-spectrometers and at the time they had a Department of Defense contract making firing systems for army helicopters...what a mix of products?

Sales and marketing would remain in Chicago and manufacturing would be moved to Forest Park, Ohio, located between Cincinnati and Dayton. But I expected relocation there was in the cards for me and my family. We continued our sales representation with O'Neill International Sales headquartered in Rockefeller Center in Manhattan. The O'Neill sales force covered the free world in, Latin America, Europe, Israel, South Africa, Australia and New Zealand. Upon meeting the firm's President,

Oscar Delgado O'Neill, Jr., a prince of a man, we soon connected and he arranged to have his sales force come to Manhattan for an introductory sales meeting. Oscar was a B-17 bomber pilot in England in World War II where he met and married his lovely British war bride Rene. Their daughter is beautiful actress Jennifer O'Neil whom I never met but, while still in New York, the president of my firm called from Chicago asking me to arrange flowers to be sent to the then teen-aged Jennifer for an occasion I no longer recall. It may have been to congratulate her for her first modeling success with Coca Cola.

We enjoyed our time in Manhattan and Mexico City with Oscar and Rene and had many business and pleasure get-togethers with them some, while entertaining government officials from the Mexican Social Security Institute. All medical instrumentation and medical supplies in Mexico had to be approved by these officials.

Everyone spoke English, the language of trade and industry. Oscar spoke Spanish and Portuguese fluently and the little Spanish I spoke was a help when off the beaten path. I would ask Lee how she said a particular word in Italian which would refresh my Spanish and that helped as I improved my pronunciation. In between business trips to Mexico City, we would slip away by ourselves to visit Taxco on our way by harrowing bus ride through the mountains to a favorite spot in Acapulco. We were told to try to get the two front seats in the bus for an exciting drive which we did whenever possible and it was a thrilling ride we always enjoyed. On the way back home, we always flew out of Acapulco non-stop to Chicago.

Our favorite place in Acapulco was the splendid Villa Vera Racket Club frequented by Presidents and Princes with private cottages and swimming pools and the first poolside bar we ever saw all, high on a hill overlooking the Pacific Ocean. Oscar recommended Villa Vera rather than the typical popular *Turista* places. Most guests were from South America and Europe, making for a more interesting experience.

The reader must realize this was in the 1960's when Mexico was a safe playground for all fun seekers from the Americas and Europe. The Villa Vera had a German executive chef who created the best food in Acapulco and the poolside bar made super Bloody Marys with the tasty Mexican "*Limone*" while Lee favored the Pina Coladas. I smile as the thought and images of my beautiful wife and all of the other lovely ladies in bikinis flash through my mind. I look at my wife now and see Lee how beautiful and how wonderful she still is and how fortunate I have been all these years to have her as my wife, my lover, my partner and my best friend.

Orders were flooding the manufacturing facility moving equipment and supplies out to the shipping dock in record numbers. This accelerated production demands placed a strain on manufacturing and raised havoc in quality control. This resulted in poorly tested medical equipment sent to dealers. The Altech Corporation, our nationwide repair service, was soon overwhelmed with repairs that really needed remanufacture. The receiving dock was overwhelmed with returned equipment faster than quality control could deal with it. Management panicked. "Vince Gallagher should be here to help with this problem." My red alert went back on...the sales force was doing an outstanding job, and the company had plenty of production and quality control people running into each other but they insisted I relocate to Forest Park, Ohio. So, we packed and the company moved us from our comfortable digs in the great town of Arlington Heights in suburban Chicago to a laid back country hamlet in between Cincinnati and Dayton Ohio. Any local area readers must realize this was back in the 1960's when there was plenty of wide open spaces in Forest Park and relatively few amenities. Even though Cincinnati at the time had two of the nation's finest French Restaurants

The corporate plan for new medical electronic products never developed so I met with their R&D people at the University of Michigan in Ann Arbor to see what they were developing for us after I had given them an approved list of competitive products we could sell. My sales force and dealers were all asking for and expecting the new products that was promised in the audio visual presentation I produced and directed with help from Dan Howard Associates a progressive advertising agency in Cincinnati. When the acquisition took place the company promised us a full Harvest Moon of new products that ended up as a total Lunar Eclipse. I am reluctant to mention the international giant in my memoir with all the failures they had in both equipment failures and management personnel.

I even convinced management to buy some competitive products to redesign and add to our line to quickly increase sales and revenue. Their R&D people felt somewhat intimidated because they had the deadly corporate virus NIH (Not Invented Here). They instead proudly showed me a small ugly air filter that could sit on a night stand and could be sold in department stores. When I saw this, I followed up on my contact with a German medical industry giant to sell under our private label some of their products on an exclusive basis to which they readily agreed. I had orders in hand for one hundred of our modified modular electrocardiographs for The Air Shields Corporation, a pioneer in the ICU (Intensive Care Unit) equipment field. Daylin Medical in Los Angeles one of the largest medical dealers on the west coast had a standing order for 100 diathermy units. All that the German manufacturer had to do was add our company logo. But it was a No Go because it was the infectious NIH virus.

I personally wrote an order for 500 thousand rolls of electrocardiogram paper for The Hospital Bureau in New York City. This was a product not made by the parent company but bought from The Nashua Corporation in New Hampshire. All we did was buy it, reship it to customers and make money on every roll we sold. It seems that the parent had a paper company somewhere on the map but ECG paper had a special coating process the parent knew nothing about and our customers wanted the paper NOW. Again, "Not Invented Here." And the parent company never invented anything. It was time for another meeting with Lee.

We discussed the many distractions in our life's adventure and decided that we no longer would be at the mercy of someone else, we would be our own bosses and make our own way in life. What successes I made for others we would do for ourselves with the best team of all...my wife Leboria Theresa Reres

Gallagher…soon to be legally changed to Lee Gallagher and a name to become well known and respected in the Philadelphia business community and later in the Real Estate profession on Philadelphia's Main Line.

More adventures, hard work, anxieties and successes awaited those two whom, as 20 year olds, kissed each other goodbye for what might have been the very last time when Vince was sent off to Korea. Now in their eighties, they still hold and caress each other and thank the Good Lord for their blessings of their long life together and for sharing this time to remember.

Don't Think "What If"…Think "What's Next!"

NATIONAL GUARD BUREAU

REPORT OF SEPARATION AND RECORD OF SERVICE IN THE ARMY NATIONAL GUARD OF THE
UNITED STATES AND THE ARMY NATIONAL GUARD OF NEW YORK

TYPE OF DISCHARGE __Honorable__

(No erasures or alterations in this entry valid)

1. NAME (Last, first, middle initial)	2. SERVICE NO.	3. GRADE	4. ARM OR SERVICE	5. TERM OF ENLISTMENT
GALLAGHER, VINCENT G.	21 ▓▓▓	MSgt	Artillery	Three Yrs.

6. ORGANIZATION Btry G, 773d AAA Gun Bn	7. DATE OF DISCHARGE	8. PLACE OF DISCHARGE
HOME STATION New York, New York	10 Sep 53	New York, New York

9. PERMANENT ADDRESS FOR MAILING PURPOSES	10. DATE OF BIRTH	11. PLACE OF BIRTH
▓▓▓▓▓▓▓	9 Feb 30	New York, New York

12. CIVILIAN OCCUPATION *(Include name and address of present employer, or if unemployed, the last employer)*

Field Representative - Household Finance Corporation

13. RACE			14. MARITAL STATUS			15. U. S. CITIZEN	
WHITE	NEGRO	OTHER (Specify)	SINGLE	MARRIED	OTHER (Specify)	YES	NO
X				X		X	

16. COLOR EYES	17. COLOR HAIR	18. HEIGHT		19. WEIGHT		20. NO. DEPENDENTS
Blue	Brown	5 FT. 9 IN.		160 LBS.		0

MILITARY HISTORY

21. DATE AND PLACE OF ENLISTMENT	22. MILITARY OCCUPATIONAL SPECIALTY AND NUMBER
11 Sep 50, New York, New York	1725 AAA Fire Control Specialist

23. MILITARY QUALIFICATION AND DATE (i. e., Infantry, Aviation, Marksmanship Badges, etc.)

Qualified Sharpshooter w/Carbine Cal .30 M1, Course B, Score 169, 10 Jan 52
Qualified Expert w/Carbine Cal .30 M1, Course A, Score 220, 31 Jul 52

24. DECORATIONS, CITATIONS, MEDALS, BADGES, COMMENDATIONS, AND CAMPAIGN RIBBONS AWARDED OR AUTHORIZED (This period of service)

Korean Sv Medal w/2 Bronze Stars AR 600-65
UN Service Medal - Cir 20 GHQ, FECOM, 16 Oct 52

25. PRIOR SERVICE (Branch of service, inclusive dates, and primary duty with MOS)

Enl NYNG 11 Sep 47 to 10 Sep 50. HD per ETS.

26.

FIRST YEAR			SECOND YEAR			THIRD YEAR			TOTAL POINTS THIS SERVICE
FROM—	TO—	POINTS	FROM—	TO—	POINTS	FROM—	TO—	POINTS	
▓	▓	▓	▓	▓	▓	▓	▓	▓	▓

27. LENGTH THIS SERVICE			28. TOTAL SERVICE FOR PAY PURPOSES			29. LATEST IMMUNIZATION DATES				30. HIGHEST GRADE HELD
YEARS	MONTHS	DAYS	YEARS	MONTHS	DAYS	SMALLPOX	TYPHOID	TETANUS	OTHER (Specify)	
3	-	-	6	-	-	20Aug52	20Aug52	3Sep52		M Sgt

31. SERVICE SCHOOLS ATTENDED AND DATES

AAA & GM Br, The Artillery School
Fire Control Electrician - T-33 Operator   1951-52

33. REASON AND AUTHORITY FOR DISCHARGE

Expiration of Term of Enlistment

34. REMARKS (This space for completion of above items or entry of other items specified in NG directives)

35. SIGNATURE OF PERSON BEING DISCHARGED (Full name)	36. SIGNATURE OF OFFICER AUTHORIZED TO SIGN (Type name, grade, and organization)
Vincent G. Gallagher	ARTHUR L. KELLY
	Capt, Arty, NYNG
	Adjutant
	773d AAA Gun Bn, NYNG

NGB FORM 22
15 NOV 48

CAUTION: NOT TO BE USED FOR IDENTIFICATION PURPOSES   ANY ALTERATIONS IN SHADED AREAS RENDER FORM VOID

CORRECTION TO DD FORM 214,
CERTIFICATE OF RELEASE OR DISCHARGE FROM ACTIVE DUTY
This Report Contains Information Subject to the Privacy Act of 1974, As Amended.

1. NAME (Last, First, Middle)	2. DEPARTMENT, COMPONENT AND BRANCH	3. SOCIAL SECURITY NUMBER (Also, Service Number if applicable)
GALLAGHER VINCENT GREGORY	NG 21	

4. MAILING ADDRESS (Include ZIP Code)
ST WOODSIDE (QUEENS) NEW YORK

5. ORIGINAL DD FORM 214 IS CORRECTED AS INDICATED BELOW:

ITEM NO.	CORRECTED TO READ
	SEPARATION DATE ON DD FORM 214 BEING CORRECTED: 9 APR 53
27	ADD: NATIONAL DEFENSE SERVICE MEDAL REPUBLIC OF KOREA PRESIDENTIAL UNIT CITATION *********************LAST ENTRY*********************

6. MEMBER REQUESTS COPY 6 BE SENT TO (Specify state/locality) _____ NY _____ OFFICE OF VETERANS AFFAIRS x YES NO

a. MEMBER REQUESTS COPY 3 BE SENT TO THE CENTRAL OFFICE OF THE DEPARTMENT OF VETERANS AFFAIRS (WASHINGTON, DC) YES x NO

7. DATE (YYYYMMDD)	8. OFFICIAL AUTHORIZED TO SIGN			
	a. TYPED NAME (Last, First, Middle Initial)	b. GRADE	c. TITLE	d. SIGNATURE
20131230	MACEWEN, DAVID K.	BG	USA Adjutant General	NO SIGNATURE REQUIRED
NARA				

DD FORM 215, AUG 2009   PREVIOUS EDITION IS OBSOLETE.   MEMBER - 4

GENERAL ORDERS)   HEADQUARTERS,
     : EXTRACT   DEPARTMENT OF THE ARMY
NO. 51)   Washington 25, D. C., 25 September 1957

REPUBLIC OF KOREA PRESIDENTIAL UNIT CITATION. The Republic of Korea Presidential Unit Citation which was awarded by the Republic of Korea to the following units of the United States Army is confirmed in accordance with AR 220-105:

10th Antiaircraft Artillery Group and
  attached units:

   Attached Units

 * * * * * * * *

773d Antiaircraft Artillery Battalion
  (90-mm)(18 Oct 52-24 Apr 53)

 * * * * * * * *

A TRUE EXTRACT COPY:

[signature]

ARTHUR L. KELLY
Capt, Arty, NYNG
Adjutant, 773d AAA Bn

REPUBLIC OF KOREA PRESIDENTIAL UNIT CITATION awarded by citation dated 16 November 1955, by Syngman Rhee, President of the Republic of Korea, for exceptionally meritorious service to the Republic of Korea during the period 11 September 1950 to 16 November 1955, inclusive, with citation as follows:
The Tenth United States Antiaircraft Artillery Group has rendered valiant and meritorious service in the defense of freedom in Korea. Joining the United Nations Forces in September 1950, the Group contributed significantly to the success of United Nations operations against the Communist aggressors. Since the cessation of hostilities, the Group has given valued assistance in preparing Republic of Korea Forces to shoulder its important responsibilities for maintaining combat readiness against the ever present threat of renewed Communist aggression. Since May 1955 the Tenth United States Antiaircraft Artillery Group has given special attention to the activation and training of the First Republic of Korea Army Antiaircraft Artillery Brigade. Various obstacles were met with efficiency and difficulties resolved with professional competence, patience and ingenuity. The outstanding services, heroism, and devotion to duty of the members of the Tenth United States Antiaircraft Artillery Group reflects great credit upon them and are in keeping with the highest traditions of the military service.

Only those units which were assigned to the 10th Antiaircraft Artillery Group prior to 27 July 1954 are eligible to be included in the above citation. Likewise, only individuals assigned or attached to the 10th Antiaircraft Artillery Group prior to 27 July 1954 are entitled to wear the Korean Presidential Unit Citation badge.

By Order of Wilber M. Brucker, Secretary of the Army:

OFFICIAL.
HERBERT M. JONES,
Major General, United States Army
The Adjutant General.

MAXWELL D TAYLOR
General, United States Army,
Chief of Staff

ARMY LESSON PLAN 1961. NOT THE RIGHT WAY, NOT THE WRONG WAY, BUT THE ARMY WAY.

PAGE 1.   PAGE 2.

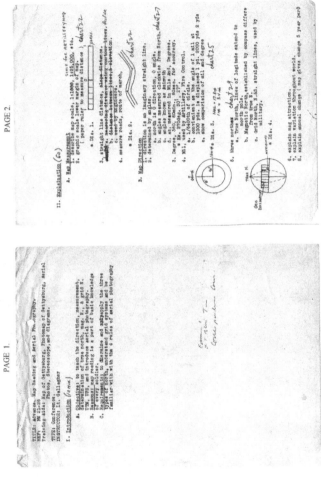

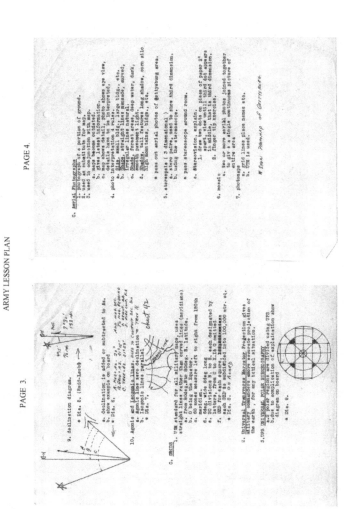

PAGE 3.

PAGE 4.

NIKE MISSILE FAMILY

AJAX   HERCULES   ZEUS

(Nike Missile Family, by U.S. Army (Public Domain), via Wikipedia Commons)

ARMY LESSON PLAN PAGE 5.

III. Demonstration & Application
    A. Demonstration will be conducted during Explanation
    B. Application will be limited to amount of people.

IV. Examination (firm)
    A. What is the scale used on all artillery maps?
    B. Give and describe the 3 types of North.
    C. Describe Agonic & Isogonic lines.
      ans. True, Mag; & Grid.
    DD.What is the standard grid system used on all U.S. maps
    E. Give the four rules of aerial photo interpretation?
      ans. size, shape, shed, shadow.

V. Discussion & Critique (firm)
    A. Review examination.
    B. Answer student questions.
    C. Discuss questions
    D. Summarize
      1. measuring distances.
      2. direction.
      3. grids.
      4. B's of aerial interpretation.

Nike Site locations are marked with dots, we occupied two sites # 99 Spring Valley, NY and #29/30 Lido Beach Long Island. Each Site occupied two locations the IFC (Intergraded Fire Control) and Launcher areas, 0.05 to 3.5 miles apart.

The Nike Hercules and Zeus had nuclear devices on site and I doubt this was widely disclosed at the time. The public were impressed when missiles were elevated during alerts and tests otherwise, there was not much to see with all the missiles hidden in underground bunkers. The IFC area displayed radar antennas that did not attract much attention.

Another hidden factor was the Booster Separation Impact Area. Within seconds after launch half of the 32 foot Ajax missile the solid fuel booster would separate and fall to earth igniting the liquid fuel onboard motor sending the missile on its way to the target. A veteran Chief Warrant Officer purchased a home in Spring Valley before the Nikes arrived and he discovered his home was in the impact area. He told this with a half-smile on his face but I can imagine his feelings during those anxious times. Thank God the Nikes never had to be fired from any of the hundreds of sites throughout North America. I would like to think that just the presence of the Nikes may have assured this.

HEADQUARTERS
42D AVIATION BATTALION
63 BABYLON TURNPIKE
FREEPORT, N.Y.

201: Gallagher, Vincent C (0)
1st Lt, O2[redacted]

17 Mar 65
Date

SUBJECT: Request for Flight Physical

TO: Flight Surgeon

1. Request that Vincent C Gallagher 1st Lt O2[redacted]
Name Rank SN
Army Aviator stationed at this installation be given a final type physical examination to determine his qualifications for continued flying status.

2. This request is initiated in compliance with the provisions contained in paragraph 15, NGR 95, dtd 6 Nov 57, Subject: Army Aviation.

3. Request that six (6) copies of this final type physical examination plus three (3) copies of Standard Form 89 be forwarded to this installation, as indicated above, for transmittal, thru Channels, to Chief, National Guard Bureau, Washington 25, D.C.

4. Class I.

FOR THE COMMANDER:

OWEN J. SCHNITZER
CAPT ARTY NYARNG
Adjutant

NOTE: Completion of item 69 SF 88, C10 AR40-500

Bn Form 8

HEADQUARTERS, DEPARTMENT OF THE ARMY
OFFICE OF THE ADJUTANT GENERAL
U. S. ARMY ADMINISTRATION CENTER
ST. LOUIS, MISSOURI 63132

6 October 1966

LO USAR:

SUBJECT: Discharge as a Reserve Commissioned Officer of the Army

TO: 1st Lt Vincent G. Gallagher, 02 ██████, Arty
    Arlington Heights, Illinois   60004

SEL SVC IDENT:

TC 411. By direction of the President, you are discharged from the United States Army Reserve, effective this date. If Reserve Identification Card, DD Form 2A (Red), is in your possession, return it to this headquarters, Attention: AGAC-P.

Relieved from   : USAR Control Group (Reinforcement)
Type of discharge   : HONORABLE - DD Form 256A
Reason for discharge: Failure to Earn Sufficient Retirement Points
Authority for discharge: Para 33f, AR 135-175

BY ORDER OF THE SECRETARY OF THE ARMY:

Adjutant General

1 Incl
DD Form 256A

DISTRIBUTION:
1 - Reservist concerned
1 - Selective Service
1 - 201 file

USAAC Form   872
1 Jun 66

from the Armed Forces of the United States of America

This is to certify that

VINCENT G GALLAGHER   02 ▓▓▓▓   First Lieutenant   Artillery

was Honorably Discharged from the

Army of the United States

on the   6th   day of   October 1966   This certificate is awarded

as a testimonial of Honest and Faithful Service

JERRY D WILEY
CAPT AGC

DD FORM 256A, 1 MAY 50

United States Army Air Defense Command (USARADCOM) shoulder
patch worn by Army and National Guard Nike Units from 1958 to 1975.

A happy day in
November 1953

Forest Park, Ohio 1968

Author disguised
as Re/Max Realtor
and mortgage
originator during
his covert years
from 1983 to 2007
on Philadelphia's
Main Line trying to
look as though he
enjoyed it

1989 A more natural and welcomed venue on
extended vacation wearing his favorite apparel for the
trail. That old army jeep hat is warm and keeps the sun
out of your eyes. Cowboy hats look great but they get
in the way when on horseback in the wilds of Alaska's
Wrangell Mountains. Offering a happy "Good
Morning" to his Horse "Sugar" before hitting the trail.

CERTIFICATE OF RECOGNITION

VINCENT G. GALLAGHER

First Lieutenant, Artillery
ARMY of the UNITED STATES

In recognition of your service during the period of the Cold War (2 September 1945 - 26 December 1991) in promoting peace and stability for this Nation, the people of this Nation are forever grateful.

SECRETARY OF DEFENSE

Acknowledgements

Many thanks to my Astoria pal Bob Dema for his help in re-visiting our youthful days. He joined the 773rd soon after it was notified of activation and served on a gun crew. He excelled as a soldier from the time we were activated, trained in Camp Stewart, and then deployed to Brooklyn and on to Korea. He even christened our buddy Max Ries on the troopship on the way to Korea which, I just recently discovered. Bob served honorably and bravely and was an outstanding soldier and a wonderful friend. In civilian life Bob achieved great success in academia in the Nassau County, New York Public School Board. He helped spark my memory and provided the only picture of the "Three Pals from Queens."

Thanks to Joseph Zurla an original guardsman from Manhattan who joined the 773rd following his older brother John. Joe was bright, smart and fluent and went on to lead the M-9 Director Section in Korea and we both returned home together. After many years I visited Joe and his wife Jackie to reminisce old times with Charlie Battery and we exchanged and nurtured each other's memories of names, places and events.

I appreciate the time son John A. Gallagher gave me from his busy schedule as a prominent New York City movie producer, writer, director and teacher for his advice while writing this reminisce. Thanks to my niece Carolyn Gallagher for sending me old family photographs I used in the book.

Mr. Jim Gandy Librarian/Archivist, New York State Military Museum offered much needed help to steer me through the approval process to use photographs of the old 12th Regiment Armory and the same to Mr. Bill Burke from the National Park Service Cape Cod Seashore who furnished photographs of the Wellfleet artillery range now part of the National Seashore.

Much appreciated help from Andrew Silverman, Esquire and his staff for assuring me the legal use of many pictures and photographs I found on line and thought would be of interest to the reader. Thanks to our good friends Andy and Beverly Colin for their taking time to read the chapters as they were written during our time in Florida when, they could have been doing more enjoyable things.

ACKNOWLEDGEMENTS

Thanks to my Cousin Elizabeth Lang and her husband and great pal Bob Lang, for their encouragement to continue when they read some of the early drafts. Sincere thanks to Angela Mondelli Ries wife of my best buddy Max Ries for her memories and for Angie and Max's daughter Liz Zakrzewski for her blessings. Early and when only a thought about writing a book, I exchanged experiences with Nick Mondelli Max's brother- in-law. Nick joined Charlie Battery sometime after the Korean War and he sparked my desire to attempt to write a more detailed narrative of my service.

I must mention my thanks to Ms. Pat Tracz Proprietor of The Photography Center in Malvern, PA for her patience and for her most welcomed professional and technical help in preparing the many photographs. I cannot forget Dan Dao our computer expert who taught me the use of flash drives to facilitate the transfer of copy from my PC to others concerned with the book...Thank you Dan.

My wife Lee is still talking to me after witnessing my outbursts of learning frustrations over MS Word, my eruptions of laughter and then, choking up unable to talk at times when tears would sneak up on me. This, as I dug deep into my past and relived my young life during those serious days with my comrades and thinking about those less fortunate than I, now, still here to write about it. Lee helped me with advice and encouragement and after all these years she is still my beautiful princess.

Thank you Katherine Mackay for your editing and inserting or eliminating pesky commas, checking the grammar and spelling and clarifying many a wandering sentence.

And lastly, and by no means least, many thanks to Rosemary Augustine, a successful author and publisher. Her patience, and professional background in writing and publishing, made me realize it was time to entrust her with this book to get it finished and printed. Although we had many starts, stops and disappointments along the way, Rosemary stepped in and literally saved the day. Rosemary has written and published 10 books of her own, so I knew I was going to be in excellent hands. Her patience and unique ability to teach those of us who know very little of the publishing process, was truly divine intervention. She made the publishing process as easy as was humanly possible for us. Lee and I are very grateful for Rosemary's presence in our lives. Without her, this memoir would never have become a book. Bless You, Rosemary Augustine.

Visit author's website which includes
interesting full color pictures, stories and books.
VinceGallagherBooks.com

Made in the USA
Middletown, DE
20 January 2020